REVOLUTION AND COUNTER-REVOLUTION IN SCOTLAND, 1644–1651

P. M. CARON

REVOLUTION AND COUNTER-REVOLUTION IN SCOTLAND, 1644–1651

DAVID STEVENSON
[1942-]

John Donald
EDINBURGH

This revised edition published in 2003 by
John Donald Publishers
an imprint of Birlinn Limited
West Newington House
10 Newington Road
Edinburgh
EH9 1QS

www.birlinn.co.uk

First published in 1977 by the Royal Historical Society, London

Copyright © David Stevenson 1979 and 2003

The right of David Stevenson to be identified as the author of this work has been asserted by him in accordance with the Copyright, Designs and Patents Act 1988

All rights reservd. No part of this publication may be reproduced, stored, or transmitted in any form, or by any means, electronic, mechanical or photocopying, without the express written permission of the publisher.

ISBN 0 85976 580 6

British Library Cataloguing-in-Publication Data
A catalogue record of this book is available from the British Library

Printed and bound by Antony Rowe Ltd, Chippenham

To Wendy

Contents

List of Maps

List of Illustrations

[BETWEEN PP. 112-113]

Conventions and Abbreviations

Dates. Old Style dates (as used in contemporary Britain) are used throughout, New Style dates as used on the Continent (ten days ahead of the Old Style) being adjusted where necessary. The new year is taken to begin on 1 January (the Scottish usage), not 25 March (English usage).

Quotations. All abbreviations are extended, but otherwise the original spelling and punctuation are retained.

Money. The £ sterling was worth £12 Scots in the seventeenth century.

References. Details of a work are normally given the first time it is cited, with short title references thereafter. All MSS cited without any location being given are in the National Archives of Scotland (formerly the Scottish Record Office). All printed works are published in London unless otherwise stated.

The following abbreviations are used.

Aber Recs — *Extracts from the Council Registers of the Burgh of Aberdeen 1625–42 and 1643–1747*, ed. J. Stuart (SBRS 1871–2)

APS — *The Acts of the Parliaments of Scotland*, ed. T. Thomson and C. Innes (12 vols., 1814–75). The new edition (1870–2) of vols. v and vi has been used.

CJ — *Journals of the House of Commons*

CSPD — *Calendar of State Papers, Domestic*

Edin Recs — *Extracts from the Records of the Burgh of Edinburgh, 1626–41 and 1642–55*, ed. M. Wood (Edinburgh 1936–8)

EHR — *English Historical Review*

Glasgow Recs — *Extracts from the Records of the Royal Burgh of Glasgow 1573–1642 and 1630–1662*, ed. J.D. Marwick (SBRS 1876–81)

HMC — Historical Manuscripts Commission. References to HMC

	publications take the form of serial number followed by the report and appendix numbers or the collection title, as recommended in *Government Publications, Sectional List,* No. 17
LJ	*Journals of the House of Lords*
NLS	National Library of Scotland
PRO	Public Record Office, London
RCGA	*The Records of the Commissioners of the General Assemblies of the Church of Scotland, 1646–52*, ed. A.F. Mitchell and J. Christie (SHS 1892–1909)
RMS	*Registrum Magni Sigilli Regum Scotorum*, 1634–51, ed. J.M. Thomson (Edinburgh 1897)
RPCS	*Register of the Privy Council of Scotland*, 2nd. series, ed. P.H. Brown (Edinburgh 1899–1908)
SBRS	Scottish Burgh Record Society
SHR	*Scottish Historical Review*
SHS	Scottish History Society
Stirling Recs	*Extracts from the Records of the Royal Burgh of Stirling 1519–1666*, ed. R. Renwick (Glasgow 1887)
TRHS	*Transactions of the Royal Historical Society*

Preface to the First Edition

This book sets out to provide a political history of the later stages of the rule of the covenanters in Scotland. My former book *The Scottish Revolution*, 1637–44. *The Triumph of the Covenanters* (Newton Abbot 1973, reprinted Edinbury 2003) traced the origins and early successes of the covenanting movement; the present volume continues the story through the years in which the movement disintegrated under pressure both from England and from within. The years it covers, 1644–51, have received surprisingly little attention from Scottish historians; though a considerable amount has been written on Montrose's campaigns and on Scottish intervention in England, even these topics have been dealt with in a very one-sided manner, being dealt with from the point of view of Montrose and of the English parliament respectively. Much new light can, I believe, be thrown on them, and indeed on the whole period, by looking at them from the standpoint of the covenanters, of their ambitions and difficulties. Abundant evidence survives, including many of the official records of the covenanting regime in the parliamentary papers in the Scottish Record Office, but little of it has ever been systematically exploited by historians. This book attempts to make use of such evidence to make sense of a sad but fascinating period in Scotland's history.

Like its predecessor this volume has its origins in my Ph.D. thesis, 'The Covenanters and the Government of Scotland, 1637–51' (University of Glasgow 1970); the acknowledgements for assistance received in the course of my work are therefore similar in both books. Professor A.A.M. Duncan and Dr I.B. Cowan of the Department of Scottish History in Glasgow proved to be the most patient and helpful of supervisors for my thesis. Dr John Imrie, Keeper of the Records of Scotland, generously gave me much advice about this period of Scottish history and its surviving records. Conrad Russell, Bedford College, University of London, provided much useful criticism and comment. The staff of various libraries and record offices anonymously provided those services, all too often taken for granted, without which no book like this could be written.

Foreword

Revolution and Counter Revolution in Scotland, 1644–1651 (1977) followed on from my *The Scottish Revolution* (1973), which is also now being reprinted. The first book followed the fortunes of the Scottish covenanters in their resistance to Charles I. Remarkable initial success was followed by unavoidable political complications, in that the very success of their revolt helped spark off revolts and civil wars in Charles's other two kingdoms, England and Ireland. Seeing Scotland's fate as inextricably bound up in the results of these struggles, the Scots sent armies to intervene in both. These were in part bold and confident moves. The calvinist ideology of the covenanters was strong, and belief that God had clearly shown them his favour and brought them success against remarkable odds was inspiring. They were God's Chosen People, and intervention in England and Ireland was God's will. His favour would again bring them victory. Others were more sober. They saw military campaigns in the other kingdoms as risky political necessities There seemed no alternatives if Scotland was to avoid invasion, threatening not just the loss of all that had been achieved in the past few years but the imposition of a crushing royal despotism which would make Scotland's pre-1637 grievances seem petty by comparison.

As either the doing of god's will or taking a calculated political risk, military interventions proved initially hopeful in their results, but disappointing in the longer term, and ultimately disastrous. In Ireland a strong bridgehead was established in eastern Ulster, but defeating the Irish catholic rebels proved impossible. Stalemate ensued, followed by military defeat in 1646. In England the north of the country was successfully occupied, and a major role was played in the English parliament's decisive victory over the king at Marston Moor in 1644–5. But once it became clear that the English parliament was on the road to victory, it emerged that it was not prepared to pay the price that it had promised in return for Scottish help—the imposition of presbyterianism in England and Ireland, and a political settlement which would protect Scotland's position within Britain. The covenanters were unable to use the fact of having a large and aggressive army in England in bargaining with parliament, because invading England had provoked royalist rebellion in Scotland. A remarkable series of victories in 1644–5 by the marquis of

Montrose threatened to destroy the covenanting regime, and had forced it to withdraw thousands of troops from England. Just when the covenanters most needed some muscle in peace negotiations in England their reputation had been shattered, and their military power seemed on the verge of collapse.

Battered and embittered, the Scots withdrew from England. Their confidence and unity collapsed. Some, though pathetically bewildered as to why god was no longer bringing them victory, believed that priority should still be given to serving his presbyterian will. But increasing numbers, particularly of noblemen, had doubts as to Scotland's divine mission. Perhaps it would be better to concentrate on political matters. As the English parliament had betrayed them, perhaps an agreement with the king could be arranged, for surely now he had been defeated he would make concessions. The 'Engagement' treaty was cobbled together and a distinctly ramshackle invasion of England undertaken in 1648—which met with total defeat. The decision to support the king had split the covenanting movement into fragments, and the 'kirk party', which put religion before all else, had bitterly opposed it. With the defeat of the noble-dominated Engagers in England, the kirk party was able to seize power in Scotland and embark on a series of thorough purges of the church, state officials, parliament and the army to remove 'malignants'. But soon the kirk party had to compromise to gain support for its continuing confrontation with the English parliament (which had complicated matters by executing Charles I and abolishing monarchy), and it drifted into an unhappy alliance with the young Charles II. This provoked English invasion and, ultimately, conquest.

Thus the subtitle of this book could well have been 'downhill all the way'. The civil wars had begun in Scotland. Now they ended there, for the English had already conquered Ireland. In trying to assert her status within the Three Kingdoms of the Isles, and then (made arrogant by success) to dominate a settlement in them, the covenanters had brought on the country the ultimate disaster of foreign conquest.

Perhaps because the years 1644–51 are ones of Scottish failure and collapse, they still tend to be shunned by Scottish historians. Since my books were first published in the 1970s, much has been written on the years of covenanting success (see the Bibliographical Update included in the reprint of *The Scottish Revolution*), but very little specifically on the years of decline. *Revolution and Counter Revolution* thus may still be regarded as the fullest account of the period, and I am delighted that this reprint is to be illustrated. Photographs I collected thirty years ago in the hope that the first edition would be illustrated now at last appear.

DS
2003

CHAPTER ONE

Civil War in England and Scotland, January 1644–September 1645

INTERVENTION IN ENGLAND AND ROYALIST REACTION IN SCOTLAND

The army of the covenant, close to its nominal strength of 21,000 men, crossed the Tweed on 19 January 1644 under the command of Alexander Leslie, earl of Leven, the old mercenary soldier who had led the Scots armies in the Bishops' Wars of 1639–40. The invading force met with little opposition until it reached Newcastle; the city refused to surrender and an assault failed,[1] so Leven and the committee of estates accompanying his army turned to consolidating their hold on Northumberand and to raising supplies there for their army.[2] They also wrote urgently demanding more men and supplies from Scotland, and entreated that the Scottish army in Ireland be transferred to England.[3] The covenanters' main executive body, the committee of estates in Edinburgh, was doing all it could to help the army, and on 1 February the convention of estates (virtually an informal parliament) ordered the northern shires which had not yet sent men to England to do so; but it also ordered all shires to prepare to raise a second levy, half the strength of the first.[4] This was evidently intended to form a reserve army which could be brought together quickly to deal with any royalist rising or invasion, and the army in England therefore opposed the raising of it for fear that it would divert supplies and recruits from England.[5]

As to the army in Ireland, the convention confirmed an earlier agreement that if the English parliament did not pay some of its arrears it should leave Ireland. But Major General Robert Monro (who commanded the army) and some of his officers were determined to remain in Ireland, and many in Scotland supported them. A joint meeting of the committee of estates and the privy council on 22 February therefore reversed the decision of the convention and instructed the army to stay in Ireland to protect protestants there and prevent any invasion of Scotland by the confederate Irish catholic rebels.[6] Before these new orders reached the army, however, three regiments had already sailed for Scotland; the others were furious at the orders but though they had been ready to disobey

Monro they did not dare to defy the committee, and therefore reluctantly agreed to stay in Ireland for the present.[7]

This was a great disappointment to the army in England. Failure to send it sufficient supplies or reinforcements either from Scotland or Ireland left it ill equipped to undertake major operations, though in April it managed to advance to lay siege to York (having left men to besiege Newcastle), where it was joined by the parliamentary army of the Eastern Association.[8] This, however, was not enough to save the army's reputation; already it was widely felt that it was a failure. In the circumstances this was hardly fair. Though it had failed to bring any large royalist army to battle and had not captured either Newcastle or York, it had shut up many royalists in the two cities and its very presence in England constituted a threat that the royalists could not ignore, and thus it relieved pressure on parliament's armies in the south. The trouble was that far too much had been expected of the Scots.[9] The covenanters, full of crusading zeal and memories of how the king's forces had fled before them in 1640, had expected their army to have an immediate decisive effect in England. The parliamentarians who had supported Scots intervention had had similar hopes, which were now dashed, while those who distrusted and feared the Scots now hastened to make capital out of their failure to live up to expectations, in the hope of preventing them gaining undue influence in English affairs.

The Scots therefore found that quick victory was no easier to achieve in religious and civil matters in England than in military ones. The general assembly had sent a distinguished team of advisers to aid the Westminster Assembly in reforming religion in England—five ministers (Alexander Henderson, Robert Douglas, Samuel Rutherford, Robert Baillie and George Gillespie) and three elders (the earl of Cassillis, Lord Maitland and Sir Archibald Johnston of Wariston). But when the first of these commissioners reached London late in 1643 they soon found that 'the best of the English have a verie ill will to employ our aid';[10] the Westminster Assembly had been set up to encourage the Scots to give parliament military help, not through any wish for immediate ecclesiastical reform. Though most of the members of the assembly favoured some sort of presbyterian system for England they were unwilling to accept the kirk as their model and wished to avoid offending the Independents unnecessarily. An English presbyterian minister could state 'that by this covenant we are bound no more to conform to Scotland than Scotland to us', an opinion that to most Scots seemed to deny one of the essential points of the solemn league and covenant. But Stephen Marshall (who had helped to negotiate the covenant) took a leading part in preventing divisions deepening and tempers rising by supporting compromise. The Independents also avoided being too outspoken; they might dislike Scots presbyterianism, but they recognised the need for alliance with the Scots until the civil war was won.[11] The Scots found that weeks passed in indecisive debates and that their influence on them was limited. But they comforted themselves with the belief that all would change once the Scottish army showed parliament how to win the war—though in fairness it must be said that they too saw the need to preserve unity until victory was in sight, and therefore resolved to avoid any public quarrel with the Independents for the time being.[12]

The alliance between the two kingdoms inevitably gave rise to a need for frequent consultations between them about civil as well as religious affairs, especially over conduct of the war and peace negotiations with the king. English commissioners were therefore appointed to accompany the Scots army in England and its attendant committee of estates, and parliament asked the Scots to appoint commissioners to reside in London.[13] This the Scots were eager to do, hoping that such commissioners 'would get the guiding of all the affairs both of this State and Church' (exactly the ambition that many English feared motivated the Scots), and on 3 January 1644 the convention of estates nominated the earl of Loudoun (chancellor of Scotland), Lord Maitland, Wariston and Robert Barclay to proceed to London to see the solemn league and covenant imposed in England, and to work to establish religious uniformity and the liberties of both kingdoms. Provided these ends were achieved they were to work with parliament to restore peace.[14] When the commissioners reached London they found much division in parliament over who should have control of the day to day running of the war, parliament or a committee, and what part the Scots should be allowed in it. In the end it was agreed that a committee of both kingdoms, on which the Scots commissioners would sit, should be established with wide powers to 'order and direct' the war. Many had wished to give such power to parliament's commander in chief, the earl of Essex, one of the main arguments in favour of this being that 'it would avoid the Scots' Power over us', an indication of how deep suspicion of the Scots was, even though they only comprised a small minority on the joint committee.[15]

The Scots members of the committee were soon busy trying to get parliament to send money and supplies to their army and in debating joint peace proposals for presentation to the king.[16] Like their colleagues attending the Westminster Assembly they did not express their views too forcibly at first, for they too expected that a quick victory by their army would bring them popularity and influence. They were soon disillusioned. Robert Baillie complained that 'we are exceeding sadd, and ashamed that our armie, so much talked off, hes done as yet nothing at all. What can be the reason of it, we cannot guesse, only we think, that God, to humble our pride . . . hes not yet been pleased to assist them'.[17] So much had been expected of the army that its moderate success was seen as complete failure.

As well as disappointments in England the covenanters had to face dangers at home caused by the activities of Scottish royalists. After King Charles I had imprisoned the duke of Hamilton in December 1643, for failing to prevent the covenanters allying themselves to the English parliament, he turned for advice to the extreme royalists who had long denounced Hamilton as a traitor and urged the need for armed resistance to the covenanters. Their spokesman was the earl of Montrose, and he quickly worked out plans for royalist risings to coincide with an invasion from Ireland, which was to be organised by the irrepressible earl of Antrim, who had recently escaped for the second time from imprisonment by the Scottish army in Ireland. Antrim had persuaded the confederate Irish to grant him the rank of lieutenant general, and then went to Oxford and presented himself to the king as being in effect the supreme commander of the Irish armies, in which capacity he offered to raise for the king 10,000 Irish soldiers for service in England and 3,000 for Scotland.[18] In spite of doubts as to Antrim's reliability Charles commissioned him on 20 January 1644 to persuade the Irish to send 10,000 men to England and 2,000 to Scotland. In planning the Scottish venture Antrim was to work with Montrose, and he was empowered to offer Major General Monro an earldom and a pension of £2,000 sterling per annum if he and the Scottish army in Ireland would declare for the king. Eight days later Antrim (now general of the Isles and Highlands of Scotland) and Montrose (now lieutenant general of Scotland) signed a formal agreement whereby Montrose undertook to do his utmost to raise forces in the north, the east and on the Borders, and declare for the king by 1 April; Antrim promised to do all he could to raise forces in Ireland and the Western Isles and invade the marquis of Argyll's estates with them by the same date.[19]

Montrose immediately began trying to obtain aid from Scots royalists in England. Probably at his suggestion those at Oxford published a declaration denouncing the covenanters' invasion of England as treason.[20] The king helped by writing to those within Scotland whom he thought remained loyal, either commissioning them to act as his lieutenants[21] or asking them to assist such lieutenants.[22] Montrose soon found many of the Scots royalists whom he approached reluctant to help him. Some were moderates who had supported Hamilton and were shocked at his imprisonment; others had fled to England out of passive loyalty to the king but were reluctant to involve themselves in plots and armed risings; and many more proved uncooperative out of personal dislike and jealousy of

Montrose, hating him as a former covenanter whom the king was now favouring above those who had always been loyal to him.[23]

Antrim too met with difficulties; it was not until late June that he managed to assemble three regiments in Ireland and shipping to carry them to Scotland, under the command of Alaster Macdonald, whose family had been driven out of Scotland by the Campbells.[24] Macdonald had landed in the Western Isles with a raiding party of Irish in November 1643, perhaps in the hope of freeing his father Col Macgillispeck (whose nickname of Col Keitach was sometimes transferred to his son) and two brothers who were being held prisoner by Argyll, but the raiders had been driven out by the Campbells in the early months of 1644.[25]

Montrose also failed to have men in arms in Scotland by 1 April. The king instructed the northern English royalists to help him, but there was little they were able to do and he got little encouragement from within Scotland. As in the Bishops' Wars the north-east seemed the most likely area for a royalist rising, but the leader of the royalists of the area, the marquis of Huntly, was an indecisive man given to relying on the advice of astrologers; he was also virtually bankrupt and his influence was weakened by family quarrels. His eldest son, Lord Gordon, had been persuaded by his uncle, Argyll, to accept command of a regiment of covenanters, whereupon his father refused to speak to him. Proceedings had been begun against Huntly for his failure to take the covenant, whereupon he had retired to his castle of Bog of Gight and refused to surrender himself.[26]

Huntly thus was not prepared to take the initiative against the covenanters though he defied them. Not surprisingly other local royalists saw this as folly; it would rouse the wrath of the covenanters without helping the king. Sir John Gordon of Haddo and a few other lairds therefore resolved on a rising as the only practical alternative to submission—Haddo was already in trouble with the covenanters, and had failed to appear before the convention to answer charges against him.[27] From the timing of his rising it seems likely that he was in touch with Montrose and therefore expected help from him and Antrim by 1 April.On 19 March Haddo and others, about a hundred men, raided Aberdeen and kidnapped leading covenanters, probably hoping that this would lead the burgh to revert to its former royalism and would encourage other royalists to appear in arms. They may also have hoped that their action would force Huntly to join them; if so, they were partially successful. Though angered by the rising he issued a declaration justifying it, but promising that those involved would submit if they were assured that no violence would be done to them. He can hardly have expected that the covenanters would agree to this, but at about this time he received a message from the king promising him aid (Charles had in fact appointed him king's lieutenant for the north-east, though he may not have known of this yet) through Montrose and Antrim, and he may have hoped to delay the covenanters by negotiations until this arrived.[28]

Having justified Haddo's raid Huntly gathered his own forces and occupied Aberdeen—as much to reassert his own authority as for any more practical reason. The burgh proved hostile through resentment at Haddo's raid and fear of the covenanters' revenge. The royalists therefore seized what arms and money they could find and quartered men on the unwilling town while occupying themselves in the congenial task of plundering local covenanters. As had happened in 1639, having occupied Aberdeen the royalists seemed to have no idea what to do next.[29]

On hearing of Haddo's rising the committee of estates in Edinburgh dispatched orders to the committees of war of the northern shires to gather forces against the rebels, but few men were sent from the south because of fears aroused by Montrose's efforts to raise men in the north of England.[30] The convention of estates met on 10 April to consider the situation; Argyll had returned from the army in England to give his advice and the commission of the kirk had already acted by excommunicating Huntly, Haddo and their supporters as well as Montrose and other royalists in England.[31] The convention appointed the earl of Callander commander of all forces to be used within Scotland; his earlier flirtations with royalists were ignored as he had a sound reputation as a professional soldier and was highly regarded by the many mercenary officers employed by the covenanters. He was a difficult, unscrupulous and ambitious man and the covenanters were probably glad to have him accept employment under them; he had, it appears, been offered the post of lieutenant general under Leven in the army in England but had refused it, insisting on an independent command. He now agreed to lead the forces sent to keep order in the south of Scotland and guard the Borders, marching into England later if necessary. The army sent to the north against Huntly was to be commanded by Argyll, technically in subordination to Callander.[32]

Three days before the convention made these appointments Montrose entered Scotland. He had managed to assemble about 800 English foot, three troops of English cavalry and about 200 Scots horse. Most of the Englishmen were unenthusiastic, ill-armed and untrained but Montrose decided to march north from Carlisle without delay since he had already failed in his undertaking to enter Scotland by 1 April. He reached Dumfries without encountering opposition but there was little sign of local support for him and his forces were dwindling fast through desertion. He could not face the forces which Callander gathered against him and therefore had to flee back into England at the end of April.[33] The army in England urged that Callander follow him to prevent him raising new forces, for with most of the army occupied in the sieges of Newcastle and York adequate forces could not be spared to hold down the large areas of northern England that the army nominally occupied. But Callander quartered his army along the Borders to prevent any further royalist incursion while Montrose took advantage of the vacuum in the north of England to recapture several garrisons from the covenanters.[34]

Meanwhile the rising in the north had been crushed almost as easily as Montrose's venture in the south. In the absence of an Irish landing or revolts elsewhere in Scotland Huntly had no plan of campaign; he showed the quality of his leadership by gloomily issuing black cockades to his already apprehensive men as a sign they were willing to fight to the death. By the end of April Argyll's forces were approaching Aberdeen from the south while to the north local covenanters prepared to attack the rebels. Huntly's army began to waste away through desertion and his friends started to 'grvge and mvrmwr with his delayis', arguing that their only hope was to attack before the convenanters' preparations were complete. But the only move he would make was backwards; as the covenanters closed in on Aberdeenn he retired northwards and Argyll occupied the burgh on 2 May. Haddo surrendered and most of the other royalist lairds followed suit or were captured, while Huntly fled to Strathnaver 'quhair he remanit, sore against his will, whil the 4th of October 1645'. The covenanters could congratulate themselves that the first royalist risings provoked by their alliance with the English parliament had collapsed almost without bloodshed.[35]

On 4 June 1644 the first Scottish triennial parliament assembled (as arranged in 1641). Apart from confirming the work of the convention which had preceded[36] it parliament concerned itself mainly with punishing those who had been involved in the recent rebellions, with providing for the Scottish armies in all three kingdoms and with considering peace proposals to be presented to the king by both kingdoms. The session lasted much longer than had been expected, for nearly two months, since discussion of peace proposals and the appointment of new commissioners to reside in London led to much dispute; but eventually Argyll and the more extreme covenanters succeeded in getting men who shared their views appointed, the nine commissioners including Argyll himself, Loudoun, Lord Balmerino and Wariston.[37] Much delay was also caused by the fact that while parliament sat there was no compact executive body to carry on the routine work of govemment; many matters of minor importance were therefore dealt with by the full parliament, or referred to specially appointed temporary committees, which often had to report back to parliament. Such methods were inefficient. The committee with the army in England complained that it had not heard from Edinburgh officially for nearly three months, while Robert Baillie complained of the lack of news or instructions from Scotland as 'a sottishness unexcusable'.[38] Clearly there was a need for a permanent general committee to sit during meetings of parliament, like the committee of estates which sat between meetings. But it was doubtless memories of the all-powerful committee of the lords of the articles through which the king had once controlled parliament that led to a general reluctance to give any committee power while parliament sat.

In dealing with opponents of the covenanters some moderation was shown, though examples were made of three individuals. Haddo and John Logie were condemned and executed for their part in the Aberdeen rising, as was William Maxwell of Middletoun for having joined Montrose in Dumfries. In addition three Scots who held important positions in the king's armies in England, the earls of Crawford and Forth and Lord Eythin, were declared to have forfeited lives and property.[39] But no attempt was made to forfeit Montrose, Huntly or other nobles who had recently been in arms against the covenants; evidently a strong body of opinion was opposed to taking drastic action against them, in the hope that they might be persuaded to submit if not made desperate by harsh action. They had already been excommunicated and had their incomes in Scotland confiscated until they signed the solemn league and covenant, and this was thought sufficient punishment for the present.

Parliament granted Crawford's forfeited title to the earl of Lindsay; he had long coveted it as it traditionally belonged to the head of the Lindsays. The new earl of Crawford-Lindsay (as he henceforth signed himself) was further favoured by being appointed treasurer of Scotland. The king was not consulted, though his approval was subsequently sought; this was a reversal of the procedure stipulated by the 1641 act conceming choosing officers of state, whereby the king should have made the appointment and parliament approved it. Parliament also ruled that the earl of Lanark (the duke of Hamilton's brother) was sole secretary of state; the king had replaced him by Sir Robert Spottiswood on the disgrace of the Hamiltons but the covenanters now bid for their support by refusing to accept the change[40] and by protesting at the imprisonment of Hamilton without trial.[41] These moves were successful. Many of Hamilton's supporters had already signed the covenants to demonstrate their disapproval of the king's action, and many of them now sat in parliament and at least acquiesced in the aid being given to the king's enemies in England; they would not have done so had the king been more sensible in his treatment of Hamilton.

In military matters parliament ordered the levying of men to reinforce Callander's army in the Borders.[42] The situation in the north of England was still confused. The English parliament opposed the withdrawal of any men from the siege of York, and the remainder of Leven's army proved insufficient to subdue Montrose. It was therefore decided that Callander should lead his army into England, deal with Montrose, and then merge his army with Leven's. On 22 June the English agreed to this, and Callander crossed the border three days later with between seven and ten thousand men.[43]

Montrose later complained that he could easily have kept Callander out of England if Prince Rupert (the king's nephew) had not called him south,[44] but in the circumstances Rupert's action was justified, for he needed all the men he could get for his attempt to relieve York from the besieging Scots and parliamentary armies. York was duly relieved, but on 2 July Rupert was crushingly defeated at Marston Moor, the greatest victory yet won by the king's enemies.

In spite of the fact that at Marston Moor the royalists were greatly outnumbered by parliamentarians and Scots they at first seemed likely to prevail. Parliament's right wing collapsed and fled, accompanied by Lord Fairfax and the earl of Leven, who were convinced that the battle was lost. But the Scots infantry in the centre stood firm, while on the left wing Cromwell's cavalry and Major General Leslie's Scots horse routed their opponents and then joined the infantry in destroying the royalist centre. Leven, whose flight had carried him as far as Leeds, lamented on hearing the news, 'I would to God I had dyed upon the place'; if there was anything more humiliating than a fleeing general being the first to bring news of his own defeat, it was a general acting thus when he was in fact victorious. His conduct was therefore an embarrassment to the Scots but Robert Douglas, his chaplain, had glib explanations for all awkward facts. If the right wing had fled it was because God (not being, in this instance, on the side of the big battalions) thought that victory would not be sufficiently glorious if his forces outnumbered those of the enemy, 'therefor he dismayed more than the halfe' of his forces so that they ran away. Moreover he wished to act as his own general and therefore caused Leven and Fairfax to flee.[45]

York surrendered within two weeks of the battle but the Scots were diverted from marching further south by the continued resistance of Newcastle. Their army therefore marched back to Newcastle, there joining Callander's army, which now merged with Leven's.[46] Marston Moor was the decisive success in England that the covenanters had long awaited to restore their reputation in London; 'behold, in a moment, when our credit was beginning sensiblie to decay, God hes come in'. But they soon found that victory did not bring them the popularity and power they had expected. In spite of their attempts to emphasise the part the Scots had played they found popular opinion far more willing to credit reports that Cromwell, already known as no friend of the Scots, was chiefly responsible for the victory.[47] Had the Scots thought more deeply about the matter they might have predicted that success would not increase their popularity; it was natural that the suspicion that they were trying to interfere in English affairs and dictate a religious settlement should increase as the power of the Scottish army grew. Yet at the same time the Scots were finding that their failure to capture Newcastle was discrediting them. The Scots army was in the unhappy situation that failure increased contempt for it while success increased suspicion of it.

THE TREATY OF UXBRIDGE

During 1644 the religious differences between the covenanters and the Independents in England came to correspond more closely than before with a division in attitudes to the civil war and peace negotiations. The Scots army had been brought into England by the 'war party' and the 'middle group' in the English parliament, against the wishes of the 'peace party' which feared that Scottish intervention would prolong the civil war and make a compromise settlement with the king impossible. But once attempts began to agree on terms for a settlement in England differences arose between the Scots and their former supporters in parliament through incompatible ambitions. The war party had wanted the Scots alliance in order to bring about complete victory in the war; but this the Scots failed to achieve, and as the war dragged on indecisively many Scots came round to supporting those in England who wanted a negotiated, compromise settlement. In politics it came to be seen that the war party wished to go further in destroying royal power than the Scots; in religion the war party included a wide variety of moderate presbyterian, Independent and sectarian opinions, and it became clear that they would not accept a strict presbyterian settlement of the type that the Scots sought.

It has recently been said that 'it became evident that the Scots were interested in something other than winning the war for an English parliament. For them the purpose of the alliance was to promote the establishment of a theocratic presbytery in England. To this they were committed by both principle and expediency'. The Scots had little concern for constitutional issues in England (which seemed of paramount importance to parliament); provided presbyterianism was established the Scots 'would have no objection to the king being restored to his full executive powers.'[48]

This statement would have been entirely acceptable to members of the war party, for it reflects their propaganda image of the Scots. It is of course true that the covenanters wished to establish presbyterianism on Scottish lines in England, but this was by no means their only ambition there. As in 1640–1 proposals for unity of religion were only one aspect of their wishes for closer union, for permanent links between the kingdoms to protect Scotland by preventing the king using English resources against her. Moreover it is overstating the case to say that the Scots were little concerned with constitutional matters in England; they were anxious to see the king's power limited, but the achievement of this was a matter in which the English parliament usually needed little encouragement from the Scots. On constitutional issues on which it was felt parliament could not be relied to act on its own—as over establishing permanent links with the Scottish parliament—the Scots did interfere. That the covenanters were not happy at the war party's plans to render the king completely powerless hardly proves that from the first they had no wish to see his power limited at all, any more than the fact that the covenanters proved most active in trying to determine the shape of a religious settlement in England proves that religion was all that they were interested in—even though it suited the war party to assert that this was the case. Moreover parliament itself had invited the Scots to help to advise it on a religious settlement, and this gave them good authority to urge their views in England; in any case religion was the concern of all men and the Scots believed they had a duty to propagate their own beliefs, whereas they showed a tendency to hold back in constitutional affairs because they recognised the strength of the argument that such matters were the concern of Englishmen alone. Thus the fact that religion came to cause most controversy between the allies does not prove that it was the most important matter to the covenanters—any more than it proves that it was most important to the English parliament.

The allegation that it became evident that the Scots 'were interested in something other than winning the war for an English parliament', which implies that this had not been known before, hardly stands up to examination. Had parliamentarians ever thought the Scots were acting in a purely selfless way they would have been remarkably naive, believing them to be acting in a way unparalleled in history. They would, moreover, have had to be both blind and deaf, for the covenanters had never made any secret of the fact that they hoped that their intervention in England in 1644, as in 1640–1, would lead to political and religious changes in England which would spread true religion and give security to their revolution in Scotland. The differences between the ultimate aims of the war party and the middle group on the one hand and the covenanters on the other had always been evident, but in late 1643 and early 1644 efforts had been made to play them down since the first priority had to be defeating the king, which was essential to the survival of both parties. Each party at first expected quick military victory. The Scots hoped that their part in this victory would then enable them to dominate a settlement in England, while the war party believed that it would then be in such a strong position that it could defy the Scots, whom it had only chosen as allies through necessity. Dislike of the Scots could be whipped up by denouncing them for interfering in England's internal affairs, even if all they were trying to do was to impose the solemn league and covenant which the English parliament had ratified. The covenanters had good reason for coming to believe that they had been double-crossed by their allies.

Failure to achieve the expected quick victory in the war led to disagreements between the allies emerging clearly before the war had ended, though the fact that it still remained to be won prevented them being pressed too far. The attitude of the Scots to the war began to change. Lack of military success by their army in England and Montrose's royalist victories in Scotland began to swing them towards desiring not a military but a negotiated settlement that would satisfy their ambitions in England and allow them to concentrate their resources against Montrose. Scots desires for a negotiated settlement were reinforced by the conduct of their allies. After mid 1644 the Independents and others in the Westminster Assembly who opposed the introduction of strict presbyterianism to England became increasingly obstructive and outspoken.[49] Disagreements with parliament itself increased during negotiations over joint peace proposals for presentation to the king, for the Scots showed themselves more ready to make concessions to the king than their English allies were; and the deeper the split between the Scots and the war party grew, the more the Scots wanted a compromise settlement. A settlement in England which left the war party, increasingly hostile to the Scots, in power no longer seemed in Scotland's interests, whereas a settlement which divided power between parliament and the king might leave the Scots holding the balance between the two, courted by both. In 1644–6 the Scots did not change their basic ambitions in England, but the methods by which they attempted to achieve them altered.

The insistence of the Scots on opening negotiations with the king infuriated the war party; and this drove the Scots into alliance with the peace party, with whom they found they had many interests in common. The peace party feared that the war party, led by religious radicals, would carry out 'a total alteration of the constitution and the subversion of the social order' and therefore 'began to turn to the Scots in the autumn of 1644 as counters . . . to the sects and the radicals'. This led to a remarkable reversal of alliances; less than a year after entering England at the behest of the war party and the middle group, the Scots had become the allies of the peace party which had originally opposed their entry into England.[50] In this reversal lay the origins of the main split in the English parliament for the next three or four years—or at least the origins of its nomenclature. The peace party, through its alliance with the Scots, became committed to a presbyterian religious settlement (though many of its members had little liking for the Scottish kirk) and hence became known as the presbyterian party. The war party and the middle group, as a counter to the military power of the Scots, created the new model army. From the first this was dominated by religious Independents, and its creators therefore gradually became known as the Independent party. These parties were relatively small; most members of parliament were permanently committed to neither. But at first the Independents could usually rely on the support of many men who were ready to vote with them 'to get rid of the Scots, to frustrate an intolerantly Presbyterian religious settlement'.[51]

Superficially, however, attempts were made to preserve some appearance of unity, though in December 1644 the Scots tried to arrange for the trial of one of their most outspoken war party enemies, Oliver Cromwell, as 'an *incendiary* whay kindleth coals of contention and raises differences in the state to the public damage'. But though the solemn league and covenant bound both kingdoms to prosecute incendiaries the Scots were disappointed to be advised that such a prosecution in England would have little hope of success.[52] The idea of proceeding against him was therefore abandoned, which the Scots must have regretted when later in the same month Cromwell was reported to have said that 'he could as soon draw his sword against them [the Scots] as against any in the king's army'.[53] Anti-Scots feeling also remained strong among some peace party supporters—some officers were reported to have threatened to join the king to prevent the Scots conquering England[54]—but gradually the willingness of the Scots to work for a compromise settlement was realised.

Cromwell might openly denounce the Scots, but most war party leaders recognised that their help was still needed. They therefore accepted the insistence of the Scots and the peace party that peace negotiations be opened with the king, hoping that they would fail and thus prove to the covenanters that compromise was impossible and that the war must continue until he was completely defeated. Joint peace proposals were sent to Charles in November 1644. In religion they demanded that he swear the solemn league and covenant, impose it on all his subjects, abolish episcopacy in England and Ireland and so reform religion in these kingdoms that unity with Scotland could be achieved, along with uniformity of church govemment. Levying and commanding armed forces in England and Scotland were to be in the hands of militia commissioners appointed by the respective parliaments; up to one third of the commissioners of Scotland were to sit and vote with the English commissioners in matters conceming Scotland, and *vice versa.* All commissioners of the two kingdoms were to meet together to settle matters concerning preserving the peace between them, to resist rebellion in or invasion of either kingdom, and to direct the war in Ireland. Thus permanent links between the two parliaments would be established and the king would be unable to use the forces of one kingdom against the other. In addition the making of war or peace with foreign states would require the joint consent of both parliaments, the education and marriage of the king's children would be arranged jointly, and negotiations would take place about free trade and commercial cooperation between the kingdoms.[55]

To the Scots these proposals to tie the kingdoms closer together in both civil and religious matters seemed of central importance in a settlement; but to the majority of English parliamentarians they seemed irrelevant complications of the issues they were fighting for and were included only to humour their allies. Negotiations on the propositions began at Uxbridge in January 1645. The lack of trust between the Scots and parliament was demonstrated when arrangements were made as to the order in which the various proposals should be discussed. It was agreed to divide them under three headings, religion, militia and Ireland. The Scots demanded that religion be debated first; only once agreement had been reached with the king on this should the other topics be negotiated on. Parliament opposed this, for fear that if the king made concessions in religion the Scots would then join him in urging parliament to compromise on other issues. It was therefore eventually arranged that each of the three topics should be discussed in rotation, three days being spent on each at a time.[56]

Luckily for the squabbling allies the king was not yet ready to try to divide his enemies by playing on the differences between them, and his refusal to make significant concessions led to deadlock and the abandonment of the treaty. During the debates the English commissioners had said relatively little, leaving most of the talking to the Scots since it was they who had insisted on having a treaty. As the Independent party had hoped, the failure of the treaty persuaded the Scots that further negotiations with the king were pointless for the present. They reported to Edinburgh with indignant surprise that Charles had not agreed to abolish bishops 'notwithstanding that the unlawfulness of Episcopacie from

Scripture and reason was cleerely evinced'.[57]

The covenanters were also encouraged to continue their alliance with parliament by the fact that the Westminster Assembly now at last seemed to be making some progress. By the end of 1644 it had approved a directory of worship and propositions concerning church government and the ordination of ministers. A special general assembly was therefore summoned in Edinburgh which accepted the documents with only minor alterations. This was a clear indication of the importance that the kirk attached to religious unity, for it was adopting for its own use standards which were the work of an English assembly (though admittedly Scots influence in it had been strong) even though this meant abandoning several details of worship traditional and well loved in the kirk.[58]

The failure of the treaty of Uxbridge and the progress over religious unity reinforced the determination of the Scots to defeat the king, but tension between them and their English allies remained. The Scots commissioners in London found that contempt for their country was increasing through their failure to defeat Montrose and the consequent weakness of their army in England; 'O! If you could gett one sound blow of Montrose, that the body of that army might come up to England'.[59] In June 1645 there were rumours that the Independents in parliament and the army were secretly negotiating with the king for the surrender of Oxford; fearing that they were trying to make a peace which would betray the interests of the Scots, Robert Baillie stirred up English presbyterians in the City to protest at any such intrigue. The rumour proved false, but Baillie's success in rousing opposition to the alleged plot reveals that the Scots did have a considerable number of supporters in London.[60]

Fortune, however, favoured the Independents. On 14 June the new model army won a major victory over the king at Naseby, raising fears that it would be able to win the war on its own and that credit for the victory would go almost entirely to the Independents.[61] For while the new model army went from strength to strength the Scots army in England achieved little. Montrose's victories made it reluctant to move far from the Borders and it was resentful of the failure of its English employers to pay it as promised. It was forced to raise provisions for itself in the north of England, a process which diverted it from military action and led to endless disputes with parliament. In March 1645 Leven reluctantly agreed to send David Leslie with several thousand men into Yorkshire, but he and the greater part of the army obstinately declined to move south;[62] when in May the committee of both kingdoms urged him to march towards the western Midlands he instead led most of his army into Cumberland and laid siege to Carlisle. On further promptings he moved south in June; but he left part of his army before Carlisle, which soon surrendered and was garrisoned by the Scots. The English parliament protested, insisting that the garrison should be English, but the Scots refused to give it up while there was any possibility of the king trying to join Montrose in Scotland. At the end of July Leven laid siege to Hereford, but he soon sent David Leslie and all the Scots cavalry back north when new fears arose that the king was trying to reach Scotland.[63] Naturally when forced to choose the army acted in the interests of its native land rather than in the interest of the English parliament; equally understandably parliament was exasperated by the army's obsession with Scottish affairs, for it tended to regard the army as a mercenary one in its employment (even though it failed to pay it) rather than as the army of an ally not entirely under English control.

MONTROSE'S YEAR OF VICTORIES: TIPPERMUIR TO INVERLOCHY

The Scottish parliament first heard of the landing of Alaster Macdonald and the Irish force sent by Antrim on 9 July 1644, and a week later it commissioned Argyll to act against them.[64] But it was not at first anticipated that the Irish would present any immediate or serious threat to the country; after all, Argyll's forces had been sufficient to drive Macdonald back to Ireland earlier in the year. Macdonald had sailed from Ireland at the end of June with about 1,600 men, perhaps a few hundred more.[65] He had landed in Morvern, expecting to be joined by Highland royalists, especially the earl of Seaforth and Sir James Macdonald of Sleat. But none appeared, for the venture seemed to have little hope of success. Discouraged, Macdonald contemplated returning to Ireland, but was prevented from doing so by the capture or destruction of the ships which had brought him to Scotland by ships of the English parliament. Rather than wait on the coast until forces could be sent against him, Macdonald marched inland into Badenoch. He managed to gather a few hundred recruits but found that most Highlanders regarded him as an invader, while the royalists of the north-east were too demoralised by the failure of Huntly and Haddo and the subsequent finings and quarterings of the covenanters to join any rising.[66]

When Montrose first heard of the landing of the Irish is not known, but he almost certainly had heard of it by 18 August when he secretly entered Scotland with only two companions; he had failed to raise revolts in Scotland to assist the Irish but could at least offer them his leadership. He ordered Alaster Macdonald to bring his men south into Atholl, and there he joined them. The men of Atholl were mainly royalist in sympathy but had regarded the Irish as foreign brigands rather than as potential allies.

Once Montrose put himself at the head of the Irish, however, most of the inhabitants agreed to join them.[67] The meeting of Montrose and the Irish saved both from failure. The Irish provided Montrose with the nucleus of an army while he, as a Scottish nobleman, provided them with some respectability and legitimacy, at least in the eyes of Highland royalists.

Like parliament, the committee of estates did not at first see the Irish as a serious menace, even after Montrose joined them; the collapse of his raid on Dumfries led to his ability being underestimated. The committee was therefore much more concerned by the possibility of royalist raids from England and by the state of the Scots army there than by the situation in the north.[68] Thus three weeks after the landing of the Irish had been reported the committee ordered men from the northern shires to be sent to join the army in England. Forces in the Borders were ordered to march to Newcastle, not against the Irish.[69] The measures which were taken against the Irish showed little sense of urgency and poor planning. It was at first left to Argyll to deal with them and then, when they moved eastwards, to the committee for the north sitting in Aberdeen. The latter prepared to defend the north-east but failed to take any precautions against the rebels moving south into shires outwith its responsibility. Not until the last days of August did the committee in Edinburgh realise the danger that Montrose might not wait in the north until forces were gathered to defeat him, and that if he chose to march south towards Perth there would be no army available to oppose him. It therefore ordered levies from central Scotland and the Lothians to assemble and gave command of them to the earl of Lothian until Argyll should return from the west.[70] The seriousness of the royalist threat was now sufficiently appreciated for an appeal to be sent to the army in England to send some cavalry back to Scotland.[71]

Montrose acted before these preparations were complete. Only levies from Fife and Perth were ready to oppose him at Tippermuir (or Tibbermore), about three miles west of Perth, on 1 September. Nonetheless the covenanters had perhaps twice as many men as Montrose's little army of about 2,500. But Montrose had the advantage that many of his men were experienced fighters, especially the Irish, whereas the covenanters' army was almost entirely composed of Lowland levies, untrained, many only recruited a few days or weeks before, 'fresh water shouldiours, neuer before vsed to martiall discipline'. They might be better armed than Montrose's men, but superior arms and numbers were outweighed by greater skill and better leadership. The levies broke on the first charge of the Irish, and were killed in hundreds by the pursuing royalists.[72] Perth surrendered and Montrose lingered there for several days. But if he was expecting his victory to bring him widespread support he was disappointed; victory supplied him with adequate clothes, arms and ammunition for his army, but with very few recruits.

As there was no sign of support for him to the south Montrose turned east, moving towards Aberdeen. But with Huntly fled and Lord Gordon commanding a regiment for the covenanters few of the royalists of the north-east were willing to join him; exceptions were the earl of Airlie and two of his sons, and Nathaniel Gordon (son of Gordon of Ardlogie).[73]

The committee of estates had feared that Montrose would advance south after Tippermuir; a proclamation therefore summoned all forces that could be raised to hurry to Stirling, and an urgent request was sent to the army in England asking that the earl of Callander and three regiments be sent to Scotland immediately. The army had in fact already dispatched three regiments back to Scotland, and on news of Tippermuir several more, along with Callander and other senior officers, were ordered to march north. But the committee in Edinburgh was anxious to weaken the army in England as little as possible; defeating Montrose was less important than defeating the king. Consequently as soon as it was realised that Montrose was not moving south the committee ordered some of the regiments from the army in England to return to it. Leven and the committee with his army stressed the need to defeat Montrose quickly, before revolt could spread, but the Edinburgh committee now insisted that forces raised under Lothian and Argyll would be sufficient to deal with Montrose; Callander was sent back to England.[74]

This indecision meant that the committee for the north was left to face Montrose without help from the south. It ordered all fencible men (able bodied men aged between sixteen and sixty) from the shires of Aberdeen and Banff to rendezvous in Aberdeen on 9 September, and Lord Gordon was appointed lieutenant general of the forces of the covenant in the north, in the hope of winning the support of the Gordons. This proved to be an error of judgement, for the covenanters of the north refused to serve under him, being doubtful of his loyalty and, in many cases, traditional enemies of the Gordons. Lord Gordon and about 3,000 men he had raised were therefore ordered not to come to Aberdeen, and most of them soon disbanded.[75]

Montrose approached the burgh on 13 September and called on it to surrender; if it did not he would allow all old people, women and children to leave, but those who remained were to expect no quarter. The burgh refused either to surrender or to send out non-combatants,[76] and Lord Burleigh (who was no general and apparently commanded simply because he was president of the committee for the north) drew up the covenanters' forces, about 2,500 strong, outside the burgh. This proved a fatal mistake, bred (like so many made in opposing Montrose) by over confidence. If the covenanters had remained within the burgh and defended it they might have been able to hold Montrose off, for he had neither the men nor the time for a siege; he had not many more than 1,500 men, since many of the Highlanders who had fought at Tippemmuir had returned to their homes with their loot.

The battle was hard fought but eventually the covenanters collapsed and fled back to Aberdeen. As at Tippermuir 'Thair was littill slauchter in the fight, bot horribill was the slauchter in the flight'. The Irish and Highlanders burst into the burgh and three days of spasmodic plundering, raping and killing ensued which Montrose made no attempt to stop.[77] It was said that he was incensed by the death of a drummer boy who had been sent into the burgh before the battle with Montrose's message and had been shot dead as he was returning, but the tone of his message suggests that from the first he had been determined to make an example of it if it resisted. Yet of all burghs Aberdeen, the largest centre of royalist sympathy in the country, least deserved such treatment.[78] His action badly damaged the cause he was fighting for; most royalists were already reluctant to join him, not only through fear of the covenanters but from dislike of the Irish catholics who formed the main part of his army. Irish catholics were already associated in the minds of Scots with stories of atrocity and massacre of protestants in Ireland in 1641. Now Montrose's failure to control them in Aberdeen made it seem that they intended to live up to their reputations.

Covenanting forces led by Argyll reached Aberdeen on 18 September, two days after Montrose had left. Understandably Argyll seems to have been none too anxious to catch up with him, and lingered in the burgh for several days[79] while Montrose was busy trying to persuade the Gordons to join him. When they refused he retired through Badenoch back into Atholl.[80] There Alaster Macdonald and many of the Irish temporarily left him to march west to attack the Campbells and collect recruits. Now that the Irish had two victories and the plunder of Perth and Aberdeen to boast of, and Montrose to lead them, they had much more success than previously in persuading Highlanders to join them. Meanwhile Montrose led the few hundred men remaining with him east into Angus for a second time, and then northwards again, while Argyll and Lothian were toiling south through Badenoch and Atholl in pursuit. By mid October Montrose was back in the Gordon country to the north of Aberdeen; he lingered too long in his recruiting and the covenanters caught up with him near Fyvie Castle, but though Argyll had many more men than Montrose he did not know this and therefore failed to press his advantage, allowing Montrose to make good his retreat after some skirmishing into Badenoch and thence to Atholl. Thus Montrose completed his second circuit of the eastern Highlands. This time Argyll made no attempt to follow but marched his army back by way of Aberdeen to bar Montrose's way south or east from Atholl. The royalists were making the covenanters' army look singularly foolish, futilely chasing them round in circles, but the process was also demoralising for Montrose's own men, since their long and exhausting marches seemed to be achieving little. At about this time therefore several of Montrose's most prominent supporters deserted him—though Nathaniel Gordon's 'desertion' may have been planned so that he could try to persuade Lord Gordon to desert the covenanters. Once in Atholl Montrose was rejoined by Alaster Macdonald and the recruits he had secured, though these only brought his strength up to about 3,000 men.[81]

The Highlanders who fought with Montrose at one time or other were drawn from many clans, but nearly all came from the lands stretching east from Mull and south-east from Skye through Lochaber and Badenoch to Atholl and the edge of the Highlands in Aberdeenshire. Most important were the Macdonalds of Sleat, Keppoch, Glengarry, Glencoe and Clanranald, the Macleans from Mull and Morvern, the Stewarts of Atholl in the east and Appin in the west, the Clan Chattan (Macphersons, Mackintoshes and Farquharsons), the Camerons, and Robertsons.[82] Most of these clans had two things in common; catholicism (or at least hatred of presbyterianism), and a hatred of the Campbells which transcended the feuds and disputes between them. Most were or feared that they soon would be threatened by the ever increasing power of the Campbells. The remnants of other clans which had already been largely broken up or absorbed by the Campbells also gave their support to Montrose, though many of them did not act until they were sure that the power of the Campbells had been destroyed—Macgregors, Macnabs, Lamonts, Macdougalls and, above all, the remnants of the Macdonalds of Kintyre and Islay.

As a result of Argyll's failure to defeat Montrose he was replaced as commander of the forces sent against him by Lieutenant General William Baillie, who was recalled from England after both Callander and Lothian had refused the command. Argyll had wished to remain as titular commander with Baillie subordinate to him, but Baillie refused to accept such an arrangement; Argyll was therefore assigned command only of the forces of the West Highlands and Isles. The committee with the army in England was still urging that all possible forces should be concentrated against Montrose, but the committee in Edinburgh continued to fear royalist invasion from England, and in any case was uncertain where to concentrate its forces. Did Montrose intend to march into Argyll, or to attack Glasgow, or to try to join the king in England? Was he expecting reinforcements from Ireland, or was he likely to try to flee to safety there? In trying to guard against all such possibilities as well as keep the Scottish armies in England and Ireland supplied the covenanters time and again failed to have sufficient forces at the right place at the right time to defeat Montrose.[83] 'This is the greatest hurt our poore land gott these fourscore yeare', complained Robert Baillie from London, 'and the greatest disgrace befell us these thousand. If we gett not the life of these wormes chirted [squeezed] out before they creep out of our land, the reproach will stick on us for ever; it hes much diminished our reputation in England alreadie'.[84] Even when the Scots stormed Newcastle on 17 October contempt for them did not diminish.[85]

On returning to Atholl after the skirmish at Fyvie Montrose intended to try to find somewhere in the Lowlands to winter his army, believing that it would be impossible to keep it together in the Highlands—a judgement with which his opponent William Baillie was in agreement. But the Highlanders and Irish were loath to leave the protection of the hills, and believed that a Highland campaign could be fought even in winter. Many were more inspired by hatred of the Campbells than by love of the king, and they therefore demanded that Montrose lead them into Argyll, claiming they could plunder enough food for the army there.[86] Eventually Montrose agreed and led his men west, plundering and burning the lands of the Campbells, who were taken by surprise and offered little organised resistance; Argyll fled as Montrose approached Inveraray. One of the Irish officers boasted that 'we left neither house nor hold unburned, nor corn nor cattle, that belonged to the whole name of Campbell' while the historian of the Clanranald claimed that during the ravaging of Argyll Montrose's army killed 895 men 'without battle or skirmish having taken place'. Such boasts may have been exaggerated, but the enemies of the Campbells showed no mercy in settling old debts. In January 1645 after 'they hade waisted Ardgyll, and leaft it lyke ane desert', Montrose's men turned north towards the Great Glen.[87]

When the committee of estates heard that Montrose was in Argyll it ordered Baillie to set off in pursuit; but the marquis of Argyll objected, and asked that instead some of Baillie's men should be transferred to his command.[88] This was agreed and Baillie returned to Perth, leaving 1,100 men with Argyll. The motive that Argyll gave for insisting on this arrangement was that the country would not be able to support all Baillie's men in mid-winter; but the real reason was doubtless that he was determined not to have any army independent of him operating in his own country; it was humiliation enough that his estates had been ravaged without having to call in a Lowland army to show the Campbells how to fight.

Montrose had by the last days of January 1645 reached Kilcumin (Fort Augustus), where he drew up a band of union for mutual defence for signature by those who joined him. Ahead of him, at the north-east end of the Great Glen around Inverness, the covenanters of the north and Moray assembled forces to bar his passage, led by the earls of Seaforth and Sutherland. Behind him Argyll occupied Inverlochy (Fort William) with about 3,000 men. Montrose's own army had dwindled to about 2,000 men, but he had the advantage of being between his enemies and thus able, if he moved quickly, to attack them separately before they could join their forces together. He resolved to deal with the Campbells first; 'I was willing to let the world see that Argyle was not the man his highlandmen believed him to be, and that it was possible to beat him in his own Highlands'.[89] Rather than move directly towards Inverlochy he chose to climb south through the mountains of Lochaber and down Glen Roy (a remarkable march in winter) in the hope of taking the Campbells by surprise. At dawn on 2 February he appeared on the hills above Inverlochy. Argyll took no part in the battle that followed, being incapacitated by a dislocated shoulder, so the convenanters were led by Sir Duncan Campbell of Auchinbreck. He just had time to draw up his men before Montrose's army fell on them. The Lowlanders fled almost at once, leaving the Campbells to stand alone; after a time they too were overwhelmed. In the battle and the pursuit that followed about 1,500 covenanters were killed, including Auchinbreck. Inverlochy Castle surrendered after the battle; the Lowlanders in the garrison were spared but all the Highlanders were killed, while Argyll fled to safety in his galley.[90]

Montrose now turned again towards Inverness. Most of the army which had assembled there to oppose him melted away at his approach, while royalists who had not ventured to do so before now hastened to join him—including Lord Gordon, persuaded to desert the covenanters by Nathaniel Gordon. But Huntly, still lurking in Strathnaver, refused to forgive his eldest son for having formerly signed the covenant; he therefore commissioned his third son, Lewis Gordon, to lead the Gordons and others loyal to him, and instructed him to have nothing to do with either Lord Gordon or Nathaniel Gordon. Huntly no doubt hoped that this would force Montrose to accept Lewis as commander of the Gordons, thus giving him (Huntly) through Lewis some control over Montrose's army. Instead his action simply caused confusion. Montrose favoured Lord Gordon and some of the Gordons rose under him, but the support they gave Montrose was often half hearted, and many others stayed at home rather than offend Huntly. Moreover many of the other recruits who joined Montrose after Inverlochy were of doubtful loyalty; men like Seaforth joined him, but only to protect their estates at a time when there seemed no possibility of resisting him.[91]

The Scottish parliament had meanwhile been meeting since early January, attempting to restore the fortunes of the covenanting cause. A committee for managing the war within and without the country (sometimes called the committee of dispatches) was elected as an attempt to establish a general executive committee during sessions of parliament, thus relieving the full parliament of many routine and minor functions[92] Much of parliament's time was spent in proceedings against those who were or had been in arms against the covenanters. The forbearance shown in the previous session had now disappeared. Decreets of forfeiture of lives, titles and property were passed against twenty-two royalists including Montrose, Huntly, Nithsdale, Aboyne, Carnwath, Airlie and Alaster Macdonald.[93] To finance the war a new tax was imposed, the monthly maintenance; though intended at first as a temporary expedient it was to be imposed regularly until 1651.[94] There was much relief that Montrose did not try to move south against Baillie's army immediately after Inverlochy, as the forces at Perth were not strong enough to oppose him. It was decided to send for 1,500 men from the army in England and 1,400 from Ireland as reinforcements, and Sir John Hurry or Urry was appointed major general of the forces in Scotland, though William Baillie objected to the appointment;[95] Hurry was a competent officer but his loyalties were doubtful as he had begun the English civil war on parliament's side but deserted to the king and then back to parliament before returning to Scotland.

After parliament rose in March direction of the war passed to three committees of estates—in Edinburgh, with the army in England, and with the army at Perth.[96] War was no longer the only serious threat the regime had to deal with. Late in 1644 an outbreak of plague had spread to Scotland from the north of England. By April 1645 it had reached Edinburgh and the committee of estates was considering fleeing from the burgh.[97] Amid the disruption and fear caused by plague in the south and Montrose in the north the covenanters were also troubled by increasingly pressing demands by the English parliament that the Scottish army in England march southwards. These were largely ignored.

A new levy of about 17,500 men was ordered within Scotland to recruit the covenanters' armies, but only a small fraction of that number ever appeared in arms.[98] The resources of the covenanters were being over strained by wars in all three kingdoms, and their military efforts on all fronts were flagging.

MONTROSE'S YEAR OF VICTORIES: AULDEARN TO KILSYTH

After Inverlochy there were no major covenanting forces left north of Perth and Kincardine to oppose Montrose. He took oaths of loyalty from Seaforth and others who had recently joined him, but he then left most of them in the north to watch the covenanters' garrison in Inverness; probably he suspected that most of them were untrustworthy and would be liabilities rather than assets. If so, he was proved right, for Seaforth soon made his peace with the covenanters and some Grants whom he did try to take with him immediately deserted.[99] Montrose moved south past Aberdeen, plundering the lands of covenanters and trying to raise recruits. He met virtually no resistance, though many covenanters defied him from the safety of their castles. Stonehaven was burnt and Brechin plundered while covenanting forces retired towards Perth. But Montrose was in no condition to attack Baillie's army; many of his Highlanders had again gone home with their accumulated loot, gravely weakening his forces. Instead of continuing towards Perth he therefore contented himself with a swift raid on Dundee. He achieved complete surprise and stormed the burgh on 4 April, but was nearly trapped there by Hurry and Baillie, escaping back to the hills and thence to Atholl with the loss of a few stragglers.[100] The covenanters, desperately in need of a success to bolster up their reputation in England, publicised Montrose's retreat from Dundee as an important victory to such good effect that the English parliament ordered a public thanksgiving for it.[101]

From Atholl Montrose sent Lord Gordon back to the north-east to gather recruits while he himself marched in the opposite direction, into the Trossachs where he was joined by Huntly's second son, Lord Aboyne, who had made his way there from England. Montrose's intention was probably to divert the attention of the covenanters, to prevent them pacifying the north-east while he was awaiting the recruits who would enable him to take the offensive. If this was the case he failed, for in his absence Baillie led forces into Atholl while Hurry marched to join the covenanters of the north-east.[102] Baillie himself considered his expedition into Atholl 'ane unnecessarie voyage' undertaken only because the committee with his army insisted on it,[103] but his presence there combined with Hurry's activities to force Montrose to cut short his wanderings. Deciding to deal with Hurry first he marched back to Atholl and then over the mountains and down the Dee, where Lord Gordon and Alaster Macdonald rejoined him. Hurry retired towards Inverness, awaiting reinforcement by local covenanters; then on the night of 8–9 May he turned suddenly, having by now perhaps 4,000 men, and marched back eastwards hoping to take Montrose by surprise. But Montrose was warned and prepared for battle at Auldearn. This was the first of his battles in which he was the attacked, not the attacker, and he arranged his small force of about 1,700 men with some skill. Hurry was lured into a trap and then attacked in flank, which threw his men into confusion; before long they were in flight and in the long pursuit that followed nearly 2,000 were killed.[104]

Baillie had meanwhile been marching north from Atholl, and Montrose was not yet strong enough to face him, and therefore drew him away southwards to prevent him remaining in the north to harry local royalists. In May and June he led Baillie (joined by the remains of Hurry's forces) on a bewildering journey through Badenoch, along the upper Spey and Dee and finally into Angus. His chances of beating the untrained levies which the covenanters were hastily assembling at Perth were good, but Baillie remained undefeated close behind him and many of his Gordons now insisted on returning to protect their homes from local covenanters. Montrose was therefore left with little alternative but to take to the hills again until his forces were strengthened by recruiting;[105] Lord Gordon was sent north and Alaster Macdonald west to find men. The latter had probably insisted on being allowed to go, for his main interest in Scotland lay in the recovery of his clan's lands from the Campbells and Montrose's endless marches did not seem to be contributing much to this. He had, however, in May achieved his other ambition; Argyll freed his father Col Keitach and his brothers in an exchange of prisoners.[106]

Montrose too was by this time thoroughly discontented with the progress of his campaign, in spite of its spectacular successes. The weeks after Auldearn had shown his weakness; he could win victories, but he had not sufficient strength to exploit them. For all his victories many of those who fought for him tended to disappear, temporarily or permanently, whenever the fancy took them, to take home their booty, protect their homes or pursue private feuds. This would not have mattered very much had he been content to confine himself to the sort of large-scale guerilla warfare he had been waging, leading raids after which he could retire into the safety of the mountains to evade pursuit and reorganise his forces. But he had come to Scotland to help the king, and Charles' first priority was winning the civil war in England. Montrose had therefore hoped to force the covenanters to withdraw their entire army from England, and perhaps to lead his army into England. After his success at Inverlochy he had believed that he would soon be in a position to enter England,[107] but in the months that followed the weaknesses of the types of soldier at his disposal, and especially their unreliability between battles, led him to change his mind. In particular he urged the need to supply him with cavalry, since his army was composed almost entirely of footmen. This was not a fatal lack while he kept in or near the shelter of the mountains, but if he was to march into the Lowlands his army would be very vulnerable without horsemen.

The king was doing all he could to get reinforcements to Montrose, but all efforts failed. The Irish confederates refused to send more men to Scotland;[108] from their point of view Alaster Macdonald's venture had failed, as it had not led to the withdrawal of the Scottish army in Ireland. From Paris Queen Henrietta Maria negotiated for cavalry to enable Montrose 'to make his victoryes profitable, as well as miraculous' by entering the Lowlands, but without success. In April he wrote in exasperation to the king that if he had had the use of 500 cavalry for one month he would by that time have been able to have joined him in England with 20,000 men. But though Charles recognised the potential value of what Montrose was doing, the English civil war was now going so badly for him that he could spare no men; he considered leading forces north to link up with Montrose but in the end did nothing.[109]

The fact that Montrose lacked the resources with which to exploit his victories was of little comfort to the covenanters, humiliated and demoralised by repeated defeats. Yet they still made no move to withdraw their armies in England and Ireland for use against him, for they remained stubbornly determined not to let his successes deprive them of the influence that they hoped their armies would bring them in these countries. In May 1645 the committee of estates was forced by plague to flee from Edinburgh. Early in June it met jointly with the committee with Baillie's army at Perth, and decided that the forces in Scotland should be dived into two, under Baillie and Argyll; the latter refused the command offered to him so Crawford-Lindsay took his place as commander of the new levies at Perth, strengthened with 1,500 trained men from Baillie's army. In return Baillie received only a few hundred raw recruits. Angered by this and by criticism of his handling of the army he tried to resign, but was forced to continue in his command as no one was willing to take his place. That the covenanters still had not learnt that their failures against Montrose stemmed partly from their over confidence seems indicated by the fact that at this critical moment they also made arrangements to send recruits to their army in England—though in doing this they may have been influenced by fears that the king would try to break into Scotland to join Montrose.[110]

Baillie marched north and was ravaging the lands of royalists in Aberdeenshire when he heard that Montrose was approaching. When he advanced towards him with about 2,000 men the royalists (about 1,500 strong) turned away as if in flight; but at Alford they halted and awaited attack. On 2 July Baillie was drawing up his forces ready for battle when the royalists fell on him, and the pattern of Montrose's previous victories was repeated; a short period of fierce fighting followed by the flight of the covenanters, who suffered heavy losses in the pursuit, while Montrose's own losses were insignificant except that, in this case, Lord Gordon was killed and he was thus deprived of his most influential ally among the Gordons.[111]

As usual the covenanters were astounded by their own defeat. 'We are amazed that it should be the pleasure of our God to make us fall thus the fifth time, before a company of the worst men in the earth', wrote Robert Baillie, though he concluded with determined optimism that the matter was 'one of the deeps of divyne wisdome, which we will adore'. The Scots commissioners in London were equally bewildered at God allowing their army to be defeated, especially as the Independent-dominated new model army had won a great victory at Naseby a few weeks before; 'We pray the Lord to discover the cause of His great wrath manifested by the continued heavy judgments of pestilence and sword, and why our forces there [in Scotland] have received defeat upon defeat even these five times from a despicable and inconsiderable enemy, while the forces of this nation obtaine victory upon victory by weak meanes against considerable and strong armyes'.[112] The morale of the covenanters was crumbling.

In his precipitate flight after Alford, William Baillie reached Stirling in time to justify himself to parliament (which sat briefly from 8 to 11 July). Criticisms of his conduct were many and outspoken, but again no one else was willing to take command of his army. Parliament therefore reluctantly approved his and Hurry's conduct and, in spite of his protests, insisted that he continue in command. Yet again orders were given for new levies (of about 9,500 men), and in addition all nobles and other landowners were to assemble in arms with all the cavalry they could muster to prevent Montrose breaking out into southern Scotland.[113] All forces—the remains of Baillie's and Hurry's armies, the levies under Crawford-Lindsay and the new levies—were now formed into a single army under Baillie; the covenanters had at last decided to concentrate all available forces in one body to prevent Montrose defeating separate small armies piecemeal. Parliament again met from 24 July to 7 August, this time at Perth; the proximity of Montrose's army (now established at Dunkeld) was judged preferable to the plague, which had now reached Stirling. Desperate new orders for levies were issued, as earlier ones had been largely ignored; any landowner who failed to appear was to suffer a fine of one quarter of his annual income. Baillie's pleas to be allowed to give up his command were at last accepted; Major General Robert Monro was to be recalled from Ireland with 1,000 men to command all forces in Scotland. But the unfortunate Baillie was forced to continue his command until Monro arrived.[114] Since the committee with the army and the main committee of estates were both now in Perth (forced there by Montrose and the plague respectively) they were combined into a single committee of estates, which an act laid down should direct the war while the general undertook the actual managing and executing of the directions.[115]

By this time Montrose was ready to renew his advance, having been joined by several hundred much-needed horsemen under Lord Aboyne. Altogether he had assembled about 5,000 men, many more than ever before, and he was determined to break the pattern of victory followed by long marches to gather sufficient men for his next attack. He knew of the defeat of the king at Naseby in June, and of the subsequent signs of collapse of the royalist armies in England. If he was to help Charles before it was too late he had to attempt to break out into the Lowlands and thence into England as soon as possible. Small scale battles on the edge of the Highlands such as he had been fighting for the past year could not help the king. Montrose at first marched to Kinross, as if to invade Fife, but he then changed direction abruptly and moved west to Kilsyth, eleven miles north-east of Glasgow, which he reached on 14 August. There he waited for the pursuing covenanters, knowing they would be forced to fight to prevent him moving south.[116]

William Baillie camped that night within a few miles of Montrose's position. It is not clear whether the single committee of estates had been intended to accompany his army or remain at Perth. In the event several of the leading nobles of the committee were with the army (some of them being colonels in it) but there was no quorum of the committee present. But nonetheless when they pressed their advice on Baillie it was hard for him to reject it; he had just been relieved of his command and was only serving until his replacement arrived. After his failures against Montrose he had neither the authority nor the confidence to insist on obedience from some of the most powerful men in the land. There had been friction between Baillie and the nobles on the march towards Kilsyth, exacerbated by personal hostility between him and Argyll. When Argyll asked what was to be done next Baillie answered 'The direction should come from his Lordship, and these of the Committee. My Lord demanded what reason was for that? I answered, I found myself so slighted in everything belonging to ane commander-in-chieffe, that for the short time I was to stay with them, I would absolutely submitt to their direction, and follow it.' Thus Baillie abdicated responsibility, choosing to interpret the act which gave the committee power to direct the war to mean that he was simply to obey orders, all decisions being made by the committee. In fact, as he well knew, it was not the committee he obeyed but a few of its members;[117] he could therefore have refused the nobles' advice on the grounds that in the absence of a quorum responsibility was his alone, and might thus have averted disaster at Kilsyth. But, bitterly resentful of criticism, he chose to sulk. Nonetheless, responsibility rests primarily on the nobles. That they should lack confidence in Baillie was understandable—it had been folly to continue him in command even temporarily once it was clear that he had lost everyone's confidence—but the fact that most of the nobles themselves had failed in battle against Montrose should have made them less arrogant in pressing their advice on him.

When Argyll asked for Baillie's advice on the morning of 15 August, Baillie insisted that the other nobles be called. When they arrived and proved in favour of advancing Baillie moved forward until he reached what he believed was an advantageous position for battle and there drew up his army. But all the members of the committee of estates present (Argyll, Crawford–Lindsay, Burleigh and others) except for Balcarres urged moving to a new position which Baillie thought very weak—they believed Montrose was trying to escape back to the Highlands and wished to cut off his flight. In spite of his conviction that the move was a mistake Baillie began to execute it. The orders to move led to some confusion, and before the manoeuvre was completed Montrose attacked. Caught off balance, the covenanters resisted stubbornly for a time but soon fled and were cut down in their hundreds. All attempts to keep part of the army together during the flight failed. Baillie, Crawford-Lindsay and Burleigh reached Stirling and tried to organise the defence of the burgh but the other nobles scattered in all directions.[118] There was now no covenanting army left in Scotland; levies being gathered in the south dispersed hastily on news of the battle. Montrose appeared to be master of the country.

PHILIPHAUGH

After Kilsyth Montrose would, no doubt, have liked to have moved on Edinburgh to establish a royalist regime; but the plague which had so long hindered his enemies prevented him. He did not dare risk the disease spreading to his army, and according to one report up to 200 people were dying daily of plague in the capital and corpses were lying in the streets.[119]

Montrose therefore led his victorious army to Glasgow and there summoned a parliament to meet on 20 October. All except those who had been 'the speciall authores and principall fomentars' of the rebellion against the king were to be pardoned if they attended.[120] Meanwhile Montrose moved his army to a camp at Bothwell.

With no army in the field to oppose Montrose many leading covenanters fled to England or Ireland. Those who remained had little choice but to submit if any royalist force approached them. The earls of Eglinton and Cassillis tried to raise men in Ayrshire, but they scattered when Montrose sent Sir Alaster Macdonald (whom he had knighted after Kilsyth) into the shire.[121] Similarly the covenanters of Fife who had met to consider what to do dispersed in confusion on a report that a party of Montrose's men were approaching.[122] Many men accepted protections from the royalists, promising loyalty in return, but few were sincere;[123] they submitted to save themselves at a time when they had no hope of resisting successfully. Paradoxically the fact that Montrose met with virtually no resistance immediately after Kilsyth was not so much a sign of support for him as of the confidence of the covenanters; they believed that their armies would soon return from England and Ireland to destroy him, so they felt no need to sacrifice themselves in desperate last ditch stands.

Montrose did, however, gain some support in the Lowlands after Kilsyth. He was joined by or offered the support of many royalist nobles who had previously passively endured the covenanters' rule, including the marquis of Douglas and the earls of Traquair, Wigtown, Annandale, Hartfell, Perth, Home and Roxburgh.[124] But few of them could provide many men for Montrose's army, for most of them had long lost much of their traditional influence through their lack of enthusiasm for the covenants, and therefore relatively few lairds and lesser men followed their lead. When the earl of Queensberry tried to join Montrose he was seized by 'some of his aune' men and sent as a prisoner to the Scots garrison of Carlisle.[125] War weariness was wide spread, and men who had avoided being levied to fight for the covenant showed no enthusiasm for fighting for the king.

Thus Montrose failed to find recruits on the scale he had hoped; moreover, the army he had was beginning to disintegrate. The Irish and Highlanders wished to leave with their loot to pursue their own ambitions; in the continued fighting in Argyll the Campbells were reported to be gaining ground. Many began to desert from the camp at Bothwell and their officers, including Sir Alaster Macdonald, pressed Montrose to allow them to go with their men to Argyll, promising to return later. Montrose was forced to agree that Macdonald and the Highlanders should leave, but insisted that the Irish remain; in spite of this Macdonald secretly took 120 of them to Kintyre with him. In this way Montrose lost over 2,000 men, nearly half his army.[126] He also had further trouble with the Gordons; Huntly, tired of sulking in Strathnaver, had decided to return to his estates, and wrote asking Aboyne, his son, to join him. Aboyne insisted on going to help his father to ensure that 'there were no new sture by the northern Couenanteres, who were yet wery strong', and when it was heard that he was leaving nearly all the Gordons went with him. Thus Montrose lost several hundred horsemen.[127] Irish, Highlanders and Gordons alike were incapable of understanding that acting to protect their particular interests in the west and north was useless if they allowed the king to be defeated in England and the covenanters to re-establish themselves in the Lowlands.

With his army thus weakened Montrose's position was precarious. Both before and after Kilsyth he had written of his expectations of entering England with a large army,[128] but he must quickly have realised that it was very unlikely that this would be possible. Nonetheless, as in the past he resolved to go on in spite of the odds against him, and decided to march to the eastern Borders to encourage the earls of Home and Roxburgh to levy men for him as they had promised.[129] He left Bothwell on 4 September, but by this time it was known that David Leslie was approaching the Borders with a large part of the Scottish army in England; Roxburgh and Home therefore decided that their best interests lay in submitting to him quickly. They made no attempt to raise men to help Montrose and did not resist arrest by troops sent by Leslie. Royalists later alleged that the two earls had been from the first in league with the covenanters, and had lured Montrose to the Borders so that Leslie could trap him; but there is no evidence for this, and the fact that the covenanters kept them prisoner for several months and only released them on caution of £100,000 Scots each suggests that they were timorous rather than deliberately treacherous in their dealings with Montrose.[130]

Though deserted by Roxburgh and Home, Montrose still hoped for reinforcement by royalist horse from England; but on 9 September the king wrote that all he could send him was his thanks, and his regrets that this was 'all my song to you'.[131] Moreover Leslie's army was probably much stronger than Montrose realised, and his intelligence was so bad that he had little idea of its movements. On 12 September he camped near Selkirk. Virtually his only infantry were 500 or so Irish, and though he had about 1,000 horse, most of them lacked training and the loyalty of many was doubtful. Montrose spent the night in Selkirk. Confused reports of attacks on some of his outposts by Leslie's men were disbelieved. It had been arranged that the royalist army should assemble at Philiphaugh, about two miles west of the burgh, the next morning. But Montrose was still at his breakfast in Selkirk when he was brought the news that Leslie's army was less than a mile away and still advancing.[132]

After Kilsyth the covenanters had immediately concluded that it would be impossible to raise sufficient forces in Scotland to oppose Montrose, and that therefore their armies in England and Ireland would have to be recalled. As Loudoun wrote to the army in England the enemy 'are now masters of the field running over and destroying the country, and will in all appearance prevail to do what they will, till God enables us to have an army in the field to oppose them'.[133] Since Montrose sent no forces east of Edinburgh while he was camped at Bothwell the committee of estates was able to reassemble on Scottish soil within a fortnight of Kilsyth; it met at Duns on 26 August, then at Floors and Mordington;[134] but the pretence that a covenanting regime still existed in Scotland meant nothing in practical terms until help arrived from England.

David Leslie had been at Nottingham with nearly all the cavalry of the army in England when news arrived of Kilsyth. He immediately resolved to march half his men back to Scotland, but on this 'being noised abroad amongst the Common Soldiers, they all openly professed that none of them would stay, but all go for relief of their Native Country', so he took them all with him.[135] At Newcastle he added 800 men from the Scots garrison to his army of nearly 5,000 horse. It was decided that he should make for Stirling, to cut off Montrose from retreat to (or reinforcement from) the Highlands;[136] as always the covenanters were confident of victory, but now they had reason to be. They probably knew of Montrose's difficulties in keeping an army together, and Leslie's army was larger than any which had taken the field against him before; moreover, it consisted mainly of disciplined veteran horsemen, not raw levies.

It had at first been intended that Leven should hasten back to Scotland after Leslie, with the rest of the army in England, but it was agreed that he should delay his march until he had satisfied the English by attempting to storm Hereford. This was not done, however; on rumours that the king's army was approaching Leven withdrew into Yorkshire and probably intended to continue northwards into Scotland.[137] But doubts as to the wisdom and necessity of this had now arisen. The Scots commissioners in London had at first agreed to it but changed their minds when their English friends begged that Leven stay, claiming that if he left the Scots would lose all that they had fought for in England for the past two years, while their enemies made no secret of the fact that they would be delighted to see their allies depart. Leven was therefore instructed to remain south of the border, though even there he could help to defeat Montrose by ensuring that the king did not join him in Scotland.[138]

David Leslie assembled about 6,000 men north of Berwick on 6 September. He was near Haddington a few days later, on his march to Stirling, when he heard that Montrose was in the Borders with only a small army. It was therefore decided to attack him directly instead of cutting him off from the Highlands, and on the night of 12 September Leslie camped about four miles from Selkirk.[139] In spite of his great gifts as a general Montrose would have had little hope of defeating Leslie's army, four times the size of his own, at the best of times, but his own negligence contributed greatly to the ease of Leslie's victory the following day. That he should have spent the night several miles from his army at a time when he knew that enemy forces were approaching, and indeed had been reported to be only a few miles away, was inexplicable folly on his part. By the time he heard, in Selkirk, of Leslie's movements his army at Philiphaugh was already under attack, having been taken completely by surprise. Most of the horsemen, untrained and doubtful of the wisdom of fighting for Montrose, soon fled. The battle was lost before Montrose arrived on the scene, but he managed to rally a few horsemen and tried to help the Irish, who had little hope of escaping on foot and were fighting stubbornly. David Leslie commented that he had 'never fought with better horsemen, and against more resolute foote'.[140] Montrose and his remaining horse soon saw that the situation was hopeless and fled. He no longer had an army. Of the Irish about 250 were killed and fifty or more surrendered on promise of quarter; most of them were then shot on the pretext that the quarter extended only to the officer who commanded them. The victors then fell on the wives and camp followers of the Irish, killing many of them.[141]

The covenanters did not at first realise the full significance of their victory. In retrospect Philiphaugh marks the end of Montrose's year of victories but that this was so was far from obvious at the time. If he could regather all the Irish, Highlanders and Gordons who had recently left him he would again have a formidable army; but it proved impossible for him to do this. They had insisted on leaving him even after his greatest victory, and showed no inclination to rejoin him when he was a defeated fugitive.

In considering the causes of Montrose's remarkable success in 1644–5 pride of place must go to his leadership, his ability to build an army from disparate elements and hold them together (even if only temporarily), persuading them for a time to lay aside narrow sectional interests and work together. From before Tippermnir until after Kilsyth he had managed to retain the initiative in his campaigns, by keeping on the move and striking at the covenanters whenever he chose, acting before they could concentrate their forces against him and using the mountains and glens of the

Highlands as safe retreats when too weak to face his enemies. They were kept constantly uncertain as to where he would strike next, and in dividing their forces in attempts to guard against all the various moves that he might make they ensured that each part of their forces was too weak to defeat him on its own. In spite of the tendency of the Irish and Highlanders who fought with Montrose to leave him to go about their own business when it suited them, they were admirably suited to the type of large-scale guerilla war in which he proved so skilled. They were used to the climate and terrain of the Highlands, to sleeping in the open and living off what they could plunder, to raiding and fighting. Once Montrose led them to the field of battle he could rely on their enthusiasm and wild charges which unnerved the peasant levies of the covenanters. True they had little understanding of strategy or tactics and on more than one occasion endangered Montrose's plans in their eagerness to get to grips with the enemy, but that was a fault which he could afford to tolerate.

Miscalculations by the covenanters also made a major contribution to Montrose's victories. The strain of supporting large armies in England and Ireland made it difficult for them to raise money, supplies and men for use in Scotland. They were over confident, certain God would bring them easy victory. Even when he failed to do so they were reluctant to weaken their armies in the other two kingdoms, for fear of losing influence in them. This was a calculated risk and it did of course justify itself in the end; Montrose was defeated without completely abandoning a military presence in England or Ireland. Finally, the leadership of the armies sent against Montrose was at best uninspired, at worse incompetent, culminating in a grand finale of muddle and stupidity at Kilsyth. Added to weaknesses of their own making, the covenanters were greatly hindered by the chance arrival of a major epidemic of plague: the disorganisation it caused increased steadily throughout 1645.

The effects of Montrose's campaigns were far reaching. Hatred of Montrose and his (to Lowland eyes) barbaric Irish catholic and Highland allies led many who in other circumstances would have supported the king to oppose his lieutenant governor in alliance with the covenanters, and to entertain doubts about a king who would employ such agents. This delayed the formation of a strong party combining moderate covenanters and royalists, such as was to emerge and lead an army into England on the king's behalf in 1648. Had such a party achieved the strength in 1646 that it did a year later it is highly unlikely that the king would have been handed over to the English parliament when the Scots army withdrew from England. It is permissible to suggest that in trying to help the king Montrose in fact helped his enemies by alienating moderate opinion in

Scotland from Charles and by weakening the influence of the Scots in England. For though Montrose did not significantly delay the defeat of the king in England he did greatly reduce the part the Scottish army played in bringing about that defeat. This the covenanters never forgave; he had forced them to weaken their army in England, and the defeats he had inflicted on them had brought them ridicule and contempt there. The emergence of anti-Scots feeling in England would probably have deprived them of the power they hoped that their military intervention would bring them, whether or not Montrose had led a royalist rising in Scotland. But most covenanters failed to recognise this, to admit that they had hoped for too much in England, and they therefore tended to put most of the blame for depriving them of the fruits of victory in England on Montrose.

Ten thousand men would be a very conservative estimate of the numbers of Scots killed in the 1644–5 campaigns. This amounted to at least one per cent of the country's population. To this must be added the substantial losses from disease and casualties of the Scottish armies in England and Ireland in the mid 1640s and the very high death toll from plague, especially in Edinburgh and Leith; few figures survive, but in the parish of South Leith between April 1645 and February 1646 2,736 inhabitants died of plague, which was evidently over half the population.[142] Material devastation brought about by the war against Montrose was widespread, mainly in the area between the Tay and the Great Glen. Royalists and covenanters plundered or systematically destroyed each other's houses, goods, animals and crops. The forces of both sides needed food and quarters and, whether among friends or foes, could seldom pay for them. Aberdeen claimed to have lost over £200,000 Scots when plundered by Montrose's men, and that burgh and Aberdeenshire claimed to have paid in money and free quarters to covenanting forces the equivalent of their monthly maintenance for seven years in advance.[143] The most systematic destruction and and killing took place in Argyll, however, and there it continued for two years after Philiphaugh.

CHAPTER TWO

The End of the Civil War in England, September 1645–January 1647

THE RE-ESTABLISHMENT OF THE COVENANTING REGIME AND THE 1646 CAMPAIGN IN SCOTLAND

While Montrose and his few remaining followers fled back to the Highlands after Philiphaugh the committee of estates busied itself in re-establishing the covenanting regime in Scotland. Plague continued to prevent any return to Edinburgh and the committee at first moved erratically, meeting at Perth, near Stirling, at Duns, St Andrews and Glasgow. No resistance was met with anywhere south of the Tay, but David Leslie and most of his cavalry were cautiously retained in the south while a force under John Middleton moved north towards Aberdeen.[1] The committee, urged on by the Scots commissioners in London, proceeded with severity against those who had collaborated with Montrose. Glasgow was first to suffer, being ordered to pay a large fine and having its magistrates and council deposed for having treated with him.[2] On 16 October the committee ordered the execution of two senior Irish officers captured at Philiphaugh; as they were Irish it was not thought necessary to try them first. Five days later the beheading of Sir William Rollock, Alexander Ogilvie younger of Inverquharity and Sir Philip Nisbet was ordered; they needed no trial as they had previously been condemned by parliament. It was agreed that those who deserved execution but were spared should be fined the equivalent of five years' rent from their estates, either as an alternative to or in addition to imprisonment or banishment.[3]

Consideration was given to sending David Leslie would be sent back to England with most of his cavalry in exchange for 2,500 of Leven's infantry, which (together with the rest of the cavalry and new levies) would operate against Montrose under Middleton. But implementation of this plan was delayed on news late in October that a body of royalist horse under Lord Digby was about to enter Scotland, hoping to find Montrose still in the Lowlands and to join him. The committee of estates feared that Digby's incursion was timed to coincide with an advance south by Montrose and Sir Alaster Macdonald, who were falsely reported to have united their forces, and therefore wrote urging Leven to bring all his infantry to Scotland.[4] In fact it soon emerged that Digby's 'invasion' was no serious threat. Discipline in the royalist forces in England was collapsing now that there seemed no hope of victory. About 1,200 cavalry raised in northern England refused to obey orders to march south, so someone had had the bright idea of seeing if they would be willing to march into Scotland instead, and Sir Marmaduke Langdale and Digby were given command of them. Digby had long urged the sending of cavalry to Montrose but he accepted the command reluctantly; it was known Montrose had been defeated (though not how seriously) and the dispirited northern horse were not the sort of force he had hoped to lead. On his march he was defeated in turn by parliamentary forces and by a sally by the Scots garrison of Carlisle. Nonetheless he managed to reach Dumfries with a few hundred men, but it soon became clear that Montrose was far away in the Highlands. Digby and Langdale therefore abandoned their men and fled by sea to the Isle of Man.[5]

Once Digby's flight became known the request for help from Leven was cancelled and David Leslie was sent back to him in England with some cavalry. The infantry Leven was supposed to send to Scotland in return were not forthcoming, however; his army was so weak that he refused to send them. He also at first ignored repeated orders from the English parliament to advance south from Yorkshire; but eventually in November he moved to besiege Newark on Trent; fear that if he refused to do so the English would declare that they had no further use for his army and order it to leave the country outweighed resentment at the way in which the needs of the army for money and supplies were being neglected.[6] Requests by the covenanters for help from the Scottish army in Ireland also proved fruitless. Robert Monro showed no sign of coming to Scotland as ordered to replace William Baillie, and his army insisted on being paid and supplied before it considered sending men to Scotland.[7]

Luckily for the covenanters Montrose proved to be a less serious threat than they at first thought after Philiphaugh, for his efforts to form a new army in the north met little success. Apart from some of the Irish none of the constituent parts of his previous armies—the Irish, the various clans, and the Gordons—had been present at Philiphaugh, so it had been feared that he might be no worse off than in the months before Kilsyth. But the Irish and the clans had no intention of rejoining him, for plundering Argyll was much more to their taste than his endless marches and counter-marches—though at least their activities prevented the Campbells from concentrating their resources against Montrose.[8] After Philiphaugh Montrose went first to Atholl, where he managed to gather nearly 1,000 men; with them he marched to enlist the help of the Gordons. But quarrels between him and Huntly fatally divided the royalists. Huntly had never forgiven Montrose for virtually kidnapping him in the First Bishops' War and was resentful of the fact that the king had made Montrose first lieutenant general and then lieutenant governor of Scotland instead of the ever-loyal Huntly himself. For his part, Montrose made little attempt to hide his contempt for Huntly; the previous year he had delayed for several months sending him a commission the king had granted him to be lieutenant of the eastern Highlands. He now wrote to Huntly, tactfully for once, promising to follow his advice; but the plan he put forward, to march on Glasgow and hold his parliament there, appealed little to the Gordons, who were worried by the advance of Middleton's men as far north as Turriff. Even once it was obvious the Gordons would not support him Montrose refused to abandon his plan; so much for his undertaking to follow Huntly's advice. He spent some weeks in the hills north of Glasgow but prudently retired on 20 November. With at most 1,000 men he had no hope of holding the burgh against the covenanters.[9] He sent direct orders to Huntly to join him but Huntly claimed his commission from the king freed him from dependence on Montrose and insisted on laying siege to castles in Moray held by the covenanters instead of supporting Montrose's latest venture, a proposed attack on Inverness. Montrose therefore withdrew to Strathspey and busied himself in trying to obtain the help of other potential royalists; few would join him, for their already low morale was further undermined by his quarrels with Huntly.[10]

While the royalists squabbled in the north the Scottish parliament sat at St Andrews (from November 1645 to February 1646). It spent most of its time punishing those who had helped Montrose and preparing new forces to be sent against him. There was, especially among the nobles, a strong party of moderate covenanters ready for some compromise with the king and the royalists in order to restore peace. But such men were leaderless; they would have followed the duke of Hamilton if the king had released him from imprisonment, but in his absence Argyll and the more extreme covenanters were able to dominate proceedings.[11] Wariston set the tone of the session with a bitter speech showing 'that the housse of parliament wes become at this present lyke Noas arke, which had in it both foull and cleine creteurs'. He demanded that there should be 'ane serious searche and enquirey after suche as wer eares and eyes to the enimies of the commonwealthe, and did sit ther as if ther wer nothing to say to them'. A committee was therefore established to check that members had not complied with the enemy; several were found guilty and expelled.[12]

Parliament was encouraged to be severe in its dealings with royalists and their supporters by the commission of the kirk and several synods which petitioned that justice be done on those whose treacherous designs and bloody practices had brought calamity; delay was displeasing to the Lord and indeed 'the sparing of Incendiaries and Malignants' in the past was largely responsible for the setbacks the covenanters were experiencing.[13] First to be dealt with were the rank and file Scots and Irish (men and women) who had been captured at or after Philiphaugh. Irish who had been in rebellion were to be summarily executed; Scots were to be given at least a semblance of a trial.[14] More substantial delinquents, men of property, were divided into three classes according to their degree of guilt. Those most guilty fell within the first class and were to be executed or, if spared, fined four to six years' rent and banned from any public office or voting in elections until peace was restored. Those in the second class were to forfeit two to four years' rent and be suspended from office at least until the next session of parliament. The least guilty, those in the third class were to be fined half a year's to two years' rent, though in minor cases the fine might be omitted and only suspension from office for a time imposed.[15]

Only four death sentences were passed by parliament, surprisingly few considering the deep bitterness against Montrose and his followers—on Sir Robert Spottiswood, Nathaniel Gordon, William Murray (a brother of the earl of Tullibardine) and Andrew Guthry (son of the former bishop of Moray).[16] Nathaniel Gordon tried to save himself and his companions by offering to arrange an exchange of prisoners with Montrose and by declaring his repentance; all he gained was the removal of his excommunication before he died. Spottiswood made a 'railing discourse' from the scaffold saying that 'their ministers that should lead them to heaven were leading them the high way to hell'. He died 'raging and railing' while Andrew Guthry died 'stupidly and impenitently' according to the minister who attended them. He had expected no better, for were not both the sons of bishops'?[17]

As in the previous three sessions of parliament a committee of dispatches was set up to act as an executive body. On its recommendations parliament reorganised the army; some regiments were to be sent to reinforce the army in England. A body of 4,300 footmen and six troops of horse were to be placed in eight garrisons north of the Clyde and Forth while 8,400 men (including 2,500 brought from Ireland) formed a mobile army to pursue the rebels in the north. The command was offered to Callander, but on his making exorbitant demands he was replaced by Middleton; William Baillie was declared to have acted faithfully at Kilsyth, the defeat having been caused chiefly by 'the wrath of god vpon the Land for our sins', but was not re-employed. New shire committees of war were established and the committee of estates was empowered to levy 10,000 men to reinforce the Scots armies in all three kingdoms. Argyll and others were sent to Ireland to persuade the army there to send men to Scotland.[18]

It is remarkable that at such a critical time, when secret negotiations with the king had already begun, Argyll should have gone to Ulster and thus cut himself off from these intrigues. It may be that he saw the landing of the troops from Ireland in Argyll as the only way of clearing the Irish and Macdonalds from his estates in the near future; and until this was done his power and influence would remain much less than they had been before Montrose had driven him from his lands. But he may also have wished to avoid having any direct part in a matter so risky as secret dealings with the king; doubtless he was kept informed of the progress of the negotiations, but there is no sign that he tried to intervene in them.

After the Scots parliament rose in February 1646 administration of the country again passed to committees of estates; one accompanied Middleton's army while the central committee, having ascertained that the epidemic of plague in Edinburgh was over, first sat there on 12 March, thus returning to the capital after an absence of ten months. In addition committees for money for the north and south of the country were established, and were soon busy fining royalists and supervising the collection of taxes.[19]

There had been several skirmishes during the winter between covenanters and royalists. Middleton withdrew from Aberdeen from October 1645 to January 1646, and in that period 'everie other day . . . divers troupes of the Gordons and Irishe wer comeing in to our town quartering and doing what thei pleasit'. The outposts of the royalists were in Kincardine Castle and Atholl; when in February a force of over 1,000 Campbells and others (most of them driven from their lands in Argyll by the Irish and Macdonalds, and wandering in search of food and royalist lands to plunder) approached Atholl it was routed by the men of Atholl near Callander, a further humiliation for Argyll. Middleton turned his attention first to Kincardine Castle. After a short siege the officers of the garrison fled and the castle surrendered; twelve of the men in it (probably Irish) were shot, and Middleton then advanced to Aberdeen.[20] There he was delayed for some weeks by lack of the cannon necessary to reduce the many royalist-held castles, but he soon found that the royalists were usually prepared to abandon them rather than stand siege, and the earl of Crawford and his forces abandoned Banff as soon as a party of convenanting horse approached. Middleton was therefore able to hold a rendezvous of local covenanters at Turriff without meeting any opposition, but he was disappointed at the numbers who attended, noting that the people were 'neither rysing for us nor against us'; all they wanted was peace and the removal of all armies, of whichever side. On 19 April Middleton received his cannon and prepared to send most of his army north to attack Montrose.[21]

Meanwhile the quarrels between Montrose and Huntly continued, fatally dividing the royalists. Montrose laid siege to Inverness with his small forces but Huntly refused to join him, arguing that instead they should march past the burgh and overcome the covenanters of the far north to encourage potential royalists there (like Seaforth) to join them. But once Middleton reached Aberdeen the Gordons reverted to their usual insistence that protecting their own lands must have first priority. Eventually Huntly did, it seems, resolve to obey Montrose's repeated orders to come to Inverness, but before he did so Middleton's army had advanced and raised the siege.[22] To complicate the confused royalist politics further the vacillating Seaforth, whose support was demanded by both royalist leaders and by Middleton,[23] tried to pursue an independent course of action, pleasing all by adopting an intermediate position. He issued a remonstrance which he hopefully sent to the committee of estates for approval, recommending as an antidote to the troubles compatible with the national covenant that the king should be invited to Scotland so that through his presence 'the Cloud of mistakes may be dispelled', peace settled, and the rebellion of those who oppressed the people punished. Continued civil war would ruin Scotland, for the countryside was exhausted by taxes and plague, much property had been destroyed, large areas wasted and burnt, and trade interrupted. Indeed 'it seemes the verie elements doe conspire our destruction by ane vnparralleled season' for the crops had been 'frosted and blasted' in the ground.[24]

Seaforth's plea for peace for an exhausted country was one with which many may have sympathised, but his remonstrance offered no practical suggestions as to how it could be brought about. He can hardly have expected the covenanters to take seriously the suggestion that all should be left to the king; in fact the committee of estates and the commission of the kirk promptly published denunciations of the remonstrance, though the latter was, rather oddly, in two minds as to whether to attribute it to God's wise dispensation in exercising his people with one trouble after another or to the inveterate malice of Satan and his instruments. But whether divine or satanic in origin, the commission was sure that it should be denounced.[25] Little more was heard of the remonstrance after this, though it may have been signed by a few royalists.

Middleton's decision, on advancing from Aberdeen at the end of April, to deal with Montrose before Huntly was influenced by the fears raised by the earl of Sutherland and other northern covenanters that Inverness would fall unless relieved quickly. Sutherland at first undertook to keep Seaforth and other local royalists from joining Montrose, but within a few days he had 'ane strange event' to relate. Seaforth had joined his forces with Montrose's and was likely to subdue all the godly of the north who would not sign his illegal remonstrance.[26] Middleton's army therefore hurried north (though he himself remained near Aberdeen);[27] it hoped to take Montrose by surprise but he got a few hours' warning and managed to gather his men together and escape across the Ness. Virtually without cavalry he could not face the covenanters and fled to the safety of the hills while the covenanters advanced triumphantly into Ross.[28] They were soon forced to retrace their steps, however, by the surprising news that the Gordons had seized Aberdeen. Taking advantage of the absence of most of Middleton's men Huntly and Aboyne had attacked the burgh on 14 May; two assaults were repulsed, the third succeeded. But as with his previous raids on Aberdeen Huntly appeared to be at a loss to know how to exploit his success, and when he heard that Middleton's army was returning he abandoned Aberdeen and withdrew to the north.[29]

When Montrose fled from before Inverness many of his men deserted him. Lord Reay was ready to rise for the king but could not spare any men to join Montrose, and his newest ally, Seaforth, did nothing to help—most of his Mackenzie levies had already deserted. Seeing little hope of recruiting in the far north Montrose therefore marched his remaining men round the south end of Loch Ness into Badenoch.[30] But there he received orders from the king (now a prisoner of the Scots army in England) to 'disband all your forces, and goe into France'; 'This at first may justly Startle you', Charles added. Not surprisingly Montrose was suspicious; he had no means of knowing the king's circumstances or what pressures were being put on him, and was concerned as to the fate of his followers. He tried to meet with Huntly to discuss the order but Huntly refused to see him, indicating that he at least would obey the king without question. This he then did, disbanding his forces by 3 June.[31] Montrose however remained determined not to 'be so base nor dishonorable to leave all who heave ingaged in the Kings service in the myre bott att least desyre that they may heave immunity for what is past', and insisted on receiving confirmation of the order. Of other Scots nobles still in arms Airlie, Lord Ogilvie and Seaforth promised to lay down arms, but Crawford resolved to follow Montrose's example.[32]

On 15 June the king renewed his order to his forces to disband,[33] but Montrose still demanded guarantees for his men. The committee of estates had already (in March) given Middleton limited powers to make terms with rebels for their submission but, as he complained, he could only offer them protection from civil proceedings and most of them feared the censures of the kirk as well as the state. Nothing was done to empower him to offer immunity from ecclesiastical censures and the general assembly warned of the evils of treating with rebels. Nonetheless on 17 June the committee of estates instructed Middleton to open negotiations. Montrose, Sir Alaster Macdonald and Crawford were not to be pardoned, but might be allowed safe transport overseas; lesser men could be pardoned.[34] The committee was clearly more interested in restoring peace in the north, which would strengthen its hand in dealing with the political situation in England, than in revenge.[35]

A messenger brought the offer of terms from the covenanters to Montrose on 8 July, and he was allowed to delay a reply while he consulted the king.[36] Charles urged him 'according to that reall freedome and frendship which is betwene vs . . . I cannot absolutly command you to accept of unhansome conditions', but he had told the covenanters that he had ordered him to accept the terms offered, and if he did not submit 'you must not expect any more treaties; in which case you must eather Conquer all Scotland, or be inevitably ruined'. On this Montrose agreed to submit, undertaking at a meeting with Middleton to leave Scotland by 1 September. He then disbanded, though Crawford and the few Irish left to him marched towards Argyll to sail for Ireland; Montrose and some of his officers waited for the covenanters to provide a ship to carry them into exile.[37]

The treaty with Montrose aroused a storm of protest from the more extreme covenanters. The 'greatest part of the honest ministers' had opposed the negotiations and the commission of the kirk now petitioned the state to reconsider the agreement, urging the need to punish rebels and murderers to avoid weakening the discipline of the kirk and exposing the country to the wrath of God. Largely through the votes of Hamilton's supporters the committee of estates rejected these arguments, but it is not surprising that as 1 September approached and no ship appeared to carry him abroad Montrose began to fear that the covenanters intended to trick him by neglecting to provide a ship and then arresting him for failing to leave Scotland on time; he wrote to Middleton that 'I hope you ar so gallant as you wold not wish to make that a snare' but no extention of the time limit was allowed. He therefore hired a Norwegian ship himself and sailed on 3 September for Bergen.[38]

Montrose's departure freed the covenanters from the most dangerous of the royalist rebels, but others remained to be dealt with. Huntly, true to his record of inconsistency, soon reversed his earlier decision to submit; he refused Middleton's offers and regathered his men, and Middleton's army was too weak and ill equipped to take effective action against him. In December 1646 he received secret orders from the king to raise forces as Charles intended if possible to come north and join him. Encouraged by this royal backing Huntly assembled about 2,000 men and occupied Banff, where he spent the winter of 1646–7.[39]

The Irish and Highland rebels in the west under Sir Alaster Macdonald were a more serious menace. In February 1646 the marquis of Antrim had at last persuaded the confederate catholics of Ireland to agree to provide money for raising 2,000 men to reinforce the Irish in Argyll. The money was probably never paid but Antrim managed to recruit between one and two thousand men and sailed with them to Argyll in May.[40] The covenanters on the other hand failed to get help from Ireland. During his stay there in April and May, Argyll could not persuade the Scots army to send troops to clear his estates of rebels.[41] Weakened by previous withdrawals of men as well as by desertion, disease and casualties the army's strength was now under 5,000 men; if as asked it sent about half its men back to Scotland it would no longer be able to play a significant part in the Irish wars. In fact even though men were not withdrawn the army was soon routed by the Irish, at Benburb in June 1646.[42]

Action against the rebels in Argyll in 1646 was therefore left to the Campbells themselves. Many had gathered in Ayrshire and in May James Campbell of Ardkinglas led these exiles in an invasion of the Cowal peninsula, which was largely occupied by Lamonts. Though the king had commissioned Sir James Lamont to act against the Campbells he had not at first risen; indeed he had fought alongside them as allies at Inverlochy. But after Kilsyth the Lamonts had turned on the Campbells; Sir James later denied the indiscriminate killing of women and children but admitted that he had 'burned all the Campbells their houses and cornes, and killed all the ffenceible and armed men hee could overtake of them', and that he had signed a band with Sir Alaster Macdonald and various Highlanders 'for the ruin of the name of Campbell'. The Campbells now came to take their revenge. Sir James and most of his leading clansmen took refuge in the castles of Toward and Ascog but on 3 June, after hearing that the king had ordered his forces to disband, they surrendered, evidently on promise of quarter. They were then seized and taken to Dunoon, where thirty-six of the most prominent Lamonts and their supporters were hanged. At least thirty-five others (perhaps over a hundred) were shot, stabbed and hacked to death by their captors in a confused melée. Sir James and some of his relatives were spared but they remained prisoners for several years, their lands being occupied by the Campbells.[43]

As well as occupying Cowal the Campbells drove the rebels from the area round the head of Loch Fyne; the synod of Argyll could meet safely at Inveraray in September though only ten ministers were present; 'because of the troubles of the countrey and of their being scattered and chased fra their dwellings, the presbyterie of Cowal haveing gon for shelter to the Lowlands, the presbyterie of Kintyre being under the power of the rebells, and none being resident in the presbyteries of Argyle and Lorn but such as wer sheltered in garesons'.[44] Reconquest of Kintyre and Islay had to be left until 1647 for (hardly surprisingly after the way in which the Lamonts had been treated) the rebels there refused to obey the king's orders to lay down their arms. Charles ordered Antrim to withdraw when he heard that he had landed with reinforcements. Antrim himself reluctantly obeyed but his men remained, under the command of Sir Alaster Macdonald, determined to retain their conquests.[45] Thus the civil war in Scotland dragged on into 1647. The covenanters could console themselves that Montrose had gone, but they were well aware that he had finally been vanquished by the king's political calculations, not by the sword as they would have liked.

NEGOTIATIONS BETWEEN THE KING AND THE SCOTS

From mid 1645 the already serious divisions between the covenanters and the English parliament grew steadily deeper. The demands of the covenanters for a negotiated settlement with the king, stilled for a few months by the failure of the treaty of Uxbridge, began again to be pressed, for the covenanters now feared that if the war continued until the king was totally defeated then most of the credit for the victory would go to the Independent party and other enemies of the Scots. In June 1645, just a week after the new model army had shown its strength at Naseby, the Scots commissioners in London urged on parliament the speedy settling of religion in England according to the covenant, the vigorous prosecution of the war (especially by supplying and paying the Scottish army properly so it could play a more prominent part) and the making of a new offer to the king for negotiations on the Uxbridge propositions. But to this and later demands parliament replied only with vague promises and did nothing.[46] Now increasingly confident of its ability to defeat the king without Scots help, parliament was no longer willing to negotiate on the basis of the propositions, being determined to demand more from Charles in civil matters than had been done at Uxbridge. Many members were not sorry to see the Scots discredited by their military failures; it was alleged that some 'prime Independents' 'did leap for joy' at the news of the defeat of their allies at Kilsyth, and 'did laugh in their sleeves at this affliction, and were glad in their souls at it'.[47] Certainly at least one parliamentarian hoped that

Kilsyth 'would rid England of "our Brethren" [the Scots], who otherwise might not so easily be got out of England', and would with luck lead the king to join Montrose. This would enable peace to be restored in England while the king and covenanters were left to fight it out in Scotland.[48] This was an absurdly naive view of the possible course of events, but well illustrates the depth of anti-Scots feeling.

When, after Kilsyth, the Scots commissioners informed the house of commons that they intended to withdraw their whole army from England they asked in addition for English military help; under the 1643 treaty they were entitled to do this, and Loudoun tried to win support for the plan by suggesting that in future the war in Scotland should be managed by the joint advice of both kingdoms. Parliament remained unmoved. The request for help was ignored and the Commons urged that when the Scots withdrew their army they should be sure to take their garrisons in Carlisle, Newcastle and elsewhere with them. Yet to some extent such anti-Scots attitudes had the opposite effect to that intended, since they led the indignant Scots commissioners to persuade Leven to remain in England with his infantry.[49] The covenanters received a similar lack of sympathy from English commissioners appointed to treat with them about the Scots garrisons and other matters in dispute; they had arrived at Berwick by the time of Kilsyth, and in the chaos following the battle negotiations with them had to be delayed; they did not meet Scots commissioners (at St Andrews) for two months, and in the interim plagued the covenanters with querulous messages, seemingly regarding the delays as evidence of ill will. And when the negotiations at last began they were abandoned after a few days without achieving anything, for the covenanters refused to remove their garrisons while their army remained in England.[50] Parliament voted the answers of the Scots unsatisfactory, but gave them until 1 March 1646 to withdraw the garrisons.[51]

The arguments over the Scots garrison were symptomatic of the increasing tension between the allies. Both foresaw that once the king was defeated there would be quarrels over a peace settlement, and that this might lead to a new war, or at least to threats of one. If this did happen then the position of the Scots would obviously be much strengthened if they still had garrisons in important English towns, though they maintained that they needed the garrisons as bases for their army. The Independents and their supporters complained loudly of the weakness and lack of success of the Scottish army in England, but the last thing that they wanted was that the Scots should be strong and successful. Denzil Holles, who supported the Scots, accused 'the violent party' (the Independents) of purposely starving the Scots army, hoping to provoke its soldiers into mutiny and disorder so as to discredit the Scots cause.[52] Certainly parliament kept the new model army comparatively well supplied and paid while allowing the Scots army to decay.

As it became clear that when the king was defeated parliament would attempt to minimise Scots influence in England and make a settlement unacceptable to the covenanters, the possibility of the covenanters making a separate peace with the king in order to bring pressure on parliament began to be considered. In June 1645 there were rumours (almost certainly false but nonetheless interesting) in London of secret dealings between the king and the Scots army.[53] At the end of July contacts were made between the king and some of the army's senior officers. The royalist Sir William Fleming (son of the earl of Wigtown) asked for a safe conduct to speak with Leven and Callander (his uncle) on matters 'worth your consideration, in relation to the public good'; the king had instructed him to make approaches for talks about a separate peace. Leven refused to take part in any political intrigue but the less scrupulous Callander, along with Lothian and Lords Sinclair and Montgomery, had several secret meetings with Fleming.[54] After Kilsyth Lord Digby wrote to Leven and Callander on the king's instructions, hoping that, demoralised by defeat, they would be prepared to negotiate; it was suggested that the armies of the king and the covenanters should be combined, in England under the king, in Scotland under Montrose.[55] Again nothing came of the king's attempts to open secret talks; Callander may have seen the letter but Leven evidently did not.[56] Montrose was soon routed by the covenanters, and the king was asking too much in return for a few vague promises; and to expect the covenanters to agree to serve under Montrose was absurd.

Rumours of a secret treaty between the Scots army and the king helped to poison relations between the covenanters and the English parliament,[57] even though the treaty failed. More successful were indirect dealings carried on cumbersomely by the Scots commissioners in London through the French agent in London, Queen Henrietta Maria and Cardinal Mazarin in Paris, and so back to the king in England. Charles had tried to negotiate an alliance with the French, but the treaty which resulted in 1644 brought him no help from France. However, Mazarin did sent an agent, Sabran, to England to attempt to arrange a peace between king and parliament and to deal with the Scots, warning them against too close an alliance with parliament for fear that Scotland become little more than a province of England. Sabran achieved nothing. Charles accused him of favouring parliament, and he found the Scots convinced that they could firmly establish Scots influence in England, but his mission did at least establish contacts between the French and the Scots.[58]

The first suggestion that France should try to help Charles by bringing about an agreement between him and the covenanters appears to have been made to Mazarin by Sir Thomas Dishington, Charles's chamberlain, in 1644; but Mazarin took no action until July 1645 when he sent an experienced diplomat, Jean de Montereul, to London.[59] Montereul quickly made contact with the Scots commissioners and with members of parliament who favoured a negotiated peace and presbyterianism. His first meeting with the Scots came just after Kilsyth, and he found them anxious for peace; they feared their English allies intended to cheat them. But in spite of their fears they would not compromise on religion.[60] The most active of the commissioners in treating with Montereul was Lord Balmerino, which illustrates the point that those who agreed to negotiate with him included the more uncompromising covenanters as well as moderates. Balmerino was one of Argyll's closest associates and he assured Montereul that he had the support of the most powerful party in Scotland. Extreme covenanters accepted the idea of a separate peace with the king not, primarily, out of regard for his interests but because they saw that the English parliament would not reform the union of the crowns or establish presbyterianism on the Scots model; it therefore seemed logical to turn to the king as an alternative instrument for imposing reform. Their eagerness to reach agreement with him was increased by rumours that the Independents were also negotiating with him for a separate peace.[61]

By mid September the Scots commissioners and the English presbyterian party (represented by the earl of Holland) had reached agreement on peace proposals to be sent to Paris; if Henrietta Maria and Charles would approve them the Scots would unite with him in presenting joint peace proposals to the English parliament, supported by France and the English presbyterian party. Balmerino at first agreed that it would be necessary for the Scots to make concessions, for only French influence could save Scotland from ruin; but once news of Philiphaugh arrived he 'did not reply with quite the same deference to the opinions of France' that he had previously shown, indicating that the covenanters only wanted peace 'in so far as it may be forced upon them by the urgency of their affairs'.[62] However, the proposals to be sent to Paris were agreed on, and were taken there by Sir Robert Moray, lieutenant colonel of the Scots Guards in France. If Charles would settle ecclesiastical matters as the parliaments and assemblies of the two kingdoms resolved, according to the practice of other reformed churches, then the commissioners gave it as their opinion that the Scots and their English allies would support the king in pressing for a compromise settlement in civil matters.[63]

The Scots were anxious to know what help they could expect from

France if their negotiations led to war with the English parliament. Mazarin therefore authorised Montereul to 'lead them to understand that . . . they will have no reason to doubt that France will assist them with banners unfurled'; this, it was hoped, would encourage the covenanters by leading them to expect military help, though Mazarin made it clear to Montereul that this would not in fact be provided. Mazarin also persuaded the reluctant Henrietta Maria to approve the proposals made by the Scots, and in November she wrote to Charles urging him to accept them,[64] but he refused. He would not establish presbyterian church government in England, claiming that even English presbyterians would 'never admit of the Scots Presbyterian way' since they wished the church to remain under parliamentary control, and he insisted that Montrose and his forces should be allowed to join him. Of these objections the first was by far the most important, but Charles remained stubborn on it as a matter of conscience; as he stated in January 1646 he would rather lose his crown than his soul. Nonetheless he still had hopes that agreement could be reached. He had again been in touch with the Scots army and claimed that David Leslie and Lord Sinclair had promised him that if he came to the army he would be safe there.[65] But at the same time Charles was also trying to open negotiations with the Independents and parliament, hoping to play them and the Scots off against each other, with each making concessions to try to outbid the other to make a separate peace.[66]

Meanwhile Montereul continued to urge the Scots commissioners to make concessions. By the end of January he had obtained verbal assurances that the king would be in safety in their army and would be received with all due respect and obedience. But they refused to put these promises into writing, giving the need for secrecy as their reason. This naturally roused fears that they were trying to gain possession of the king without providing him with any written guarantees, so that new concessions could then be forced from him.[67] Charles himself remained determined never to give way on some points; 'the nature of Presbyterian government is to steal or force the crown from the king's head. For their chief maxim is (and I know it to be true), that all kings must submit to Christ's kingdom, of which they are the sole governors'. 'I hold it [presbyterian government] absolutely unlawful, one chief (among many) arguments being, that it never came into any country but by rebellion'. His Roman Catholic wife little understood such scruples, since for her all forms of protestantism were equally heretical, so she can hardly have been pleased when he informed her that he saw little or no difference between setting up presbyterian government and submitting to the church of Rome.[68] The king's attitude justified the suspicions of the covenanters; since he held presbyterianism to be absolutely unlawful, how long would his conscience allow it to continue in Scotland, whatever he promised? The fact that he appeared equally willing to treat with either covenanters or Independents hardly increased confidence in his sincerity. When he informed the Independents that the Scots and the French were making an alliance against them[69] it simply demonstrated that he could not be trusted to keep negotiations secret and would probably pass on all they said to him to the covenanters.

The instructions that the Scottish parliament sent its commissioners in February 1646 contained no mention of the negotiations between Montereul and the king, for most members evidently knew nothing of the matter. But the difficulties over a peace settlement were well known, and the Scots parliament now moved further away than ever from terms likely to be acceptable to the English parliament. Not only were their commissioners to urge a peace based on the Uxbridge propositions, but if the king accepted those concerning religion concessions might be made to him in civil matters 'where there may be greater Latitude without sin than in maters of religion'. All that should then be demanded in civil matters would be such things as 'may be a fundation of a firme and just peace' though they might not 'come the Length' of the proposition.[70] To many English parliamentarians this would seem to threaten all they had fought for in constitutional matters.

Unlike the Scots parliament the committee of estates which sat after it rose was fully informed as to the secret negotiations. Additional instructions to the commissioners ordered 'You shall conferre with Monsieur Montereule upon his negotiations from France; you shall heare his propositions and draw the same to as neir a point as you can', though nothing was to be concluded without the consent of the committee. If the English ordered the Scots army to leave this was to be, in effect, refused.[71]

In March Loudoun conceded on behalf of the Scots commissioners that Charles need not actually sign the solemn league and covenant, though he was to impose it on his subjects, and that he would not be forced to abandon his friends, though Montrose would have to go into exile. If he undertook to accept the Uxbridge propositions the Scots army would receive him with honour and would guarantee his safety. Leven and the committee of estates with the army had agreed to send cavalry to meet the king when they heard he was approaching. With these promises Montereul travelled to Oxford to negotiate with the king.[72]

The conduct of the English parliament was meanwhile spurring on the Scots to negotiate with Charles by showing that it wanted to be rid of its Scots ally. Though it did not yet venture to demand that the Scots army leave England it continued to complain of its lack of success, giving the impression that it was a useless burden on the country, and it demanded changes in the army's composition. The 1643 treaty had spoken of the army containing 3,000 horsemen, but it had been able to send nearly 5,000 to Scotland after Kilsyth and musters taken near Newark in January 1646 (excluding the Scots garrisons and other forces in the north of England) had shown that the army consisted of 4,136 horsemen, 2,836 foot (both exclusive of officers) and fifty officers and men of the artillery train. Parliament claimed that so many horse were useless at a siege, and demanded that they be reduced to 3,000. The Scots rightly pointed out that the treaty did not restrict the number of horsemen, and that in any case Callander's army had subsequently been invited into England, containing an unspecified number of horse.[73] Therefore none of the Scots horse were disbanded, and the army failed to remove its garrisons in the north by 1 March as parliament had demanded. Arguments also arose about the Scots army in Ireland; attempts were made to force it to give up Belfast to parliament, and on rumours that it was to be reinforced English commissioners complained that this would be destructive of the service[74]—though only a few months before they had opposed the weakening of the army by withdrawing men to Scotland.

The English parliament was well aware that the Scots were dealing with the king, though they continued to deny it.[75] Parliament was now considering in detail the form of presbyterian church government to be established in England, and the system it favoured further inflamed the quarrels with the covenanters. For though the Westminster Assembly was willing to recommend a system on the Scottish model parliament would not accept it. The Scots found to their dismay that most of the presbyterian party members whom they had regarded as allies against the Independents were tainted with Erastian ideas in that they were determined that the church would be dependent on parliament. However, the Scots views on church policy had significant support in some quarters in England—from many ministers and from the City of London—and this encouraged them to continue trying to persuade parliament to establish what they saw as a true church.[76] The very term 'Erastian' had only obtained its modern meaning—as a general term of abuse for ideas which seemed to exalt state over church—in the previous few years in the hands of Scottish ministers in London,[77] and they and the rest of the covenanters remained determined not to compromise on the issue. The two swords, temporal and spiritual, must each be supreme and independent in its own sphere; church government must be free from state or lay control (though in Scotland this was the theory but not, in reality, the practice). It must comply with the principle of parity among ministers and combine this with central control through a hierarchy of church courts. But though the English parliament was willing to set up the framework of courts it insisted on limiting their powers in ways which seemed to the Scots to remove essentials of a true church. An ordinance of August 1645 indicated that ministers would form only a minority of members of the courts, and that a national assembly would only meet on parliament's orders.[78]

The covenanters were appalled at this watered-down presbyterian system but parliament would not alter it. Worse followed in November. Not only did parliament vote in favour of some sort of compromise between the presbyterian and Independent systems, but the Independents felt powerful enough to reject this and demand toleration. However, in this at least the covenanters had the support of the English presbyterians, for they too were determined that there should be one national church and no toleration. Finally, in March 1646 parliament passed a comprehensive ordinance for setting up a presbyterian system; all church courts were to be subordinate to parliament and their powers were to be strictly limited.[79] Robert Baillie s verdict on it was widely shared by his countrymen. 'The Pope and the King were never more earnest for the headship of the Church than the pluralitie of this Parliament . . . The Erastian and Independent party joyning together . . . to keep off the [presbyterian] Government so long as they were able, and when it was extorted, to make it so lame and corrupt as they were able'.[80]

The covenanters were equally disappointed by parliament's plans in civil affairs. When in February it at last produced proposals for presentation to the king (as the Scots had been pressing it to do for many months) they found that nearly all the significant divergences from the propositions of Uxbridge seemed designed to weaken the union between the two countries. 'We cannot bot observe, that the most material Additions, Omissions, and Alterations . . . betwixt these and the Propositions formerly agreed upon do trench upon the joynt Interests of both Kingdomes, and tending to the lewsing of the Bands, and weakening of the Sinewes, of our happy Union'. But all attempts to get parliament to alter the proposals failed. It was a sad comment on two and a half years of attempted co-operation between the two kingdoms in the war against the king that parliament could now argue with some plausibility that relations between the countries would be better if links between them were kept to a minimum, all thoughts of closer union being abandoned.[81]

Some of the papers presented to parliament by the Scots commissioners were published with a preface by David Buchanan, a Scottish writer, explaining how parliament's new proposals differed from the Uxbridge propositions. In religion the demands made on the king were now very vague, but parliament would not make them more explicit. Parliament now proposed that the militias of the two countries should be entirely separate; and it claimed permanent power over the militia whereas the Scots wished it to revert to the king after a set time. There was no longer to be consultation between the kingdoms in making peace or war, or in raising or disbanding forces.[82] This was a reasonable summary of the changes parliament had made, but the Commons chose to find it insulting and ordered the pamphlet to be burnt by the common hangman; only a more moderate motion of the Lords that only the preface be burnt prevented the Commons having burnt official papers presented to parliament by its nominal allies.[83] Moreover in reply to the pamphlet the Commons issued a declaration showing that they had no intention of compromising with the Scots. Though support for the solemn league and covenant was re-affirmed this was done in terms which brought no comfort to the Scots; the Commons would do nothing 'repugnant to the true Meaning and Intention thereof', but added that it was presumed that 'no Interpretation of it (so far as it concerns the Kingdom of England) shall by any be endeavoured to be imposed on us, other than we ourselves do no be suitable to the first just Ends for which it was agreed', for the covenant was 'only to be expounded by them by whose Authority it was established in this Kingdom', that is, by parliament.[84] In other words, the Scots could interpret the covenant as they liked, but their opinions would carry no weight in England.

No wonder the Scots commissioners concluded gloomily that there was no possibility of agreeing peace proposals with parliament and that a strong party in England was trying 'to bring in confusion, both in Church and State'. All they could suggest to improve the situation was the reinforcement of the Scots army in England since 'the esteeme of our affaires is very much proportioned to the strength or weakness of our army'. The only hope of overcoming their enemies seemed to be to persuade the king to join their army and come to some agreement with them; unless this was done he might join the new model army instead.[85] To the English the plots of the Scots with the king might seem treachery; to the covenanters it seemed that the betrayal had come from parliament altering the demands to be made of him, thus forcing them to turn to him. If they could not get closer union in religion and other spheres, which they saw as vital to Scotland's future security, through alliance with parliament, then it was logical to seek it in alliance with the king instead.

When Montereul arrived in Oxford late in March 1646 he found the king suspicious but willing to negotiate. If the Scots would assure him that he would be safe in their army he would come to it. The Scots reply to this is lost, but it was sufficiently encouraging for Montereul to promise Charles that the Scots would receive him as their sovereign and that he would be free in conscience and honour. They would join him in working to protect him and his party, to the utmost of their power, using their armies to assist him in recovering his just rights and in procuring a well grounded peace. In return Charles agreed that he would receive instruction on presbyterian government and would strive to content the Scots in anything not against his conscience.[86]

It is hard to believe that if the Scots commissioners really did make the promises which Montereul told the king of, they ever had any intention of keeping them; but it is quite possible that Montereul, eager to persuade Charles to join the Scots army, exaggerated the concessions he had been offered. On 2 April Montereul left Oxford for the Scots army near Newark; the king was to follow when he heard that the Scots had ratified the agreement.[87] But when Montereul reached the army it denied knowledge of the agreement between him and the Scots commissioners in London. Balmerino soon arrived, but he showed little enthusiasm for persuading the army to receive the king on the terms agreed, though he did say the terms would be adhered to. Montereul tried to inform the king of the situation, but the committee of estates with the army refused to allow this, doubtless hoping that if Charles did not receive any warning from Montereul he would come to the army without it having to confirm the promises made to him.[88] However, Charles wisely remained in Oxford, and gradually Montereul persuaded some of the Scots nobles to swear to uphold the promises made to the king, though they insisted on making two major exceptions. They refused to contemplate any of the king's forces joining their armies, though Montrose would be allowed to go into exile; and the king would have to agree to establish presbyterian government in England, whatever his conscientious scruples.[89]

When Montereul at last managed to get a message to the king explaining the difficulties which had appeared Charles concluded furiously that 'in short, the Scots are abominable relapsed rogues . . . they have retracted almost everything which they had made him [Montereul] promise me'. But he had to do something, for he was in danger of being trapped in Oxford by advancing parliamentary armies. He first resolved to negotiate with the new model army but it rejected his offers. He therefore fled from Oxford disguised as a servant, with only two companions. At first he moved towards London, considering whether to try to treat with parliament, but then turned northwards and sent a message to Montereul asking for written assurances from the Scots. The committee with the army, however, refused to put anything into writing; the most it would do was to accept a paper by Montereul in which it undertook that the king would be treated honourably, would not be pressed to act contrary to his conscience, and that if the English parliament refused to restore him to his just rights the Scots would declare for him. Unfortunately neither the exact wording of these conditions nor the way in which the Scots assented to them is known, but Charles judged them acceptable enough (though he had little choice) for him to arrive at Montereul's lodging near Newark on 5 May.[90]

THE PROPOSITIONS OF NEWCASTLE

Nobles accompanying the army hurried to the king as soon as they heard of his arrival. Lothian demanded that he at once surrender Newark, sign the solemn league and covenant, agree to establish presbyterian government in England, and order Montrose to disband. When Charles refused, pointing out that he had come to the army on conditions agreed, Lothian expressed surprise, claiming that he and the committee of estates with the army knew nothing of this. Montereul detailed his negotiations with the Scots commissioners in London but Lothian argued that the committee was not bound by their actions; he denied that Charles had been invited to come to the army.[91] Thus the king found that he had been tricked; in the face of Lothian's bland denials he had no written proof of his claims. In all but name Charles was now a prisoner.

The covenanters were exultant; surely possession of the king would restore their fortunes? They would persuade him to accept their peace proposals and could then use his influence to help them to impose a settlement in England. Of course they did not publicly admit this. Lothian wrote to the English commissioners saying that the king's action had 'overtaken us unexpectedly' and 'filled us with amazement and made us like men that dreame'.[92] The English parliament also was told that there had been no secret agreement with Charles.[93] However, as news that the king had joined the Scots army spread so inevitably did belief that he and the Scots had made a secret bargain against English interests. The Scots commissioners in London had predicted that the event would bring them the support of a large party in the English parliament and wide public support.[94] Instead the immediate effect was to increase fear, distrust and hatred of the Scots. On 6 May the Commons voted that disposal of the king was a matter for the English parliament alone, and that he should be taken to Warwick Castle. Further, it was voted that the general, Sir Thomas Fairfax, should dispose of his forces as he thought fit. If approved by the Lords this would have left the new model army free to march to interpose itself between the Scots army and the border, a move which the Scots commissioners had foreseen and feared. But an immediate military confrontation was averted by the Lords ordering Fairfax not to move his forces and refusing to agree to the king being taken to Warwick.[95]

Probably at the instigation of Independents hoping to prove that the Scots commissioners were plotting with the king, guards in London seized a messenger leaving for Scotland with their letters. On 8 May these were read in the Commons and one of them, from John Cheisly (the commissioners' secretary) was found so offensive that his arrest was ordered; he had described with satisfaction reactions in the Commons to the news that the king had joined the Scots army—the consternation, fear and anger of the Independent party, the happiness of those more friendly to the Scots. 'A wittie gentleman said this day, lett us send to the Scottishe armie, to disband ther supernummarie hors',[96] the joke being that the Scots and their friends believed that parliament would no longer dare to risk offending them with niggling complaints over the proportion of cavalry in the Scots army. But in spite of the anger aroused by the letter the Commons seems to have been embarrassed by the interception of the correspondence of their allies, and perhaps there was a wish to avoid provoking the Scots too far. It was voted not to decipher a coded letter to the committee of estates, most of the letters were soon returned, Cheisly was freed, and the Lords later ordering the arrest of the captain of the guard who had seized the letters.[97]

Alarmed by the possibility of being cut off from Scotland by the new model army, the Scots withdrew with the king from before Newark, having persuaded Charles to order it to surrender. On 13 May he arrived at Newcastle, which the army made its headquarters while negotiating with him. It was soon found that Charles had no intention of making any significant concessions; he again refused to take the covenant and though he wrote to both London and Edinburgh declaring his willingness to negotiate he did so in terms so vague as to be almost meaningless, though he did for the moment at least accept military defeat, ordering all his forces in England and Scotland to disband.[98] If the Scots were disappointed by the king's reluctance to make concessions, he was disillusioned by their conduct; he found that they would 'absolutely hinder my being any more king in England than they have made me in Scotland'.[99] But he still had hopes that in time he would be able to build up a party among them to support him. In particular he was encouraged by Lanark's offers to serve him. Charles did not trust him but decided to show favour to both him and his brother, Hamilton. The latter had been freed from imprisonment in April when parliament captured St Michael's Mount in Cornwall, and not surprisingly he was at first reluctant to have anything more to do with the king's affairs, but Lanark persuaded him that it was his duty to aid the king in spite of the way he had been treated.[100]

Charles also retained hopes that France would bring her influence to bear in Scotland in his favour, but as usual France was willing to help only with words. When de Bellièvre was sent to England as ambassador in June he was instructed to inform the Scots that France was offended at their treatment of the king but he was also told that France did not consider herself bound to help him, and he was to tell Charles to make the religious concessions demanded by the Scots.[101]

Meanwhile the covenanters maintained their pressure on Charles. Argyll had hurried back from Ulster and joined the other nobles in urging him to accept the covenant and their proposals for church government in England. If he did this the Scots would reinstate him on the English throne, either by joint consent of both kingdoms or with Scots help against the English parliament if it did not co-operate. But Charles stubbornly refused to give way on religion.[102] Possession of the king thus quickly became a liability to the Scots rather than an asset; they had gained no advantage from it and it aroused increasing resentment in England. On 19 May the Commons voted that parliament had no further need for the Scots army; again only the moderation of the Lords prevented a crisis, by declining to accept the vote.[103] Fuel was added to the flame of anti-Scots feeling in the Commons by the publication of a letter written by the king in April claiming that he had received promises from the Scots army that it would assist him in recovering his just rights; few believed the hasty denials issued by the Scots commissioners.[104] The covenanters were now in the unhappy position of having their negotiations with the king revealed, while his refusal to make concessions deprived them of any advantage to offset the odium thus incurred.

Having failed to make an alliance with the king the covenanters turned hurriedly to reassuring the English parliament of their loyalty to the alliance between them, declaring their willingness to agree on peace proposals.[105] Parliament was in no mood to make concessions but, as a result of the disastrous failure of their intrigues with the king, the Scots were. They feared that unless they consented immediately to whatever parliament proposed they would be denounced as enemies of peace and that parliament might then negotiate with the king without consulting them.[106] On 14 June the committee of estates in Edinburgh therefore authorised the commissioners in London to agree to whatever proposals parliament produced, though they were to declare that they did this to demonstrate their desire for peace, not because they approved of them.

Two days later the general assembly gave similar advice; it would be lawful for the sake of peace to consent to proposals on religion which did not fully satisfy the kirk, provided that the commissioners stated that they would continue to press for further reform.[107]

In accordance with this advice the Scots commissioners (reinforced by Argyll) resolved to accept parliament's proposals without alteration but with all 'the circumspection we could thinke upon' in making it clear that they consented but did not approve.[108] This they proceeded to do on 25 June.[109] Argyll made a speech urging the need for uniformity of religion instead of lawless liberty, though he admitted the necessity of some measure of toleration. Above all he stressed the need for unity between the kingdoms, one in language, religion, king and covenant, on one island, differing only in name. He denied that the Scots were supporting the king, they had a natural affection for him but personal regard would never make them forget that the safety of the people was the supreme law. After Argyll's speech the commissioners gave in a paper explaining that the proposals on religion came 'short of what was wished' and that some were inconsistent with the word of God, but that they accepted them for the sake of peace.[110]

Thus one of the consequences of the king having joined the Scots army was that it led the covenanters, for fear of quarrelling with parliament without gaining the king, to accept peace proposals which were largely the same as those which they had denounced in March and April. The proposals now agreed (soon to be known as the propositions of Newcastle) were sent to the king on 13 July. They provided that he should sign the covenant and agree to it being imposed on his subjects. Religion in England and Ireland was to be reformed in conformity with the covenant and as parliament agreed; the work of bringing about uniformity with Scotland would also be advanced. As for the militia, the armed forces of England would be controlled by parliament for twenty years before reverting to the king. Leading officials and judges would be nominated by parliament. Similar provisions concerning the militia and officials would apply to Scotland if the Scots parliament thought them necessary. As had been agreed in the 1641 peace treaty, conservators of the peace would be appointed by both kingdoms to meet together to maintain peace between them.[111]

In limiting parliamentary control of the militia and in providing for conservators the propositions of Newcastle went some way to meet the objections of the Scots to the propositions produced in March, but not very far. The terms concerning religion were studiedly vague; upholding the covenant meant little since parliament had asserted its right to interpret it as it wished. The undertaking to appoint conservators had been ignored in 1641 and probably would be ignored again. It is hardly surprising therefore that even after accepting the propositions the covenanters continued to press their own terms on the king, promising him their support in return for his acceptance of them. Alexander Henderson (the most widely respected Scottish minister; a convinced covenanter but no fanatic) exchanged a series of papers with the king on the religious points at issue,[112] but the only result was that each man came to have some personal regard for the other. The general assembly sent a team of ministers to assist Henderson but they had no more success; Andrew Cant, 'aye very forward and zealous, being of a fiery temper', proved a liability by simply infuriating Charles, though Robert Blair got on well enough with him to be appointed his Scots chaplain when Henderson died in August.[113]

Charles was prepared to talk, to gain time during which he hoped the Scots would fall out among themselves and with the English parliament, but he had no intention of conceding anything. He distinguished four parties or factions among the Scots—Montrose's, the neutrals, the Hamiltons and the Campbells. Montrose's faction, that of the extreme royalists, was excluded from all power, but the neutrals and the Hamiltons were prepared to keep in touch with it and might perhaps eventually come to some agreement with it. The disorganised and fluctuating group the king called the neutrals attempted to remain on good terms with all the other factions; it stood for a moderate settlement and included Callander and Dunfermline, both of whom had offered their services to the king. The neutrals had much in common with the third group, the Hamiltons, differing from them mainly in being unwilling to accept the leadership of Hamilton and Lanark. Charles believed that the Hamiltons had the support of most of the nobles and were the strongest party on the committee of estates in Edinburgh, but unfortunately the committee with the army at Newcastle and the Scots commissioners in London were mainly supporters of the Campbells, who were led by Argyll and Loudoun. Moreover most of the lairds and burgesses of Scotland, as well as the ministers of the kirk, supported the Campbells 'so that in voting these are strong enough for the other three'. Neutrals, Hamiltons and Campbells all offered to help the king, and he hoped to play them off against each other to his own advantage.[114] In fact the king had really no choice as to which faction to support. The neutrals, with weak leadership and vague policies, were too nebulous a group for him to rely on, the Campbells would never support him while he refused to make concessions in religion, so inevitably he was thrown back on the Hamiltons. He also had hopes of winning over at least part of the Scottish army in England; his offers and promises may have tempted David Leslie for a time.[115] But Leven and over a hundred officers waited on the king to beg him to comply with the just desires of his parliaments in what was probably meant to be a demonstration that he had nothing to hope for from the army.[116]

THE DISPOSAL OF THE KING

Even before Charles knew of the contents of the propositions of Newcastle he was convinced that they would be unacceptable. He still maintained that presbyterian church government was destructive of monarchical government. Royal power would mean little 'if the pulpits teach not obedience (which will never be if Presbyterian government be absolutely established)'. As for the covenant it did 'not only make good all theire former rebellions, but lykewais laies a firm and fructful foundation for such passetymes in all tymes to come'.[117] But to reject the propositions outright would be impolitic; he therefore resolved to delay a full answer for as long as possible.

Commissioners from the English parliament arrived in Newcastle with the peace propositions late in July. The Scots begged him to accept them, Loudoun bluntly warning him that if he refused he would lose all his friends in England, 'And if your Majesty lose England by your wilfulness, you will not be permitted to come and reign in Scotland'.[118] But Charles's reply to the proposals was little more than an evasion; he needed time to consider, and asked meanwhile to be allowed to go to London.[119] 'The King's answer hes broken our heart; we see nothing but a sea of new more horrible confusions' lamented Robert Baillie. But at least the covenanters were pleased by one part of the king's reply; they supported his request to be moved to London[120] as this seemed to present a painless way of getting rid of him. They had now accepted that possession of him was a liability, and that they would probably have to withdraw their army from England without reaching agreement with him or the English parliament, and they were determined not to let him come to Scotland to intrigue against them, perhaps involving them in war with England.

Unfortunately, however, the English parliament was opposed to allowing the king to return to London since it feared his plottings, and the Scots were in no position to insist on it. There was talk in London of passing resolutions 'of a high nature' against Charles, and of demanding that the Scots surrender him immediately and withdraw their army from England, under threat of sending the new model army against them. To reduce tension the Scots commissioners hastened to give assurances that their army would leave as soon as it was given satisfaction for its arrears of pay, and indicated that when it left it would not take the king with it.[121] The question of how much was owed to the Scottish army had already led to heated arguments but in September a compromise settlement was agreed; parliament would pay the army £400,000 sterling, half before it withdrew.[122] The fact that the army was not to leave until paid such a huge sum, which would take several months to raise, gave the covenanters time to negotiate on the disposal of the king, for though they were resolved to leave him in England they still claimed an interest in him as king of Scotland. The delay also gave them time to treat with him in the hope of at last persuading him to make the concessions which would enable them to help him against the English parliament. But as usual Charles was hopelessly optimistic, confident that the delay would be to his advantage. In this case he had some justification, for an increasing number of moderate covenanters were coming to find the idea of abandoning their native king to a hostile English parliament distasteful. To threaten the king with being left was one thing; actually to do it was quite another.

Early in August 1646 Hamilton and Lanark went to Edinburgh to try to persuade the committee of estates to retain the Scots army in England until a peace settlement was reached there. The more extreme covenanters argued that this would involve them in a new war with England on the king's behalf, and this they would not accept unless he signed the covenant.[123] This attitude prevailed, and on 7 August instructions were sent to the Scots commissioners which clearly contemplated surrendering the king; if 'which God Forbid', parliament demanded the king then they were to ask for an undertaking that his freedom and honour would be preserved, that he be disposed of in a way consistent with the security of the kingdoms, and that his right to the crown of England would not be questioned.[124] Probably at the insistence of the supporters of Hamilton (who was not a member of the committee of estates since he had been a prisoner in England when it had been appointed) a joint meeting of the committee, the committee for money and the privy council was held on 18 August to consider the matter further; the privy council had only met occasionally since 1643, and was now revived to lend its traditional authority to an important decision. But the joint meeting reached no final decision, contenting itself with sending yet again to the king to beg him to accept the propositions of Newcastle.[125] He proved as obstinate as ever, arguing that though a peace might be 'slubbered up' on the basis of the propositions it could not be durable. This was reported to another joint meeting on 17 September.[126]

By this time Hamilton's conduct since his release in April was leading to the renewal of hostility to him by many royalists. As in 1641–3 his policy was to court moderates among the covenanters since he believed the king could not succeed without their support, but it raised suspicions that his professions of loyalty to the king were insincere and that he was interested only in his own advancement. Old rumours that the Hamiltons thought themselves to have a right to the throne of Scotland revived; de Bellièvre reported that of the leaders of the two main parties in Scotland one (Argyll) wished to do without monarchy while the other (Hamilton) wished the throne for himself.[127] Hamilton thus failed to win the support of either extreme royalists or of extreme covenanters for a compromise settlement with the king.

De Bellièvre exaggerated Argyll's position. It was true that he was willing that Scotland should continue to be ruled by the estates, being a monarchy in little more than name; but he saw no reason to complicate matters by questioning the existence of monarchy. Charles himself continued to have no doubt that the covenanters were determined to destroy 'the essence of Monarchy (that is to say, reduce my power in England to what they have made it in Scotland)'. He was 'more and more assured that nothing can be expected of the Scots'.[128] Yet at least the covenanters were not prepared to destroy the form of monarchy, and there were now fears that some English parliamentarians were aiming at this. The Scots commissioners in London therefore asked for advice early in September. If the English seemed to be ready to depose the king or to abolish monarchy how far were they to go in protecting him? Should they refuse to negotiate on the removal of the Scots army until parliament declared that it would do nothing prejudicial to monarchical government and would complete the reformation of religion according to the covenant?[129]

The committee of estates and privy council replied that the army was to leave England as soon as it was paid, and that all possible means were to be used to preserve the union between the kingdoms. In other words, no considerations of the king's safety were to be allowed to lead to a quarrel with England. The commission of the kirk gave similar advice concerning religion; less weight was to be placed on achieving full uniformity of church government than on preserving peace and union.[130]

Meanwhile the English parliament was becoming increasingly impatient at the failure of the Scots to state clearly if and when they would hand over the king, and resolved that it had the sole right of disposing of him (which the Scots indignantly denied); any debate concerning the king should not delay the removing of the Scots army.[131] The covenanters' position was set out in speeches by Loudoun to a committee of both houses. Disposal of the king was 'a matter very ticklish' but he insisted that is should be settled by both kingdoms. Restraining Charles was a cure worse than the disease, therefore he should remain free (as the covenanters maintained that he was in his stay with their army). If he was left free he must either go to Scotland or come to his parliament in London. The former was full of dangers, especially since Irish rebels still possessed 'the Mountains and High Lands, which are the strong-holds, and never conquered parts of that Kingdom'. Therefore he should be allowed to come to London as he desired, Loudoun concluded. The Scots thus insisted that the king remain in England; parliament welcomed this but were anxious to keep him away from London, maintaining still that it alone had the right to decide his fate.[132]

Charles was at last beginning to take seriously the idea that Argyll would not, and Hamilton could not, help him unless he made concessions—which, nonetheless he refused to make, for he could not really believe that he would not be allowed to go to Scotland.[133] No doubt he believed that those who accepted offices and pensions from him would feel some obligation to serve him, and many covenanters took advantage of the king's position to beg favours from him; thus he ratified Crawford-Lindsay's appointment as treasurer, appointed Glencairn justice general and accepted Wariston as king's advocate.[134] But such enforced generosity brought him little support.

The Scots parliament assembled on 3 November 1646 but it did not discuss the urgent questions of the king and the removal of the army from England for over a month. This was probably because a committee 'for the burdens and pressors' of the country was set up to consider the state of all three kingdoms and act in routine matters without reference to parliament, being thus the successor of the earlier committees of dispatches.[135] From the first this committee was, it seems, mainly concerned with discussing the king and the army, and until it reported the full parliament avoided these topics. Instead parliament concerned itself with lesser matters; the most important of these was the ratification of the agreement which had allowed Montrose to go into exile. The commission of the kirk denounced the treaty for having pardoned many 'drunk with the blood, and rich with the spoyles of thousands of our deir brethren', even though some had previously been sentenced to death. In spite of this protest parliament approved the treaty and a long list of pardons granted by Middleton.[136]

The outcome of this dispute well illustrates the limitations of the power of the kirk. The great majority of Scots were in favour of the treaty, desires for peace outweighing wishes for vengeance. Against this the general assembly and the commission proved powerless, for they had few lay allies on the issue. On other issues, where the good of religion was more clearly involved, the kirk's influence could be decisive, but in general the ministers were far from being the dictatorial rulers of the country that royalists found it convenient to represent them as being. Without lay support they were ultimately powerless, though they could raise much controversy and embarrass the regime.

Feeling in parliament in favour of supporting the king against the English parliament and of maintaining the army in England was fairly strong, though perhaps often based on sentiment rather than reason. In arguing in favour of refusing to withdraw the army, Hamilton, with some success at first, played the part of the defender of true religion by stating that it should not leave England until religion was fully reformed there in conformity with the covenant;[137] Argyll and his supporters were thus made to seem careless of the interests of the kirk since they urged the army's removal. Both parties acted in the belief that if the army stayed in England Scotland would in all likelihood find herself involved in a new war with the English parliament on behalf of the king.

At first it seemed that the Hamiltons would prevail. On 15 December the committee for burdens resolved that a declaration in favour of monarchical government being continued in King Charles should be issued, and demanded that he be allowed to go freely to London. But the Hamiltons' triumph was short lived, for the mood of the committee the next day was very different. It then voted that the king must approve all the Newcastle propositions; if he refused, the government of Scotland would be settled without him, he would not be allowed to come to Scotland, and she would not intervene in England on his behalf even if he were deposed. The debates before these votes were heated—'I never remember to have seen anything carried with so much violence and bitterness', Lanark related.[138] The main influence in bringing about the sudden change in attitude was probably a warning from the commission of the kirk which was read to the committee; this was clearly a matter which concerned religion, and the kirk's attitude already had strong lay support from Argyll's party. Hamilton's claim to be working in the best interests of religion was rejected; former enemies of the covenant who seemed to have laid aside their former practices were still in fact secretly seeking their own ends. Satan was not sleeping though he did not appear as a roaring lion. These secret enemies were trying to destroy the covenant and the union between the kingdoms under pretence of preserving religion and the king. The kirk therefore desired that Charles should not be allowed to come to Scotland until he took the covenant, for otherwise he would violate it and try to cause divisions; if he would not satisfy the just desires of his people then they would be obliged to uphold the covenant without him.[139]

Parliament decided on 24 December to make a final attempt to persuade the king to accept the propositions. Charles was to be told (in accordance with the committee's decision) that unless he agreed he would not be allowed to come to Scotland, and the covenanters would not help him if the English parliament excluded him from government. Scotland would 'continue the government of the kingdome without him, as hes bene done thir yeiris bygane'. Final preparations for withdrawing the army in England were ordered, and the Scots commissioners were to arrange jointly with the English parliament for the disposal of the king if he still refused to make concessions; all authorised by the covenanters were to be promised free access to him.[140]

The details of the payment and removal of the army were agreed with the English on 15 December, and soon afterwards it was decided that the king should be moved to Holmby House; the Lords said he should await disposal by the two kingdoms but the Commons repeated their objections to the Scots being allowed any say in his fate.[141] If this tempted any covenanters to consider refusing to surrender him, Charles' own attitude gave them no encouragement. His second answer to the Newcastle propositions (issued on 20 December) was as evasive as the first.[142] Granting presbyterian church government was the only thing that could save the king, remarked de Bellièvre, and it was the only thing he would not grant, for he confided that he discovered 'daily more and more that he had committed a great sin when he abolished, seven years ago, the Scottish bishops and established Presbyterianism in their place'; he was now being justly punished for this.[143]

During December Charles toyed with plans to escape from Newcastle, but they came to nothing.[144] He was still vainly hoping to induce some or all of the Scots army to refuse to abandon him, while at the same time he sent a message to Huntly asking him to remain in arms in Scotland; the messenger he used was Robin Leslie, a brother of David Leslie, and Charles still believed he could win over the latter. On his behalf de Bellièvre offered Leslie a large pension and the title of duke of Orkney, but the bribes were refused. The covenanters knew that there was talk of the army refusing to leave the king in England, but if they took it seriously it can only have encouraged them to hurry its withdrawal before discontent came to a head.[145]

On 16 January 1647 the Scottish parliament at last reached a decision on the king's future, after hearing from the commissioners sent to him that he would not make concessions. A vote was taken on whether or not he should be left at Newcastle. Crawford-Lindsay, the president of parliament, showed where his sympathies now lay by trying to get this changed to 'Whither or not his Majestie who wes our Native King and had done so great things for the good of Scotland and thrown himselff upon ws for shelter should be delivered up to the Sectaries avowed enemies to his liffe and Government', but the vote was taken on the original question. The result was a majority in favour of abandoning the king. Hamilton and

Lanark expressed their horror, while Crawford-Lindsay declared his dissent and only signed the act on the understanding that this would not be taken to indicate his approval of it.[146] A declaration by parliament explained that the king had come to the Scots army promising satisfaction (in fact he had only promised all just satisfaction) but had then failed to give this. He had expressed a desire to be near his English parliament, and Scotland had therefore agreed that he should go to Holmby House until he satisfied both kingdoms.[147] A request was sent to the English parliament that no peace should be made by one kingdom without consent of the other and that a committee of both kingdoms should be appointed to attend Charles to continue to press the propositions of Newcastle on him and, if he still refused them, to determine what to do to strengthen the union.[148]

On hearing that he was to be left to fall into the hands of the English the king tried to delay matters further by writing to Crawford-Lindsay suggesting new negotiations. But the committee for burdens ruled that the letter was a private one not addressed to parliament, and therefore refused to consider it.[149] The English parliament hastened to give the Scots the empty reassurances that they sought; no peace would be made without consent of both kingdoms, and meanwhile no changes would be made in the form of government in England.[150] On 30 January, the first £100,000 sterling due to the Scots having been paid, the Scots army marched out of Newcastle, leaving the king to fall into English hands, though two Scots commissioners remained with him. On 3 February payment of the second £100,000 was completed, and within a few days all Scots troops had left English soil, after a stay of almost exactly three years.[151]

Did the Scots sell their king to the English? The statement that they did was widely accepted at the time, and Charles himself contributed to the story by remarking that they had sold him 'at too cheap a rate'.[152] Certainly the fact that the Scots had possession of the king may have made the English parliament more willing than it would otherwise have been to offer as much as £400,000 sterling to the Scots, but the covenanters avoided suggesting that their actions with regard to the king would be in any way influenced by the amount offered. Moreover the Scots had shown themselves anxious to get rid of the king from early August, supporting his request that he be allowed to go to London; this was long before the amount the Scots army was to be paid was settled (mid September) or the details of payment were agreed (December), which was hardly the way to drive a good bargain. Once Charles had refused to make the concessions demanded of him by the Scots he was an embarrasment to them; it was the refusal of the English parliament to allow him to come to London that prevented the covenanters parting with him long before their army was paid. As far as both the covenanters and the English parliament were concerned the removal of the Scots army from Newcastle and the fact that the king thereby passed into parliament's custody were completely separate events. Nonetheless the two matters were outwardly so closely related that the charge that the Scots sold their king seemed plausible. And to another charge connected with their treatment of the king the covenanters certainly were guilty; they had lured him to their army with promises to preserve his freedom and safety, but then made him a prisoner and eventually handed him over to his enemies. They in turn, however, could complain that Charles' own promises of concessions had turned out to be meaningless; and, as Argyll later wrote, 'what could Scotland doe in such a case but as they did?'[153] The king had refused the propositions of peace offered to him by the parliaments of both kingdoms, and was clearly working to increase the divisions between them to bring about a new war from which he hoped to benefit.

Leaving the king in England solved for the Scots the short-term problem of how to rid themselves of him, but it brought solution of the long term problem of how to make a permanent peace settlement in England and Scotland no nearer. Moreover, as time was to show, no matter how many resolutions might have been passed that it would be illegal to intervene to help the king if he were ill treated or deposed in England, most Scots were not prepared to see this happen, and many felt leaving him in England had been dishonourable and left them with some responsibility for him. But in the circumstances of the time the three estates of the Scottish parliament had decided that preserving the alliance with the English parliament was more important than upholding the rights of a king they could not trust.

CHAPTER THREE

The Engagement, January 1647–September 1648

THE END OF THE WAR IN SCOTLAND

Once the army had withdrawn from England the question arose of what should be done with it. Hamilton's faction wished to retain it in arms; encouraged by growing sympathy for the king, they hoped to use the army to help him, though Hamilton continued to bid for the support of covenanters by claiming that the army was needed to complete reformation in England. Argyll on the other hand feared that the increasing royalism would involve Scotland in a new war; therefore he wanted to disband the army to prevent it being misused, retaining only a relatively small force for use against the rebels in the north. Publicly he argued that the army was an unnecessary burden on the country. After debate parliament adopted Argyll's policy, ordering the reduction of the army to only 1,200 horse, two companies of dragoons and 6,000 foot. Nominal command of this 'new model' army (as it was called) was given to Leven, but as he had virtually retired effective command was in the hands of Lieutenant General David Leslie, with John Middleton and John Holborne as majors general. Argyll managed to control the choice of men to be kept in arms and excluded all suspected of royalist sympathies. As David Leslie showed himself increasingly ready to follow Argyll's lead the latter was able to create an army on which he could rely.[1]

The Scottish army in Ireland remained there when the army in England withdrew, and soon caused further disputes with the English parliament. It no longer had any hope of taking the offensive but was determined to remain in Ulster until its arrears were paid. But the English were in no mood to be generous. In March 1647 the Commons resolved that England was no longer able to pay the army; it should therefore return to Scotland, after which payment of arrears would be arranged. Not surprisingly the army had little confidence that it would ever see its arrears unless it insisted on being paid before it left, and it was given a respite by the refusal of the Lords to accept the Commons' vote until August. The army then resolved not to leave before being paid, and the committee of estates supported this decision; the army was weak, but it might nonetheless prove useful as a bargaining counter or as a source of reinforcements.[2]

While David Leslie's army was being formed the question of negotiating with rebels again arose. The kirk remained strongly opposed to a treaty but parliament favoured leniency for the sake of restoring peace quickly; it confirmed that Montrose, Sir Alaster Macdonald, Huntly, Aboyne, Crawford and Sir John Hurry would not be pardoned, and recommended that Lord Reay and his supporters should not be pardoned until they withdrew from lands claimed by the earl of Sutherland which they occupied, but sentences formerly passed against various other royalist nobles were now cancelled and it was agreed that most rank and file rebels might be spared.[3] Leslie marched first against Huntly, moving north from Montrose on 10 March. Castles still held by royalists such as Wardhouse and Lesmoir promptly surrendered, all Irish found in them being immediately executed, and in general resistance was slight. Huntly himself withdrew without a fight into the mountains of Badenoch, and Leslie wisely decided against trying to follow him with his whole army. He therefore established a garrison at Ruthven in Badenoch and marched most of his men south to Dunblane preparatory to moving into Argyll, leaving Middleton and a small force to pursue Huntly and settle the north-east.[4]

Leslie's army was by now badly under strength, and morale was low enough for the kirk to regret that there was 'not greater alacritie and chearfulness in the souldiers of this new modell'. At Dunblane the army demanded payment of arrears, but then suddenly on 17 May marched west without its pay, to escape the unseen enemy which still pursued the covenanters—plague.[5] Though the epidemic was almost over in the south-east, plague reached Glasgow late in 1646, Aberdeen by April 1647; by the end of the year Aberdeen and the neighbouring villages of Footdee and Torry had recorded 1,740 plague deaths, while two thirds of the population of Brechin are said to have died within four months. St Andrews was infected by June, Perth by July. For the rest of the year plague raged widely in the north and west, disrupting public life and hindering the recovery of areas devastated by war.[6]

It was clear from the start that little mercy would be shown in the campaign in Argyll; the Campbells had suffered terribly and were intent on revenge. When Montereul suggested that Sir Alaster Macdonald and his men should be allowed to leave Scotland, Argyll declared that the only debate over the fate of Alaster would be 'as to whether they would make him shorter or longer than he was', whether he would be beheaded or hanged.[7] The rebels had wintered in Kintyre, but seem to have done little to prepare themselves to resist the covenanters.[8] Leslie and Argyll entered

Kintyre on 24 May, charging and scattering about 1,300 rebels, killing sixty or eighty. That night Macdonald, his father Col Keitach and most of the Irish and Macdonalds fled to Islay, leaving many of their Highland allies to fend for themselves. About 300 of them retreated to Dunaverty castle. An attempt by Leslie to storm the castle failed, though about forty of the defenders were killed, but the survivors soon surrendered unconditionally. Leslie resisted the pressure of those determined on vengeance for several days, but then gave way and allowed most of the garrison to be massacred.[9]

After some delay caused by lack of supplies—food, cannon, ammunition and ships—the covenanters crossed to Islay in pursuit of the rest of the rebels. There they found that Sir Alaster Macdonald and nearly all the Irish had fled to Ireland, leaving Col Keitach behind in the castle of Dunyveg.[10] The garrison soon ran short of water, and Col Keitach was foolhardy enough to come out 'desyreing speech of ws without anie assurance', offering to negotiate. This was refused, but he was allowed to return to the castle. Emboldened by this, Col soon appeared again, in search of another commodity the garrison was short of—whisky; surprisingly he was again allowed to return safely, but when he appeared for more on 1 July he was made a prisoner. The leaderless garrison then agreed to surrender on terms, which Leslie offered since he lacked supplies necessary for a prolonged siege; 176 fighting men surrendered their weapons and agreed never to carry arms in Scotland again.[11]

Sir Alaster Macdonald having escaped him, Argyll took his revenge on Col, having him hanged, and soon Sir Alaster too was dead, killed in battle in Ireland.[12] Once Islay was cleared of rebels Leslie turned his attention to Mull. Sir Lachlan Maclean of Duart claimed not to have been in arms since Montrose had disbanded, but the covenanters plundered widely, insisting that he surrender all his castles and all Irish on his lands—who were promptly killed. After this Leslie brought his army south to Stirling, though Middleton was still pursuing the elusive Huntly in the north. He was captured at last in November though his son Aboyne escaped to France. Some wished to execute him immediately but it was decided to leave his fate to parliament when it next met, though two of his most loyal supporters, the lairds of Harthill younger and Newtown-Gordon younger, were executed.[13] In the far north Lord Reay fared no better than the other royalist rebels; when in October part of the garrison of Inverness was sent against him he submitted and left the country, dying abroad in 1649.[14]

Thus by the end of 1647, for the first time for three and a half years, there were no enemies of the covenant in arms in Scotland. But the plague still spread in the north and had followed Leslie's army into Argyll.[15] Devastation was widespread and bands of robbers, men uprooted by the civil wars, still troubled the Highlands. Restoring the exhausted countryside was a slow and laborious business.

POLITICAL CHANGES IN ENGLAND AND SCOTLAND

In March 1647 the Scottish parliament reappointed the former commissioners in London to negotiate with the king and the English parliament; this avoided disputes over the choice of new commissioners, but it was significant that it was decided to send Lauderdale to England ahead of the rest, for of all the commissioners he had shown himself most inclined towards favouring the king in recent months. This was therefore a triumph for Hamilton. New instructions to the commissioners also indicated a somewhat more favourable attitude to the king. They were still to work for presbyterian government and reformation according to the covenant in England, but they were to press the king to swear the covenant or 'at Least give his consent that it may be confirmed as a Law', which suggested that he might be allowed to evade swearing it himself. If Charles accepted the Newcastle propositions the English parliament was to be desired to restore him to power; even if he refused the commissioners were to do what they could to prevent anything being done to his disadvantage.[16]

Members of parliament were by now fairly clearly divided into two main factions or parties, led by Argyll and Hamilton, though the facts that both were devious men concerned to conceal their motives and that they remained outwardly on good terms led many to suspect that they were really allies plotting together but pretending to represent different policies to achieve some obscure advantage.[17] Both claimed to be working to uphold the covenant and the rights of the king, and both were sincere; but in the last resort Argyll was prepared to see the king deprived of some of his rights if he would not take the covenant and establish presbyterianism in England, while Hamilton was prepared to compromise on these religious issues if this was the only way of helping the king. The concern the covenanters expressed for Charles was not simply hypocrisy, though it seemed so to many. The English could point out the illogicality of demanding that the king's just rights in England be protected when he had been deprived of all power in Scotland. The Scots urged that the king be allowed to go to London, but had refused to let him come to Edinburgh. They expressed concern at the English parliament restraining him, but had themselves kept him prisoner at Newcastle. This was all certainly inconsistent, but the covenanters had some justification for their attitudes. It was now becoming clear that some English parliamentarians were prepared either to depose the king or remove him from power permanently, and this was something that even the most extreme covenanters would not accept. They could not bring themselves to agree to accept the logical conclusion that if Charles would not in any circumstances grant the concessions they insisted on, then he should be deposed or otherwise excluded from power.

In part this attitude was the result of history and tradition. England had many national and constitutional myths which were independent of the monarchy: myths and traditions of fundamental laws and Magna Carta, of a free constitution which had existed before the Norman conquest and, above all, of the powers and privileges of parliament. On the other hand though the covenanters talked sincerely of fundamental laws and liberties of the subject, these were in Scotland abstractions which had little popular appeal. The Scottish parliament had not (until the previous few years) achieved anything like the importance, the central place in national life, of its English counterpart, though the tradition that the estates had a right to some say in government was a long one. The strongest constitutional myth that the Scots possessed was that of an unbroken line of over one hundred kings stretching back to the distant past. Pride in this myth had been increased by James VI's accession to the English throne, and most Scots still took pride in the fact that the king of England was a fellow Scot. Were they to stand idly by while the English dethroned their compatriot, the head of their ancient line? In helping the English parliament the covenanters had never contemplated the king's deposition, and many must have argued that since they had unwittingly helped to reduce him to a position in which it was possible to depose him, it was their duty to ensure that this did not happen. Moreover, the Scots clung tenaciously to the principle of union with England as something vital to Scotland's security, and now that the English parliament was showing hostility to the idea of closer union the Scots had to fall back on upholding the union of the crowns as the one existing link between the two kingdoms.

Thus the immediate reaction in Scotland to leaving the king in England had been to swing the balance in parliament of the rival claims of upholding kirk or king slightly in the latter's favour; Argyll complained that 'I can hardlie expres . . . the difficulties sum men are put to, to carie on business her'.[18] A new committee of estates was chosen in March, shortly before parliament was dissolved, and the Hamiltons claimed that the majority of members supported them; a sign of the times was the election to the committee of Traquair, the arch incendiary of 1637–41. Argyll's supporters admitted that most of the nobles on the committee would vote with Hamilton but maintained that half the lairds and three-quarters of the burgesses would follow Argyll.[19]

In England too the withdrawal of the Scots army brought about significant political changes. Many parliamentarians had given their support to the Independent party through determination not to allow the Scots to dictate a peace in England, but many of them opposed the radicalism of the Independents' religious and other policies. Now that the Scots had withdrawn and surrendered the king they swung back to favouring a moderate presbyterian settlement negotiated with the king, and were prepared to work in alliance with the Scots to achieve this. English presbyterian party leaders thus turned out to have calculated correctly when they had urged the Scots to remove their army and abandon the king, as this would increase support for a presbyterian settlement in England.[20] Even before the king had left Newcastle for Holmby House a group of presbyterian peers resolved to open secret negotiations with him on the basis of the establishment of presbyterian government for three years and parliamentary control of the militia for ten; and the presbyterians and other groups opposed to the Independents quickly came to have a majority in both houses of Parliament.[21] The body most likely to interfere with a presbyterian settlement was obviously the new model army, which remained Independent in sympathy. Parliament therefore resolved to disband most of the army; but this was undertaken in such a tactless way (without payment of arrears) that the army united in opposition to the presbyterian party majority in parliament and prepared to resist.[22]

All this was a source of satisfaction to the king, who as always hoped to benefit from divisions among his enemies. On 12 May he issued a new answer to the Newcastle propositions, offering presbyterian government for three years and to give up the militia for ten; thus his paper was really not so much an answer to the propositions as to the proposals of the presbyterian peers, which he now largely accepted. The presbyterian party in parliament declared its willingness to accept the king's concessions as the basis of a new treaty,[23] while the Scots commissioners (led by Lauderdale) indicated that the concessions were at least a move in the right direction.[24] Parliament now favoured bringing the king to London (as the Scots had long urged). In secret talks between Lauderdale and presbyterian leaders the fear that the new model army might seize Charles was discussed, together with the possibility of bringing a Scots army into England to save him from the army, or of sending him to Scotland.[25] Four months previously the English presbyterians had supported the Independents' demands that the Scots leave England without the king, yet now they were ready to consider inviting the Scottish army back as an ally to protect them and the king.

Rumours of the plans of the presbyterians and the Scots to secure the king and make a peace unacceptable to the Independents soon reached the new model army. To prevent this, elements of the army acted as their opponents had feared and seized Charles, carrying him to Newmarket on 4 June. The Scots commissioners protested vigorously, undertaking that if necessary Scotland would join England in rescuing him;[26] the army's action naturally brought them and the English presbyterians closer together, and they jointly dispatched Dunfermline to France to urge Henrietta Maria to send the young prince of Wales to Scotland to lead an army into England on the king's behalf.[27]

In talking of sending a Scots army to help the king Lauderdale was promising more than he could perform, for neither Argyll nor Hamilton was willing to support such action. The committee of estates discussed the seizure of the king on 11 and 22 June but no decisions were taken, probably because neither party leader was present, though members were strongly of the opinion that Lauderdale had acted without authority in offering Scots help for the king. On 1 July Hamilton was present, and by that time indignation at events in England had been increased by the interception of letters from the Scots commissioners by soldiers of the new model army. Yet the committee took no action on either 1 or 6 July, on the pretext that reports of the situation in England varied.[28]

Why did Hamilton, so forward in professions of his wish to help the king, not press for intervention in England? It was not, as Montereul still suspected, because he was secretly in league with Argyll,[29] but rather because he was so much opposed to Argyll. At heart he did favour sending an army into England, but if such a policy was implemented at this time the nucleus of the army sent would be David Leslie's army, recently modelled into a force loyal to Argyll. If this army was to rescue the king he would be little better off than before. Unless he then accepted the religious demands of the extreme covenanters he would simply exchange one captivity for another. Hamilton had therefore decided that he must oppose intervention in England until Leslie's army could be disbanded or purged, and this would not be until it had completed its campaign in the west. Thus it appeared that Argyll's party was more eager to help the king than the royalist Hamilton, its main interest in intervening in England being in overthrowing the Independents, which it believed would be in the king's best interests. In the committee of estates on 6 July Argyll's supporters suggested some increase in the size of the army, for defence against the country's enemies in England, but the Hamiltons opposed the idea, stressing that no specific request for assistance had come from the king.[30]

Hamilton's attitude may well have been justified by the king's own, for it seems probable that Charles had no wish to be rescued by the Scots. He had, after all, just spent nine months in their hands without reaching any agreement with them. He therefore favoured an English solution to his problems, trying to turn to his own advantage the increasingly bitter quarrels between the army and the Independent party on the one hand, and the presbyterian party on the other. On 26 June eleven prominent presbyterians withdrew from parliament after being denounced by the army, and parliament's attempts to regain possession of the king were thwarted; the army allowed him to be moved to Richmond but came with him, thus threateningly moving nearer to London. Presbyterians at first seemed determined to resist, and stirred up riots in London on 26 July which led about sixty members who supported the Independent party to flee to the army. But after this brave start resistance soon crumbled; the presbyterians, seeing themselves as resisting the illegal violence of the army in the name of law and order, were not willing themselves to resort to force, and early in August the army occupied the capital without a fight. The Independent members returned while the presbyterian leaders again withdrew, and though the army still could not always rely on the support of a majority in parliament direct opposition to it collapsed. The covenanters were horrified; they believed that a little more resolution on the part of the presbyterians, 'one stout look more', would have broken the power of the Independents. For lack of it the new model army was now 'master of all'.[31]

The army now produced its own terms for a settlement, the heads of proposals, which made provision for the existence of a form of episcopacy combined with toleration but demanded strict limitations on the king's civil power. The king, meanwhile, had begun to show himself more favourably inclined than before to Lauderdale's offer (renewed on 22 July, again without authority) of a Scots invasion of England. But Lauderdale's negotiations were abruptly cut short when he arrived at Woburn Abbey to see the king on 30 July; the guards decided to prevent him meeting the king, and early next morning hustled Lauderdale out of bed and ejected him from the abbey. The Scots complained furiously but got no satisfaction. Another such outrage occured in August when John Cheisly was arrested in Newcastle while carrying letters to Scotland.[32]

Meanwhile the committee of estates continued to debate indecisively the English army's seizure of the king. On 14 July it received the advice of the kirk, which denounced English sectaries and Independents and urged the necessity for religious unity between the two kingdoms as a protection for religion in Scotland. 'Befor our vnion with that nation vnder one King, the influence from thence in the revolutions and alterationes of Religion was alwayes powerfull upon us, and since that tyme wofull experience hes taught it to be such as first overturned the govemment of the Church, and corrupted the worship of God, and did afterwards well nigh cary vs bak unto Rome itself'. Scotland was always going to be influenced or infected by events in England, and therefore had a vital interest in the work of reformation there. This left little doubt that if necessary the kirk would favour military intervention in England to overthrow the Independents and rescue the king from them. Only one minister, George Gillespie, 'who was indeed of good parts, but bold beyond all measure, withstood these Inclinations, and represented, that the greatest Danger to Religion was to be feared from the King and the Malignant Party', not from the Independents.[33]

On 17 August Argyll took his seat on the committee of estates for the first time since he had marched west with the army in May, and decisions now at last began to be made, which suggests that they had been delayed until he was present, though the fact that John Cheisly had been freed and now reported in detail on events in England may also have been influential. New instructions to the commissioners in London were quickly approved; parliament was to be desired to invite the king to London out of the power of the army so that both kingdoms could again present the propositions of Newcastle to him. Two extra commissioners were to be sent to England, Loudoun and Lanark, to tell the king of the committee's concern for his safety, its wish for peace and that he might be restored to his throne. The choice was clearly a compromise; Lanark would represent his brother Hamilton, Loudoun his kinsman and ally Argyll. But the message they were to deliver to Charles was too royalist for Argyll, who therefore protested that none of the instructions should be taken to imply any engagement in a war between the kingdoms or weakening of the union between them. Hamilton then disarmed such suspicions by declaring himself in favour of this protest, adding that neither should the instructions be held to prejudice the king; the protest was then adopted almost unanimously. Thus out-manoeuvred, Argyll tried to get it suppressed, but without success.[34]

Now that the campaign against the rebels was over the problem of what to do with David Leslie's army became acute. Argyll maintained that it should be kept in arms and reinforced in view of the dangers to king and religion, while Hamilton argued that it should be disbanded since there was no use for it and it was a burden on the country. On 8 September Argyll was absent and Hamilton's views prevailed; the committee voted that the army should be disbanded on 20 October. But, with its habitual reluctance to make a final decision on anything, a more frequent (better attended) meeting was summoned for 12 October to reconsider the vote.[35]

The departure of Loudoun and Lanark for London was delayed (evidently because, after the treatment of Lauderdale at Woburn Abbey, guarantees of their safety were demanded) but the Hamiltons secretly sent Robin Leslie to the king to tell him of the almost universal opposition in Scotland to the actions of the English army and that a Scots army would have entered England by this time if he had let it be known that he favoured such action. The fact that Hamilton was in fact for the moment opposing such intervention was not mentioned, though a letter from Lanark to the king contradicted Hamilton's message by stating that the delay in helping the king was caused by the strength of opposition to such action except 'at the old rate of satisfaction in Religion and the Covenant'.[36] Charles commented on the discrepancy and urged Lanark to come to him to explain it.[37]

Meanwhile in London parliament was preparing to present the propositions of Newcastle to the king again; the Independents and new model army allowed this because they knew Charles disliked the propositions and hoped that he would react to them by favouring their rival heads of proposals, which he had previously rejected. Lauderdale and the other Scots commissioners joined in the offer of the propositions reluctantly, perhaps because they knew Charles would reject them.[38] This he duly did on 9 September, stating that the heads of proposals were a more satisfactory basis for a peace. This was what the army had hoped for, and it immediately reduced the chances of the king receiving prompt help from Scotland.[39] Nonetheless it was resolved to continue negotiations with him; late in September new instructions were approved for Loudon and Lanark, who were now about to depart as a letter promising them free access to the king had been received from the English parliament. They were to press that the king go to London to negotiate on the basis of his paper of 12 May (which had offered presbyterian government in England for three years) and were to do all they could to prevent any negotiations on the heads of proposals. Argyll feared that this did not go far enough in ensuring that religion would be protected but the committee refused to alter the instructions, referring them to the 'more frequent' meeting on 12 October; Argyll's demand that the order for disbanding the army be cancelled was similarly refused.[40]

Lanark and Loudoun apparently travelled to England separately.[41] On his way south Loudoun spent a night with the earl of Roxburgh, who told him of the secret plans of the Hamiltons to ensure that the army would be disbanded. 'I find noe meanes wilbe left unassayed to disband our present Armie. The burthen of the kingdom will be pretended as the sole caus'; those who wished to help the king would be better to have a new army than to 'keip up that Armie who delyvered up the king, whom he can hardly trust'.[42] Both Hamilton and Argyll therefore prepared for a trial of strength on 12 October. Fifty-three members of the committee of estates were present on that day, sixty-one two days later, perhaps the largest number ever to attend a meeting of the committee. As throughout the year, the divisions between the two main factions were remarkably close, but on 15 October an act was passed relating that because of the imminent dangers to king and religion the army would be kept on foot until the Scottish parliament met in March 1648. This was a triumph for Argyll, but the act was passed only by a single vote, and only after the army had agreed to accept a reduction in pay.[43]

THE ENGAGEMENT

The fact that Argyll had prevented the disbanding of the army did not alter the fact that negotiations with the king were now in the hands of Lauderdale (who earlier had been over ready with promises of Scots help for him), Lanark (who had long favoured helping him) and Loudoun (who, though he normally supported Argyll, was no extremist and was full of concern for the king). Moreover the king's praise for the heads of proposals made the three Scots nobles more willing than they might otherwise have been to make concessions, for they were convinced that for the king to make a peace on the basis of the proposals would be disastrous both for him and for Scotland; Loudoun remarked that they gave neither God nor Caesar his due.[44]

They first met the king at Hampton Court on 22 October and gave him to understand that if he satisfied them concerning religion he would be master of Scotland.[45] Charles still was not sure that he had more to hope for from the Scots than from the new model army, but he did authorise them to have secret talks with the marquis of Ormond, his lord lieutenant of Ireland. Ormond had just handed Dublin over to the English parliament to prevent it falling into the hands of the confederate Irish, but he now undertook that if the Scots invaded England for the king he would return to Ireland to lead a royalist campaign there.[46] Some days later Lanark and Lauderdale felt able to urge the king to flee with them; he refused, but in further talks he accepted the idea of flight and of going to Scotland, though Lauderdale warned him that unless he made concessions in religion he would be a prisoner there. Charles suggested going to Berwick, and the two nobles approved the idea. The English would not be able to claim that he had deserted the kingdom, yet he would be out of the power of the new model army, would be conveniently situated to negotiate with the Scots, and could easily withdraw into Scotland if threatened. The king duly fled from Hampton Court on 11 November, but then instead of making for Berwick he showed his lingering distrust of the Scots by turning south, ending up in Carisbrooke Castle on the Isle of Wight, where he was soon again a prisoner; he had hoped the governor of the island would declare in his favour or help him to escape to the Channel Islands or France.[47]

From Carisbrooke Charles hopefully directed a new peace offer to the English parliament, offering presbyterian government for three years, combined with toleration, preparatory to a final settlement.[48] Needless to say this was not satisfactory to the Scots commissioners, who complained that the offer 'hath infinitely disabled us to serve You'. In religion it was less acceptable than his paper of 12 May since toleration of heresy and schism was now proposed.[49] Charles then (on 29 November) glibly tried to explain away his offer to the English; he might offer many things in order to begin negotiations which he would alter later. To persuade the Scots to reopen talks with him he praised a paper they had presented to parliament stressing their desire for peace, complaining of the hard usage Charles had received and asking that he be allowed to come to London. This, he now announced, 'is as full to My sense, as if I had penned it My Self. And let me tell you, that it will turn to the greatest Honour (I say no more) that ever befell you; wherefore I conjure you by all that is dear to wise or honest men, that you adhere close and constantly to it'. Having ignored the advice of the Scots that he go to Berwick, Charles was now being forced to look to them for help, for the English parliament had ignored his new offer and was instead preparing its own proposals, the four bills; the new model army had also refused to negotiate with him.[50]

The three Scots nobles were eager to respond to the king's advances, for they had no more liking than he for the four bills, which had little to say about religion, 'the *Unum Necessarium*; we ought to build the House of God before our own', and virtually nothing about the covenant and the treaties between the kingdoms. They were also unsatisfactory concerning the power of the crown and 'the Union and joint Interest of the Kingdoms'.[51] But such arguments carried little weight in the English parliament, which interpreted them as a claim that the Scots had a right to a say in English affairs. The English republican Henry Marten was soon to denounce the Scots answer to the four bills in a pamphlet flatly contradicting Scots assumptions about the nature of their involvement in England. They only had the right to join in counsels 'with a Committee of ours in ordering and disposing of such Auxiliary Forces' as Scotland had formerly sent to England. Their 'devout-like and amicable Endeavours' to try to settle peace and religion in England, for which they expected thanks, were 'Intrusions into Matters unconcerning you'; apart from the war the kingdoms had no common interests requiring joint action. 'You affirm that the Covenant . . . makes you co-partners with us in everything there mentioned' but 'I do not conceive the parties to that League intended thereby to be everlastingly bound to each other'. It was merely a joining in war to suppress a common enemy; the war being over the covenant was irrelevant, as out of date as 'an Almanak of the last year'. The demands the Scots were making were more exorbitant than those of the king.[52]

Parliament itself simply ignored the Scots answer to the four bills, and continued preparing to present them to the king. This raised the fear in the minds of the commissioners that unless they could quickly reach agreement with the king parliament would force him to accept the four bills or would take punitive action against him; either course would lead to a settlement which ignored Scotland's interests. Loudoun at least still had doubts as to how to act; on 30 November he wrote worriedly that 'Wee intend to goe to the king if wee can . . . it is to be feared that the gudeman of Ballengight [the king][53] will not come the length he should so it will be hard to Resolve what should be next. Bot wee shall with gods assistance endeavour to doe our dewtie . . . Althoughe I must confes I never hade so many difficulties as at this time'.[54] In spite of his doubts he joined the other two nobles in welcoming the king's letter of 29 November, and in suggesting that he again try to reach Berwick. Once there he could treat with his affectionate Scots subjects; 'You already know upon what terms you can engage them, either to restore You, or fall with You'. But these terms, based on the propositions of Newcastle, were still unacceptable to Charles, though he was told that there was no hope that Scotland would help him on easier ones.[55]

The Scots nobles were anxious to go to Carisbrooke to negotiate with the king personally but feared that parliament would suspect (rightly) that they hoped to arrange a separate peace with him. They therefore remained in London until English commissioners left to present the four bills to Charles, and then set out after them, ostensibly merely to protest against them in the king's presence.[56] This delay in the arrival of the Scots was turned by the king to his own advantage, for he almost certainly persuaded them to make concessions by pretending to be about to accept the four bills. The bills were first presented to him on 24 December;[57] two days later he and the Scots nobles signed the Engagement, a treaty by which the king was to receive Scots military aid in return for concessions that he had first offered months previously, on 12 May.

By the terms of the Engagement the king agreed to confirm the solemn league and covenant in the English parliament, but neither he nor his subjects were to be constrained to take it. Presbyterian church government in England he confirmed for three years only, prior to a final settlement by an assembly of divines, parliament, and the king: meanwhile Independents, heretics and schismatics were to be suppressed. Thus the Scots at last abandoned the religious demands of the propositions of Newcastle; Charles' stubbornness had brought its reward. In civil matters he promised to ratify the acts of the 1644–7 Scots parliament and to settle the debts due by the English parliament to Scotland. 'According to the intentions of his father' he would 'endeavour a complete union of the kingdoms, so as they may be one under his Majesty and his posterity', or would at least establish free trade between them. Thus the Engagers remained true to the covenanters' belief that a closer union was necessary to solve the problems raised by the union of the crowns. In return for these concessions Scotland would undertake to bring the king to London for a personal treaty with parliament. If this was not granted peacefully Scotland would send an army into England to preserve religion, defend the king and his authority, and restore him to his government. In additional articles Charles promised that in future Scots would be employed equally with Englishmen in foreign negotiations, and that Scots would sit on the English privy council and *vice versa.* Scots would also be employed in places of trust around the king, queen and prince of Wales, and the king or prince would reside in Scotland as frequently as was convenient.[58]

Early in December Loudoun, Lanark and Lauderdale had told the king that Scotland would not help him unless he made concessions concerning religion. Yet now they had agreed on an Engagement in which it was they and not Charles who made concessions sanctioned neither by the committee of estates nor by the kirk.

THE RECEPTION OF THE ENGAGEMENT IN SCOTLAND

After signing the Engagement the king rejected the four bills, whereupon the English parliament passed a vote of no addresses; no approaches were to be made to him without its leave and no message from him would be considered. It was well known that his intransigence was due to the fact that he was contemplating a secret treaty with the Scots, though not that he had actually signed such a treaty, and the vote was doubtless partly intended to thwart the treaty. Anger at the plotting of the Scots was also expressed in the abolition of the committee of both kingdoms;[59] it had long been of only minor importance so its suppression was a gesture intended to indicate that parliament was no longer prepared to consider the Scots even as nominal allies.

Details of the signing of the Engagement were brought to the committee of estates in Edinburgh on 21 January by Sir John Cheisly;

previously he had been a supporter of Argyll but he had helped to draft the Engagement, being rewarded by the king with a knighthood and the office of master of requests.[60] Along with Traquair and Callander, who had also been at Carisbrooke, he spread the good (though false) news that the king had given complete satisfaction to Scotland's desires.[61] Loudoun, Lauderdale and Lanark left London on 24 January; for the first time for four years there were to be no Scots commissioners in London. They had been holding secret talks with English royalists and presbyterians on risings to coincide with a Scots invasion, and on their journey north they confided in other royalists, some of whom followed them into Scotland. Even before the Engagement had been signed Lanark had been in touch with Henrietta Maria and other royalists in Paris who were now busy trying to raise arms and money for the cause.[62] Loudoun and Lauderdale reported to the committee of estates on 10 and 15 February, the latter denouncing the English for their breaches of the covenant and claiming that there were four things that they would not tolerate—the covenant, presbyterianism, monarchical government, and Scotsmen! The committee approved their conduct and expressed itself in favour of the Engagement;[63] in the resentment that events in England had aroused the fact that the Scots commissioners had exceeded their instructions was ignored. But actual implementation of the treaty was delayed until parliament met on 2 March, and meanwhile vocal opposition to it emerged. The commission of the kirk demanded that it be consulted before decisions were taken concerning religion; when it heard of the king's concessions it declared them inadequate, destructive of the covenant and presbyterian government. Loudoun, Lauderdale and Lanark therefore wrote urgently to the king begging him to make further concessions to satisfy the ministers as this was 'the only means to procure Unanimity', but he refused.[64]

Many ministers who had favoured invasion of England in 1647 since it then appeared that such a venture would be in the hands of Argyll's party and be primarily concerned with overthrowing the Independents, quickly changed their tune when they heard the terms of the Engagement; they began to stress the need for peace and unity, arguing that in spite of the many faults of the Independents there was no justification for a war. They now said 'loudly that God is powerful enough of Himself to punish the Independents, without requiring help from men.' Following the lead of George Gillespie, who had opposed intervention in England even in 1647, the 'Clergy (for the most part) have (upon the activity of the malignants) changed their note, and are now for peace', while the women of Edinburgh and Leith 'who carry a great Sway, especially at home, do cry for peace, and say their husbands shall not fight'.[65]

In the committee of estates Argyll, Lothian, Balmerino, Balcarres and others supported the ministers; a war would ruin both kingdoms and allow anti-Christian malignants to gain power.[66] But the king's concessions had won over enough of Argyll's former supporters to give the Engagers an unshakeable majority. The even balance between the two main parties which had been so notable a feature of the committee in 1647 had been destroyed.

Argyll's party held meetings to discuss how to react, and it was rumoured that 'it was proposed that the army of Scotland should imitate that of England';[67] in other words, that David Leslie's army should overawe the estates into rejecting the Engagement. Argyll also had talks with English commissioners who arrived in February to try to dissuade Scotland from intervening in England—with the help, it was said, of large sums of money for distribution in bribes. It was also hoped that the money owed to Scotland by the English parliament (especially the £200,000 sterling still due to the former army in England) would restrain the Scots, but the commissioners found the committee in no mood to be swayed by such financial considerations—it virtually ignored their presence in Edinburgh. The English parliament had neglected to reply to papers from the Scots in the last months of 1647 and the committee now repaid the insult.[68]

When parliament met on 2 March it quickly became clear that it contained a substantial majority in favour of the Engagement. Now that there seemed to be some real chance of helping the king, royalist nobles who had previously taken little part in public affairs attended; it was said that all but ten or eleven of the fifty-six nobles present, more than half the shire commissioners and nearly half the burgesses favoured the Engagement, giving Hamilton a majority of thirty or thirty-five votes. All disputed elections were decided in favour of his supporters.[69] The fanatic Wariston had sat in the previous parliament for Midlothian; now he got a seat only through the marquis of Argyll, who had him elected for Argyll after selling or giving him the island of Shuna to provide him with the necessary property qualification.[70] An immediate triumph for Hamilton was the election of Loudoun to be president of parliament, for the other three candidates were all followers of Argyll.[71] Parliament proceeded to approve the conduct of the former commissioners in London, which amounted to approval of the Engagement itself.[72] The kirk stressed its inadequacy where religion was concerned and warned of the hidden danger from 'secret malignants, discovenanters, and bosome enemies' who had opposed the covenant but now pretended zeal to invade England to impose it; parliament promised to consider these arguments but asked that they should not be made public.[73]

On 10 March a committee for dangers, remedies and duties was appointed to consider the dangers threatening religion, covenant, king and monarchical government; of eighteen members only five were of Argyll's party, and it was said that Argyll himself would not have been elected if Hamilton (anxious to prevent an open quarrel so soon) had not supported his membership.[74] But this did not disguise the increasing bitterness between the factions, which now manifested itself in a series of duels. The first was between David Leslie and Lord Sinclair. Leslie had earlier complained that Sinclair had called him a perjurer and traitor for promising the king safety in the Scots army in England and then abandoning him. Sinclair had been imprisoned until he apologised, but a few days after his release fought a duel with Leslie, though (as with the others in the series) there was evidently no bloodshed. At about the same time those hereditary rivals of the west, Eglinton and Glencairn, fought; the former opposed the Engagement, the latter supported it. But it was the third encounter which won most attention. While talking in parliament to Crawford-Lindsay (who was emerging as a leading Engager), Argyll understood him to claim to be a better man than he was. Crawford-Lindsay refused to explain what he had said but stated that 'whatever it was, he would make it good with his sword'. The two men arranged to fight on 13 March, but were parted by friends before 'they began their play'. The final duel was between Lords Cranston and Kenmure.[75]

The Argyll duel led to wild rumours and confusion. The commission of the kirk seems to have feared that it was part of some plot to dispose of Argyll and stifle opposition, for on hearing of the duel it published its denunciation of the Engagement.[76] This aroused the indignation of the prevailing party in parliament, but it continued its efforts to win the support of the ministers; the committee for dangers produced a declaration on the reasons for undertaking a war which gave more emphasis to the need to enforce religious reform than to help the king.[77] However, the fact that at the same time three of Argyll's supporters were removed from the committee prevented this doing anything to reassure the ministers. Moreover, it was ruled that the committee's meetings should be in secret and that it had power not only to consider what to do to prevent malignants or sectarians from garrisoning Berwick and Carlisle but also to act on its own in the matter. By treaties of 1641 and 1643 neither country was to garrison these towns, yet now the committee was given power to seize these gateways into England if it saw fit. Argyll and his supporters denounced the grant of these new powers to the committee as being illegal, a breach of the 1640 act abolishing the lords of the articles;[78] when the protest was ignored he and more than forty others walked out of parliament while Loudoun (whose enthusiasm for the Engagement was already waning) declared that he signed the act granting the new powers 'as seruant to the hous, not as his oune opinion'. Many Engagers were eager to take this opportunity to rid themselves of all opposition in parliament by resolving to refuse to allow those who had left to return but Hamilton and Traquair argued that this would encourage their enemies by showing how divided opinion in Scotland was, so Argyll and his supporters were summoned and told 'thatt you should sitt doune in your places', which they did.[79]

The kirk also denounced the new powers of the committee, as being 'of exceiding dangerous consequence', and produced a list of demands that would have to be satisfied before the kirk could support a war. The English breaches of the covenant must be specified, and it must be declared that the establishment of the covenant and presbyterian government in all the king's dominions was being sought. The king's religious concessions must be declared unsatisfactory, and malignants and non-covenanters must not be accepted as allies in any attempt to help him.[80] By this time the organisation of petitions against the Engagement had begun, and its opponents were meeting nightly in the Tailors' Hall in Edinburgh to co-ordinate opposition. The most influential petition, it was hoped, would be that from David Leslie's army; if the majority of officers of the only armed force in the kingdom denounced the Engagement parliament could hardly ignore them. But largely through the efforts of Middleton the unity of the army was broken; Leven, Leslie and Holborne signed the petition but Middleton and Sir Alexander Hamilton (general of the artillery) refused, and Middleton persuaded many to sign only with an addition stating that they would obey parliament even though they opposed the Engagement. Rather than present the petition in this emasculated form the anti-Engagers suppressed it. Thus the army that Hamilton had so feared in 1647 that he had refused to declare in favour of helping the king proved divided and unwilling to interfere in politics.[81]

The Engagers were also encouraged by the arrival of Sir William Fleming, sent by Henrietta Maria and the prince of Wales; he spent a month in discussions before returning to France with requests for money, arms, ammunition and ships, and an invitation to the prince to come to Scotland (though Montereul recommended that he should not entrust himself to the Scots).[82] Fleming also carried private instructions from Callander, who presented himself as being primarily responsible for any help that might reach the king from Scotland. He and his friends, he claimed, held the balance of power between the evenly matched parties of Hamilton and Argyll, so by supporting Hamilton they swayed the balance in the king's favour. He therefore wished to negotiate separately with the queen and the prince, and he asked them to state who they thought should lead the army to be raised for the king, obviously hoping that he would be their choice.[83] Callander was much exaggerating his power, but during the previous year he and Traquair had emerged as leaders of a group of royalists who distrusted Hamilton and wished to pursue a more openly royalist policy, without wasting time trying to conciliate the kirk before helping the king.[84] But even without their votes Hamilton held a majority in parliament and they could hardly vote with Argyll. That their claim to hold the balance of power was thus false was apparently realised, for nothing came of his attempt to deal directly with the prince. Nonetheless Callander had too much support among royalists for Hamilton to ignore him; in trying to win the maximum of support for the Engagement he therefore had to attempt simultaneously to please the kirk and extreme covenanters on the one hand, Callander and his royalists on the other.

On 11 April parliament approved an act setting out breaches of the covenant and treaties by England and demanding reparation. The act was intended both to satisfy the kirk and to provide a justification for war by making demands that the English were bound to reject. The English army and parliament alike were denounced for hindering reformation of religion, failing to impose the covenant, and treating with the king without Scots consent. Scotland could not be secure while the sectarian army mainly responsible for such actions prevailed; it must therefore be disbanded and the king be allowed to come to London for a treaty.[85] That this was purely a propaganda document was admitted by Lanark: 'You may possibly think our demands concerning religion impertinent: I doe soe too. Yet certainly they are most necessary at this time and the more unreasonable the better, for then we are sure to have then denyed and without a pretext of religion it is impossible to engage this Kingdom'. As the kirk feared, to the Hamiltons religion was no more than a pretext, but the contents of the act made it difficult for supporters of the kirk to vote against it. In the event only four did so, including Argyll, Cassillis and Wariston; the rest of Argyll's party felt obliged to vote for it. This was a triumph for the Engagers, but its price was that they temporarily lost the support of Callander and Traquair, who so disapproved of even the pretence of making war to uphold the covenant that they abstained.[86]

The kirk was not so easily confused by a cloak of religious zeal, and pointed out the inconsistency of the act. Why were only the English being asked to impose the covenant and reformation and not the king as well? If the Engagers were going to war for the sake of religion if the English refused their demands, how could they act in alliance with a king who had refused the same demands?[87] Regardless of such protests the Engagers began open preparations for war, appointing new shire committees of war and shire colonels on 18 April to train and arm men; as a sop to the kirk all those guilty under the first and second classes of the 1646 act of classes were excluded. Two days later parliament approved a declaration that Scotland would undertake a war unless its demands were met; but by this time Argyll's supporters had been persuaded that outward expressions of concern for religion were not enough, and more than forty of them again followed him out of parliament when the declaration was voted on.[88] The kirk also reacted sharply, writing to all presbyteries accusing parliament of deciding religious matters without consent of the kirk; it also again stressed the inconsistency of the Engagers; they complained of breaches of the covenant in England but it was also being broken in Scotland, and true zeal should 'strike equally on both hands, beginning to reforme at home'. Some latitude might be allowed to sectaries in England since some was being allowed to malignants in Scotland. The commission of the kirk was 'not convinced of any just grounds of war'.[89]

On the very day that this paper was issued the first act of war took place, the seizure of Berwick. Hundreds of English royalists and disbanded parliamentarian soldiers had made their way to Scotland, seeking to join the Engagers, and demands by the English commissioners in Edinburgh that they be deported had been ignored.[90] It was presumably the committee for dangers which decided to assemble these English soldiers and use them to occupy Berwick and Carlisle; in this way the towns could be secured while denying that Scotland was responsible. Sir Marmaduke Langdale occupied Berwick on 28 April; Sir Philip Musgrave entered Carlisle the following day.[91]

THE LEVYING OF THE ARMY OF THE ENGAGEMENT

On 4 May, over four months after the Engagement had been signed, the Scots parliament at last gave orders for the levying of a new army, 27,750 foot and 2,760 horsemen, who were to rendezvous in their shires by the end of May. David Leslie's army was to be absorbed into the new one, and approaches to the Scottish army in Ireland gave hopes that it would send men to join in invading England.[92] General officers were appointed a week later; Leven, no friend of the Engagement, was persuaded to resign the post of general and was replaced by Hamilton—to the disgust of Callander, who had to be content with being second in command as lieutenant general. David Leslie and John Holborne were offered the posts of lieutenant general of the horse and major general of the foot respectively in the hope of persuading them to support the Engagement, but they refused to serve, so Middleton and William Baillie (unemployed since Kilsyth) were promoted to lieutenants general of the horse and the foot.[93]

The kirk hastened to denounce the levies: 'we cannot in our conscience allow either ministers . . . or any others whatsoever, to concurre and co-operate in the Engagement', for pretence of religious zeal hid malignant designs.[94] To counter this, parliament wrote to presbyteries placing blame for opposition to the Engagement on favourers of sectaries and haters of monarchical government. The kirk was encroaching on the rights of the estates: 'what can be more civill then to determine what civill dewties wee ought to pay our king or what civill power he ought to be possessed of'. It was to be hoped that the kirk 'will never be guiltie nor fall into the Episcopall disease of medling with civill effaires'.[95]

It was now being found (as so often in the past) that theories of the relations of church and state based on the idea of two swords or kingdoms, temporal and spiritual, each exercising jurisdiction in its own sphere and supreme in it, ultimately broke down through the impossibility of fixing an exact demarcation between the two spheres acceptable to both. Almost any question had some civil and some religious aspects. As each sword claimed supremacy in its own sphere, each inevitably felt that it had the authority to decide what fell within it. The kirk claimed that the distinction between the jurisdictions was clear, but though it proved this in theory to its own satisfaction, in practice its definitions were ambiguous and unhelpful. Thus Alexander Henderson had stated that there was nothing so ecclesiastical that it did not in some way belong to the jurisdiction of the magistrate, and nothing so secular that it did not concern the kirk. Yet he dismissed the suggestion that this could lead to confusion and rivalry between church and state as false and malicious; the church was solely concerned with the spiritual aspects of all things, the state with secular aspects.[96] Similarly George Gillespie asserted that to both powers 'is in some way intrusted the keeping of both tables of the Law', but went on to claim 'yet by marvellous vast differences are they distinguished the one from the other'; the magistrate is concerned with the outward things of the church, the ministry is concerned with the internal, spiritual part of civil government. Ministers should interpret the word of God to the magistrate and 'show the magistrate his duty, to wit, how he ought to govern the commonwealth, and in what manner he ought to use the sword'. Though the kirk had no powers of compulsion, it was lawful for subjects to resist tyranny or abuse of power by magistrates. Here in fact Gillespie was upholding the supremacy of the ecclesiastical sword over the civil; his position was virtually that of Andrew Melville.[97]

Thus the spokesmen of the kirk gave no clear answer to the problem of deciding between the rival claims of church and state, denying that such a problem existed except through malice, but in effect they assumed the supremacy of the kirk by taking it for granted that it should define the jurisdictions. Moreover, it was the kirk's duty to testify to the truth, showing magistrates how to act, and subjects had the right to resist abuse of power by magistrates. Combining these ideas the kirk was claiming the right to preach rebellion whenever civil magistrates ignored its advice.

The levying of the army provided the first opportunity for gauging the relative strengths of Hamilton's Engagers, and their opponents supporting Argyll and the kirk, in the country as a whole. Parliament adjourned on 11 May until 1 June to allow members to help in levying men, a committee of estates being left in Edinburgh to co-ordinate its work; all its members were probably Engagers except for Argyll and Wariston, neither of whom took their seats.[98] The commission of the kirk proved to have the support of the majority of local church courts; most synods and many presbyteries petitioned against the Engagement. But lay opinion was more evenly divided; some committees of war, including those of Fife and most of the western shires, petitioned against the treaty but others supported it—as did a petition of Fife lairds who opposed their committee of war.[99] Argyll did what he could to hinder levies, and it was rumoured that he was in contact with leaders of the Independents and sent Major Archibald Strachan to Cromwell to desire him to send part of his army to Scotland to join in suppressing the Engagers.[100] This was probably untrue (though Strachan evidently did go to England and join Cromwell's army) but Argyll may well have suggested that part of the English army should quarter just south of the border to terrify the Engagers and encourage their opponents. An Englishman in Edinburgh made just such a suggestion; if 5,000 or more men were sent to the Borders 'the honest partie here will take such a course as shall put you out of great opposition or danger heare, and this is noe dreame—make use of it'. If it was not done the Engagers would soon invade England.[101]

Opposition to the levies were strongest in Fife and the west, especially Galloway and Ayrshire; orders had to be issued forbidding men to leave the country since many were crossing to Ireland to avoid being levied. Late in May Argyll met Eglinton, Cassillis and some local ministers in Irvine, and there is little doubt that if they had decided on rebellion they could have raised large forces in the west; the seething discontent only needed leadership. But they decided that the time was not yet ripe, and opposition was therefore mostly confined to obstructing the levies as much as possible without openly defying parliament. There were a few exceptions. Edinburgh women assaulted the provost and shouted abuse at Hamilton, and Holburne's regiment mutinied after Holburne, his lieutenant colonel and all the captains resigned rather than support the Engagement.[102] The regiment was soon reduced to obedience, however, and was sent to help to subdue Glasgow, where the magistrates refused to obey parliament and raise levies. James Turner, who commanded the forces in Glasgow, soon found that quartering eight or nine soldiers in a house for a few nights was 'ane argument strong enough . . . to make the hardest headed Covenanter in the toune to forsake the kirk', and the burgh's council and magistrates were deposed.[103]

In the face of widespread passive resistance levying proved a slow and difficult process. Only a few thousand men can have been ready in arms by the time appointed, the end of May, and though the officers of the Scottish army in Ireland agreed to contribute 2,100 men (together with forces raised by protestant settlers in Ulster) they insisted on pay and supplies before the men were sent.[104] When parliament reassembled on 1 June the gathering of local levies into an army began. Since the Engagers had no need to fear royalist risings in the north most of the garrisons there were withdrawn. All forces were to march towards the Borders 'and such vther places in the kingdome as will not obey the orders of parliament'; as these areas were mainly in the south-west it was here that the Engagers began to assemble. It had probably already been decided to invade by way of Carlisle as royalism was strong in the north-west of England. Ministers who stirred up opposition to levying were to be arrested, and all Scots were to take an oath to defend parliament and obey its acts—in effect an oath to support the Engagement.[105] In the event it was not enforced.

The Engagers now showed how little they really cared for the breaches of the covenant and treaties which, they had claimed, were the grounds for war with England, by failing even to consider the English reply to their demands. On 6 May the English parliament had gone a long way to meet the demands, promising not to alter the fundamental government of the kingdom, to preserve the covenant and treaties inviolably, and to offer to the king jointly with the Scots the terms previously offered to him at Hampton Court in September 1647 (in essence the propositions of Newcastle).[106] Yet on 7 June the Scots parliament refused even to consider these concessions, on the technicality that they were not worded in the form of an answer to their demands. It was apparently this which led Loudoun to break finally with the Engagers; when parliament adjourned on 11 June he did what Argyll, Wariston and others had done a month before—retired to his home and refused to take any action which might imply support for the Engagement.[107]

A new committee of estates was appointed to prosecute the war once parliament rose; most of its members were of course Engagers but their leading opponents were also included, though they refused to take their seats.[108] They also continued their refusal to rebel against the regime; Argyll's conduct in this time of crisis, his withdrawing from Edinburgh to wait on events, may be paralleled by his actions at other critical points in his career—his refusal at first to support the covenanters, his failure to sign the covenant for some time after joining them, his sojourn in Ulster in 1646 while secret negotiations were taking place with the king in England. The comparison with Oliver Cromwell's well known tendency to wait on providence, to wait until events made God's will clear to him, is striking.

Other anti-Engagers were not so patient; it was possible for nobles and lairds to bide their time, for the Engagers were content to leave them alone to avoid driving them to resistance, but lesser men were liable to be forcibly enlisted to fight in a cause they believed to be evil. The meeting in May in Irvine which Argyll had attended and other such consultations led to rumours that a rising was being planned, and when local ministers arranged for communion to be celebrated at Mauchline kirk on 11 June large numbers of armed men assembled in the parish; how far this was spontaneous, how far incited by the ministers is not clear. But though armed and mostly mounted, the men were leaderless; local nobles and lairds met near Kilmarnock on 10 June but decided against a rising. When Middleton and some Engager troops of horse arrived on 12 June to investigate the situation they found about 2,000 men drawn up on Mauchline Moor to oppose them, accompanied by several ministers, who advised them to scatter. But before they could do so a confused skirmish was fought in which several of the 'slashing communicants' were killed and many captured. Wisely, moderation was shown; most prisoners were released on promising obedience to parliament. A few officers were sentenced to death but promptly pardoned. At least four ministers were taken to Edinburgh for trial but in the end they were allowed to return to their homes.[109]

By their firm but not vindictive action at Mauchline the Engagers suppressed a potentially dangerous rising before it really got started. But the west remained 'very readie for new commotions'; many of the Clydesdale horsemen who had fled from Mauchline were said to have made their way to Galloway. Over a large area levying was at a standstill. Proclamations were needed to order inhabitants of Glasgow who had fled to return and to forbid flight to Ireland. Most of the ministers of the presbytery of Lanark fled to avoid being forced to acquiesce in the levying. The committee of estates recommended Hamilton to establish garrisons in the west to restore order, but this was not done; it might have provoked civil war, and it would have tied down men urgently needed for the invasion of England.[110] Even in the north-east where support for the Engagement might have been expected to be strong the levies met with opposition; the area had not yet recovered from the fighting of 1644–7 and had no enthusiasm for a new war. Many royalists distrusted Hamilton, while others who were willing to fight had taken part in royalist risings and their services were therefore refused in an effort to demonstrate to the kirk that the Engagers were not associating with malignants; for similar reasons the Engagers did not release Huntly from imprisonment. Twenty-four Mackenzies and other followers of the earl of Seaforth claimed that, though they were anxious to fight, the clansmen would only serve under Seaforth; but in spite of this the Engagers would not accept the latter's services for fear of alienating moderate covenanters.[111] There was also trouble about getting help from the army in Ireland since two regiments opposed the Engagement, and the others only co-operated after being sent large sums of money and being promised that the men sent back to Scotland would be commanded by George Monro (Robert Monro's nephew and son in law) with the rank of major general.[112]

The delays in raising men led to arguments among the Engager leaders. Lanark insisted that all resistance to levying must be suppressed before an invasion of England began; this would also give time for arms and ammunition being sent from Holland to arrive. But Lauderdale held that it was necessary to enter England as soon as possible; the longer they delayed the less the support they would find there, for many English royalists had proved too impatient to await the coming of the Scots, and a series of uncoordinated local risings had easily been crushed. Unless the Scots acted quickly the remaining royalists would also be defeated. Hamilton was convinced by these latter arguments and decided on immediate invasion, ordering a rendezvous at Annan on 4 July.[113] A declaration justifying the invasion was issued and George Halyburton was dispatched to England with copies of it and letters to the king and parliament. The most important part of his mission was kept secret; he carried letters to English royalist and presbyterian leaders asking for their support. But he was searched on his journey and the letters discovered; he was therefore allowed to deliver his messages to king and parliament but prevented from communicating with anyone else.[114]

THE INVASION OF ENGLAND

The committee of estates divided itself on 3 July, part going to join the army at Annan.[115] It had been hoped that levies, Leslie's army and men from Ireland would provide at least 40,000 men, but less than half that number, perhaps little more than a quarter, appeared. Most of those who did assemble were completely untrained, ammunition was short and there was no artillery, as the general of the artillery, Sir Alexander Hamilton 'being groune old and doated, had given no fitting orders for these things'. None of the men from Ireland had yet landed.

However, Hamilton decided against further delay and crossed the border on 8 July to help Sir Marmaduke Langdale and English royalists who were in danger of being defeated by Major General Lambert's parliamentarian forces. Once he had entered England however, Hamilton proved to be in no hurry, since he still hoped for reinforcements and supplies from Scotland; he stayed near Crofton Hall for nearly a week before advancing to near Penrith, where he settled for another three weeks.[116]

The efforts of the committee of estates in Edinburgh to hasten reinforcements after the army had little success, for in the absence of the army there was no force available to enforce levying. In mid July Sir William Fleming arrived with badly needed arms and ammunition, which were sent after the army; less welcome were the demands that he brought concerning the terms on which the prince of Wales would come to Scotland. The prince and his mother demanded that he should be free to choose whom he wished to accompany him, that he should be free to go where he wished and consult whomever he chose. He was not to be pressed to take the covenant and was to have freedom of worship. Many of the Engagers were alarmed at these conditions; they did not dare to make them public for there would be strong opposition to allowing him to use Anglican worship, and some of the demands showed a distrust of the Scots which would be resented.[117] Lauderdale was especially upset, for unlike Hamilton and Lanark, whose professed zeal for religion was largely a matter of expediency, he had really believed that the Engagement served the best interests of the kirk. Yet now there seemed a danger that the Engagers would come to an agreement with the prince on terms which he believed would be damaging to religion. To prevent this he suggested that he himself should be sent to negotiate with Prince Charles. The Hamiltons agreed—partly, it was said, because they were tired of Lauderdale's scruples and were glad 'to have him out of the way, that they may rule all without any impediment, which is impossible (while he is present, at least) to bad ends'. Instructions were therefore given to Lauderdale on 31 July to find the prince and invite him to Scotland.[118]

The prince was cruising off the mouth of the Thames with ships of the English navy which had recently mutinied against parliament. Lauderdale soon persuaded him to come to Scotland, and to use the form of worship established there. This was the main concession he had hoped for, and one which the king had forbidden his son to make. But a new difficulty arose; the sailors whose mutiny had won the fleet for the prince wished him to remain with them; there was talk of throwing Lauderdale overboard if he tried to take him away. Rather than lose his fleet the prince decided to delay joining the Scots, so Lauderdale sadly left him and made his way to Holland to try to win support for the Engagers there.[119]

Meanwhile the general assembly had met in Edinburgh, on 12 July. Ominously for the Engagers it elected George Gillespie moderator. The committee of estates offered hopefully to explain the lawfulness of the Engagement, but the assembly ignored the suggestion and proceeded to denounce it as unlawful.[120] The committee retorted that this had not been proved and challenged the assembly to prove that 'the kirk hes interest in the undertakings and ingadgements in warr'.[121] This was again ignored, but the ministers nonetheless were faced by the harsh truth that, in spite of their protests, 'Our State hes now found, which scarcely could have been believed, that, contrare to the utmost endeavours of the Church, and all their friends, they can raise and maintain ane army, and doe what they will at home and abroad'.[122]

This triumph of the state was, however, precarious, and its continuance clearly depended on the success of Hamilton's army in England; and the work of reinforcing that army was making little progress. On 31 July order was given for an additional levy of 1,369 men to remain in Scotland under Lanark to guard against active resistance to the Engagement,[123] but this inevitably meant that fewer men were available to be sent to the army in England. At least the long delayed men from Ireland were now landing, but mismanagement rendered their presence pointless. Major General George Monro came to Hamilton (who had now reached Kendal) at the beginning of August to ask for orders concerning his men from Ireland, but a dispute over precedence at once arose. Monro claimed to be directly dependent on Hamilton, and therefore refused to take orders from the lieutenants general. The importance of the dispute was magnified by Hamilton's handling of it. Instead of deciding for or against Monro's claim he weakly evaded the issue by ordering Monro to return to his men and retain them in the Borders, ostensibly to guard an artillery train which it was hoped would soon be sent.[124] Thus Hamilton parted his squabbling generals at the cost of denying his army badly needed reinforcements.

After some argument among the remaining generals it was decided that the army should continue south through Lancashire rather than cross the Pennines into Yorkshire (which Lambert had expected).[125] The Engagers knew little or nothing of Cromwell's movements, and Hamilton allowed his army to straggle southwards in a long and disorganised column, much of it dispersed foraging, as if he had no reason to fear attack. On 16 August Callander, Middleton and most of the cavalry were near Wigan while Hamilton and most of the infantry were about twenty miles to the north, near Preston. On hearing a rumour of Cromwell's approach Callander returned to Preston to consult Hamilton.

Cromwell had meanwhile joined his forces with Lambert's and was advancing across the Pennines. On 17 August he fell on an English royalist force under Langdale a few miles to the east of Preston. Hamilton at once sent orders to Middleton to bring the cavalry back to him and ordered Baillie to support Langdale. But Callander then intervened, arguing that the Scots infantry would have no chance of withstanding Cromwell's cavalry and should therefore be withdrawn south of the River Ribble to await Middleton's arrival with the Scots horse. Hamilton allowed himself to be persuaded and the Scots infantry retreated across the river, leaving Langdale's royalists to their fate. Baillie proposed to make a stand just south of the river but Callander was again ready with disastrous advice and persuaded Hamilton to withdraw southwards under cover of darkness. The losses of the Scots were so far very slight, but the army was demoralised by its abandonment of Langdale, by its retreat without a fight, and by the fact that Cromwell now cut it off from Scotland. It fled south in pouring rain on 18 and 19 August, suffering heavy losses in a rearguard action at Winwick. On Callander's advice Baillie and the infantry surrendered at Warrington; many of the men had thrown away their arms or run out of ammunition. Cromwell left Lambert to continue pursuit of the Scots cavalry while he himself turned north to deal with George Monro; during 17–20 August he estimated that he had taken 10,000 prisoners. In the next few days Middleton and many of the Scots horsemen were captured, and many more deserted. At Uttoxeter Hamilton finally admitted defeat, signing terms of surrender with Lambert on 25 August; Callander made off on his own and escaped to Holland. Lambert then turned to rejoin Cromwell in trying to cut George Monro and English royalists who accompanied him off from Scotland.[126]

THE WHIGGAMORE RAID AND THE TREATY OF STIRLING

News of Hamilton's defeat led to open revolt in the west of Scotland against the Engagers; within a few days several thousand men from Ayrshire and Clydesdale were moving towards Edinburgh in what became known as the whiggamore raid. They were led by Loudoun, Eglinton, Leven and David Leslie, and Cassillis soon followed with men from Galloway. Whether they had led the revolt from the start, or simply put themselves at the head of a spontaneous rising, or one encouraged by lairds and ministers, is uncertain. The anti–Engagers later claimed that the rising had been planned and the date for it fixed before Hamilton's defeat in England, but this may have been simply an attempt to restore their credit by suggesting that they had not ingloriously awaited the defeat of the Engagers by English Independents before rising in arms to support the kirk.[127]

News of 'some stirring of the well affected people of the West' first reached Edinburgh on 28 August, and the committee of estates immediately sent orders to George Monro to gather his men from Ireland and any other remnants of Hamilton's army he could find (except for the garrisons of Berwick and Carlisle) and assemble them at Berwick. Forces raised under Lanark to keep the peace in Scotland were to rendezvous at Jedburgh. Thus the Engager regime gathered its forces on the eastern borders to defend itself.[128] The apprehensive committee sent Sir Adam Hepburn of Humbie and Sir William Lockhart of Lee to the forces from the west to represent to them the danger of civil war and express willingness to do all it could to satisfy their just desires; while negotiations took place they were asked to advance no further. Lanark had opposed this conciliatory move, wishing instead to seize Perth and Stirling and raise the Highlands and north for the king, but he was overruled.[129]

The westerners replied (on 3 September) that they were engaged in removing the dangers to kirk and kingdom and would act in accordance with the covenants, and continued their advance; this message was drafted by Sir John Cheisly, knighted by the king when the Engagement had been signed but now among its enemies.[130] On this the committee of estates abandoned Edinburgh and joined Lanark and Monro in the Borders rather than risk capture by the westerners, who entered the burgh a few days later. From Duns leading Engagers (Crawford-Lindsay, Lanark, Glencairn) wrote to the commission of the kirk asking it to help remove the differences between church and state and restore unity, but the kirk's reply was uncompromising; breaches between men of differing principles could not be patched up.[131] On 8 September the Engagers again sent Humbie and Lee to the westerners, with articles for a peace, but the terms asked were hopelessly optimistic, including demands that no Engager should be punished and that the committee of estates should meet freely. This would have allowed the regime to continue in power, and was rejected by the kirk as involving approbation of the Engagement. George Gillespie denounced compromise as 'a backsliding into that very sinne which was especially pointed at and punished by the prevalency of the Malignant party'; God had allowed them to prevail for a time to show the consequences of not excluding them from power and to punish the failure to exclude them. 'O that there were such a spirit at least in such of our Nobility as stand for the Trueth that they may take more of God's counsell, and leaue lesse to their owne reason and understanding'.[132]

In spite of the fears of the kirk negotiations were eventually arranged, but the position of the Engagers' forces was rapidly becoming untenable, for Cromwell was now approaching. They therefore took the westerners by surprise by marching their forces round Edinburgh and seizing Linlithgow from them.[133] Yet the westerners quickly agreed to arrangements for a new treaty, during which neither side was to move its forces, for they feared the Engagers might march to try to raise new forces in the north. By this time forces gathered by Argyll were approaching Stirling from the west, and though the westerners promised that they would not enter the burgh the Engagers feared that they would do so, and thus cut them off from the north; they therefore marched from Linlithgow on 12 September to forestall them; Argyll's men were surprised and scattered with heavy losses and Stirling was occupied.[134] Though angered at this further breach of the treaty the westerners again hastened to renew negotiations, for they believed that the only way of persuading Cromwell not to enter Scotland would be to show him that the Engagers had disbanded, and this could be more quickly achieved by a treaty than by force. Most Engagers also favoured negotiation; their cause was clearly lost and they wished to prevent a civil war embittered by English intervention, though Lanark and Monro wished to fight on. Talks soon began with the westerners' representatives—Cassillis, Wariston, Cheisly and Robert Barclay.[135]

The westerners also sent, on 15 September, Sir Andrew Ker and Major Archibald Strachan to Cromwell, to assure him that no treaty would be made with the Engagers unless they agreed to disband and relinquish power; Scotland would then be ruled by those who had opposed the Engagement. In any such treaty England's interests would be protected; Berwick and Carlisle would be surrendered as soon as possible. If the Engagers would not submit 'we are confident that the Houses of Parliament and their Armies will be ready to assist us with their forces, to pursue them as common Enemies to both Kingdoms'. The English were therefore desired to 'be in Readiness to concurr with us, when we shall give them a Call'. The westerners thus hoped that Cromwell would not enter Scotland unless they asked him to do so. He replied (18 September) that he was glad to hear that power was to be entrusted to those who 'we trust, are taught of God and seek His honour', but he claimed that the Berwick garrison was still receiving supplies from Scotland, and the Engagers were still in arms at Stirling with 'much of Scotland at their backs' in which to recruit a new army, while the westerners were not yet strong enough to force them to submit. He therefore thought it necessary to advance into Scotland with his army 'to the end we might be in a posture more ready to give you assistance'.[136]

When the westerners' leaders (now calling themselves the committee of estates) heard that Cromwell's men were already marching into Scotland they sent Argyll and others to beg him not to bring in his whole army but only 'such a partie as give least offense to this Kirk'; Argyll was also to order the Engagers in Berwick and Carlisle to surrender and was to ask (at the request of the kirk) that presbyterian ministers accompany Cromwell's men, the preaching of 'strange opinions' among them being forbidden.[137] He first met Cromwell on 21 September, but he failed to get agreement that only part of the English army should cross the border—virtually all of it was over already—and the Berwick garrison refused to surrender.[138] To provide evidence for Cromwell of their sincerity in wishing to exclude the Engagers from power the westerners' committee of estates passed an act on 22 September declaring that, to prevent imminent dangers and so that affairs would not be managed by those whom England esteemed enemies, the committee would in future consist only of those members appointed by parliament in June who had opposed the Engagement. The fact that Hamilton had had Argyll and other opponents elected members in the hope of conciliating them now enabled them to give their seizure of power a cloak of legality. In future all elected to be burgh councillors or magistrates, and all commissioners to parliament, were to be enemies of the Engagement.[139]

Now that Cromwell's army was camped in Scotland the need to persuade the Engagers to disband was more urgent than ever; Argyll wrote desiring the committee to 'speidily put ane end to your treatties with those at Stirling', since the burden of supporting the English army was fast ruining the country.[140] The picture often painted of Argyll encouraging the English to enter Scotland to support his seizure of power[141] is thus false. He and his supporters were confident of their ability to suppress the Engagers without outside help and would have preferred Cromwell to have remained south of the border—though they would certainly have accepted his help if the Engagers had rallied and looked like regaining power. The Independent English might be marginally less offensive to Argyll and the ministers than the malignant Engagers but they had no wish for them as allies, and once the English entered Scotland they worked to get them removed as soon as possible.

The Engagers had now been negotiating for more than ten days, spinning out the treaty to give them time to recruit men in the north.

Many royalists whose aid the Engagers had previously rejected were gathering to oppose the English, and it was said that many clan chiefs and others had combined and 'entred into a Confederacy, to invade fall upon and destroy the Lord Marques of Argyles lands'.[142] The Edinburgh committee of estates therefore declared on 25 September that unless the Engagers accepted the terms offered promptly force would be used against them.[143] Under this threat they gave way and signed a treaty two days later. Considering the bitterness of feeling against them the terms were fairly generous, reflecting the wish of their opponents to get them disbanded quickly so as to be rid of Cromwell's army. All forces, including those of the anti-Engagers, were to disband by 10 October. No Engager who accepted the treaty would be injured in life, estate, title or freedom, though all who held public offices were to forbear to exercise them until parliament met in January 1649 to settle all civil matters, while the kirk dealt with religious ones.[144]

So ended the disastrous nine month history of the Engagement, an attempt to re-establish the king's power in England with the help of the covenanters by falsely persuading them that the Engagement was equally concerned with the king and the covenant. At least this is what the Engagement had meant to the Hamiltons and to those covenanters who had seen through their pretences and opposed them. For the Hamiltons the demands for religious reform in England were a matter of expediency, though they differed from the king in that Charles would probably have insisted on disowning the covenant and restoring episcopacy (in England at least) as soon as possible, whereas the Hamiltons were prepared to keep up the pretence of acting for the covenant semi-permanently to retain the support of covenanters. Loudoun and Lauderdale on the other hand had genuinely believed when they signed the Engagement that, though it involved making concessions to the king, it served the best interests of both king and covenant; so did the many moderate covenanters who joined them in defying the ministers and supporting the Engagement. They had decided that they must trust the king, as the only alternative appeared to be to abandon him entirely to the English parliament and army. The trust was misplaced. Charles remained as firmly convinced as ever that the covenants were incompatible with monarchical authority, and that episcopacy was the only form of church government pleasing to God. Once re-established in England he would have taken the first opportunity to use the kingdom's resources to regain his authority in Scotland. The argument that presbyterianism in Scotland could never be secure unless the king was deprived of power to use English resources to attack it still held good. By the time of the Engagers' defeat at Preston the covenanters among them were beginning to recognise this; the king and the Hamiltons could not be trusted. Loudoun had already deserted the Engagers and Lauderdale was wavering as the reiterated argument of the ministers that the Engagers were compromising religion became increasingly plausible. Hamilton's hasty invasion of England with a completely inadequate army had no hope of success unless it provoked large scale royalist risings there. Once these failed to take place he must have known that he was lost; his incompetent generalship only hastened the inevitable. Yet he could not have delayed his entry into England without running the danger of seeing his movement in Scotland collapse as covenanters deserted it.

The failure of the Engagement marked the final failure of the policy Hamilton had pursued since 1641 (interrupted by his imprisonment in 1644–6). Persuaded by the Bishops' Wars that the covenanters could not be overthrown by force he had worked to gain Scots help for the king in his quarrel with the English parliament by persuading the covenanters that their best interests lay in aiding him. The solemn league and covenant and the subsequent invasion of England, the abandonment of the king in England, and the failure of the Engagement marked three successive defeats for his efforts to persuade the covenanters that the king was trustworthy.

Nonetheless, the shortcomings of Hamilton and the ultimate failure of the party which he built up in 1647–8 should not be allowed to disguise the significance of the events of these years. Scotland had seen what has been called 'a limited but dramatic counter-revolution'.[145] Moderates, covenanters and royalists, had won control of the government for the first time since the covenanters had seized power in 1638–9. This had owed less to Hamilton's leadership than to circumstances—growing sympathy with the king, disillusionment with the English parliament and army, and conservative reaction to years of disorder and uncertainty. The counter-revolution had been achieved constitutionally, by votes in the committee of estates and parliament; for the moment it had failed but it was notable that, for all the divisions among its supporters and the hostility of many to it, the fact was that it had only been destroyed within Scotland after it had met with military disaster in England.

These facts were ones of which the new 'kirk party' regime must have been painfully aware, though its supporters could console themselves by arguing that the temporary success of counter-revolution had only been made possible by false pretences, by its leaders disguising its nature. The pretence could not have been kept up indefinitely, and once the real intentions of its leaders were revealed the counter-revolution was doomed.

It has sometimes been said that the acceptance of the Engagement by many moderate covenanters represented a recognition by them that their aspiration to impose presbyterian church government on England was unreasonable and indeed unachievable; 'the Scots acknowledged (though as yet very grudgingly) that the people of England might have some say in the choice of a constitution for their own church'.[146] But the covenanters had never denied this. Certainly they had demanded the introduction of presbyterian church government in England, but they had never insisted that it be an exact copy of the kirk's government. So long as it was similar in essentials they were quite prepared for the English parliament and the Westminster Assembly to decide its exact form. Moreover, though the Westminster Assembly was strongly influenced by the Scots it is nonetheless remarkable that the kirk adopted for its own use the Westminster standards (directory of worship, catechisms and confession of faith) drawn up by an English assembly. The kirk showed more flexibility and willingness to compromise for the sake of unity with England than it is usually credited with.

Nor, on the other hand, did covenanters who accepted the Engagement abandon hope of permanently establishing presbyterian government in England. The Engagement is often read as if it stated that presbyterian government was to be established for three years, and then replaced by a different system. In fact there was nothing to prevent the system adopted in the final settlement from being presbyterian, and this is what the covenanting Engagers hoped for; did not the treaty specifically state that the system finally adopted would be that 'most agreeable to the word of God', a phrase that to all covenanters could only mean presbyterian government? In accepting the Engagement covenanters conceded that they would help the king before he promised the permanent establishment of presbyterianism in England, but this did not lessen their determination to exact such a promise from him eventually. They accepted an alliance with him even though his religious concessions did not go so far as they wished partly because they thought he was being unjustly treated by the English, partly because they hoped he would later make further concessions, and partly because they now saw the Independents as a more formidable enemy to presbyterianism than the king. Indeed it may be said that by the Engagement the Scots, far from resolving to reduce their interference in English affairs, actually pledged themselves to increase it, for they undertook to impose a king, a political settlement and a closer union as well as a form of church government.

The fact that Hamilton and Lanark had to pretend to be working for king and covenant jointly in order to win the support of moderate covenanters inevitably meant that they could not seek or accept the help of the royalist malignants who were their most natural allies, and even raised the suspicions of some royalists that they were betraying the king, while their efforts to conciliate such royalists led covenanters like Loudoun to distrust them. As with all Hamilton's schemes suspicion as to his sincerity proved a major handicap. Ministers might be appalled that he could win enough support to invade England in spite of their opposition, but even without defeat in England his triumph would probably have been short lived, being based on intricate political juggling. It took the conduct of the extremists of the kirk party in their two years of power after Preston to persuade the majority of the three estates in Scotland to abandon the covenants, or at least only to express support for them as a matter of expediency, as Hamilton himself had done.

CHAPTER FOUR

The Rule of the Kirk Party, September 1648–September 1650

THE CONSOLIDATION OF THE REGIME AND THE EXECUTION OF THE KING

Though the Engagers had agreed to disband their forces the position of the new kirk party regime in Scotland remained precarious. Only a small proportion of the nobility supported it and it was uncertain whether or not the royalists of the north (who had begun raising men for the Engagers) would accept the treaty. Moreover, by the treaty the committee of estates had agreed to disband its own forces; new forces could then be raised but there would be an interval in which the regime would have to rely on Cromwell's army for protection. But such dependence was almost as bitter to many as the former subjection to the Engagers, and no regime which relied on an English army to keep it in power could hope for much popularity.

Disbanding of forces was carried out according to the treaty, except that the committee evidently retained a few hundred men in arms, and that George Monro tried to lead some of his men back to Ireland; but he soon learned that troops of the English parliament had dispersed the remnants of the Scots army in Ireland, and he therefore disbanded and fled to Holland. Monro, along with Lanark and Crawford–Lindsay, refused to declare acceptance of the treaty to the committee, but the other leading Engagers did so.[1] On 4 October the committee renewed its act of 22 September excluding all Engagers from exercising any office or taking part in elections before parliament met.[2] On the same day Cromwell arrived in Edinburgh to ensure that the settlement made would be acceptable to England. His emotional protestations of good intentions and hopes that they would join in the work of the Lord impressed some of the leaders of the kirk party, but Robert Blair warned them not to be fooled; Cromwell was 'an egregious dissembler, and a great liar. Away with him, he is a greating [weeping] devil'.[3]

Cromwell indicated that he was not satisfied that enough had been done to prevent Scots malignants regaining power and again threatening

England; 'I hold myself obliged, in prosecution of my duty and instructions, to demand . . . that you will not admit or suffer any that have been active in, or consenting to, the said Engagement against England, or have lately been in arms at Stirling or elsewhere in the maintenance of that Engagement, to be employed in any public place or trust whatsoever'. In reply the committee of estates swore that it would do its utmost to exclude Engagers from public places, adding that it hoped that the English parliament would be willing to help in this work if necessary. On this Cromwell declared himself to be content; both he and Lambert seem to have been impressed by the conduct of Argyll and the kirk party, and to have hoped for a lasting alliance with them.[4]

That the new regime in Scotland recognised that it was at least temporarily dependent on English support was shown by the fact that when Cromwell left Edinburgh on 7 October and marched back into England he left behind him Lambert with two regiments of horse and two companies of dragoons at the request of the committee of estates. Lambert remained for about a month; on 7 November the committee thanked the English parliament for his assistance but stated that it was no longer required. The English soldiers must have been glad to leave for they had met with general hostility, being abused in the streets of Edinburgh and robbed of their horses and arms in the country. The committee apologised, offering compensation, but it must have been thankful to see the last of its unpopular allies.[5]

Did Cromwell, in his private talks with Argyll, reveal plans to try and to execute the king? After the execution royalists were quick to suggest as much, and that Argyll had consented to such action.[6] It is very hard to believe that this was so; even if (which is unlikely) Argyll himself favoured execution he must have known that it would rouse bitter hostility in Scotland and increase the political difficulties of the kirk party. It may well be, however, that Cromwell got Argyll to admit in general terms that kings might be tried for their crimes; this would be in accordance with the kirk party's opposing the king's execution but refusing to deny that kings could be tried and avoiding calling his death murder.

It is hard to avoid the conclusion that Cromwell was very easily satisfied by the assurances of the kirk party. He insisted that Engagers be excluded from power but he withdrew from Scotland without exacting any guarantee that the new regime would not prove as hostile to a settlement in England dominated by the new model army as the old Engaging regime had been. Argyll and others may have given private promises of good will but they can have left him in little doubt that they still maintained their demands for religious reform on presbyterian lines in England. Perhaps in the first flush of victory over the Engagers Cromwell overlooked the fact that his and the kirk party's ideas of the work of the Lord were incompatible; on a more practical level he probably over-estimated the extent to which the kirk party would be dependent on English help to keep itself in power.

Once the forces of the Engagers had disbanded the committee of estates got down to work restoring order and strengthening its hold on the country. On 7 October it reinforced itself by appointing eighty new members, only eight of whom were nobles. A week later a new levy of 2,730 foot and 620 horse was ordered, to join 700 men already in arms who presumably had not been disbanded according to the treaty. It was ruled (at the desire of the kirk) that those levied were to be carefully chosen, men loyal to the kirk and the good life, as testified by their ministers. New shire committees of war were appointed to supervise the levying.[7] Not all were satisfied, however, that the levies would provide adequate defence against malignants. On 17 October the gentlemen of Argyllshire commissioned Argyll and others to attend a meeting of the western shires on 22 November to form an association 'for the good of religioune, king and kingdome'. This was the first meeting of the Western Association, modelled on the military associations of the English parliament and intended to co-ordinate the military action of the strongly covenanting west. Failure to act together had prevented effective opposition to the Engagers; now if a new malignant regime were to establish itself in Edinburgh the west would be united in opposing it. Where the initiative for founding the association came from is obscure; it may well have been from the nobles who had led the whiggamore raid, but Argyll is the only one of them whose name can be connected with it with certainty. In December the committee of estates agreed to supply the association with arms and ammunition, but it disappears from view in 1649 as there was no need for its services; only in 1650 did it become a major force in Scottish politics.[8]

The defeated and demoralised Engagers proved no immediate danger. Parliament was summoned to meet on 4 January 1649 and preparation of cases against Engagers who held public offices began.[9] There is no evidence that Engagers tried to take part in shire elections of commissioners to parliament, and though there was trouble in several burghs—Glasgow, Lauder, Aberdeen, Dumfries and Banff—over the election of magistrates there was no direct defiance of the regime and the disputes were all settled to the satisfaction of the kirk party.[10]

The work of making contact on behalf of the new regime with the English parliament, the king and the prince of Wales (now back in

Holland) was begun by the kirk. On 11 October it commissioned Sir John Cheisly and Robert Blair to go to London with instructions similar to those issued on many previous occasions—to work for uniformity of religion according to the covenant. If possible they were to urge on the king the propositions of Newcastle and the covenant. The prince was to be told of Scotland's unshakable loyalty to his father in spite of his deplorable support for the Engagement.[11]

The state also employed Cheisly to approach the English parliament, and he was urged to emphasise the part the westerners had played in overthrowing the Engagers, and that they had resolved on a rising before they heard of Hamilton's defeat in England. By this time the English parliament had reopened negotiations with the king, and Cheisly was to see that Scotland's interests were protected in them. To indicate the kirk party's continued opposition to those who had invaded England Cheisly was to ask that the Engaging nobles, officers and gentlemen of Hamilton's army who had been captured should remain prisoners in England to prevent them raising new troubles in Scotland. To disarm English fears of Scots plots letters from the committee of estates to the king and the prince were to be shown to parliament prior to being delivered. Before he had known that the Engagers had been defeated the king had requested that Sir James Carmichael (the treasurer depute) be sent to him to discuss the situation in Scotland. As Sir James had been an Engager he was unacceptable to the kirk party, so his son Sir Daniel was sent to the Isle of Wight instead to press the propositions of Newcastle on Charles, and James Carmichael (probably another son of Sir James) was sent to Holland to the prince; there were disturbing rumours that Engagers who had fled there were trying to organise an invasion of Scotland, and the prince was warned not to be seduced by evil counsel.[12]

None of the missions, to king, prince, and English parliament, had any success. Neither king nor prince was ready to make concessions to the Scots, and parliament refused them any part in negotiations with the king or in the settlement in England. Attitudes to the Scots had changed in response to the Engagement. Reaction to Scots activities had been partly responsible for the emergence of the Independent party in parliament in 1644–5; in 1648 reactions to the Scots had helped to bring about the collapse of that party. The old 'war party' and 'middle group' alliance which had created the Independent party had broken down once it became clear that the Engagers intended to invade England. Exasperation with the king and his plots with the Scots led the radicals of the Independent party to determine that Charles should be brought to justice and that the Scots should be resisted. But the more moderate 'Independents' of the old middle group had reacted differently. Fearing that defeat of the Scots and the trial of the king would open the way to more radical changes in church, state and society than they wished, they had urged that war should be averted through new negotiations with the king which would separate him from his Scottish allies. To achieve this the middle group had swung back to alliance with the presbyterian party. But the middle group and the presbyterian party had failed to forestall Hamilton's invasion, and the war made the split between them and the radicals wider than ever. The latter, with the army's support, held the king responsible for the new war; a settlement was impossible until he had been brought to justice. The middle group on the other hand asserted that failure to reach agreement with the king had caused the war, and that the war therefore emphasised the need to negotiate a settlement with him to restore peace and stability. Presbyterians and middle group therefore demanded punishment of royalists and that no concessions be made to the Scots, but still wished to treat with the king.

They got their way, defying the radicals and the army, and opened negotiations with Charles.[13] In this they had the support of the kirk party, for though they refused the Scots a part in the treaty at least they favoured a moderate settlement and presbyterian church government (though of an erastian sort) in England.

The radicals and the army, however, refused to accept the policy now being pursued by the English parliament. At the beginning of December army officers carried the king off from Carisbrooke and the army occupied London. The Commons defiantly declared Charles' answers to their demands to be grounds for a settlement, whereupon by 'Pride's purge' the army excluded from the house those members most in favour of a settlement.[14] The kirk party indignantly denounced the purge, but ironically their own purge, their exclusion of Engagers from power, may have had something to do with convincing their opponents in England of the practability of purging the Commons. A month before, Cromwell had written of how in Scotland 'a lesser party of a parliament hath made it lawful to declare the greater part a faction, and made a parliament null, and call a new one, and to do this by force . . . Think of the example and consequences'.[15]

Even before Pride's purge Cheisly and Blair had written to the kirk of the shortcomings of the peace the English parliament seemed likely to conclude with the king; there was nothing in it to protect Scots interests and the covenant was 'vtterly slighted'.[16] The committee of estates sent Lothian and William Glendoning to join Cheisly in trying to protect Scots interests; if Charles would accept those of the propositions of Newcastle that concerned religion they were to urge parliament to restore him to his royal dignity and office.[17] Pride's purge rendered these instructions obsolete; there was no question of treating with the king, for preparations were being made for his trial. The Scots commissioners found themselves faced with a dilemma. If they failed to protest at the purge and the trial they would be held to condone them; but the only body they could protest to was parliament, and if they did that they would seem to acknowledge its legitimacy in its purged condition. This would be a breach of the covenant as it included an undertaking to uphold the rights of parliament.[18]

The commissioners overcame their scruples sufficiently to write to the Commons condemning the purge and warning that trial of the king 'cannot but continue and encrease the great distractions of these Kingdoms', but the letter was laid aside unread. On 9 January the Scottish parliament sent new instructions to its commissioners defining the attitude they should adopt towards the king's trial. They were not in any way to justify his proceedings, and were to declare that the Scots were not satisfied with the concessions he had made. Nothing was to be done that might lead to a breach between the kingdoms, and any intention of meddling in anything which concerned England alone was to be disclaimed. But they were to insist that Scotland had an interest in the king and were to ask that the trial be delayed for this and 'any other saiff reasons which shall there come to your thought . . . Bot without offering in any reasons that princcs are exempt from all tryell of justice'. They were to dissent from any sentence against the king's life, and protest if anything was done to alter the fundamental government of England. Later they were authorised to negotiate with General Fairfax and Cromwell for the safety of the king. Meanwhile, to still rumours that the Scots had some secret understanding with Cromwell, all members of the Scottish parliament took an oath that they had had no knowledge of or part in purging the Commons or the trial of the king.[19]

In accordance with their instructions the Scots commissioners made further protests to the Commons, asserting that both kingdoms had 'an unquestionable and undeniable interest in his person as King of both', but these were ignored, as were approaches to Fairfax and Cromwell. Charles I was beheaded on 30 January.[20] The Scots had done all they could to save him, but the impact of their protests had been weakened by their avoidance of justifying Charles' conduct and by their tacit admission that kings could be tried. No condemnation from Scotland, however, no matter how outspoken, would have had any effect, for the English regime was determined not to allow the Scots to influence it, and was confident that the kirk party's position in Scotland was so weak that it could not afford to quarrel with England. This proved to be a miscalculation.

THE PROCLAIMING OF CHARLES II AND THE PURGING OF THE ENGAGERS

During the session of the Scottish parliament which sat from January to March 1649 only sixteen nobles took their seats, whereas in the session which had approved the Engagement fifty-six had sat, a striking illustration of how weak support for the kirk party was among the nobility. The tone of the session was set at once by Wariston, who gave a 'long tedious speich' denouncing the leading Engagers. Argyll spoke at length on the same theme, dividing the Engagers into classes according to their guilt. Perhaps even more influential was the dying testimony of George Gillespie; failure to carry out a thorough purge of malignants would bring the wrath of God on the country.[21] These sentiments led to a new act of classes, modelled on the 1646 act directed against those who had supported Montrose. The first class of the new act comprised the general officers of Hamilton's army, all officers who had fought at Mauchline Moor or Stirling, those who had helped bring forces from Ireland, leading promoters of the Engagement, and all who had been active in Montrose's rebellion, even if they had taken no part in the Engagement. All such persons were barred for life from holding offices or taking any part in public affairs. Lesser offenders fell into classes two (barred from office for at least ten years) and three (barred for five years, or less if parliament agreed). A fourth class (barred for one year) consisted of office-holders guilty of moral rather than political offences.[22]

Much abuse has been heaped on this act as unreasonably severe; it has been called '*a reductio ad absurdum*' of the 1646 act.[23] This ignores the fact that the 1646 act fined delinquents and left them open to execution or imprisonment as well as excluding them from office. It is true that the 1649 act made many Engagers irreconcilable to the kirk party regime, but it had to be passed to implement the promise made to Cromwell that those involved in the invasion of England would be removed from power. Even without this promise, however, the kirk party would have purged its enemies, to gain revenge and secure its own position; it was not moderation that kept it from fining, imprisoning or executing enemies but the fact that the Stirling treaty had guaranteed that Engagers would not be punished in persons or estates. As it was parliament partly evaded this by ruling that Engagers should be responsible for paying all the monthly maintenance for March to October 1648 which should have been paid by non-Engagers.[24]

Engagers who had not declared their acceptance of the treaty were summoned to find caution to keep the peace and to acknowledge the legality of the regime, for it was rightly feared that some to them still hoped to regain power with the help of the royalist and Engager exiles in Holland. Late in 1648 Lanark had sent James Mowbray to Prince Charles to inform him of his eagerness to serve him and to denounce Lauderdale's conduct of the earlier negotiations with him; to have insisted that Charles conform to presbyterianism in Scotland was unreasonable. In contrast he, Lanark, invited him to Scotland without imposing conditions, and would meet him with an army of ten or twelve thousand men.[25] Messengers from Argyll (Mungo and William Murray) made rival bids for the prince's favour, promising that if he came to Scotland the kirk party would raise an army to restore his father's rights in England.[26] The prince wisely took little notice of either message; Lanark was in no position to help him and Argyll was clearly trying to lure him to Scotland in the hope that once there he would prove more pliable than his father. Instead he decided to send Lauderdale to Scotland to report on the situation there. On the pretence that he was only coming to settle his private affairs, Lauderdale managed to obtain a pass from the kirk party. As he had long been disillusioned with the Engagement and was on bad terms with most royalists, it was perhaps hoped that he could be persuaded to submit to the regime. Lauderdale himself would have liked to do this, and then work to bring about an agreement between it and the prince, but on his arrival in January 1649 he found that the act of classes would exclude him from office for life, and that the kirk would demand a public confession of his fault in supporting the Engagement. Even Loudoun had had to repent publicly and Balmerino warned Lauderdale 'There will be a penitential speech expected of yourself'.[27] He refused to submit to this humiliation, and parliament therefore sent troops to arrest him and Lanark; it was rumoured that it had been decided to hand them over to the English. But even kirk party nobles like Balmerino and Cassillis opposed this, and the latter sent a warning to Lauderdale that he was to be arrested. He and Lanark therefore fled to Holland,[28] thus relieving the regime of their embarrassing presence.

On news of the execution of Charles I the Scots parliament adjourned for two days, after which it had Charles II proclaimed king of Great Britain, France and Ireland since his father had been, as it was tactfully put, 'removed by a violent death'. But before being admitted to the exercise of his royal dignity the new king must give satisfaction concerning religion, union and the peace of Scotland, according to the covenants. For some even these limitations were not enough; Patrick Gillespie (brother of George) and James Guthrie, two of the most extreme ministers, 'were passionate against the proclaiming of the King, till his qualifications for government had first been tryed and allowed'.[29]

By proclaiming Charles II king of all his father's kingdom, not just of Scotland, the kirk party broke the informal alliance with the English parliament which had overthrown the Engagement. To have continued the alliance would have lost the kirk party much of its support in Scotland, for opinion was unanimously hostile to the execution of the king. But the end of the alliance nonetheless left the regime more isolated than before. It could no longer count on English help in defeating any rising of Scots malignants, and the king's death made such a rising more likely than before as many royalists held the kirk party partly responsible for it. Reaching agreement with the new king to forestall rebellion by his supporters and to help to unite the country in case of war with England thus became a matter of urgency.

Yet even in these dangerous circumstances the kirk remained determined to make no compromise in religion. Some members of parliament may have wished to show some flexibility, but they knew that they were dependent on the support of the ministers. The kirk wrote to the new king desiring him to agree to establish presbyterian government and the solemn league and covenant in all his kingdoms,[30] and parliament set out the terms on which the state would admit him to office. He must agree that all future kings would swear at their coronation to observe and preserve religion as then established in Scotland and to rule according to the word of God and the constitutions of the kingdom, and he must accept the covenants and the obligation to advance them in all his kingdoms. He was not to bring evil councillors to Scotland, and was to undertake to agree to anything else for the good of the kingdom. Clearly it was planned that he should be no more than a figurehead.[31]

It was intended that the commissioners already in London—Lothian, Cheisly and Glendoning—should proceed to Holland to lay these demands before the king, but the English parliament inadvertently thwarted this plan. It had followed up the execution of Charles I by abolishing both the monarchy and the house of lords. The commissioners protested at such alterations in the fundamental government of the country and demanded the acceptance of Charles II as king; they then prudently hastened to Gravesend, hoping to have sailed before the English could react to this denunciation.[32] But the Commons reacted more quickly than they had expected, rejecting the Scots paper as an impertinent meddling which assumed Scotland 'to have power over the Lawes and government of this Nation' and showed that the Scots still pursued the ends which had led the Engagers to invade England. The arrest of the commissioners was ordered, and they were seized on board ship at

Gravesend. The English at first hoped by their violent reaction to the paper to force the Scots regime to repudiate it, for fear of provoking English hostility. But the Scots parliament refused to be intimidated and demanded that its commissioners be freed, though it also stressed its wish for peace and union, disclaimed any intention of invading England like the Engagers, and denied that the paper which had caused this incident contained grounds for a new war; there were disturbing rumours that English forces were assembling for an attack on Scotland.[33]

The English eventually released the Scots commissioners, but meanwhile new ones had been chosen to go to Holland. It was intended that Balmerino should lead them, but he died suddenly and was replaced by Cassillis, who was to be accompanied by Alexander Brodie of that Ilk, George Winrame of Libberton and Alexander Jaffray. Cassillis, Libberton and three ministers, James Wood, Robert Blair and Robert Baillie, were appointed to represent the kirk.[34]

By this time the purging of office-holders who had supported the Engagement was well under way. Since the new king had not been admitted to office, parliament decided to fill vacant places itself, seeking royal consent later. Of the officers of state only Loudoun (chancellor) and Sir John Cheisly (master of requests) retained their offices. Lanark (secretary) and Glencairn (justice general) were replaced by Lothian and Cassillis respectively. The only three officers of state who had, by judicious trimming, managed to remain in office since before the beginning of the troubles in 1637 were all removed; Roxburgh (keeper of the privy seal) was replaced by Sutherland, Sir John Hamilton of Orbiston (justice clerk) by Hew Campbell of Cesnok, and Sir James Carmichael (treasurer depute) by his son Sir Daniel. Crawford-Lindsay was deposed as treasurer and the treasury put into commission. Wariston replaced Gibson of Durie as clerk register while Thomas Nicholson took over Wariston's old place of king's advocate. Eight new ordinary lords of session and two new extraordinary lords were appointed to fill vacancies caused by the purge. Purging of lesser office-holders was entrusted to the officers of state and the committee of estates.[35]

These purges of office-holders were by far the most thorough since the start of the troubles. Until the overthrow of the Engagers there appears to have been much continuity in minor places and offices. Those prepared to serve whatever regime happened to be in power had been allowed to do so; turning them out of office now merely made enemies of men who would have been happy to serve the kirk party. Both in purges of office-holders and of the army the kirk party added unnecessarily to the already widespread hostility to its rule. But it argued that it was better off without

(ABOVE) GOD'S WARS

Print by Wenceslaus Hollar. In the far north a hand bearing a sword (A) threatens Scotland with civil war, and the lion of Scotland (B) turns to face the threat. At (C – inset) the riot in Edinburgh in July 1637 against the prayer book is depicted, while at (D) the covenanters confront Charles I's army on the borders in the First Bishops' War of 1639, and agree the Pacification of Berwick. At (E) half a spread eagle, which hovers over England fanning the flames of war, is a reminder that Britain's wars are a part of a much greater European conflict, the Thirty Years War. At the bottom of this detail from a much larger print, armies clash and ships fight at sea as the English civil war rages (1642 onwards).
British Museum, Department of Prints and Drawings

(RIGHT) JOHN LINDSAY,
EARL OF CRAWFORD-LINDSAY (DIED 1678)

Portrait dated 1663. The white staff he carries indicates his office of Lord Treasurer (1644–1661–3).
Scottish National Portrait Gallery

JOHN CAMPBELL,
IST EARL OF LOUDOUN (DIED 1664)

Medal by Abraham Simon, mid 1640s. Copies cast in lead, silver and gold survive.
British Museum, Department of Coins and Medals

JAMES, IST DUKE OF HAMILTON (DIED 1649)

Portrait after Anthony van Dyck, dated 1640. Hamilton was executed in London after leading the Engagers' invasion of England.
Scottish National Portrait Gallery

WILLIAM HAMILTON, 1ST EARL OF LANARK AND 2ND DUKE OF HAMILTON (DIED 1651) AND JOHN MAITLAND, 2ND EARL AND 1ST DUKE OF LAUDERDALE (DIED 1682)

Portraits by Cornelius Jonson van Ceulen. Hamilton died of wounds after the battle of Worcester. *In the Collection of Lennoxlove House, Haddington*

THE
INDEPENDENCY
OF
ENGLAND
Endeavored to be maintained
By *HENRY MARTEN*,
a Member of the Parliament there,
Againſt the Claim of
The *SCOTTISH* Commiſsioners,
In their late
ANSWER
UPON THE
Bills and Propoſitions
SENT
to the KING in the Iſle of *Wight*.

THE INDEPENDENCY OF ENGLAND

Title page of an English pamphlet, 1647. The title suggests a two-fold threat to England from the stance taken by the Scots in peace negotiations with Charles I. On the one hand a threat is seen to political independence, on the other to the English puritans known as the Independents.

(LEFT) MEDAL COMMEMORATING JAMES, 1ST MARQUIS OF MONTROSE, EXECUTED IN 1650

In some copies the reverse of this silver medal is plain, but this example is inscribed

> Treu Pellican who
> shilit [split] his blood
> To save his King
> and do's [do his] Country good

The spelling errors suggests that the engraver could not understand English. The pelican was regarded as a symbol of blood sacrifice, or even of Christ himself, as it was believed to peck its own neck to provide blood to feed its chicks.
Hunterian Museum, University of Glasgow

(RIGHT) THE MAIDEN

The Scottish beheading device used to execute a number of royalists, including the marquis of Huntly (1647).
The Trustees of the National Museums of Scotland

(RIGHT) THE CORONATION OF KING CHARLES II AT SCONE, 1 JANUARY 1651

Medal commemorating the event designed by Sir James Balfour of Denmylne, the Lord Lyon King of Arms, and cast in gold and silver. On the reverse the defiant lion of Scotland brandishes a thistle.
Hunterian Museum, University of Glasgow

(BELOW) THE CORONATION OF KING CHARLES II AT SCONE, 1 JANUARY 1651

Dutch print by Huych Allaerdt. The scene is imaginary, but full of symbolic meaning. On the right (background) the marquis of Argyll places the crown on the king's head. On the left (foreground) 'Ireland' buckles on the king's armour and 'Scotland' hands him a pistol.
British Museum, Department of Prints and Drawings

THE BATTLE OF DUNBAR, 3 SEPTEMBER 1651, BY PAYNE FISHER

The English army is shown on the right, with the Brox Burn running from top right to bottom centre. The English have crossed the burn and are advanced uphill against the Scots, whose cavalry is beginning to flee.
Sutherland Collection, Ashmolean Museum, Oxford

LEATHER GUNS

Designed by James Wemyss, General of the Artillery in Scotland 1649-51, these light leather-cased cannon were designed to provide highly mobile artillery for the covenanters' army. Barrel lengths vary from 2 (?) to to 5 feet, and one, two and four barrel versions survive. (The stands shown are modern).

The Trustees of the National Museums of Scotland

the support of time-servers and potential malignants. To employ them would not only be disgraceful but dangerous; had not the Engagement shown the dangers of trying to advance the cause of the covenants in alliance with hypocritical malignants? God would give victory to a pure minority, purged of sinners, in preference to a malignant majority, as the defeat of the Engagers had proved. The blinkered vision of the extreme covenanters was blind to the fact that if victory was a sign of divine approval then the fall of the Engagers indicated that God favoured the Independents rather than the kirk party.

NEW RADICAL POLICIES

It was not only in purging that the 1649 parliament proved the most radical since the troubles had begun. Until the fall of the Engagers power among the covenanters had remained firmly in the hands of the nobles. Ministers, lairds and burgesses had all played important parts, and no regime could have survived without their support, but they had nearly always deferred to the authority of the nobles, accepting them as natural leaders. Even the ministers, so often held to have been the wielders of the real power throughout the 1640s, had usually taken care to ensure that they had the support of Argyll and the other covenanting nobles. The years 1637–41 had seen constitutional and religious revolutions in Scotland but the vested interests of the three estates, especially of the nobility, had prevented significant social change. But gradually support for the covenants among the nobles had declined, especially after the signing of the solemn league and covenant in 1643; an increasing number of nobles was discredited through involvement in royalist risings and attempts to compromise with the king. Now involvement in the Engagement had discredited the great majority of politically active nobles. Leadership still nominally lay in the hands of Argyll and his few noble supporters, but now as never before they had to consider and give way to the opinions of the other estates and, above all, to those of the more extreme ministers.

Unlike the nobility, the other two estates had been able to replace by elections those who had been purged from parliament or were unwilling to serve in it while it was dominated by the kirk party. But here too there does seem to have been a change; the social positions of the new commissioners have never been analysed, but it seems that in many cases vacancies were filled by electing men who would not previously have been regarded as suitable to sit in parliament, men of lesser status. They were, obviously, still lairds and burgesses, members of the aristocracies of their shires and burghs, or they would not have been qualifed to sit; but they were nonetheless often lesser and poorer men than those they replaced. In part this was doubtless simply the result of the stock of men of what would previously have been considered sufficient status to sit becoming exhausted after years of turmoil with many becoming disillusioned and withdrawing from politics, or being excluded (from voting as well as being elected) because of their association with royalists or Engagers; the electors therefore had to turn to lesser men. But there seems also to have been a deliberate turning to such lesser men since their betters seemed to have failed, just as so many of the covenanting nobles had failed, to bring peace to the country without betraying what the covenanters had fought for. Much of the former covenanting leadership had been discredited through taking part in the counter-revolution of 1647–8. The counter-revolution had been destroyed from outside (by defeat in England) and from below (by resistance to levying and the whiggamore raid). Some of the nobles and the greater lairds and burgesses supported and provided leadership for the new kirk party regime, but there were not enough of them to fill parliament and its committees; some commissioners therefore had to be recruited from below; not from far below, but the change was nonetheless significant. Many of the new commissioners were less rigidly committed to the *status quo* in society than their predecessors had been; they had no intention of altering the basic structure of society, in which they benefitted from a relatively privileged position, but they were prepared to support many reforms which had not previously been advocated by the covenanting regime, or which had only received half-hearted support—especially reforms which had been held back because they conflicted with the interests of the nobles and great lairds and burgesses of the earlier covenanting lay establishment.

Furthermore, the lesser men who now sat in parliament seem to have been much more open than their predecessors to domination by the ministers; after all, ministers had led opposition to the Engagement when lay leaders had failed to do so, and in any case such lesser men had probably always tended to pay more attention to their ministers than their betters had. Measures advocated by the ministers for years which parliament had previously ignored or suppressed were now to receive general support, and the direct influence of the kirk in political matters increased greatly. The new regime could remain in power (at least temporarily) in spite of the opposition of all but a few nobles, but it could not afford to alienate the general assembly or the commission of the kirk.

This trend, the replacement of original revolutionary leadership by new leaders from lower in the social structure, men who had not previously taken a prominent part in national politics and who support more radical policies than their predecessors, is of course a well known phenomenon.

Such 'a displacement of leadership is a common feature of revolutions'. Ironically for the kirk party the nearest parallel in time and place to this revolution in Scotland was provided by England, where many of the radical members of parliament who supported Pride's purge, the execution of the king and the establishment of the commonwealth were 'men from outside the normal political establishment'.[36]

The new power and confidence of the ministers after the fall of the Engagers was clearly seen in their demand that lay patronage in the appointment of ministers to parishes be abolished as a thing often complained of, contrary to the word of God and the constitution of the kirk, and a corrupt and unlawful custom. It was true that many ministers had long disliked patronage and questioned its lawfulness, but no serious attempt had been made to have it abolished; Alexander Henderson had referred to it as existing 'by toleration of that which they cannot amend'.[37] It had not been a matter worth risking losing the support of the lairds and nobles over, especially as such lay covenanters had no objection to the rights of non-covenanting patrons (including bishops and the king) being taken over by presbyteries. In 1642 Argyll on behalf of himself and other noble elders in the assembly stated that they would give up their rights of patronage provided that in return ministers did not seek any increases in stipends, but nothing came of this. The assembly did lay down that patrons should choose ministers from a list of six (later reduced to three) names drawn up by the presbytery, but this had little effect at a time when it was hard to find suitable applicants to fill vacancies. The following year a petition to the assembly complained of ministers being intruded against the will of congregations but the noble patrons got it suppressed. After this there is no sign of any move to abolish patronage until 1649; ministers recognised that they were dependent on the support of nobles and lairds who were strongly opposed to abolition.[38]

In 1649 however the situation was very different. The ministers now had the initiative, and the nobles no longer had power to resist them; on 9 March at the kirk's request parliament abolished patronage. Some nobles and lairds protested that this was derogatory to the rights of their estates and walked out, but Argyll, Loudoun and Wariston voted for the act—they 'durst doe no wtherwayes, lest the leaders of the church should desert them, and leaue them to stand one ther auen feeitt, wich without the church non of them could weill doe'.[39]

The removal of patronage interfered with the rights of many lairds as well as those of nobles; in the matter of the feudal superiorities of kirklands lairds took advantage of the weakness of the nobles to advance their own ends. By Charles I's act of revocation of 1633 it had been ruled that the feudal superiority of former kirklands then held by laymen belonged to the crown, but that the feu duties paid by the lairds and lesser men who had actual possession of the lands should continue to be paid to the lords of erection (who had previously possessed the superiorities) until the crown redeemed them. In the event Charles I had been able to redeem very few of the feu duties, and after the troubles had begun he had tried to win support, or to reward support already given, by making new grants of the superiorities and feu duties to nobles. Though the lairds had not (as Charles had hoped) shown gratitude to him for annexing the superiorities to the crown, they opposed his granting them back to the nobility. In parliament in 1647 and 1648 petitions in the name of the lairds had demanded that the grants by the king be cancelled, and no new ones be made in future. In 1647 many shire and burgh commissioners had supported these demands, but the nobles had almost unanimously opposed them; there was as yet no sign that division on the issue corresponded at all with the division between Argyll's party of extreme covenanters and Hamilton's of moderates and royalists. Balmerino led opposition to the lairds, and Argyll arranged a compromise whereby decision was delayed.[40]

By March 1648 however the issue had become a party one. Agitation for the cancelling of the king's grants of superiorities was led by lairds meeting in the Tailors' Hall; it was no coincidence that those organising petitions against the Engagement met in the same place. But parliament was dominated by Hamilton's party, and the petition against the grants was laid aside without any action being taken; many nobles hoped to gain such grants by persuading the king that grants would increase their influence over the lairds and thus increase their power to help him.[41]

A year later, with only a few nobles sitting in parliament, circumstances favoured the lairds, who produced petitions (one of which was said to have had the support of 900 persons from fourteen shires) denouncing the king's grants to nobles as subjecting vassals of kirklands to slavery. An act was therefore passed on 8 March, which ratified the revocation's declaration that superiorities belonged to the crown, and that feu duties should remain in the hands of the lords of erection until the king bought them. But, with some exceptions, grants by the king of such superiorities were cancelled, and it was now declared that vassals of kirklands might buy their own feu duties from the lords of erection if they wished; the right of the king in turn to buy them from the vassals was affirmed, but the lairds must have hoped that the effect of the act would be to free them from all feu duties on kirklands.[42]

Other reforming acts of the 1649 parliament are less clearly the result of the weakness of the nobility in parliament but do owe something to the new power and influence of the kirk. New provisions for the augmentation of the stipends of ministers fall into this category.[43] Moreover, since the fall of the Engagers the kirk had shown more interest in the material welfare of lesser men, tenants and the poor, than previously. The commission of the kirk had begun to petition against the burden of taxation, oppression of tenants by soldiers, officials and landlords, and similar grievances.[44] The kirk's concern led to the passing of an act anent the poor on 1 March; the problem of the poor had been growing increasingly serious as levies, taxes, plague, and war with its plundering and destruction had caused disruption and hardship. Grain prices, low in the mid 1640s, had doubled since 1646, reaching record heights in 1649–50.[45] The new act related the misery of large numbers of the poor to lack of an orderly way of providing for them, to 'the shame and reproach of our christaine professioun which obleidgeth us to the relieff of our poore brethrene'. In future each parish was to make a list of its poor twice a year. If voluntary contributions were insufficient to provide for them the privy council or the committee of estates would stent the parish or the presbytery. Heritors who dealt harshly with their tenants, thus impoverishing them, were to pay more than others—virtually a way of fining unjust landlords. A similiar discrimination was to govern the distribution of money to the poor; not only were the able bodied who could work to be excluded (as was traditional) but the pious poor were to receive more consideration than the vicious.[46]

After further urgings from the kirk, parliament in May set up a committee to consider ways of remedying grievances and the sufferings of tenants through oppression by their masters and soldiers, their sufferings being 'the guiltines and sins of your Lordships and such as rule in the land'. In July parliament agreed to appoint, in cooperation with the kirk, commissioners in each presbytery to investigate all complaint, wrongs and grievances against masters, collectors of taxes, officers and soldiers. Orders were given for the immediate remedy of the most common grievances. Attempts to revive justices of the peace were also connected with the desire to settle grievances and injustices at a local level. Appointments of justices had ceased after the troubles began, and an order by parliament in 1647 that they be revived had been ignored. Now, in March 1649, parliament instructed members of the shire committees of war to act as justices. Later the 1617 act concerning justices was renewed and appointment of new justices began.[47] Reforms in the law were also ordered. A commission for surveying the laws had been proposed in 1639[48] but nothing had been done; now parliament appointed a commission for revising the laws, so that there would be 'a constant certane and knowne modell and frame of Law according to equitie and Justice established be publict authoritie and published to all his Maiesties Leidges'. The laws were to be drawn up into a book to be ratified by king and parliament, all unprofitable and superfluous laws being omitted. The years 1649–50 also saw harsh action by the court of session against malpractices by lawyers and perjury by witnesses.[49]

THE ASSAULT ON SIN AND WITCHCRAFT

The increased concern of the kirk for the poor and the oppressed was connected with a new urgency shown in the work of moral reform. It was now eleven years since the national covenant had been signed, yet there was no sign of the improvement in morals which it had been hoped would follow from reformation in accordance with it. There had been slackness in searching out and punishing sin, a situation disgraceful to Scotland and displeasing to God. Montrose's victories, plague, the covenanters' failures in England and the Engagement might all be God's punishment for such laxity. The kirk party therefore embarked on a concentrated assault on sin in the hope that this would lead God to bring it success. Moral as well as political offenders were purged from the army and civil offices. The kirk petitioned parliament to take action against various sins, as a result of which acts were passed in February 1649 'against Witches and Consulters, against fornication, against remissions for capital crimes, against swearing, drukennes, scolding, and other prophannes, against clandastine mariages, scandalous persons, goeing of mylnes, salt pans, and fishing on the Sabbath day', while new acts against adultery and incest were to be passed in the next session.[50]

To many, however, it seemed that sin was fast increasing in spite of such action; 'as for adulterie, fornicatioun, incest, bigamie, and uther uncleanes and filthynes, it did nevir abound moir nor at this time'.[51] It is possible that this was true, in reaction against the puritanism of the covenanters, but it seems much more likely that it was not the case that sin was more common, but that it was being unearthed and punished more zealously than ever before. Contemporaries might think that the more sin was punished, the more there was of it to punish, but in reality it was probably only the detection rate that was rising.

The most unpleasant aspect of the assault on sin was the great increase in the persecution of witches in 1649–50. Little has been published on the history of witchcraft in Scotland above the level of anecdotes about individual cases; general conclusions therefore can at present only be tentative, but it is worth trying to indicate how far the Scottish evidence is compatible with recent interpretations of witchcraft in England.[52]

In Scotland as in England, belief in witchcraft was almost universal, and persecution from the Reformation to the late seventeenth century was endemic. Popular belief in England was basically in the ability of witches by charms and curses to harm or kill men or their animals. In this lay the origin of most cases. But once investigation began another type of belief was sometimes added by the lawyers and clergy involved; this was the belief, imported from the continent, that witchcraft entailed a compact with the devil and devil worship at gatherings of many witches, the witches' Sabbath. Those accused sometimes really believed themselves to have power to do evil. Others came to believe that they must be witches in the course of interrogation. But most were forced into confessions incorporating the preconceptions about witchcraft which they shared with their persecutors, sometimes with the addition of the imported continental beliefs. Prosecution usually began with accusations by those who thought themselves bewitched or by their families. Though the nature of the accusations might alter once clergy and lawyers became involved, it was rare in England for the initiative to come from above (from lawyers, clergy or government) in a prosecution, or for prosecutions to be influenced by political events. Persecution was steady and unspectacular, not a matter of periodic witch crazes. On the continent on the other hand the initiative did tend to come from above and cases tended to be concentrated in certain periods.[53]

The underlying beliefs in Scotland were similar to those in England, but it does seem that the type of persecution differed, at least in emphasis. The initiative, both in individual cases and in general encouragement of persecution, more often comes from above. Two other aspects of Scottish witchcraft cases are logically connected with this. First, allegations of devil worship, compacts and witches' Sabbaths are much more common in Scotland, a feature also partially explained by the fairly frequent use of torture, usually sleep deprivation, to exact confessions. Secondly, intensity of persecution fluctuates much more widely than in England; there are periodic witch crazes, and they seem to bear some relation to political and religious developments.

The peaks of persecution in Scotland come in the early 1590s, 1643–4, 1649–50 and 1660–3.[54] In the first of these periods continental witch beliefs first become widespread in Scotland, through James VI's acceptance of them.[55] The trials which sparked off this craze were at least in part politically motivated, involving charges of treason. Later the persecution acquired a momentum independent of official encouragement, dying down after 1597—at about the same time that the bitter struggle between James and the presbyterians for control of the kirk decreased in intensity.

The relatively small craze of 1643–4 came at a time of acute tension through disputes over how to react to the civil war in England. The years 1649–50 saw the kirk party struggling to retain power, and 1660–3 the restoration of the monarchy and of episcopacy. All these were thus periods of crisis, and it seems very likely that these crises were related to the witch-hunting epidemics by more than chronological coincidence, even though the exact nature of the relationship remains obscure.

The 1649–50 witch craze was undoubtedly to some extent inspired from above. Parliament, the privy council, the committee of estates, the general assembly and the commission of the kirk all showed interest in pursuing witches in the 1640s, and this interest intensified in 1649[56]—in striking contrast to contemporary England where the parliamentary regime showed very little interest in such matters.[57] The witch craze probably had its origins in the determination of the kirk party to suppress all forms of evil and sin; denunciations by ministers of sin in general and of witchcraft in particular doubtless stirred up members of congregations to make accusations.

In Scotland, as in England,[58] witches were very seldom blamed for large scale disasters as opposed to the misfortunes of individuals; plague, harvest failure, defeat in battle and so on were recognised as acts of God. Yet there was a link between the persecution of 1649–50 and the disasters which had afflicted the country since 1644. If God was, by these disasters, punishing the covenanters for their failure to root out sin, surely pre-eminence should be given to extirpating witchcraft, for what could be more sinful than the compact with the devil which it was supposed to involve a hellish counterpart to the covenants with God?

However, a simple equation of zeal in witch-hunting with extreme presbyterianism[59] will not work even for 1649–50, let alone for other periods. Certainly one finds some strongly covenanting areas, Fife and the Lothians, providing a greater concentration of cases than any other part of the country, but the even more strongly covenanting south-west provides relatively few cases. Nor is there any concentration of cases in areas where there were many anti-covenanters, nor any other indication that enemies of the regime were apt to be persecuted as witches. It may be that some of the most ardent persecutors were supporters of the kirk party; but the minister of Inverkeithing, responsible for intense local persecution, was suspended from the ministry in 1649 for various offences, and was deposed in 1650 for neglect of his spiritual duties.[60]

Accusations were normally first considered by the kirk session. It or the presbytery then petitioned parliament, council or committee of estates to appoint commissioners to try and to burn the suspects, from whom confessions had usually already been exacted.[61] Those who confessed under interrogation or torture often implicated others, who in turn made further accusations, until it seemed that the evil was spreading fast throughout the country. In July 1649 parliament agreed that witchcraft was increasing daily in the land, though some doubted if it was quite as widespread as confessions suggested; on 20 July parliament insisted on hearing evidence against thirty witches before it would appoint commissioners to burn them, whereas previously such commissions seem to have been granted almost automatically, and on 7 August it ordered committees of war to find out whether torture had been used on those suspected or found guilty, and to report to the committee of estates before executions were carried out.[62] Again, on 6 November when ordering the trial of thirty-eight witches the committee of estates specified that no torture was to be used to make them confess. Clearly even supporters of the kirk party were beginning to suspect that the witch epidemic was, partly at least, being manufactured (in all good faith) by ministers and others through their methods of dealing with suspects. Nonetheless, persecution continued unabated; in August to December 1649 the committee granted commissions for trying nearly 150 witches, and in May 1650 parliament ordered the trial of fifty-four more. After Cromwell invaded Scotland two months later it was rumoured that the devil had carried 2,000 witches to meet him.[64]

How many witches were strangled at the stake and their bodies then burned in Scotland in 1649–50 is impossible to say; certainly many dozens, perhaps hundreds. Most were the wives, widows or daughters of people of humble status, though some were men or boys and a few were of higher status; the magistrates of Inverkeithing refused to arrest their own wives when they were accused, while Margaret Henderson, widow of the laird of Pittaro, fled from the burgh to escape trial, only to be captured and die (by her own hand, it was suspected) in prison in Edinburgh.[64] Much about this witch craze is obscure; the suffering involved is all too clear.

All the regime's purging, punishing and persecuting simply increased its unpopularity without making the kingdom noticeably more godly. Yet to a few it seemed (at least in retrospect) almost a golden age; 'this seems to me to have been Scotland's high noon. The only complaint of prophane people was, that the government was so strict they hade not liberty enough to sin'.[65]

PLUSCARDINE'S RISING AND THE TREATY OF THE HAGUE

While ministers fought witches, the devil's minions, in the Lowlands, the army was engaging a more substantial enemy in the Highlands. Though the feared invasion by royalists and Engagers from Holland had not taken place it was still rumoured that a royalist landing was intended, and there was widespread unrest and hatred of the kirk party regime in the Highlands. In the far north the master of Reay (who became Lord Reay on his father's death in February 1649) and his men were again in arms against the earl of Sutherland over the possession of Strathnaver. The execution of Charles I brought more general unrest to a head. On 9 February the magistrates of Inverness informed parliament that they had heard that their burgh was to be the first objective of an invasion from abroad; on this and other reports an act putting the kingdom in a posture of defence was passed.[66] The committee of dispatches was well informed of where the danger lay, for it summoned Lewis Gordon (Huntly's heir since the death of Lord Aboyne in exile), Sir Thomas Urquhart of Cromarty, Sir Thomas Mackenzie of Pluscardine (brother of Seaforth, who had joined Charles II in Holland), Mackenzie of Redcastle and other Mackenzies to come to Edinburgh to sign bands of loyalty;[67] within a few days all those summoned were in rebellion. A troop of horse was sent to Inverness to strengthen the garrison and David Leslie was summoned to Edinburgh to give his advice.[68]

On 22 February about 700 horsemen, mainly Mackenzies and led by Pluscardine, Redcastle, Cromarty and Colonel John Monro of Lemlair, seized Inverness. On hearing of this, parliament ordered the raising of 5,440 horse and about 13,400 foot for defence against invasion—by royalists in the north or by the English in the south. David Leslie was sent north with whatever troops he could gather, with power to pardon all who had not taken part in previous rebellions. Meanwhile Pluscardine and his supporters were finding little enthusiasm for their action; the regime might be unpopular but the rebels seemed to have so little chance of success that few joined them. There was also some doubt as to why they had rebelled; the fact that they demolished the fortifications of Inverness suggests that the story that they hoped to hold it as a base for a royalist invasion was false, and that the motive was in many cases the determination of local clans that Inverness should not be fortified and permanently garrisoned by any regime.[69]

Pluscardine established a committee of war which hopefully sent out orders for payment of taxes in the northern shires but these were almost entirely ignored and on Leslie's approach he abandoned Inverness and withdrew into the mountains. Leslie pursued him into Ross but then learnt of a new danger; the men of Atholl had risen in arms for the king, led by Lord Ogilvie and Major General Middleton (who had escaped from imprisonment in England). Moreover the garrison of Stirling Castle had been stirred into mutiny by the malignants and had disarmed its officers. Only prompt action by Major General Holborne persuaded the mutineers to submit. Whether or not the Stirling mutiny, the rising in Atholl and the action of Pluscardine had been coordinated is impossible to say, but it must have looked to Leslie as if they were, He hurriedly offered favourable terms to most of those who had joined Pluscardine; Cromarty, Lemlair and others agreed on 21 March to submit and gave assurances for their future good behaviour in return for pardons.[70] Leslie feared the committee of estates might think he had been too generous and therefore emphasised the weakness of his position. He had fewer than 800 men, and they were suffering from the cold and could find little food. The rebels had retired to the snowy mountains where he was unable to follow them, and his presence was needed further south to deal with the men of Atholl. As Pluscardine and the Mackenzies remained in arms Leslie left three troops of horse in Ross to prevent them from venturing out of the mountains. Having thus settled what he called the 'hubbub about Inuerness' he marched quickly to prevent the Atholl royalists moving south.[71]

The main sufferer from the seizure of Inverness was Huntly, who (having been captive in Edinburgh since 1647) had had nothing to do with Pluscardine's exploit. But the bitterness roused by yet another royalist rising in the north drew attention to the almost forgotten prisoner, still under sentence of death for his rising in 1644. What better gesture to indicate determination to exact obedience and punish offenders of all ranks than to execute him? The kirk was consulted and replied grimly 'it is clear from the Word of God that murtherers should die without partiality'. The nobles in parliament opposed the execution—no noble had yet been executed in Scotland during the troubles—but were over-ruled; Huntly was beheaded on 22 March.[72]

The Atholl men proved as irresolute as the rebels in the north and hurried to submit to Leslie. Lord Ogilvie and Middleton fled and most of the gentlemen of Atholl signed bands to keep the peace on 31 March.[73] The crisis seemed over. But then in mid April Pluscardine's rebellion revived, and he was joined by Ogilvie, Middleton and Lord Reay. They marched into Badenoch and were there joined by a party of Gordons under Lewis Gordon, the new marquis of Huntly. Now totalling over 1,000 men, the rebels camped at Balvenie, near Dufftown. Leslie, however, was now moving north from Atholl and the rebels hastily sent Pluscardine and Middleton to negotiate with him, perhaps hoping to persuade him to declare for the king.[74] But they had neglected to consider the threat of the three troops of horse under Colonel Gilbert Ker and Lieutenants Colonel Halket and Strachan which Leslie had left in Ross, probably considering them too small a force to be dangerous. Though outnumbered more than ten to one (the officers put their strength at 120 horse and twelve musketeers) the three troops followed the rebels and fell on their camp at Balvenie on 8 May, achieving complete surprise. Sixty or eighty rebels were killed and about 800 (including Lord Reay) captured. Such was the 'Bourd [mock battle] of Balvenie'. After it Huntly, Ogilvie, Pluscardine and Middleton quickly submitted on promises that they would not be punished in life, liberty or estates; Reay and other prisoners were sent to Edinburgh. Some Irish, stragglers from Montrose's army, had fought with the rebels and were captured; the committee of estates ordered that they should 'bee putt to present execution, to bee done upon them be there associat rebells of the Clankenzie' in the hope that the resultant ill-feeling would prevent future cooperation between Irish and Mackenzies.[75]

Even though the risings in the north had collapsed, further troubles were feared. It was said that agents of Montrose were at work in the north, and that Dutch merchants were smuggling in arms and ammunition. Work had begun in March on fortifying Leith and Burntisland, and this was continued as a matter of urgency;[76] to fear of attack by ships of the English commonwealth there was now added fear of attack by the king's ships, for by the end of May the negotiations with Charles II in Holland had broken down.

When the Scots commissioners had arrived in Holland in March they had found the king's advisers at the Hague divided into several factions over how he should go about regaining his thrones. Some of the English and several Scots (including Montrose, Sinclair and Napier) advised Charles to go to Ireland, to join the catholic Irish and Ormond. Others urged him to invade Scotland to overthrow the regime, arguing that the kirk party was untrustworthy and that in any case it was so weak that alliance with it would be a liability. Some Engagers, Lauderdale, Lanark and Callander included, did argue in favour of alliance with the kirk party, however, and urged the king to go to Scotland and take the covenants. Lauderdale at least was sincere in this, but the others calculated that once established in Scotland Charles would be able to overthrow Argyll and the kirk and thus change the nature of the regime. Lanark was thus following the policy that had brought his brother Hamilton to disaster, of trying to fool covenanters into supporting the king. He inherited his brother's title as well as his policy, for Hamilton was executed by the English for treason in March, having been tried under his English title of earl of Carnbridge. The new duke's life at the Hague was made difficult by Lauderdale, who constituted himself Hamilton's covenanting conscience to keep his royalist tendencies in check; it was said Hamilton would incline more to the king 'were it not for the violence of Lauderdale who haunts him like a fury'.[77]

Callander's motives at this time are as hard to discern as those for much of his conduct. At the Hague he was said to form a faction of his own with Seaforth, a man long known for his wavering indecision; they made an odd and ineffecutal partnership. Montrose was said to appear to abhor 'even the most moderate party of his countrymen'; he saw military action as the only way to establish an acceptable regime in Scotland. The king showed favour to this point of view by renewing his father's commissions to Montrose as lieutenant governor and captain general of Scotland, but he may only have done this in the hope that it would frighten the kirk party into making concessions to him.[78]

The Scots commissioners were first received by Charles II on 27 March, in his bedchamber; it had been decided that no ceremony or respect should be shown in receiving them and that Charles should avoid acknowledging the legality of the parliament which had sent them.[79] They began by demanding that Montrose be removed from access to the king, but Charles refused to respond until he heard the other demands that they had to make. Not until 5 April did the Scots agree to this while Montrose was still being consulted by him. They then related that Scotland had done its utmost to preserve his father, and intended to serve him with the same faithfulness (a promise which can hardly have much encouraged their new king). But, the commissioners related, the estates considered it necessary that he make certain concessions before he was restored to his just rights; these were then detailed, based on their instructions from parliament, and the need for haste was stressed 'before Democracy or any new modell of government under the name of an Agreement of the people, or any other name' was settled in England.[80] When the king tried to get them to say unambiguously that they had no other demands to make they proved evasive, accusing him of repeating questions they had already answered. When he tried to make them call his father's execution murder they would do more than express their 'deep sense of that horrid fact against the life of your Royall Father', which was hardly satisfactory.[81] Neither party was being entirely honest. The covenanters wished to retain the right to make further demands after Charles reached Scotland; the king had no intention of accepting demands which would have left him virtually powerless but wished to avoid openly rejecting them and to divert attention to the evasiveness of the Scots. By renewed favour to Montrose he indicated that he felt there was little hope of reaching agreement with the kirk party; Montrose was authorised to negotiate with foreign powers for help for an invasion of Scotland, and was appointed admiral of Scotland.[82]

Before giving a final answer to the commissioners Charles asked his leading Scots supporters to give him their advice. Hamilton, typically, excused himself from answering as he was not acquainted with all the relevant circumstances. Lauderdale proposed that Charles accept the religious demands so far as they concerned Scotland, and offer to settle religion in England in a free parliament.[83] Montrose suggested that the king accept the national covenant out of expediency, but denounced the solemn league and covenant as so full of injustice, violence and rebellion that it would be shameful and ruinous to agree to it—'it is the same thing as if they should desire to undo you by your own leave and favour'. In demanding concessions before admitting the king to office the covenanters were trying to turn hereditary right into conditional election. 'Your Majesty does clearly see they resolve that you should signify nothing' and should therefore 'trust the justice of your cause to God and better fortunes; and use all vigorous and active ways, as the only probable human means that is left to redeem you';[84] in other words, Charles should use force against Scotland.

When at last, on 19 May, Charles gave a direct answer to the Scots commissioners it was clear that he had accepted much of Montrose's advice. He would do all he could in honour and conscience to satisfy them, but only if they undertook to help him to avenge his father and recover his rights in England. He would confirm the covenanters' civil and ecclesiastical revolution in Scotland up to 1641, as his father had done, and would pass an act of oblivion, but he could not impose the solemn league and covenant on England and Ireland without consulting their parliaments. Needless to say this did not satisfy the commissioners; Charles I had made greater concessions in the Engagement. They therefore returned to Scotland empty handed early in June. This they regretted, for they had been much impressed by the person of their new king, finding him of 'a very sweet and courteous disposition', 'one of the most gentle, innocent, well inclyned princes', though surrounded by a 'very evill generation' of advisers who led him astray. Scots alienated by his father's cold reserve were favourably impressed by Charles II's more informal and friendly manner, and still hoped that he would prove more pliable than his father. But he showed no sign of deserting his evil counsellors, writing to Montrose, 'I will not determine any thing, touching the affairs of that Kingdom [Scotland], without having your advice'.[85]

On adjourning in March the Scots parliament had agreed to reassemble in May, in the hope that it could ratify a treaty with the king. Instead the new session soon learnt that the negotiations had failed. The regime of the kirk party thus remained isolated as it had been since the execution of Charles I, fearing attack from the king and Montrose on the one hand, from the English on the other. The latter threat had temporarily abated as Cromwell was undertaking the conquest of Ireland, but it was feared that once he had completed that task he would turn his attention to Scotland.

Yet the Scots parliament refused to compromise with the English commonwealth; when the English suggested a treaty of friendship the Scots replied that they would not negotiate unless the English parliament disowned its own recent proceedings in executing the king and abolishing the monarchy and the house of lords.[86]

In view of the dangers to Scotland, common sense and worldly wisdom suggested that the Scots should maintain as large an army as possible. But the kirk continued to demand a thorough purge of the army 'by reason of the Malignancie, insolence, and profanity of many that are members thereof'; the arguments against purging were 'meerlie politick' and failure to purge would be a neglect of duty exposing both army and kingdom to God's wrath. The 'Bourd of Balvenie' increased the force of the kirk's reasoning, for did it not show, as the ministers had predicted, that God would give a godly few victory over a multitude of malignants? Archibald Strachan certainly interpreted the victory in this way, writing in favour of purging that 'The Lord hath shown what he can doe by a few'; even if Montrose landed 'ther shalbe no need of the levy of Knavis to the work tho they should be willing'. A small, carefully chosen army was preferable to a mass levy.[87]

Parliament accepted such arguments and on 21 June ordered the purging from the army of any who had had any part in royalist risings or the Engagement, or who had otherwise shown themselves disaffected. Most of the infantry whose levy had been ordered in February had never been raised, so new orders were given in August to levy more than 10,000 men.[88] But the orders for purging and for raising new men soon proved incompatible, for there were not enough godly men willing to serve; even the few thousand already in arms contained many defined as malignants. Years of intermittent warfare in the three kingdoms had created a class of semi-mercenary soldiers in Scotland, men uprooted from their homes by war and dependent on employment as soldiers for their livelihood, willing to serve for or against king or covenant as occasion offered. Having little interest in the cause for which they were fighting they tended to be undisciplined, looting and oppressing those on whom they were quartered, whether friend or foe. No matter how often the kirk and the estates ordered that those levied should be godly, loyal and moral, it was always much easier to raise such veterans, who would enlist willingly, than reluctant if godly peasants. It is easy to sneer at the stupidity of the covenanters in weakening their armies by purging in 1649 and 1650, but had they failed to try to prevent them oppressing the people, and to try to ensure that those who fought for the covenants really believed in them, they would no doubt be accused of hypocrisy.

The kirk was as zealous in purging itself as in purging the army. The general assembly met in July and August 1649, and it not only deposed seven ministers and confirmed the deposition of ten others for having supported (or failed to denounce) the Engagement, but also appointed commissions of zealous young ministers to carry out purges in areas where support for the Engagement had been strong.[89] There was much controversy in the assembly over how ministers should be appointed now that patronage had been abolished. In the end it was agreed that the kirk session should elect a minister but that the presbytery would try his qualifications and, if satisfied, admit him. Moreover if the congregation disagreed with the session's choice the presbytery would judge between them.[90] The abolition of patronage gave general satisfaction, but at least one minister wanted to go further, and demanded that parliament should restore all teinds (tithes) to the kirk. This was bitterly opposed by Argyll, Cassillis and all other elders in the assembly, some threatening to 'make the sword decide that question', and it won little or no support from other ministers. They well knew the limits of the kirk's power even under kirk party rule; to have demanded the return of all teinds would have lost it the support of most of its lay adherents.[91]

Before dissolving the assembly published its analysis of the state of the kingdom in the form of a warning. English sectaries looked on Scotland 'with an evill eye' as upon these who stand in the way of their monstruous and new fangled devices in Religion and Government', while malignants still worked against the covenants and the king had rejected the kirk's just desires. If Charles II invaded Scotland it would be a religious duty to resist him. Many 'do so much dote upon absolute and Arbitrary Government for gaining their own ends' that they would admit the king unconditionally, but the magistrate's power was from God and limited by him, as well as by the mutual obligations between him and his people. Duty to the king was subordinate to defence of the covenants and liberties of the kingdom.[92]

From this it seems that the kirk was of the opinion that no new approach should be made to the king for the time being. Argyll, however, favoured new negotiations. His motives are not altogether clear, but he probably disliked the dependence of the regime on the kirk and the undermining of the status of the nobility. Recent events in England, where the house of lords had been abolished after the execution of the king, as well as developments in Scotland may have convinced him that kings and nobles had more interests in common than he had previously thought; to refuse to admit a king by hereditary right to office might lead to a questioning of the inherited rights of the nobility. Moreover he doubtless hoped that if he was responsible for bringing about an agreement between king and kirk party then he would be the power behind the throne. Encouraged by letters from the king (brought by William Murray), he therefore proposed in parliament that Lothian should be sent to Charles to reopen negotiations. Parliament at first agreed, but then found that he had not consulted Loudoun or any of his other kirk party allies about the plan. This raised suspicion of his motives, and parliament resolved on 7 August that though an approach should be made to the king it should be by Libberton, not Lothian; and the instructions given to him were so uncompromising (though not so harsh as those proposed by the kirk) that there seemed little point in Libberton's going at all.[93]

Parliament also proved deeply divided on other matters. In July nearly half the members refused to attend for nearly a fortnight in opposition to a proposal that the proportion of the total monthly maintenance payable by the eastern shires should be increased since the western shires had been paying more than their fair share. Previously nothing had been done to rectify the situation because the east had been over represented in parliament through the disproportionate number of nobles from that area; now few nobles were present, and many of those who were came from the west and forced a change. This was not the only crisis raised by financial matters; on the last day of the session, 7 August, nearly all the burgesses walked out of parliament in protest at an act to reduce interest rates.[94]

Thus when parliament rose the regime of the kirk party was still isolated, open to invasion by both royalists and English and faced with widespread hostility within Scotland, especially among the nobility. Yet instead of uniting in the face of such dangers the regime weakened itself by purges and by squabbles over taxation and negotiations with the king.

NEGOTIATIONS WITH THE KING AND THE LANDING OF MONTROSE

Once parliament had risen the committee of estates proceeded with the tasks of purging minor officials[95] and summoning former Engagers whose loyalty was doubtful to sign a declaration denouncing the Engagement and promising to keep the peace.[96] The committee sat in Perth in late August and early September to order Highland Engagers to sign, but had only very limited success. Many from the southern and eastern fringes of the Highlands signed, but none of the chiefs from the west did so, and the committee had to leave it to Argyll to try to get signatures from Badenoch and Lochaber.[97] Hand in hand with the work of trying to ensure loyalty to the regime went moral reform. Purging of the army for both moral and political reasons proceeded spasmodically, but met with many difficulties; the purging of David Leslie's own troop of horse had to be stopped because after nine troopers had been ejected the rest threatened to disband rather than await the disgrace of being purged. Leslie tried to get purging left in the hands of army officers, but on 8 January 1650 a new committee for purging containing members of the committee of estates as well as officers was appointed.[98]

The most important matter requiring the attention of the committee of estates in August 1649 was Libberton's mission to the king. Libberton was reluctant to go, in spite of parliament's orders, and the committee was divided as to the wisdom of sending him; but finally on 12 September he was instructed to try to get a satisfactory answer from the king to the demands formerly presented to him at the Hague. If Charles would acknowledge the legality of the Scots parliament and of the committee and grant all that was desired of him, persons of 'greater eminencie' would be sent to invite him to Scotland. Yet though Libberton was now fully instructed another month passed before he sailed (on 11 October), a delay partly caused by a rumour that the king had landed in Ireland.[99] On reaching Holland Libberton found that Charles had moved to Jersey. Before following him he tried to persuade some of the exiled Engagers to submit to the kirk party, but found them unwilling to make the public recantations which would be demanded of them. He had more success in talks with English presbyterian exiles; they promised that their supporters in England would work to restore the king if he came to an agreement with the Scots.[100]

The long delays before Libberton reached the king proved in some ways to be to the kirk party's advantage, for in the interim events in Ireland forced the king to see a treaty with the Scots as the most likely way of regaining his thrones. When he had broken off the treaty at the Hague he had intended to go to Ireland to join the Irish catholics; his lord lieutenant, Ormond, had signed a treaty with the confederate catholics whereby they were to work jointly to reduce Ireland to obedience to the king. But by the time Libberton arrived in Jersey Cromwell had conquered much of Ireland.[101]

Charles and his council therefore resolved in January 1650 that an agreement with the Scots would be an effectual means of saving Ireland, recovering England, and bringing the regicides to justice.[102] But in spite of this Charles refused to recognise the legality of the Scots regime (which Libberton's instructions made a pre-condition a treaty); the most he would do was to address letters to the committee of estates, the commission of the kirk and Argyll, asking that a treaty be held at Breda, hoping that the Scots would accept this as involving recognition of the regime though he himself believed that it did not do so.[103]

Libberton reported back to the committee of estates on 5 February 1600,[104] and there was much dispute over whether or not to send commissioners to Breda. Argyll and most of the nobles strongly favoured agreement with the king; they thirsted after the young king so 'that the government might run in the old channel' and be largely a matter for king and nobles. Under the kirk party the nobles 'doubted their own safety till they were settled upon that rock', the rock of religion and laws confirmed by the king.[105] Argyll stated that he would rather have no king than prejudice religion, but many in the kirk party suspected that he aspired to the role and power of king-maker. They therefore pointed out that there was no sign of a change of heart in the king; he was still surrounded by royalists and continued to support Montrose. He would try to trick the Scots with fair promises, and it was urged that in a new treaty the demands made of him should be even more stringent than before.[106]

The matter was decided on 21 February after 'a great and hott dispute'. The extremists argued that Charles had not recognised the legality of the regime and that no negotiations should take place until he did so, but Argyll and the other nobles got this proposal defeated; of fourteen nobles present only one (Cassillis) voted with the extremists. As parliament was due to meet on 7 March the extremists then argued that commissioners should not be sent to the king until after parliament met; 'Mighty tugging and heate at this', but they were again defeated, in spite of the fact that they produced a copy of a letter from the king to Montrose telling him to proceed with plans to invade Scotland as this might scare the Scots into making concessions. 'Yet all was waved and put by, and voted to send presently'. In discussing instructions to be given to commissioners there was 'scarce a word but underwent a dispute'. In the end it was agreed to make the same demands as had been made at the Hague, but the extremists succeeded in getting it decided that the commissioners should not have power to conclude a treaty; any agreement would have to be ratified by parliament.[107]

The choice of commissioners to go to the king clearly indicates a compromise, three representing each of the main factions in the kirk party. Lothian, Libberton and Sir John Smith favoured Argyll's policy of making some concessions if necessary; Cassillis, Alexander Brodie of that Ilk and Alexander Jaffray adhered to the uncompromising extremists. Cassillis and Brodie had been already chosen by the kirk to represent it in the negotiations along with three ministers—John Livingstone, James Wood and George Hutcheson.[108] In the event the commissioners failed to leave before parliament met, and parliament added to their instructions. Charles was to be required to cancel any commissions he had granted to Montrose, to disclaim Ormond's treaty with the Irish catholics, and to swear never to tolerate catholicism. He was to acknowledge the lawfulness of the Scots parliaments held since 1641 and to agree (as his father had done) that all matters civil and ecclesiastical should be settled in parliament and the general assembly respectively. Once he had made these concessions he should be invited to Scotland, but he was to be told he would have to sign the covenants and a declaration promising to work to implement them and to impose presbyterian government and the Westminster standards in all his kingdoms. If possible Charles was to sign the covenants before he left Holland; at the latest he was to sign as soon as he landed in Scotland, for he would not be admitted to the exercise of his royal power before he did so. Finally, parliament ordered that the treaty should be limited to a maximum of forty days; it then prorogued itself (after a session lasting only two days) until 15 May, hoping that by then the results of the treaty would be known.[109]

Within days of these final instructions being given to the commissioners to negotiate with Charles II, Montrose returned to Scotland to attempt to overthrow the regime. Since the king had broken off the treaty at the Hague in May 1649 Montrose had been busy trying to raise men and money in Brandenburg, Denmark and Sweden.[110] As an advance party he had dispatched the earl of Kinnoull with about eighty officers and one hundred Danish soldiers, together with arms and ammunition. They had landed at Kirkwall in Orkney on 5 September and set about raising and training men while waiting for Montrose to join them with reinforcements. But as so often in the past the royalists weakened themselves by squabbling; Kinnoull's uncle, the earl of Morton, claimed to be deeply insulted at not being given command of the royalist force, as he was the most powerful man in Orkney. To placate him Kinnoull agreed to hand over the command until Montrose arrived. To make matters worse both Kinnoull and Morton died suddenly in November, but luckily Kinnoull's brother and heir soon arrived and took over command, holding the royalists together over the long winter. Montrose at last arrived, with about 1,200 men, in mid March 1650; Lord Eythin, his lieutenant general, was soon to follow with more men.[111]

It was not until Montrose reached Orkney that he received a letter the king had written to him in January explaining that he was reopening negotiations with the covenanters but wanted Montrose nonetheless to 'proceed in your business with your usuall courage and alacrity' in order to terrify the kirk party into making concessions. He promised to do his utmost to protect Montrose's interests, but the king's news left him in a precarious position.[112] If the king reached agreement with the Scots the price would certainly include orders to Montrose to withdraw from Scotland, and few royalists would be willing to join his invasion while the king was treating with the kirk party. But Montrose decided to proceed with his invasion, hoping by quick success to overthrow the regime before the king signed any agreement with it. The only alternative seemed to be to reconcile himself to more years of exile.

News of Kinnoull's landing in Orkney had reached Edinburgh on 27 September 1649. The committee of estates had immediately ordered David Leslie to send forces north; but he was also to ensure that the west coast was protected from the threat of royalist invasion from Ireland.[113] This latter fear had been aroused by the activities of Major General Sir George Monro. After he had fled to Holland on the fall of the Engagers Monro had been knighted by Charles II and sent to Ulster to organise a royalist revolt among the protestant settlers there. In this he at first had considerable success, and it was feared that he intended landing in Scotland. Many inhabitants of Ulster who would not join him fled to Scotland, where several hundred were recruited into Leslie's army. But not all the refugees were well inclined to the Scots regime; it was reported that some of them, along with Scots royalists, were trying to make their way north to join Kinnoull.[114] In the last months of 1649 the threat posed by Monro was removed, for his forces in Ulster were dispersed by Cromwell's army, but this sent a flood of malignant royalist refugees to Scotland.

David Leslie found great difficulty in gathering forces against Kinnoull, for there was little enthusiasm for a new civil war.[115] He had neither the men nor the equipment necessary to invade Orkney, and it was impossible to keep his forces in the north during the winter. He therefore retired southwards late in November, though some garrisons and a few troops of horse were left behind.[116]

THE TREATY OF BREDA AND THE DEATH OF MONTROSE

The Scots commissioners had their first meeting with the king at Breda on 19 March, and from the first Charles must have been encouraged by the obvious divisions among them. Lothian and Libberton had suggested that Hamilton, Lauderdale and other Engagers should be invited to take part in the treaty but the extremists had indignantly vetoed this. They were pleased when the moderates agreed that Cassillis should be preses or president of the commissioners, but this proved a miscalculation; as preses Cassillis could only vote if the votes of the other commissioners were equal, and of the other five only two (Brodie and Jaffray) were extremists. The moderates thus had a permanent majority. Admittedly the five kirk commissioners were all extremists, but they were anxious to avoid interfering in civil affairs. The extremists noted bitterly that Lothian and Libberton had private meetings with the king, and complained that Charles would have accepted all their demands if the moderates had not shown how eager they were to reach agreement with him.[117]

The main points on which the king stuck during the negotiations concerned his taking the covenants and disowning the treaty with the Irish, though he was anxious to convince the commissioners of his good intentions; 'The King strokes them till he can get into the saddle, and then he will make them feel his spurs',[118] which was exactly what many Scots feared. Charles replied on 17 April to the demands made of him by presenting his own demands; most of them were promptly refused. Three days later he announced his willingness to sign the declaration subjoined to the covenants, but, as the kirk commissioners were quick to note, he said nothing about signing the covenants themselves. Moreover he would not disown the Irish treaty, though in the end he did secretly promise that he would abandon it if, once he reached Scotland, parliament still desired him to do so. The forty days allowed for the treaty were now running out; on 29 April the state commissioners therefore hurriedly invited the king to Scotland in return for the concessions he had promised. He accepted the invitation on 1 May and the commissioners' secretary, James Dalrymple, was sent to Scotland to ask parliament to ratify the agreement.[118]

In issuing the invitation the anxiety of the commissioners to reach an agreement had led them to exceed their instructions; the king had not disowned the Irish treaty or agreed to sign the covenants. Though Cassillis and Brodie had signed the invitation to the king in their capacity as state commissioners (presumably because all were expected to sign once a majority had agreed to do so), as kirk commissioners they joined the three ministers in writing to the kirk urging it to do all it could to prevent the invitation from being ratified. Livingstone listed additional reasons, apart from the limited nature of the king's concessions, for his and his colleagues' dissatisfaction. It was obvious that Charles had made concessions for the wrong reasons, out of expediency rather than conviction, that he was acting 'rather as a politician than as a convert'. His real attitudes were revealed by his continued use of Anglican worship, by his 'balling and dancing till near day', by his suggestion that all parties, including Montrose and the Irish catholics, should combine in his service; he might have added also by his mistresses and bastards. Livingstone therefore denounced the state commissioners for issuing the invitation.[120]

In accepting Charles's limited concessions the state commissioners may have been influenced to some extent by fear and uncertainty concerning Montrose. In fact by the time the invitation was made Montrose was a defeated fugitive. On 9 April he had ordered his major general, Sir John Hurry (the former covenanting general) to land on the mainland with some of his forces, to prevent the covenanters of Sutherland from occupying Caithness. Montrose expected immediate help from the Mackays and Seaforth's Mackenzies, but though Seaforth had been generous in professions of goodwill to Montrose he had not accompanied him to Orkney and there is no evidence that he ordered his clansmen to cooperate. Lord Reay, chief of the Mackays, had been in prison in Edinburgh since the battle of Balvenie, and both clans were demoralised by that defeat. Few men from either clan joined Montrose. He had offers of assistance from further south, from Huntly, the Earl Marischal and John Middleton, but the committee of estates was keeping a close watch on them and other suspected royalists.[121]

Montrose soon joined Hurry on the mainland and advanced his forces to Carbisdale, on the border of Ross and Sutherland.[122] The committee of estates learned that Montrose had landed on 16 April and immediately ordered David Leslie to march against him.[123] A rendezvous of the army was arranged at Brechin on 25 April, and Archibald Strachan was sent to take command of the troops of horse that had wintered in the north. Strachan quickly gathered five troops (including the three that had fought at Balvenie the year before) and advanced into Ross with about 230 men. At Tain he held a council of war with Sutherland, Monro of Lemlair (who had returned to his allegiance as a covenanter after taking part in Pluscardine's rising) and other local covenanters. They decided that Strachan, with the troops of horse and a few hundred local footmen, should advance towards the royalist position.[124]

When Strachan was six or seven miles from Carbisdale on 27 April his scouts reported that a party of Montrose's horse was approaching. Strachan promptly hid all but one of his troops of horse; as he had hoped, the royalist party returned to Montrose and informed him that there was only one covenanting troop in the vicinity. He was, it appears, preparing to advance and attack this troop when all Strachan's horse appeared and fell on the royalists before they had time either to form up to resist the attack or to withdraw to the woods and hills. Many of those he had levied in Orkney fled almost at once, some of the Danes resisted for a time but then they too broke. The covenanting footmen soon arrived and joined the cavalry in cutting down the fleeing royalists. Of perhaps 1,200 men with Montrose, 400 to 500 were killed, 200 drowned in the River Shin and over 400 captured. The covenanters claimed that they lost only one trooper, who was drowned. Montrose himself escaped, but most of his officers were captured. On news of the defeat his remaining forces in Caithness withdrew to Orkney and from there escaped abroad.[125]

Thus ignominiously ended Montrose's last campaign, freeing the covenanters from the fear that he would again humiliate them in a civil war. In 1644–5 he had had the enthusiastic and experienced Irish to join with the clansmen in attacking the raw levies of the covenant. The Danish and German mercenaries he used in 1650 were no substitute for the Irish; and the covenanters, no longer trying to support armies in England and Ireland as well as in Scotland, could send veteran cavalry, completely confident that God would give them victory, against him. Even in 1644 Montrose had had difficulty in persuading royalist inclined clans to rise; in 1650, after they had been demoralised by long years of defeat, it had proved impossible.

About a week after the battle Montrose was captured by Neil Macleod of Assynt and delivered to David Leslie. Treated with ignominy on his long journey south, Montrose's dignified bearing won him considerable popular sympathy.[126] This was probably partly the result of the growing unpopularity of the rule of the kirk party; he would have found far less sympathy had he been captured in 1645 or 1646 when hatred of him was at its height. He reached Edinburgh on 18 May and was driven to the tolbooth tied to a cart driven by the hangman, while Argyll, Loudoun and Wariston watched from the windows of Moray House. Again his bearing softened the bitterness felt by many onlookers for the man previously held responsible for years of bloody civil war. Before he was brought before parliament he was warned that the king had reached agreement with the Scots at Breda, and that he should therefore 'be spairing in speaking to the King's disadvantag. . . in his own justifcation';[127] he therefore tried to justify himself without stating that he had acted under a commission from the king. This final service to his king, however, had no influence on his fate. No matter what justification he might have pleaded his fate was certain, for the covenanters were determined to have their revenge. Order was given that he should be executed on 21 May in accordance with the sentence passed on him in 1644. He was to be hanged, since this was held more disgraceful than beheading, and his head was then to be displayed over Edinburgh tolbooth, his limbs in Stirling, Glasgow, Perth and Aberdeen.[128]

Argyll abstained from taking any part in these proceedings against Montrose, a forbearance that Montrose's son repaid in 1661 by abstaining from voting for Argyll's execution.[129] There is no evidence that Argyll thought that Montrose did not deserve to die, no sign that he argued against the execution, but he probably did think it impolitic, as it might lead to the breakdown of the treaty with the king. Argyll's credit with the kirk party had already been undermined by his enthusiasm for bringing the king to Scotland and by rumours that he hoped to marry his daughter to the king,[130] and nothing he could have done could have saved Montrose. In these circumstances he judged it best to try to win the king's approval by having no part in Montrose's death while avoiding further offending the kirk party by not actively opposing the execution.

Montrose died with dignity and courage.[131] Argyll, remarking on 'the tragik end' (a surprisingly charitable phrase), regretted that Montrose knew 'how to goe out of this world, but nothing at all how to enter in ane other, not so much as once humblling himself to prayer at all on the scaffold'. He was to express a related sentiment shortly before his own execution in 1661, saying 'he would not die as a Roman braving death, but he would die as a Christian without being affrighted'.[132] This sums up many of the differences between the two men. Montrose was a sincere Christian, but religion did not play a central part in his life and thought. His ambitions were 'Roman', of this world, concerned with glory and honour, with true service to his king. He prepared for death as if it were essentially a matter of leaving this world. Argyll certainly did not lack worldly ambition, the wish to advance his clan and make himself the most powerful man in Scotland. But in spite of this religion, his long hours of private prayer and his personal relationship with God, formed the real centre of his life. He wished to die with dignity, but this was a matter of far less importance to him than his reception in the next world.

Some of Montrose's leading followers soon followed him to the scaffold. Sir John Hurry and Captain John Spottiswood (nephew of Sir Robert, executed after Philiphaugh) were beheaded on 29 May. Hurry died penitent, Spottiswood 'in a furey and rage, almost distracted of his witts'. Sir William Hay of Dalgety and Colonel William Sibbald both died unrepentent on 7 June. Finally, on 21 June Alexander Charteris was beheaded. Most of the common soldiers captured at or after Carbisdale were sent to serve in Scottish forces in France, though about forty Orkney men who had been forced to serve Montrose and had families dependent on them were allowed to return to their homes.[133]

The haste with which Montrose was executed, only three days after reaching Edinburgh, was probably connected with the negotiations with Charles II. Nothing he could have done would have helped Montrose, but it was judged best to present him with a *fait accompli* before he had time to intervene. Before signing the agreement of 1 May at Breda the king had probably received some sort of vague undertaking from the Scots commissioners (or perhaps from Argyll through his agent, William Murray) that Montrose would be allowed to disband and withdraw from Scotland, as he had done in 1646.[134] But such an arrangement would only have been acceptable to the kirk party if Montrose had been at the head of an army, threatening to repeat his exploits of 1644–5. Once he had been defeated and captured his fate was certain.

On 3 and 5 May Charles II had written letters and instructions to be carried to Montrose by Sir William Fleming. A public letter informed him that Charles had reached full agreement with his Scots subjects, and ordered him to lay down arms and withdraw himself and his forces from Scotland. A private letter promised that the king would do all he could to protect Montrose's interests; he hoped soon to be able to employ him again and meanwhile had set aside a large sum of money for his maintenance. Fleming was to explain to Montrose that agreement with the Scots seemed 'the only probable human means to recover our other kingdomes'. Montrose's venture 'hath not answered either his or our expectations'; through no fault of his own he had failed to invade Scotland as soon or with as large forces as had been hoped, and there was therefore no hope of reducing Scotland to obedience by force. Charles delayed the dispatch of these letters to Montrose; probably he wished to be sure that the Scottish parliament had ratified the agreement of 1 May before instructing Montrose to disband. On 8 May he gave Fleming a letter addressed to parliament stating that Montrose had been ordered to disband and asking that he and his followers be allowed to leave Scotland. The next day Charles added instructions to Fleming to ascertain whether or not parliament would confirm the 1 May agreement before he gave Montrose his orders to disband—and also, presumably, before he gave parliament the letter of 8 May. If parliament rejected the agreement, or appeared only to be negotiating so that the king would order Montrose to disband, then Fleming was to tell Montrose to remain in arms.[135]

On 12 May the king issued yet another set of instructions to Fleming, together with a new letter to parliament. The text of the letter has not survived, but it is clear from the outcome that in it the king to some extent disowned responsibility for Montrose's actions. It seems likely that the Scots commissioners had persuaded the king to substitute this new letter for that of 8 May, arguing that the earlier letter would cause offence and damage the king's cause, since in it he implicitly admitted that Montrose had invaded Scotland on his instructions. But rumours that Montrose had been defeated were now reaching Holland, and Charles was only prepared to disown Montrose (to please the Scots) if he was sure that this could not hurt Montrose. He therefore ordered Fleming only to deliver the letter disowning Montrose if he was still at the head of an army; if he had been defeated the letter was to be suppressed.[136]

It has usually been assumed that the letter which Charles, on 12 May, ordered Fleming to suppress if Montrose was defeated was the letter of 8 May, in which Charles had asked that Montrose be allowed to leave Scotland in safety;[137] but the natural interpretation is that the instructions of 12 May refer to the letter of 12 May. In other words Charles did not tell Fleming to suppress a letter which might have helped Montrose but a letter disowning him, a very different matter.

Whether Charles intended Fleming to deliver the letter of 8 May in place of that of 12 May if Montrose had been defeated is not clear. In the event it seems that Fleming did not reach Edinburgh until on or just before 25 May, some days after Montrose's execution. Allegations by later historians (but not by any contemporaries) that Fleming arrived before Montrose's death but then sat back and did nothing to save him are almost certainly unfounded.[138] That Montrose might be dead by the time Fleming landed was a circumstance that had not been allowed for in his instructions, and he evidently decided that since he was too late to do anything to help Montrose he could best serve the king's interests by delivering the letter of 12 May disowning Montrose to parliament, together with a copy of the letter of 5 May ordering Montrose to disband. According to a contemporary summary of the 12 May letter the king denied in it that he had been accessory to Montrose's invasion, and it is said that Argyll confirmed in parliament that this was so, stating that Lothian had written from Breda saying that Charles had said that he was not sorry that Montrose had been defeated as he had ordered him not to invade Scotland.[139] Whether these are accurate summaries of what Charles had written and said remains uncertain; it may well be that, since it could no longer harm Montrose, the extent to which Charles had disowned him was exaggerated to parliament to help to overcome the suspicions of those doubtful of the wisdom of treating with the king.

Although Charles had only agreed to disown Montrose provided this could not harm him, it was nonetheless a shabby reward for years of loyal service. But Montrose had implicitly accepted the risk of being thus disowned when he had proceeded with his invasion after Charles had clearly warned him that he regarded the invasion as no more than a threat to force the covenanters to make concessions at Breda. Once established in power in Scotland Charles hoped to be in a position to employ Montrose again. But the defeat and execution of Montrose before the king had time to intervene, and Fleming's subsequent delivery of the letter disowning Montrose, made Charles' sins of omission (his failure to insist on a clear guarantee of Montrose's safety before he reached agreement with the Scots on 1 May) and political manoeuverings appear as sins of commission, as if he had cynically disowned Montrose and abandoned him to his fate because he had become a political embarrassment likely to prejudice his treaty with the kirk party.

News of the agreement of 1 May had reached Edinburgh a few days before parliament met on 15 May. It was known that Montrose had been defeated and captured, so fear of him was no longer a consideration that would help the king to win concessions. Parliament promptly insisted that explanations must be added to the king's concessions to make them more explicit and binding; these were detailed in new instructions to the commissioners in Breda agreed on 17 May.[140] These stated uncompromisingly that only the king's complete acceptance of the demands formerly made could satisfy the kirk and kingdom; he had already agreed to follow the advice of parliament and the kirk, and this was the advice they now gave him. Only if the king accepted explanations to the agreement would the invitation to come to Scotland be ratified. The explanations included that all assurances made to the king were dependent on his completely satisfying church and state, and that undertakings to help him recover his English and Irish thrones did not bind Scotland to make war on his behalf until parliament and the general assembly had judged its lawfulness and necessity. All guilty under the first and second classes of the 1646 and 1649 acts of classes were to be banned from access to the king. Charles must sign the covenants as well as the declaration subjoined, and must disclaim the Irish treaty.[141]

The kirk also wrote to its commissioners in Breda of its exceeding dissatisfaction with Charles' concessions, especially with his trying to evade personal acceptance of the covenants. The new instructions from kirk and state were dispatched on 21 May; Arthur Erskine of Scottiscraig and James Dalrymple were sent north with copies in case the king had already sailed (his ship would make for the north to avoid interception by the English navy) while a Scots merchant took copies to Holland.[142]

Parliament was right to fear that Charles would try to come to Scotland before the invitation was ratified. The prince of Orange had provided a ship, the *Skidam*, and by 1 June all the Scots commissioners had gone on board except for Cassillis and Lothian, who remained on shore with the king. The new instructions from Scotland were then delivered, and those on board went ashore, determined to get satisfaction from the king before sailing. But they were diverted by bad weather, and when they reached the shore they found that Lothian had insisted on going on board with the king and many of his malignant supporters, in spite of the new instructions. Cassillis had then been persuaded to follow them. The moderates among the commissioners who had come ashore, Libberton and Smith, followed the nobles aboard, but Brodie, Jaffray and the three ministers at first refused. Livingstone in particular was determined not to sail for Scotland until Charles had given satisfaction, for otherwise 'we were taking along the plague of God to Scotland'. After some toing and froing all agreed to go on board again, though Livingstone only on the understanding that he would be allowed to go ashore if he wished; but once they were on board, the ship immediately sailed.[143]

With the new demands from Scotland the king had also received news of Montrose's death, but this did not deter him from sailing; probably he justified his continued dealings with those who had just executed the greatest of his supporters by the argument that a temporary alliance with the kirk party based on expediency was the best way to establish himself in power and thus put himself in a position to exact revenge eventually. The *Skidam* was delayed at Heligoland for several days, and there the Scots commissioners at last persuaded Charles to make the extra concessions demanded by parliament. They had been divided on whether to press the demands on him; Lothian and Libberton were for doing nothing until the king landed in Scotland, but the usual three to two majority of the moderates among the state commissioners (Cassillis being the non-voting preses) was reversed when Smith joined the extremists Brodie and Jaffray in insisting that the king give way. Charles at first said he would rather turn back,[144] but when the bluff failed he signed the concessions, though he did not sign the covenants themselves until the *Skidam* anchored at Speymouth on 23 June.[145]

A COVENANTED KING

The king landed at Garmouth the next day, and parliament and the kirk were informed that he had done all that was required of him 'for the outward part' except that he was still accompanied by malignants.[146] The qualification 'for the outward part' removed all sense of triumph from the kirk party's achievement. It was a hollow victory since it was obvious that the king had complied unwillingly and would revoke his concessions if he was ever given a chance of doing so. Several of the commissioners, at the time or in retrospect, believed that they had acted wrongly. Cassillis was unhappy at the extra concessions forced from the king. Livingstone lamented 'the guilt, not of the commissioners only, but of the whole kingdom, of the State, yea, of the Church' in extorting oaths from the king though they knew that they were no evidence of a change of heart. Jaffray thought 'we did sinfully both entangle and engage both the nation and ourselves, and that poor young prince to whom we were sent; making him sign and swear a covenant, which we knew, from clear and demonstrable reasons, that he hated in his heart'. Jaffray had gone so far as to urge

Charles not to sign the covenants if his heart was not satisfied.[147]

While the king was on his way to Scotland parliament had continued to argue about policy, especially about attitudes to the king's malignant supporters and whether war should be made on England immediately. Callander had arrived in Edinburgh in May, perhaps sent by the king to see if such a notorious former Engager would be allowed to remain there; the nobles in parliament favoured allowing him to stay, but the votes of the lairds and burgesses brought about his expulsion.[148] The greatest disputes were over the need for an immediate levy to reinforce the army. The nobility argued for a new levy but the other estates opposed it, fearing that a new army would tend to favour the king; instead they demanded a more stringent purging of the army already on foot, and even got a committee appointed to purge parliament itself. Nothing came of this, but on 21 June it was voted that a committee to purge the army be established.[149]

By this time, however, it was becoming clear that the English commonwealth was not going to give the Scots time to consider at leisure whether to invade England or not. Cromwell had been appointed general in place of Fairfax, who refused to lead an attack on Scotland; as the Scots had invaded England in 1648 and were now preparing a new invasion, Cromwell had satisfied himself that an attack on them would be a defensive war.[150] The Scots parliament wrote rather naively to its English counterpart enquiring whether it intended to invade Scotland, hopefully pointing out that under the 1641 peace treaty this would require three months' notice,[151] but it also prudently pressed on with the work of fortifying Leith and Edinburgh.[152] Opposition to new levies quickly collapsed once it became clear that English invasion was likely; only six votes were cast against an act of levy passed on 25 June. Orders for a second levy were given a week later. Altogether over 36,000 men were to be raised to join the few thousand already in arms under David Leslie. The kirk evidently agreed to the levies, but suspicion remained that it would be impossible to keep such a large force free from malignants who would fight the English for the wrong reasons, through nationalism and the wish to restore the king instead of to advance the cause of the covenants and a covenanted king.[153]

News that the king had landed was generally greeted with joy; his landing was officially celebrated in Edinburgh with ringing of bells and firing of salutes. But the kirk party was too suspicious to celebrate wholeheartedly; the popular reaction to the king's arrival seemed excessive. There was dancing for most of the night in the streets of Edinburgh and the 'pure kaill wyfes at the Trone' made bonfires with their baskets and stools.[154] But how many were greeting the arrival of the king whom they hoped would overthrow the kirk party, rather than the alliance between king and kirk party?

From Bog of Gight on 26 June Charles sent to Argyll to assure him of his friendship and to ask him to come north as soon as possible; whatever secret contacts there had been between the two men they had been sufficient for the king now to look to Argyll for help. He asked him to ensure that none of those who had come with him from Holland should be expelled; or at least that he should be notified privately of any who must leave instead of being humilated by the public removal of his friends. But Argyll's resolution in parliament in favour of delaying the removal of malignants from the king was defeated. At this he was 'exceedingly unsatisfied', but could do nothing to prevent both parliament and the kirk sending to the king to persuade him to abandon malignant company. In the end he was allowed to retain some of his English malignant friends (including the duke of Buckingham), but all the prominent Scots were forced to leave. Some, including Hamilton and Lauderdale, managed to remain in Scotland, but they were not allowed to approach either the court or the army; Carnwath unwisely appeared in Edinburgh and was promptly imprisoned.[155]

On 4 July parliament unanimously ratified the treaty with the king, and declared that he should at once enter into the exercise of his royal power; he was to be crowned on 15 August (the kirk was already busy revising the coronation ceremonies to remove 'superstitious solemnities'), to which date parliament prorogued itself after appointing a committee of estates by whose advice Charles was to govern.[156] In practice the fact that the king had been declared to have entered into his government made no difference to him. After he had given way at Falkland to the purging of his court he had no one whom he could trust to consult, and the committee of estates ruled the country without reference to him. He was allowed some freedom of movement but the kirk party feared that he might prove too popular if allowed to come to the capital or the army; he was told he could come to the army when the condition of affairs required it, but no indication was given of when this was likely to be.[157] The kirk was equally suspicious. In a private meeting before the general assembly Livingstone told leading ministers of Charles' conduct in Holland, and especially of how he had insisted on taking communion kneeling. It was decided to keep this and other uncomfortable facts about the new covenanted king secret from the assembly, lest they lead it to reject the treaty with him.[158]

On 22 July Cromwell crossed the Tweed with about 16,000 men. Leven had tried to lay down his office as general on account of his age and infirmity but parliament insisted that he remain in office because of his great reputation; David Leslie therefore continued to command the army as his deputy. By the end of July he had about 15,000 men with whom to oppose the English.[159] Many were ill-armed and untrained, but their morale was high; there was far more enthusiasm for a war against English invaders than there had been a few months before for a civil war against Montrose. Leslie had decided on his strategy some time before; a line between Leith and Holyroodhouse had been strongly fortified and the Scots army retired behind this, Berwickshire and East Lothian having been stripped of food and other supplies likely to be of use to Cromwell before being abandoned. The English would either have to make a frontal attack on Leslie's fortified position or try to outflank it by marching between Edinburgh and the Pentland Hills; if they took the latter course they would risk being attacked in flank themselves or having their supply routes cut.

The Scots strategy meant that at first Cromwell met with very little opposition, and he reached Musselburgh on 28 July. The next day he reconnoitred the defences, attempting without success to tempt the Scots into sallying out to attack him in the open. When this failed he withdrew, and during his retreat Scots cavalry attacked his rearguard and raided his camp at Musselburgh.[160] After writing to the kirk beseeching it to 'in the bowels of Christ, think it possible you may be mistaken' in opposing him Cromwell withdrew to Dunbar to provision his army. Not surprisingly the kirk indignantly rejected the idea that it might be wrong—'Would you have us to be scepticks in our religion'?[161]

The first round of the campaign had clearly gone to the Scots, but the kirk party continued to weaken itself by internal disputes over the army and the position of the king. On 28 July Wariston proposed that a sub-committee be appointed to meet with senior army officers to decide how to dispose of the forces; David Leslie strongly opposed the idea, but two days later Wariston got his way.[162] Meanwhile Charles was growing increasingly discontented at his position as a figurehead. A proclamation was issued in his name in which he explained how he had been enlightened by God and had taken the covenants; he was willing to make a settlement in England based on the propositons of Newcastle and would pardon all except regicides. But the king was only shown the proclamation after it had been published.[163] Lothian urged that the king be invited to come to the army, but a decision was delayed, whereupon he warned that the king might come of his own accord.[164]

This was exactly what happened. Having received an invitation from some officers of the army and been encouraged by Eglinton, Charles appeared at Leith the next day. His arrival was greeted by most of the army with great joy, leading Wariston to bewail that the royal presence was giving the army 'carnal confidence' outweighing confidence in God, an ominous sign. Charles' appearance threw the committee of estates into confusion, as it feared that his presence would encourage many malignants to come to the army, which might be brought to serve the cause of the king instead of that of God. He was too popular for the kirk party to allow him to remain. Wariston, Brodie, other members of the committee and the kirk informed him that if he stayed with the army he would discourage the godly from fighting and rouse the wrath of God, who was jealous of his glory and would be angered if rivalled in popularity by the king. Eventually Charles reluctantly consented to leave; he could not yet afford to break with the kirk party. On 2 August, 'sore against his auen mynd' he left Leith for Dunfermline.[165]

The kirk party was badly shaken by the evidence of the king's popularity. A new proclamation ordered the removal of all malignants from the army, and between 2 and 5 August about eighty officers were purged.[166] Wariston led those who demanded a far more comprehensive purge of all ranks, no matter how much this reduced the strength of the army; had not the example of Carbisdale been added to that Balvenie in showing that God would give small armies victory over great ones provided the former were godly enough? Reliance on big battalions revealed again the sin of carnal confidence. As for the English, God would 'by a few muddle them away', throwing them into confusion so that a few of the godly could rout them. Wariston had the support of Sir John Cheisly, of Archibald Strachan and Gilbert Ker and of the more extreme ministers led by Patrick Gillespie. But opposition was strong. Both Argyll and Leslie were against too thorough a purge, and significantly they were supported by some of the ministers who had been the recognised leaders of the kirk throughout the 1640s—David Dickson, Andrew Cant and Robert Douglas now joined the moderates of the kirk party in arguing that the religious qualifications of those who were to be privileged to fight for the cause should not be set too high. Yet in the end Wariston got his way, and by far the most thorough purge of the army yet undertaken began on 16 August. By the end of the month several thousand officers and men had been expelled, fatally weakening and demoralising the army; this was a remarkable testimony to the extremists' confidence in God and lack of worldly wisdom.[167]

Arguments over strategy and control of the army also persisted. Many of the king's supporters wanted the army to march into England by way of Carlisle, hoping to draw Cromwell out of Scotland after them, but the extremists were suspicious of the motives behind this proposal; was not the desire to enter England influenced by hopes that once there the army would be joined by the king's malignant and royalist allies? Wariston argued that even though the English had invaded Scotland the justice of invading England was not clear. The idea was therefore abandoned and Leslie was allowed to continue his policy of remaining on the defensive in prepared positions. He also got his own way over control of the army. The committee which sat with the officers to consider the disposal of forces was abolished on 5 August, and Wariston and Cheisly were blamed for hindering the general officers in carrying out their duties.[168]

The fears raised by the popularity of the king had led to thorough purging. They probably also occasioned the revival of the Western Association. Nominally the new association was formed to protect the western shires from the English,[169] but it was also inspired by fear that Charles and the malignants would win control of the army (as the Engagers had done in 1648); the west was now preparing to oppose malignant Scots as well as sectarian English. Some at least of the extremists of the kirk party were moving towards the conclusion that alliance with the king would inevitably in the end mean the triumph of the malignants, so that to fight for the king would do more harm than good. Much as they might hate Cromwell and Independency, they might be lesser evils than king and malignancy. In July Wariston, Strachan, Ker and others of their faction had secret talks with officers of Cromwell's army, expressing their dislike of seeming to be working in alliance with malignants.[170]

To try to allay such fears among the extremists that Charles would revert to malignancy it was decided to draw up a new declaration for him to sign. Among added humiliations he was to express regrets for the faults of his father, the idolatry of his mother and his own early sins. The committee of estates and the kirk both sent commissioners to Dunfermline to demand that Charles sign the declaration, though Robert Douglas (moderator of the commission of the kirk) opposed the declaration and refused to press the king to sign. Charles bluntly refused to accept the declaration, whereupon some of the extremist army officers stated that they would not fight unless their scruples were removed. To try to satisfy them the kirk declared that in supporting the war against the English it was not espousing the cause of the malignant party, and that it would not own the king and his interest unless he owned the cause of God. The committee of estates gave its support to this statement but it was agreed that it should be kept secret, being shown only to the officers who were demanding satisfaction, as many moderates thought that it was too severe. But the extremists proceeded to publish it.[171]

Thus the first results of the new declaration pressed on the king were the opposite of those intended, emphasising the deep divisions among Scots as to what they were fighting for. Charles held a meeting of his privy council (the first since his arrival in Scotland) to advise him what to do. It proposed that he should give way and sign the declaration, though first trying to get some changes made in it. But the council also advised the king to move to Perth, no doubt because he would there be well placed to negotiate with the royalists of the north, and to retreat among them if he decided to break with the kirk party.[172] The kirk agreed to some changes in the declaration, but not enough to satisfy the king, and new demands were made on him for a further purge of his household. A petition from some officers renounced any intention of fighting for a malignant cause and demanded purging of the army. With church, state and part of the army all threatening to desert the king unless he signed, the collapse of the alliance of expediency between him and the kirk party seemed at hand. Argyll had opposed the declaration but now urged Charles to sign it as the only way to prevent fatal divisions, assuring Charles that once he entered England he would have more freedom; for the time being it would be best to submit to the extremists, the madmen.[173]

In spite of this the king prepared to leave for Perth without signing, asking that all forces being raised in the north be assembled at Stirling. Not surprisingly the committee of estates refused to allow this, for it was obvious that Charles was hoping to form a northern army loyal to his interests.[174] But at the last minute, on 16 August when Charles was 'readie for hors bak', about to leave Dunfermline for Perth, new commissioners from the kirk arrived. After a long conference the king gave way and signed; but he then immediately left for Perth.[175] He had not abandoned hope of creating a royalist army, and now signed yet another piece of paper to which he had no intention of adhering in the hope of lulling the suspicions of the kirk party for a time.

The English invasion had provided a convenient excuse for postponing the coronation;[176] if the kirk party came to break with the king it would be easier to disown him if he had not been crowned. Refused permission to visit his capital or his army, with his crown withheld, the position of the king was not enviable. With his household purged of friends and packed with spies Charles had difficulty even in writing private letters, because 'evre since I came hether I have bine so narowly watched'; 'I dare not say any more for they are so watchful over me that I doe nothing but they observe it'. When he wished to send a messenger to Ireland he and his few remaining trusted servants had to hold a secret meeting at night when the rest of the court was asleep.[177]

On 11 August Cromwell advanced from Dunbar, probing westwards south of Edinburgh and then turning northwards. After several hard-fought minor engagements he retired on 27 August, first to Musselburgh, then to Dunbar. His army had suffered heavy losses from sickness in unusually bad weather, and he was again short of supplies. This time the whole Scottish army (though it too was short of supplies) followed close on the heels of the English, and established itself on Doon Hill a few miles south of Dunbar, commanding the road to Berwick which ran between the hill and the sea. Further down the coast Scots forces blocked the road at Cockburn spath. If Cromwell tried to withdraw into England he would be delayed at Cockburnspath while the Scots army on Doon Hill fell on his army in flank and rear.[178]

Cromwell's position if attacked in Dunbar was strong, but he could not afford to remain there on the defensive for long, cut off from all but seaborne supplies. 'We are', he wrote on 2 September, 'upon an engagement very difficult. The enemy hath blocked up our way... through which we cannot get almost without a miracle. He lieth so upon the hills that we know not how to come that way without difficutly'.[179] The Scots by now had nearly twice as many men as Cromwell, over 20,000 to his 11,000. It seemed that they only had to wait on Doon Hill until shortage of supplies forced the English to try to slip past them, and then to fall on them. But though David Leslie might have been content to do this the committee of estates and the ministers were impatient, and it was evidently on their advice and orders that he moved his army off the hill on 2 September to straddle the Berwick road along the Brox Burn and try to capture Broxmouth House;[180] Leslie later stated that he had not had 'the absolut command' of the army before the battle.[181] The move from the hill was not quite so foolish as it is often represented as having been. After pursuing Cromwell back to Dunbar with an army twice the strength of his it was not only fanatics who thought that the moment of victory had come and that Leslie should retain the initiative by preparing to attack the English before they had time to fortify their position. Moreover, to wait on Doon Hill until the English chose to leave Dunbar might well have proved fatal; by great efforts 20,000 Scots had been gathered, but they would soon have begun to melt away through sickness and desertion if left on the bleak hillside exposed to the wind and rain. With their great numerical superiority they were confident that they could meet the English in open battle. They thought they had Cromwell on the run, and when they moved off the hill they little expected that he would turn and attack them. English captured by the Scots found them—including Leslie himself—completely sure of victory. Leslie had certainly wished to remain on the hill, but there is no evidence that he opposed the move with much vigour or thought it likely to be disastrous. After the battle he blamed his defeat on the slackness of his men in failing to stand to arms on the night of 2–3

September, and on the failure of officers to stay with their men.[182] The cause of these failings was doubtless the purging of the past few weeks which had left the army dangerously short of experienced junior officers. In a wet and stormy night too many officers left their men, and when Cromwell attacked at dawn many of the Scots were caught off their guard and without their officers.

At four o'clock on the morning of 3 September Cromwell's cavalry crossed the Brox Burn and fell on the Scots right wing between the Berwick road and the sea. The Scots were soon driven back, their front swinging round until it was parallel to the road, their backs to Doon Hill. After a time the cavalry broke and fled, and the English closed in on the infantry. The Scots foot, many of them new levies with no experience, proved no match for Cromwell's veterans; some regiments surrendered, others fought almost to the last man. About 4,000 Scots were killed and 10,000 captured while Leslie fled to Edinburgh with about 4,000 men.[183] Nearly 200 Scots colours were captured to be added to about eighty-five taken two years before at Preston.[184]

With considerable insight Cromwell predicted the likely result of the battle. 'Surely it's probable the Kirk has done their do. I believe their King will set upon his own score now, wherein he will find many friends. . .'[185]

CHAPTER FIVE

The Cromwellian Conquest, September 1650–December 1651

GROWING OPPOSITION TO THE REGIME: THE START

News of the disaster at Dunbar, brought by David Leslie and his fleeing men, caused panic in Edinburgh and a hasty retreat towards Stirling began at once. The burgh magistrates and many inhabitants joined in the flight, though perhaps more left for fear of being branded as compliers with the enemy than through fear of the English. The kirk session of South Leith did not meet again for more than a year since the minister and most of the 'honest inhabitants' had fled, while no marriages took place in Edinburgh 'for manie months becaus there was no pastours remaining in the citie'. Many local ministers took refuge in the castle but Leven, its governor, retired to Stirling; the castle's garrison was therefore left to resist the English under his deputy, Lieutenant Walter Dundas, younger of that Ilk.[1]

An emergency meeting of the committee of estates at Stirling on 5 September dispatched urgent orders to the shires for new levies, and attempted to organise resistance to the English south of the Forth. A few weeks before the Western Association had offered to raise larger levies than those which had been ordered at that time; in return it had apparently demanded that these forces should form a virtually independent army under commanders acceptable to the association. The committee of estates now accepted this offer and dispatched Colonels Archibald Strachan and Gilbert Ker to the west with Sir John Cheisly. Colonel Robert Halket soon joined them, which meant that the three military heroes of the kirk party were now commanding the army of the Western Association. Allowing this was to prove unwise, as in effect it gave the extremists of the kirk party their own army, but at the time the need to raise forces to oppose the victorious English outweighed all other considerations. Sending Strachan and Ker to the west also had the advantage of preventing them quarrelling with David Leslie, for they blamed him for the defeat at Dunbar and refused to obey his orders. But their appointment to command the western army inevitably alienated those nobles and lairds who believed themselves to be the natural leaders of such local forces. Eglinton was busy raising men on his estates, but disbanded and left rather than serve under such upstarts.[2] In 1648 the forces raised in the west to overthrow the Engagers had been led by nobles and senior officers; the new army of the Western Association had no noble support, no officers above the rank of colonel, and very limited support among the larger lairds. Its strength lay in the enthusiasm of many ministers, and of their supporters among lesser lairds, heritors, burgesses and farmers.

In the face of widespread criticism of his conduct at Dunbar David Leslie tried to resign, but the committee of estates refused to allow this; there might be doubts about his ability but there was no one generally acceptable to replace him, and the king's advice that arguing about responsibility for Dunbar would lead only to discord and further defeat was timely.[3] But the need to build a new army round the few thousand men that Leslie had managed to keep together reopened more urgently than before the divisive question of the qualifications of those who should be allowed to serve. To the king and his supporters, and to an increasing number of moderates in the kirk party, it seemed obvious that purging had failed. Engagers and malignants should therefore now be admitted to serve in defending their country. The extremists argued that on the contrary Dunbar had proved their point; a large and inadequately purged army had been defeated by an English army of half its size, clear proof that numbers alone were not enough to bring victory. But few found this argument convincing, and the defeat was therefore a great blow to the prestige of the kirk party; most Scots put the blame on its purging and interference in military matters. Nonetheless the extremists stubbornly demanded even more thorough purging of both army and court. As support for them in the country dwindled it became ever more urgent for them to exclude all their enemies from any position from which they could challenge the power of the kirk party.

The first meeting of the commission of the kirk after the flight from Edinburgh was not held until 11 September, but some days before that a few extremist ministers met and agreed on a paper of reasons for a fast, which they then sent to the presbyteries. The main causes of the Lord's anger, they decided, included the continued ignorance and profanity of most Scots, the sins of the king's family (which he had not fully repented), and his behaviour in bringing many malignants with him to Scotland. The attitude of senior officers 'who thought that we could not be served but by ane numerous armie' was condemned, together with the owning of the king's quarrel by many without clearly subordinating it to religion and the liberties of the kingdom. When the commission met it approved this paper, probably partly for fear of causing divisions by rejecting it after it had been distributed to the presbyteries. A suggestion by the king that Engagers should be employed in the army was refused; only individuals who had given full satisfaction might be admitted. Further purging of Charles' household was demanded and the sins of the country and its rulers were denounced, especially the king's guiltiness in taking the covenants 'vpon politick interests, for gaining a crowne to him selfe rather than to advance Religion and righteousnesse'.[4] But though the commission in some respects thus supported the extremists, and declared its approval of the work of Strachan and Ker, it was worried by the fact that many of the more godly of the officers and men of the main army at Stirling were leaving to join the westerners without orders.[5] Moreover, many ministers both on and off the commission disapproved of its extreme statements. Ministers in Fife refused to read the reasons for a fast in their kirks, complaining of the presumption of the few ministers who had sent it to the presbyteries, and the synod of Fife declared in favour of a more general employment of Engagers in the army.[6]

The increasing power of the western army and the refusal of the kirk party to compromise meant that the king at first derived little or no benefit from Dunbar, though he was reported to have rejoiced at the defeat of his 'enemies' there. Royalists, both English and Scots, did the same. 'Upon the Route at Dunbarr' noted one of Cromwell's officers, 'the royall partie were much comforted in seeinge us destroy their enemy, as well as ours'.[7] On the day of the battle Charles had written to the Netherlands lamenting his plight: 'nothing could have confirmed me more to the Church of England then being here seing theire hipocrisy'. He asked the prince of Orange to 'send hether a smack or a hering buss with five or six men', to stay in Montrose harbour on the pretext of waiting to carry a messenger to Holland.[8] The king was ensuring that if his position became intolerable he could escape abroad. Argyll now spent most of his time with Charles at Perth, trying to persuade him to submit entirely to his influence. He well knew that his future power depended on this, for the kirk party no longer trusted him and the royalists would never forgive him for the part he had played in the troubles. On the pretext that the honours of Scotland (crown, sword and sceptre) were not safe in Perth, Argyll persuaded the king and committee of estates to entrust them to his care. He then secretly sent them to Balloch Castle on Loch Tay. On 24 September he got Charles to agree to create him a duke, a knight of the garter and a gentleman of the bedchamber whenever Argyll thought fit.[9] But in spite of such outward signs of royal favour Argyll must have realised what events were soon to prove: that the king still hated and distrusted him.

Late in September the committee of estates ordered the purging of twenty-four persons from the king's household; most of his few remaining personal servants and friends were to be expelled.[10] This was the last straw that decided Charles to flee and either raise a royalist army or escape to Holland. He had allied himself to the kirk party, in spite of its humiliating demands, because this seemed the most likely way of regaining his thrones. Dunbar had made it clear that the kirk party was incapable of helping him effectively, so Charles opened secret negotiations with various royalists scattered in the north. A plot for a *coup d'etat* on 3 October was organised. On that day the king's horse-guard was due to be purged, and the guards were to arrest the purgers (including Wariston and Brodie) and declare for the king. Meanwhile he was to have left Perth, ostensibly to go hawking, and Highlanders who had gradually been infiltrated into the burgh were to seize it, and would be joined by the earl of Atholl and other royalists. Huntly, Airlie, Lord Ogilvie, Marischal and Middleton were to hold separate royalist rendezvous while Lord Dudhope seized Dundee. With nearly all David Leslie's army gathered at Stirling only three weak regiments of horse quartered in Angus under Robert Montgomery (Eglinton's son) would be available north of the Tay to oppose the royalists.[11]

However, the plot was thrown into confusion by the king's indecision. The day before the rising was due to take place Charles let the duke of Buckingham into the secret, and he in turn told Lord Wilmont. These English nobles then combined to persuade him not to involve himself in such a rash venture. Orders were therefore sent cancelling the rising, but by this time rumours about the plot were circulating and those involved in it began to fear that their activities would be discovered and punished. They demanded that the king act, urging that unless he did so the kirk party would imprison him (or even hand him over to Cromwell) and hang his servants. Under this pressure Charles changed his mind again, and on the night of 3–4 October he sent to some of his supporters asking for advice; but before they could answer he suddenly left Perth with a few servants. He was probably still undecided as to whether to join the royalists or flee to Holland; only two days before he had written to one of his agents arranging that a considerable sum of money be sent to Holland for his use. Near Dundee he met Lord Dudhope, who took him to Cortachy Castle at the mouth of Glen Clova. Later he retired up the glen with a few Highlanders and others who had joined him, and spent the night at Clova.[12]

The king's orders and counter-orders had created confusion among royalists. Erskine of Dun, not knowing that the king had cancelled the rising planned for 3 October, had approached Perth on that day with other royalists, but had not sufficient forces for an attack. Next day they heard of Charles' flight and marched after him to Cortachy, from where they appealed to Middleton to join them.[13]

As soon as it had been realised in Perth that the king had fled, Loudoun had summoned a meeting of all available members of the committee of estates and other 'well affected' persons. They decided to send Sir Charles Erskine of Scottiscraig and others to find Charles and tell him of the committee's grief and amazement at his behaviour. He was to be begged to return and assured of the loyalty to him of the committee and the army. Once he returned it could be resolved, with his advice, how to restore him to his other thrones.[14] Clearly submission and apology would be expected of the king, but the committee also seemed to promise that he would be more consulted about affairs than previously. Officers sent by Robert Montgomery were first to find the king, on the morning of 5 October 'laying in a nastie roume. . . ouer weiried and werey fearfull'. Scottiscraig soon joined them and Charles was persuaded to return to Perth.[15]

On news of the king's submission most of the royalists who had been gathering in arms disbanded; two hundred Fife royalists who had been making for the Earl Marischal's stronghold of Dunnottar returned to their homes, and the king's horse-guard, which had been moving to join the royalists of Atholl, turned back. The earl of Atholl was said to have had a thousand men in arms, but the king ordered him to disband.[16] On 7 October the king apologised to the committee of estates for his actions, claiming that he had been led astray by evil counsel and fear that his person was in danger. But even in making this submission Charles gained an important concession. It was the first time that he had been permitted to be present at a meeting of the committee, and from this time onwards he was allowed to attend all meetings. Thus his abortive flight, 'the Start' as it soon became known, 'proved, contrary to the expectation of wise men, very much to his majesty's advantage'. However angry the committee might be at his conduct, it could not afford to drive him to break with the kirk party, for by this time it was only the claim to be acting in the king's name that allowed it to remain in power.[17]

The regime also indicated that it recognised its own weakness by showing leniency towards the royalists. Many of them refused to disband until an act of indemnity had been passed; several covenanters had been killed in a skirmish. The committee at first agreed to an indemnity for the men of Atholl only, and sent Sir John Brown of Fordell with forces against the other royalists. The Atholl men duly disbanded but on 21 October Sir David Ogilvie fell on Sir John Brown's regiment at Newtyle in Angus and scattered it. The committee therefore instructed David Leslie to proceed to

Angus to disperse the rebels, taking with him all forces north of the Forth except those necessary to protect Stirling and Fife from the English. On 24 October Leslie passed through Perth with 3,000 horsemen.[18]

Two days before, Middleton had sent Lord Ogilvie and Major General Jonas van Druschke (a Dutch mercenary) to the king to promise to obey his orders. He also wrote to Leslie explaining the grievances of the royalists; as Scotsmen they wished to be allowed to fight against the English and were willing to fight under his command; they had no wish for civil war. Middleton enclosed a copy of what became known as the 'northern band', signed by Huntly, Atholl, Seaforth, Middleton, Sir George Monro, Mackenzie of Pluscardine, van Druschke and other royalists; they bound themselves not to disband without common consent but stressed that they were not trying to create divisions in the country, and swore to maintain religion as established in Scotland, the solemn league and covenant, and the freedom of subjects.[19]

The kirk party rightly suspected that this declaration of good intentions was no more sincere than the king's own promises, and insisted that Charles send positive orders to the royalists to disband; but in order to persuade the rebels to submit without a fight it was conceded that they should have the benefit of an act of indemnity similar to that granted to the Atholl men. In a treaty with Leslie signed at Strathbogie on 4 November the royalists agreed to lay down arms.[20]

The agreement was timely, for it allowed David Leslie to hurry his forces south to deal with a new threat to the authority of the committee of estates from (both geographically and politically) the opposite quarter, from the extremists of the south-west.

THE REMONSTRANCE AND THE COLLAPSE OF THE WESTERN ASSOCIATION

Meanwhile, luckily for the quarrelling Scots, Cromwell was not strong enough to attack their position behind the Forth; his victory at Dunbar had not cured his shortages of men and supplies. On occupying Edinburgh he had invited the burgh's ministers to come out of the castle, promising them freedom of worship (though not freedom to rail or 'overtop the civil power'), but they had refused, whereupon he entered on a written controversy with them and the garrison commander over the merits of their respective causes. On 17 September he advanced to within a mile of Stirling but, failing to lure the Scots out to fight, retired a few days later. He then had boats collected as if he intended a landing in Fife, but this too came to nothing. In mid-October he briefly occupied Glasgow but then withdrew.

The object of this excursion was probably to test opinion among the extremists of the Western Association. The visit was well timed from this point of view, for the Start and the risings of the royalists in the north had scandalised many in the west, dispelling any faith that remained in the promises of the king for whom they were nominally fighting. Cromwell must have been satisfied with what he learnt from his march west, for as he advanced the western army had moved south towards Dumfries.[21] This may have been partly a response to reports that English forces were gathering near Carlisle as if for an invasion,[22] but is seems that the westerners were also motivated by a wish to avoid having to fight Cromwell. This was the result not of fear but of doubt; was it right to oppose Cromwell in alliance with a malignant king? Cromwell sent to Strachan and Ker offering to negotiate, but it seems that though they were willing to talk with him they were restrained from doing so by Wariston and Cheisly. However, Cromwell had confirmed that he would probably meet little active resistance in the west, and after he returned to Edinburgh Strachan entered into a written discussion with him. The committee of estates soon learnt of this but, anxious not to antagnonise the westerners, refused to let David Leslie punish this near treason. Instead commissioners were sent to try to persuade the westerners to co-operate with the main army at Stirling against the common enemy.[23] There can however have been little hope of success, for by this time the more extreme of the westerners had in effect disowned the king.

The westerners had become increasingly vocal and critical of the regime during October. On 2 October the synod of Glasgow and Ayr sent a remonstrance (inspired by Patrick Gillespie and James Guthrie) to the committee of estates, lamenting the conduct of both church and state towards the king, especially in admitting him (in name at least) to the exercise of his royal govemment before sufficient trial had been made of his sincerity.[24] News of the Start reinforced belief that the cause of God was being betrayed, and many of the westerners met in Dumfries to discuss the situation while Cromwell was in Glasgow. On 17 October they approved a remonstrance of the gentlemen, commanders and ministers attending the forces of the west.

This new remonstrance was partly based on the declaration of the kirk of 13 August (threatening to disown the king's cause unless he signed the declaration that had been submitted to him), partly on the reasons for a fast issued after Dunbar, and partly on the Glasgow and Ayr remonstrance, but it went further than any of these papers. The greatest sin of the land discovered by the 'remonstrants' was the signing of a treaty with Charles II without evidence of a change of heart in him. He had shown his insincerity by supporting Montrose and the treaty with the Irish papists, by his suggestion that malignants be employed in the army and by the Start. The remonstrants therefore disclaimed all the guilt and sins of the king and his house, renouncing his interest in the quarrel with the English. The committee of estates was denounced as guilty of an intention of invading England and imposing a king on a kingdom which was not subordinate to Scotland in a war which had not been declared lawful by either parliament or the general assembly. Many breaches of the covenants were detailed; insufficient purging, the oppression and covetousness of the rulers of the land, who had used public service for dishonest and private gain. Finally, the remonstrants disclaimed any intention of falling into the opposite error from allying themselves with malignants, that of following in the footsteps of the English sectaries; they would not change the fundamental government of the kingdom or undertake 'any levelling way'.[25]

Thus though the remonstrants still accepted Charles as king of Scotland they believed that he should not be allowed power until he proved himself worthy. They would fight to expel English invaders for religious and national reasons, but denied that Scots had any right to impose a king on England. In effect, though they would never have admitted it, the remonstrants were, at least temporarily, abandoning the claim that Scotland was bound by the solemn league and covenant to impose her religion on England. As in 1648 those who opposed the imposition of a malignant king on England out of fear of a royalist triumph found that, whether they liked it or not, they were implicitly accepting the triumph of the Independents in England.

The western remonstrance was probably mainly the work of Patrick Gillespie; Wariston and James Guthrie were both present in Dumfries and approved of it, but both later denied having had a hand in drafting it. It was said that one of the reasons for the remonstrance's outspokenness was to still Strachan's scruples at opposing Cromwell. If this was so the attempt was a failure, for Strachan evidently refused to accept the remonstrance,[26] and within a few weeks he gave up (or was deprived of) his command in the western army. But the intentions of the remonstrance had been far wider than the satisfying of one man. It was a declaration of faith by the godly who refused to compromise either with malignants or with Independents, and put their faith in the victory that God would surely bring them and their army.

It is hard to judge how widespread support for the western remonstrance was. No noble countenanced it. A few lairds emerged as its principal lay exponents—Campbell of Cesnok, Cunningham of Cunninghamhead, Maxwell of Nether Pollock, Mure of Glanderston, Dalrymple of Stair and

Sir John Cheisly—but their numbers were limited and they were confined to the south-west. Among burgesses the remonstrants were strongest in Glasgow, but they also had the support of two of the best known merchants in the country, Sir James Stewart, provost of Edinburgh, and former commissary general and treasurer of the excise, and Robert Farquhar, former provost of Aberdeen, who had served the covenanters well in the north-east.[27] They were, however, isolated individuals and their support did little to help the remonstrants. The same was often true of ministers outside the south-west who supported the remonstrance; they had little popular support, for opinion was moving increasingly in favour of the king, or of peace and quiet above all else. Even in the south-west it seems likely that disillusionment was widespread, in spite of all the efforts of the remonstrant ministers to stir up the people.

The western remonstrance was presented to the committee of estates at Perth on 22 October by Sir George Maxwell of Nether Pollock, while Patrick Gillespie presented the Glasgow and Ayr remonstrance. Special meetings of the committee and the commission of the kirk were summoned for 14 November to consider them,[28] and in the interim efforts were made to persuade the remonstrants at least to modify their position, but without success. New papers from the western forces on 30 October stated bluntly that it was manifest that the king was opposing the cause of God; he should therefore be excluded from power. A few days later remonstrant ministers met in Glasgow, calling themselves the presbytery of the westem army. Representatives of the association and the army were also meeting in the burgh, and the ministers tried to persuade them to sign the remonstrance. Few would do so, and thus, far from uniting the association in a common cause, the remonstrance divided it. The association also broke with those who tended to favour Cromwell; two officers were cashiered for corresponding with him and Strachan was evidently imprisoned.[29]

On and after 14 November the committee of estates and the commission of the kirk debated the remonstrance. The commission, anxious to heal divisions, tried to bring about a compromise; if the remonstrants would agree not to insist on an answer to the remonstrance from the committee, and would desist from preaching in favour of it, then the committee would refrain from denouncing it. At first the remonstrants seemed inclined to accept this, but in the end they rejected it.[30] The committee therefore resolved to issue an answer, proroguing parliament from 20 November (the date on which it was to meet by the last of four prorogations since Dunbar) until 26 November, so that there would be time to do this.[31]

The debates in the committee were heated. Argyll, Balcarres and

Lothian led in denouncing the remonstrance while Wariston argued passionately against its being condemned. An answer was agreed and sent to the commission of the kirk on 25 November, along with papers accusing Patrick Gillespie and James Guthrie of contriving divisions in church, state and army. To the anger of Eglinton the terms in which the remonstrance was rejected were very moderate; even so, twelve members of the committee (including Cassillis, Lords Burleigh and Arbuthnot, Wariston and Sir James Hope of Hopetoun) voted against the answer. Most of them were not remonstrants, but felt some sympathy for their point of view and believed that a condemnation would do more harm than good.[32] The answer opened mildly; the committee was willing to investigate and punish faults in its own actions and members, and was willing to be lenient and gentle though it found much to dislike in the remonstrance. But the remonstrance was scandalous, injurious to the king and prejudicial to his authority. It held seeds of division, tended to the breach of the treaty of Breda, and strengthened the hand of the English invaders. Honest men who had been ensnared by it would be free from censure, but not those who persisted in supporting it. The kirk was asked to join in condemning it in so far as it concerned religion.[33]

This the commission was very reluctant to do. There was a strong minority of remonstrants on the commission and it was clear that to denounce the remonstrance would cause a deep split in the kirk. The commission therefore would only announce its provisional opinion, delaying a detailed examination until the remonstrants had explained their intentions. The remonstrance contained many sad truths, but it encroached on the authority of the general assembly and was apt to cause divisions. In spite of the studied moderation of this statement about sixteen of the thirty-eight ministers present, and two out of nine elders, protested against it, and most then withdrew from the commission. The protest was led by James Guthrie; from the first he and Patrick Gillespie had been the leaders of the movement. Both were young men whose reputations dated from the purges after the fall of the Engagers in 1648, but the remonstrants now also included Samuel Rutherford and Andrew Cant, two of the best-known names in the kirk since the beginning of the troubles.[34] But most of the recognised leaders of the kirk gave their support to the commission.

Having rejected the remonstrance, the commission proceeded to try again to show that it had some sympathy with the remonstrants by informing parliament that there was much truth in the remonstrance and lamenting the indemnities given to royalist rebels, the slowness in purging the king's household, and the secret sins of members of parliament.[35] For the two parties now emerging in the kirk did not really differ over what the sins and faults of the time were, but over how best to deal with them. None could doubt the insincerity of the king's promises, but was it best to work in alliance with him to overthrow the English Independents, or to break with him and hope that this would persuade Cromwell to withdraw from Scotland? The moderates of the kirk party favoured the former policy; they retained the hope of ultimately converting the king to their own way of thinking, lured on by the fantasy that if he was restored in England through their agency he would fulfil his promises (or at least that they would be in a position to force him to fulfil them) to impose the solemn league and covenant and presbyterian church government there. However unrealistic these hopes might be, they seemed the only possible chance of imposing the covenant in England and protecting the revolution in Scotland. The remonstrants were more practical; they would accept the presence of an Independent regime in England, at least for the time being, and though they did not contemplate doing without the king entirely they were not so naive as to continue to expect his conversion. They saw the folly of hoping that restoring him in England would help the kirk, since it was proving impossible to keep him to his promises even while he was still in Scotland; how much harder would it be once he was established in London?

As soon as the commission of the kirk had condemned the remonstrance parliament began proceedings against the western army, which was held responsible for having sponsored it. Perhaps as a final test to see if any service could be expected from it, the committee of estates had ordered Colonel Gilbert Ker to relieve Borthwick Castle, which was holding out against Cromwell. Ker refused, on the grounds that his forces were insufficient; but he added significantly that in any case he saw no advantage to the Lord's work in such an action. He affirmed his willingness to serve the king, but only providing that 'the King himselfe be a servant to the King of Kings'.[36] This made it clear that the western army, at least under its present leadership, was no asset to the regime. Parliament therefore ordered the dispatch of Robert Montgomery westwards, giving him command of all forces in the west. He was to supersede Ker, peacefully if possible, by force if necessary, and was to gain control of or disband the western army.[37]

Cromwell meanwhile had spent most of November consolidating his hold on the south-east, where small-scale guerrilla resistance by the Scots had developed; bands attacked English outposts and ambushed parties of Cromwell's men. To put an end to this Cromwell concentrated on capturing the castles still held by the Scots, which often served as bases for such activities. In Dirleton he captured the best-known of the Scots guerrillas, Captain Watt, and had him shot. But others continued to plague him, especially the daring Augustine, a German mercenary whose most notable exploit was to break through the besiegers of Edinburgh castle and reinforce the garrison early in December. Late in November Cromwell moved west with Lambert and most of the English cavalry;[38] as in October, he probably wished to see how the westerners would react, and perhaps hoped to establish a few garrisons. What he did not know was that as he moved west Robert Montgomery was marching from Stirling to replace Ker in command of the western forces.

News of Montgomery's intentions at last stung Ker into action against the English. Early on 1 December he launched an attack on what he thought was a small force of English occupying Hamilton. In fact Lambert was in the burgh with a large body of cavalry. In this, their first and last battle, the forces of the Western Association were completely routed. Ker was wounded and captured and Robert Halket fled. The English made little attempt to follow up their victory; Cromwell again visited Glasgow briefly but then retired to Edinburgh, leaving a garrison in Hamilton.[39]

After the defeat at Hamilton the Western Association collapsed and its leaderless forces disbanded, though some of the men may have joined Robert Montgomery, who withdrew northwards. The association had already been divided and demoralised by the remonstrance and the reluctance of some of its members to fight Cromwell, and (whatever zealous ministers might urge) few saw any hope of success for a policy of defying both Cromwell on the one hand and the committee of estates on the other. The disappearance of the Western Association was probably as welcome to the king and parliament as to Cromwell—perhaps even more welcome, since Cromwell had had hopes of reaching agreement with it. Parliament declared the association void and forbade the formation of any such body in future.[40] But the fall of the association did not undermine the confidence of the remonstrant ministers; they remained as determined as ever to do their duty by denouncing the errors of the times. As the remonstrance had stated, they did not judge the merits of their cause by its worldly success.

RESOLUTIONERS AND PROTESTERS: THE FALL OF THE KIRK PARTY

The loss of the south-west added to the strength of the arguments of the king and his friends that to oppose Cromwell successfully the strictness of the qualifications for those allowed to serve in the army must be relaxed. After much soul searching and pressure from parliament, the commission of the kirk decided on 14 December that it was the responsibility of parliament to use all lawful means for defence against the sectaries. The enemy possessed much of the kingdom, and there was no possibility of preserving the north or freeing the south unless there was a more general levy than previously. Therefore the kirk could not oppose the raising of all fencible persons for defence against the enemy, though at least officers were to be men of known affection to the cause, and persons forfeited, excommunicated, profane or enemies to the cause were to be excluded.[41]

Had the remonstrants not withdrawn from the commission two weeks previously these 'public resolutions' would probably never have been passed. The split in the kirk thus helped to open the way for a flood of malignants to pour into the army, for once parliament had the kirk's grudging admission that malignants might be employed it used this to justify the employment of all and sundry, regardless of the kirk's limitations. Yet if the English were to be resisted it is hard to see what else the kirk could have done. Whether the ministers liked it or not the war had become for most Scots primarily a national one, for king and country against English invaders, not a religious one; and to most moderate ministers to let malignants fight through such mistaken motives seemed a lesser evil than allowing the English to conquer the country.

How far events since Dunbar, the antics of the remonstrants and the need to resist invasion, had altered opinion in parliament was seen on 20 December when colonels were chosen to command the new levies being raised, supposedly in accordance with the kirk's resolutions. Most of the new colonels were men with royalist records, Engagers or even men who had fought for Montrose. They included Crawford-Lindsay, a leading Engager; Atholl, Marischal and Lord Ogilvie who had been in rebellion in the north only two months before; many Highland chiefs, and others who, at best, had never shown zeal for the covenants. Loudoun and the kirk protested strongly, but without effect. An act of levy ordered the raising of all fencible men north of the Forth; lip service was paid to the conditions recommended by the kirk, but it was obvious that under such colonels these would count for little.[42]

The kirk was meanwhile declaring itself satisfied with the repentance of increasing numbers of Engagers and royalists. Even before the resolutions of 14 December it had recommended the employment of Linlithgow and Dunfermline, Lords Montgomery, Yester, Cranston and Cardros, and of many lairds and officers. In February 1651 Tullibardine and Lord Ogilvie were also recommended, Hamilton and the marquis of Douglas in March, Erroll, Glencairn and Lauderdale in May. Once the moderates on the commission, the 'resolutioners', had admitted that others than the godly might be employed they found it hard to justify excluding anyone. 'Behold a fearfull sinne! The Ministers of the Gospell ressaved all our repentances as unfained, thogh they knew well enough they were bot counterfeit; and we on the other hand made no scruple but to declare that Engadgment to be unlawfull and sinfull, deceitfullie speaking against the dictates of our oune consciences and judgements'.[43]

The public resolutions of 14 December further deepened the split in the kirk. The 'protesters', those who protested at the conduct of the resolutioners, were led by the remonstrants but included many who had not been willing to accept the remonstrance. On 7 January 1651 the commission of the kirk warned all ministers to avoid complying with the sectarian army or speaking against the public resolutions,[44] but already protests against the resolutions had begun to appear. The first was from the presbytery of Stirling; it was also the best known, for the English printed and distributed copies of it in order to encourage discord among the Scots. In any case, as Stirling was the headquarters of the army it was particularly embarrassing for the regime that the protesters should prevail there, and the burgh's ministers, James Guthrie and David Bennet (both ardent protesters) soon became central figures in the controversy. In January the presbyteries of Paisley, Glasgow, Irvine, Ayr, Hamilton, Lanark, Aberdeen and Deer, and the synod of Glasgow and Ayr, submitted protests against the resolutions. But the synods of Fife, Angus, Moray and Perth and the presbytery of Chanonry declared their support for the commission and its resolutions.[45] The distribution of these declarations for and against the resolutions shows clearly that the protesters' strength lay in the south-west, that of the resolutioners in the north and east; at this stage the areas of the south-east under English control took little part in the quarrel. The protesting presbyterias of Aberdeen and Deer seem to mar this pattern, but they were dominated by ministers imposed on parishes by the extremists, and there was no local popular support for the protesters in them.

The resolutioners tried to bring about reconciliation with the protesters at a meeting in January 1651 but failed. The commission then ordered Guthrie and Bennet not to preach against the resolutions; they refused to obey and appealed to the next general assembly. The committee of estates then intervened, accusing them of preaching against the resolutions of both church and state and obstructing the levies. They were finally persuaded to appear before the committee in Perth and were forbidden to return to Stirling, an order which they denounced as prejudicial to the liberties of the kirk.[46]

Cromwell inevitably benefited from the religious and political disputes among the Scots. Some extremists came to regard his regime as at least marginally preferable to that of the malignant king; others despaired of victory and decided to submit to him. One of those thus demoralised was Walter Dundas, who insisted on surrendering Edinburgh Castle on 24 December though there was no immediate military need for him to do so. He wisely remained in Edinburgh, for his countrymen denounced him as a traitor; there had been little hope of relieving the castle, but for it to fall so soon was seen as a national disgrace. 'It was alwayes before called the Maiden Castle, but henceforth term it the Prostitut Whore'.[47] Strachan had already made his peace with Cromwell, and Swinton of that Ilk and several army officers soon followed. Alexander Jaffray, provost of Aberdeen, had been captured at Dunbar and (after conversations with Cromwell and other Independents) came to believe the kirk guilty of various errors. He later became a quaker, along with Brodie of that Ilk and others exhausted by years of war and disillusioned with an authoritarian kirk. Others became Independents, and there is also some evidence suggesting that the reaction against the kirk may have led to an increase in catholicism in Scotland at this time.[48]

Desertions to the English gave rise to a great deal of fear and suspicion in Stirling; who would be next to betray king and covenants? The English were reported to be boasting that they had the same key to Stirling castle that they had had to Edinburgh, and the fact that the garrison was commanded by Major General Holborne, long known for his sympathies with the extremists in the kirk, lent some credibility to the story. He was cleared of any treachery after an investigation; but all the same he was relieved of his command, being replaced by Lord Drummond.[49] Further fears of treason were aroused by the activities of three brothers, Sir John Hope of Craighall, Sir James Hope of Hopetoun (both ordinary lords of session) and Sir Alexander Hope, who proposed that the king should abandon the parts of Scotland already occupied by Cromwell as well as England and Ireland; better half a cloak than no cloak at all. Charles angrily retorted that he would be hanged first, and proceedings were begun against the brothers; but these were soon abandoned, for they would serve only to emphasise the disunity among the Scots.[50] One of those most suspected of treachery was Johnston of Wariston, but after the surrender of Edinburgh castle he was sent (as clerk register) to treat with Cromwell for the return of the public records of Scotland, which had been in the castle. In March he succeeded in getting them shipped to Burntisland, but they were almost immediately recaptured by an English ship when an attempt was made to send them by sea to Dunnottar. Wariston managed to persuade Cromwell to part with them again in June, but he himself prudently remained behind in Edinburgh, for it was widely believed that he was plotting the betrayal of Stirling and other burghs to the English. The records were transported to Stirling, where they were captured for a third time by the English a few months later.[51]

Parliament ended its session on 30 December 1650 after agreeing that the king should be crowned at Scone on 1 January; fasts had already been held in preparation for this, one being for the sins of the royal family.[52] In spite of this additional humiliation, however, the king's position was becoming steadily stronger. The kirk party since its breach with its own extremist wing had become increasingly dependent on him. The levies under royalist colonels were daily strengthening Charles' hand, and the kirk party well knew that if it drove him into a new Start that would lead to a royalist rising which would almost certainly be successful. Argyll continued his efforts to dominate the king, proposing that Charles should marry his daughter. Though the king can hardly have seriously considered such a marriage he placated Argyll by writing to his mother in Paris asking for her consent; predictably she advised against it.[53]

As if to symbolise the role to which he aspired, that of king maker, it was Argyll who placed the crown on Charles' head at Scone. Other parts of the ceremony must have been equally distasteful to the king. He was not annointed, as that was regarded as a superstitious ceremony. Robert Douglas preached that though the king was the keeper of both tables, civil and ecclesiastical, he 'hath not absolute power to do what he pleaseth', for he was tied by the conditions of his covenant with his people. Certainly kings receive their crowns from God and are accountable to Him; but not only to Him, for 'totall government is not upon a king'. There are inferior magistrates who share in government. A king who tries to overthrow religion, laws and liberties must be opposed, by force if necessary, for obedience to a king is subordinate to obedience to God.[54]

The new committee of estates which parliament had appointed before it rose on 30 December contained no protesters and few who had any sympathy with them; on the other hand the royalists and Engagers now being admitted to the army were still barred from civil office, and the committee was therefore composed of the more moderate adherents of the kirk party.[55] But opinion was still moving in favour of the royalists and the committee feared that when parliament next met it would try to force the kirk to agree to royalists sitting on the committee. Parliament was due to meet on 5 February, but the committee apprehensively prorogued it, first to 21 February then to 13 March.

On 11 March Loudoun, Cassillis 'and ther factione' tried again to delay the meeting of parliament, but were out-voted by those who favoured at least some relaxation of the exclusion of royalists from civil power, arguing that this was essential if the English were to be opposed successfully.[56] The time of the committee was mainly taken up with military preparations. Middleton and Holborne were appointed lieutenants general of the cavalry and infantry respectively; as the one had only a few days before been relaxed from excommunication for malignancy, and the other had been relieved of command of Stirling castle for fear that he betray it to the English, the appointments graphically illustrate the width, and the unnaturalness, of the alliance against the invaders. Sir John Brown and Robert Montgomery were chosen as majors general of the cavalry, and (later) Scott of Pitscottie and Thomas Dalyell of the Binns majors general of the foot.[57]

There were three ways in which Cromwell could attack the Scots positions: by shipping his men across to Fife, by a direct attack on Stirling, and by crossing the upper Forth, above Stirling. In January a force led by Major General Monck tried to land at Burntisland (which seemed to confirm rumours that the bailies of the burgh had been plotting to betray it to the English) but retired when it met with resistance.[58] Cromwell moved west early in February, evidently intending to cross the upper Forth (perhaps in conjunction with a landing in Fife) but was forced to turn back by bad weather.[59] Later in the month he fell ill, and did not fully recover until June. During his illness the English army remained inactive. The Scots were too weak to take much advantage of this, but a force from Stirling raided Linlithgow on 14 April, and Robert Montgomery probed south-west with his cavalry, forcing the English to withdraw their garrison from Hamilton. English troops from Carlisle which had occupied Dumfries retreated hurriedly. Montgomery's father, Eglinton, and two of his brothers were sent after him to try to raise new forces in the west, but they were captured by an English raid on Dumbarton after being betrayed by a spy. The attempt to raise levies in the west therefore collapsed, but Robert Montgomery had opened a way into England if the Scots decided on an invasion. Cromwell realised this, and ordered English forces to draw together near Carlisle.[60]

When parliament met at Perth on 13 March the fears of the kirk party were soon realised. On a motion from the king parliament voted in favour of asking the kirk whether persons debarred by the acts of classes could be admitted to the committee of estates. There was much debate as to the exact form the query should take; some wanted it put in a way which would invite a negative answer, but it was decided that it should be whether or not it was sinful or unlawful, for the more effectual prosecution of the public resolutions, to admit persons to be members of the committee who had been excluded by the acts but had given satisfaction to the kirk.[61] Cassillis angrily accused the malignants of dealing craftily with the regime. First they had begged merely to be allowed to remain quietly in their homes and not be banished. They had then asked to be allowed places in the army. Now they demanded places on public judicatories. Some kirk party nobles supported a proposal by Lothian that instead of admitting malignants to the committee it should be abolished. This would kill two birds with one stone as far as such nobles were concerned; their rivals, the majority of nobles who had royalist leanings, would continue to be excluded from power, while in the absence of the committee the privy council, dominated by kirk party nobles, could be revived to take its place. Ever since the fall of the Engagers the kirk party nobles had been resentful of their declining power and prestige, of the tendency of lairds and burgesses to ignore their advice. Now these estates were swinging towards the other extreme and were increasingly royalist—or at least increasingly convinced of the necessity for an alliance with the royalists. By abolishing the committee of estates the kirk party nobles evidently hoped to monopolise power to the exclusion of the other estates (and, indeed, of most of their own estate) at least between sessions of parliament, for traditionally the privy council was dominated by the nobility. The king also supported the idea, hoping a council would be easier to control than the committee. However, the proposal was rejected; the lairds and burgesses had no intention of agreeing to such a reduction of their powers.[62]

In spite of pressure from parliament, the commission of the kirk refused to give a direct answer to the query as to membership of the committee of estates. On 22 March, however, it offered a compromise; it thought it reasonable that those who had already been admitted to serve in the army should be free to sit on any committee established for managing the army. Thus it could be argued that they were still to have only military, not civil, power. In spite of protests from ten kirk party nobles parliament resolved to act on this concession; Loudoun and Lothian bitterly rebuked the king for agreeing to this, accusing him of deserting his best friends, those who had brought him to Scotland, in favour of those who had led astray and ruined his father. The new committee for managing the affairs of the army included Hamilton, Douglas, Crawford-Lindsay, Glencairn, Atholl, Lauderdale and other royalists, as well as many members of the kirk party; it was to concern itself with raising and drawing together forces and supplying them; but it was not given power to control the movements or actions of the army.[63] Though king and parliament had taken full advantage of the kirk's concession by appointing the committee they still were not satisfied, and proceeded to demand that the kirk agree to the repeal of the acts of classes. Parliament then adjourned (until 17 April) after appointing a committee of estates made up, like its predecessors, of supporters of the kirk party.[64]

The kirk protested at the appointment of so many royalists and Engagers to the army committee. Just as parliament had used the commission's resolutions of 14 December as an excuse to appoint royalist army officers whom the kirk had never intended to qualify, so now it had taken advantage of the suggestion of an army committee to appoint many unsuitable persons to sit on it.[65] The kirk party supporters who had been given places on the army committee refused to take their seats as this would imply approval of so many royalists having been appointed. Therefore until parliament next met (23 May) a royalist-dominated committee for managing the affairs of the army met in Perth (or in Stirling on a few occasions),[66] while the kirk party's committee of estates sat in Stirling and also mainly concerned itself with military matters. Each committee pointedly tried to ignore the existence of the other. Needless to say this was not the most efficient way of raising forces against the common enemy.

During May Middleton brought the forces of the northern shires to Stirling, though he had obtained few men from the west; Argyll had delayed sending out his levies and neighbouring clans feared to march to Stirling until the Campbells did so, for fear that Argyll would take the opportunity to overrun their lands. Commissioners were sent to scour the north for food; the more men assembled at Stirling the harder it became to feed them, and it proved impossible to gather any reserve magazine to feed the army once the campaign began. On 17 May only six days' food was available for the army, and the shortage would have been much more acute if the levies had produced anything like the numbers of men hoped for. In spite of all efforts there were probably fewer than ten thousand men gathered in and around Stirling.[67] Meanwhile the higher command of the army was becoming increasingly top-heavy as efforts were made to satisfy all who aspired to be general officers. Leven was confirmed as general, though active service was not to be demanded of him, and the king was appointed commander in chief. In addition in May there was an abortive attempt to appoint Callander field marshal. The duke of Buckingham was chosen to command the English royalists and deserters from Cromwell, with Edward Massey as his major general. Apart from the king, Leven and these two English officers, the army had at least five majors general (Brown, Montgomery, Pitscottie, Dalyell and van Druschke) and three lieutenants general (Leslie, Middleton and Holborne) to command about 10,000 men.[68] By contrast the 20,000 men who had invaded England in

1644 had needed only one general, one lieutenant general and one major general.

As had happened before the previous session, parliament's meeting on 17 April was prorogued by the committee of estates, first to 21 May then to 23 May, for fear that it would rescind the acts of classes. The committee pressed the kirk for a reply to parliament's query about the acts, evidently hoping for a negative answer.[69] The commission prevaricated, not giving an answer until 24 May; even then it rather evaded the issue by claiming that it had not the power to determine whether or not the acts should be repealed; but as an answer was insisted on it declared that persons formerly excluded from office might be employed without sin if they were of good affection to the cause, provided certain conditions were first fulfilled. Parliament must undertake never to repeal any laws formerly passed in favour of religion and reformation and swear never to avenge itself on those who had opposed the Engagement. In addition parliament was asked not to admit suddenly large numbers of leading royalists to offices and places. This was a futile hope. In effect the commission was sadly resigning itself to the fact that a royalist regime would soon supersede that of the kirk party, and was trying to ensure that this led to as little change in the position of the kirk as possible. The resolutioners recognised that their action (in virtually saying that it was up to parliament to repeal the acts of classes if it wished) made reconciliation with the protesters impossible, and they therefore acted to try to exclude them from the approaching general assembly by instructing presbyteries to cite ministers who opposed the public resolutions to appear before the assembly, which would mean that they would not be eligible to sit in it.[70]

On 30 May parliament passed an act containing most of the guarantees the kirk had asked for; all formerly excluded from parliament were to sign a band which included the guarantees before being allowed to take their seats. The acts of classes of 1646 and 1649 were then, on 4 June, at last repealed.[71] Royalist nobles had already begun to sign the band to qualify themselves for civil office. The names of those who first signed, on 2 June, evidently included Hamilton, Huntly (whose title had been restored to him by parliament), Crawford-Lindsay, Lauderdale and Atholl, for they were all appointed members of the committee of estates on 3 June. Other members included Douglas, Wigtown, Annandale, Callander, Tullibardine, Hartfell, and Lords Lindores and Belhaven, all of whom signed the band on that day.[72]

The kirk party members of the new committee did not continue their earlier refusal to sit with royalists, for that would have been to surrender power completely. But in spite of their presence the new committee was dominated from the first by the royalist and Engager nobles. The kirk complained that in choosing members men of known faith and integrity had been passed over while others who notoriously lacked these qualifications had been appointed; the committee replied blandly that it knew of none of its members who had not been constant to the cause of the covenants.[73]

As well as rescinding the acts of classes parliament passed an act against the western remonstrance; those who did not renounce it would be proceeded against as seditious persons. Only Loudoun, Argyll, Cassillis and three burgesses voted against this, and even they did so because they thought it impolitic, not because they supported the remonstrance. As parliament (which adjourned on 6 June) and the committee of estates had no control over the south-west where support for the remonstrance was strongest there was little they could do to enforce the act—especially as no attempt appears to have been made to exact obedience from ministers, presumably to avoid charges of encroaching on the liberties of the kirk. But many of the leading lay remonstrants eventually signed a band renouncing the remonstrance. Sir James Stewart, Robert Farquhar, Maxwell of Nether Pollock, Campbell of Cesnok, Dalrymple of Stair, Cunningham of Cunninghamhead, Mure of Glanderston and several other lairds submitted; those who refused to do so included Sir John Cheisly and some prominent Glasgow burgesses.[74]

The general assembly met at St Andrews on 16 July. The protesters reacted to the attempt to exclude them from membership by demanding that the resolutioner members of the commission of the kirk should themselves be excluded, so the assembly could try them for their scandalous proceedings. 'Immediately there arose a great number on both sides, with a great heat and fury'. Andrew Cant, Patrick Gillespie and James Guthrie made 'feirce and bitter' speeches for the protesters, while James Wood and Robert Baillie spoke for the resolutioners. With the help of Balcarres, the king's commissioner (the first to be present at an assembly since 1643) the resolutioners managed to get the assembly formally constituted and Robert Douglas elected moderator; there were many disputed elections from presbyteries to be settled, an indication of how deeply the kirk was now divided even at the local level.[75] But before the assembly could reach any decisions news arrived on 20 July that the English had been victorious in a battle at Inverkeithing. The assembly met at midnight and adjourned until 22 July at Dundee. Fearing that this might be his last chance, Samuel Rutherford gave in a protestation denying the legality of the assembly, signed by himself and twenty-one other protester ministers two days before. They then withdrew from an assembly which, they asserted, was not free;

the letter from the commission to the presbyteries for citing protester ministers to appear before the assembly was a prelimitation.[76]

When the assembly reconvened in Dundee nearly half the members who had been in St Andrews were absent, though it was not clear how many had withdrawn through support for the protesters, how many to avoid having to take sides in what was now virtually a schism in the kirk, and how many through fear of the English enemy. Balcarres began by deploring Rutherford's protestation as derogatory to the freedom of the assembly and offered the king's help in punishing protesters; here the moderator interrupted, desiring him to cease as this was a purely ecclesiastical matter. Later Balcarres intervened again, urging that a 1638 act for excommunicating those who denied the lawfulness of an assembly should be enforced. The moderator replied that they knew what to do with their own acts; 'this was by way of a nipp'. However bitter the feelings of the resolutioners towards the protesters, they had no wish to involve the state in the quarrel, especially now that it was dominated by the king and royalists. Guthrie, Gillespie and John Simpson were deposed from the ministry and other protesters were summoned to answer for their actions, though it was noticeable that Rutherford and Cant were not among them;[77] they were too famous and venerable to be proceded against and it was probably hoped that once the zealous young leaders of the protesters had been dealt with, the older men would agree to a reconciliation.[78]

The schism which now split the kirk had, clearly, been brought about primarily by events since the mid 1640s, by divisions over how to react to political developments which threatened to destroy all that the covenanters had fought for. But differences of outlook which contributed to the split can be traced much further back, to earlier quarrels within the kirk. It is no coincidence that nearly all the 'radical party' ministers of the early 1640s and before became protesters rather than resolutioners (the only major exception being that David Dickson supported the resolutioners).[79] This radical minority had led active resistance to royal religious policies in the 1620s and 1630s. After the troubles began in 1637 it had been able to dominate the kirk, by providing leadership and through the support of lay covenanting leaders. But by 1650–1 the radicals had lost lay support; though supported by many extremist young ministers, they could not prevent the infiltration of the kirk party regime by royalists. Nor could they stop the majority of ministers rejecting their leadership and accepting the royalist revival on grounds of political necessity.

Before the beginning of the troubles what the radical ministers had seen as corruptions in the kirk had led them to hold coventicles or prayer meetings outside the normal worship of the kirk; they had still recognised the kirk as a true kirk, which they should remain within and strive to reform. But after 1650 the protesters reacted to corruption in the kirk by virtually seceding from it and setting up their own organisation, which claimed to be the true kirk. Rival kirk sessions in the same parish, rival presbyteries and, eventually, rival general assemblies were to emerge as the protesters refused to submit to the authority of the majority in the kirk.

CONQUEST

All the efforts of king, parliament and committee of estates failed to gather at Stirling an army large enough, or well enough equipped and supplied, to take the initiative against Cromwell. In June David Leslie complained at the endless delays; even the relatively small numbers of men at Stirling were near starving and many lacked clothes or arms.[80] The army advanced to Torwood, about seven miles south-east of Stirling, on 28 June but it was not ready for a general advance; when Cromwell's forces approached early in July Scots outposts in Falkirk withdrew. After some skirmishing Cromwell moved west towards Glasgow and his cavalry reconnoitred across the upper Forth as if an attack was intended there.[81] In fact Cromwell's movements were a blind, designed to divert the attention of the Scots from the east. A month before the Scots had strengthened their Stirling army by with drawing ten regiments of horse from Fife.[82] Cromwell had probably heard that Fife had thus been left almost defenceless; after tricking the Scots into expecting an attack in the west he hurried back to Edinburgh, and on 17 July sent a force across the Firth of Forth to occupy the Inverkeithing peninsula.

The Scots were taken by surprise, allowing the English three days free from attack to reinforce their expeditionary force before about 4,000 men under Holborne and Sir John Brown approached. By this time the English had 4,000 or 5,000 men in Fife under Lambert, and on 20 July they attacked and routed the Scots. Perhaps as many as half the Scots were killed. Brown was mortally wounded; Hector Maclean and his regiment of about 500 of his clansmen were killed almost to the last man, refusing to flee or surrender. Holborne was widely blamed for the disaster and again accused of treachery; though cleared by an enquiry he resigned his command.[83] On news of Lambert's victory the Scots army marched hastily back from Torwood through Stirling towards Fife; but when they heard that Cromwell had advanced from the south to Bannockburn they turned back to Stirling. Having thus prevented the Scots from concentrating their forces against Lambert, Cromwell hastened back to Edinburgh and greatly reinforced him. By the end of July Cromwell himself was in Fife with 14,000 men, leaving only eight English regiments south of the Forth. On 1

August he appeared before Perth and the garrison surrendered the next day.[84]

Thus within two weeks the military situation in Scotland had changed completely; after months of inactivity Cromwell had fooled the Scots as to his intentions and then, by establishing himself in Perth, cut them off from all hope of reinforcements and supplies from the north. The price that Cromwell paid for this breaking of the military deadlock was that he left the way open for the Scots at Stirling to march into England; he had not sufficient forces to cut them off from the north and to prevent them from moving south at the same time. But he calculated that this was a risk worth taking, for he was confident that the Scots would find little support in England and that they could be defeated there far more conclusively than if he attacked Stirling from the south, leaving the Scots free to retreat northwards. Spreading the war to England would thus hasten its conclusion.

The Scots reacted to Inverkeithing and the loss of Perth exactly as Cromwell had hoped. They had little choice but to remain in Stirling until attacked or starved into submission, or to move south towards England in a last desperate attempt to restore their fortunes. On 31 July king, army and part of the committee of estates left Stirling, camping that night at Cumbernauld. From there Charles issued instructions to leading royalists who were to remain in Scotland with part of the committee—Crawford-Lindsay, Marischal, Glencairn and Balcarres. They were to raise as large an army as they could, under the command of Crawford-Lindsay, and use it to attempt to drive out of Scotland whatever English forces remained there and did not follow the main Scottish army into England. Care was also to be taken to prevent any insurrection in Scotland. Clearly the king feared that the kirk party would try to seize power again and perhaps reach agreement with the English once the royalist army had entered England, as had happened in the whiggamore raid of 1648.[85] The king and the royalists had no illusions about their chances of success. Morale was low and men deserted by the thousand, especially after the defeat at Inverkeithing. As Hamilton wrote, 'we must either starve, disband, or go with a handful of Men into England. This last seems to be the least Ill, yet it appears very desperate to me'.[86]

When Charles crossed the border he probably had less than 13,000 men under his command. The army commanders tried to keep their spirits up by convincing themselves that this lack of numbers was positively an advantage; all the half hearted and those of doubtful loyalty had left. 'This is a natural purge, and will do us much good.' Even so, Hamilton related that Lauderdale and others 'are now all laughing at the ridiculousness of our condition. We have quit Scotland, being scarce able to maintain it; and yet we grasp at all, and nothing but all will satisfy us, or to lose all. I confess I cannot tell you whether our hopes or our fears are greatest: but we have one stout argument, despair; for we must now either stoutly fight it, or die'.[87] The fears rather than the hopes were soon realised. Very few English joined the king (partly through dislike and suspicion of his Scottish allies) and there were arguments about whether the army should march on London or make for Wales. Cromwell caught up with the Scots at Worcester, concentrating about 31,000 men against them. About 2,000 Scots were killed and near 10,000 captured in and after the battle which followed. Only a few individuals escaped back to Scotland or abroad, though these included the king himself.[88] When, after he reached France, it was suggested that he should return to Scotland he said he would rather be hanged first.[89] He had seen enough of Scotland and its people to last him a lifetime. Yet thousands of Scots had just died for him, including the duke of Hamilton, who was mortally wounded at Worcester.

As soon as Cromwell had taken Perth and confirmed that the Scots army had marched from Stirling he had hurried back to Leith and thence into England, leaving Monck with five or six thousand men to proceed against Stirling. The burgh quickly surrendered but the castle held out until a mutiny in the garrison forced it to capitulate on 15 August. This freed Monck to march back to Perth on his way to Dundee, while a few troops of horse were sent to police Glasgow and the south-west to prevent any attempt to raise levies there.[90]

The committee of estates left in Scotland had fled into Angus when Monck advanced on Stirling. As the king had suspected, the kirk party had hoped to gain control of the committee now that Charles and many of the royalist nobles were away in England, but it was soon discovered that Crawford-Lindsay had been appointed to command all forces in Scotland with instructions to prevent the kirk party re-establishing itself. After bitter disputes over the command most of the kirk party members withdrew from the committee, though Loudoun tried to bring about reconciliation and was with the committee as late as 24 August, after which he left to try to persuade Argyll to return to it. From Dundee on 20 August the committee called on all Scots who had any sense of religion and loyalty to rise in arms at once to free the kingdom from the handful of the enemy who remained within it.[91] But almost immediately it showed that in fact it was well aware that Monck had more than a handful of men by fleeing from Dundee as he approached; Monck summoned the burgh to surrender on 26 August.[92]

The committee of estates met at Kirriemuir on 24 August; or rather, members of the committee met for there was not a quorum present, there being no burgesses.[93] Four days later the remnants of the committee were at Alyth, sixteen miles north-west of Dundee, with a few hundred soldiers and members of the commission of the kirk. Their presence was betrayed to Monck and he resolved to destroy this nucleus before a new Scots army could form round it. Seven or eight hundred English horse raided Alyth; they took the Scots completely by surprise and captured nearly all the members of the committee and the commission present, including Leven, Crawford-Lindsay, Marischal, Lord Ogilvie and Robert Douglas.[94] Dundee was stormed on 1 September, about 800 Scots being killed in fierce fighting, including some women and children during the plundering and looting which followed the storm.[95]

This was the last major engagement of the campaign in Scotland, but it was some months before the English could adequately occupy all Lowland areas, let alone Highland ones, and some attempts were made in the north to raise new levies and maintain a regime. Thus a few members of the commission of the kirk met in Aberdeen on 2 September and later further north, but more for 'encouraging and strengthening one another' than to conduct any business. Balcarres and a few members of the committee of estates who had escaped from Alyth fled north and on 31 August six members (not a quorum) met in Aberdeen. Balcarres joined his men to levies raised by Huntly and tried to maintain the pretence of a royalist regime; a party of English cavalry occupied Aberdeen for a few days early in September to hinder their activities but soon withdrew southwards.[96]

A rival to Balcarres' royalist remnant of the committee had by this time appeared in the west. On news of the capture of most of the royalist committee at Alyth, Loudoun (as chancellor) summoned all remaining members of the committee to meet on 5 September at Killin on Loch Tay, a central position safe from attack by the English. Balcarres refused to attend, suggesting that Loudoun and his adherents should join him in the north-east instead. Nonetheless Loudoun managed to assemble a substantial committee at Killin by 10 September; seven nobles (including Argyll and Lothian), three lairds and three burgesses. The following day they wrote to Balcarres commanding him to bring all the forces he could to Dunkeld by 24 September. Huntly and the forces of Perthshire and Angus were also to rendezvous there. But the committee also gave orders that its own next meeting was to be at Dumbarton on 25 September; how the levies were to be kept together at Dunkeld while their commanders met at Dumbarton was not explained. Balcarres at first agreed to bring his men to Dunkeld, and the Mackenzies were busy raising men in the north, but in the end no rendezvous took place.[97]

At Dumbarton the committee found the English too close for safety and adjourned its meeting to Rosneath. Parliament was due to meet in Stirling in November and Loudoun was anxious that the disintegrating committee should alter the place of meeting to somewhere not controlled by the English while there was still a quorum present. But the committee refused to act until it had again retreated, to Rothesay on the island of Bute. From there on 15 October the committee hopefully summoned parliament to meet at Finlarig (near Killin) on 12 November though, as Loudoun had feared, a quorum was no longer present. The committee lingered on at Rothesay for a few days more before dissolving, not to meet again until 1660.[98] It was obvious that the situation was hopeless and that the country, exhausted and defeated, wanted nothing more than peace. It was only Loudoun's insistence that had led to the summoning of parliament at Finlarig, and when he arrived there he found that only three nobles (Home, Callander and Lord Cardros) and no members of the other estates were present. Most of those summoned were in English hands or were busy trying to make their peace with the conquerors. Argyll had written to Monck on 15 October suggesting negotiations to prevent further bloodshed. He agreed, provided Argyll did all he could to prevent the Finlarig parliament from meeting, a condition also demanded of others who wished to submit. In the event Argyll did not finally make his peace with the English until August 1652, but he made no further attempt to resist.[99]

In the east Huntly and Balcarres remained defiant for a few weeks longer, though causing more harm to their countrymen than to the enemy, as they needed to extort money and plunder food for their forces. Huntly signed articles with the English at Aberdeen on 21 November, Balcarres at Elgin on 3 December. English forces quickly garrisoned Inverness and marched into Ross, Sutherland and Caithness, 'so that all the Lowlands of Scotland (south and north) submitted themselves to the power of the English',[100] though a few castles still held out—the Bass Rock until March 1652, Dunnottar until May 1652. It was to be some years before the English hold on the Highlands was complete, but the rest of the country, exhausted by war, shattered by religious and political divisions, and demoralised by defeat, was completely subdued.

'Thus, with the losse of the libertie of my nation, I end both this year one thousand six hundred fiftie-one, and my collections, having neither hart nor incouragement to proceed therein'.[101]

CHAPTER SIX

The Scottish Revolution

FROM REVOLUTION TO COUNTER REVOLUTION

The solemn league and covenant and intervention in the English civil war are often regarded simply as disastrous miscalculations which ruined the covenanting movement; over-confidence instilled by earlier successes led the covenanters to attempt more than could possibly be achieved. There is some truth in this, but for adoption of the policy represented by the new covenant to be regarded as a misjudgement on the part of the covenanting leadership it is surely necessary to be able to point to some alternative policy which might have been more likely to have served the same purpose—the bringing of security to the covenanting revolution in Scotland. No such option was available; the only alternatives open to the covenanters were to intervene in England, or virtually to surrender by passively awaiting destruction. Charles I's promises could not be relied upon, so victory for him in England (which seemed inevitable unless help was sent to parliament) would almost certainly be fatal to the covenanters in Scotland. Intervention in England therefore seemed unavoidable. Many of the covenanting leaders were well aware of the risks entailed, but the risks of not intervening were even greater. It was a matter of rational political calculation, not blind religious zeal.

This does not mean that the religious ambitions stressed in the new covenant were insincere or unimportant. Securing true religion in Scotland and reforming religion in England were certainly of central importance to the covenanters. Hindsight shows that this primary place given to religion in the alliance was quickly to undermine it; in the years ahead it was to be religious differences that caused most bitterness between the allies. Yet at the time giving such prominence to religion seemed to have many advantages. What stronger basis for an alliance could there be than religion, transcending any secular disagreements? In both kingdoms episcopacy and popery seemed to many the main enemies, and Scots presbyterians and English puritans had a great deal in common. It was not obvious that presbyterian church government as it existed in Scotland in

1643 would prove unacceptable in England. Finally, since the national covenant had been so successful in uniting Scots against their king it was natural to assume that a new covenant was the best way of uniting both kingdoms against him.

Yet it is true that it was clear even before the new covenant was first signed that it would not be so acceptable, even within Scotland, as its predecessor had been. Hamilton had had the support of many moderate covenanters as well as that of royalists in opposing alliance with the English parliament. He had won the votes of the majority of nobles in the convention of estates, leaving Argyll victorious only through the support of most lairds and burgesses. The position of Argyll and his noble colleagues as natural leaders of the regime was not challenged, but they can hardly have been happy at being reliant on the support of men from lower down the social scale in order to overcome the majority of their own estate. The king's arrest of Hamilton, which drove many moderate nobles into active support for, or at least acquiesence in, intervention in England was an unexpected stroke of good fortune for Argyll and the regime he dominated, increasing its social respectability.

Intervention in England predictably provoked royalist revolt in Scotland. Though this won less support than might have been expected (through royalist distrust of Montrose, hatred of his Highland and Irish troops, and disgust at the arrest of Hamilton) it nonetheless had much greater success than could have been predicted. Montrose's military genius, the quality of his despised Highland and Irish troops and the failure of the covenanters to concentrate sufficient forces against him led to his great series of victories. Yet in the end his spectacular victories were deprived of value by the fact that support for him was so limited. He failed to inspire royalist risings south of the Tay, and even after Kilsyth had, to all appearances, left him master of the country, he failed to win the whole-hearted support of many royalists and moderates. Indeed, far from encouraging royalism in Scotland Montrose's campaigns consolidated opinion in favour of the covenanters. Many might think it wrong to help the king's enemies in England, but few would fight for him in Scotland while Montrose was his lieutenant general. Ironically Montrose's most significant achievement was to weaken and delay the emergence of royalist reaction in Scotland—though admittedly he made it all the harder for the covenanters to resist it when it did come, since they never lived down the humiliating defeats he had inflicted on them. In particular, Argyll's reputation as a leader and as the most powerful man in Scotland was permanently damaged by his flights from Montrose's army and by the terrible mauling inflicted on the Campbells. Large areas of his estates were devastated, and even armed resistance was not crushed until late in 1647.

This was of great importance once Montrose was defeated and disillusionment with the English parliament grew in Scotland, accompanied by growing sympathy for the king's plight in England, for Argyll, his reputation shattered, proved unable to control many men who had previously supported him. Hostility to the English parliament spread as it became clear that it wished to give the Scots as little say in English affairs as possible. The achievements of the Scottish army in England were minimised, implementation of the solemn league and covenant was evaded, new concessions from the king were demanded, while the rise of Independency and sects gave rise to fears of religious and social anarchy in England which might spread to Scotland. By 1648 fears for the king, for the covenant and of anarchy had brought together a strong party of moderate covenanters (including the majority of the covenanting nobles) and royalists under Hamilton in an unnatural alliance, intent on imposing king and (as many still hoped) covenant on England. Argyll proved able to win the support of only a minority in parliament, and with his estates devastated was unable to contemplate armed resistance to the royalist revival. Leadership of opposition to the Engagers' counter-revolution was thus left to the kirk. Ten years after the troubles had begun church and state held their first open trial of strength, and the state (dominated by the nobility) won. Their counter-revolution was only rendered abortive by defeat in England, which allowed the supporters of the kirk to seize power in Scotland.

The defeat of the Engagers and their exclusion from power left only a few nobles supporting the new kirk party regime; not only were these nobles few in number but their estate had been discredited by the desertion to the Engagement of the majority of the nobility. The kirk party nobles therefore quickly found that their natural right to leadership was seriously questioned for the first time since the troubles had started. They were no longer trusted. The power of lairds and burgesses had increased correspondingly, and many of them were probably men of lesser status than their predecessors in parliament, as successive purges of royalists and Engagers had excluded many of the greater lairds and burgesses from power. The kirk party representatives of these two estates showed a greater tendency to defer to the advice of the ministers of the kirk, as the name given to their 'party' indicates. They also, feeling the need to counter-balance the hostility of the nobility, showed themselves ready to seek popular support not just by appeals to the cause of God and patriotism but by concessions admitting the hardships being suffered, by promises to investigate grievances and give protection against bad masters. This change in social outlook represented by the kirk party regime was admittedly limited, but nonetheless it was important, and was seen as such at the time. As in many revolutions, the failure of the original revolutionary leadership to provide the victories promised, together with an attempted counter-revolution, had led to its being partially displaced by more radical leadership from lower in society.

Not surprisingly even the kirk party nobles were suspicious of a regime which distrusted them and undermined their rights. Argyll and others began to fear that by destroying the king's power they had begun a process which was now inevitably destroying the nobility and the whole social order—as royalists had claimed would happen since the troubles began. The horrid example of England loomed large. Resistance to the king there had led to his execution, the abolition of monarchy and the house of lords, and the rise of a variety of subversive ideas about religion and society. Was not, perhaps, the only way to save Scotland and her nobility a partial restoration of royal power, which then could be used to uphold the revolution of 1638–41 in Scotland while correcting the kirk party's excesses? It was probably to this period that Argyll referred when, though admitting that 'the Nobility of Scotland, have always bickered with their Princes, and from the insolency of that Custome, not any of our Kings have been free', he claimed that he had not previously thought that the covenanters' actions would have dangerous results, since true religion confirmed men in obedience to established government.

> I did not look upon our intended Reformation as any way taxable, since it had the whole stream of universal consent of the whole Nation; I never thought of those dire Consequences which presently followed, till by that confusion my thoughts became distracted, and my self incountred so many difficulties in the way, that all remedies that were applyed did the quite contrary operation.[1]

There was much truth in what Argyll said, though he was clearly trying to justify himself. Years of confusion seemed to be bringing a permanent settlement no nearer and had brought a party to power in Scotland which, however laudable its religious complexion, was dangerous to the established order of society. Finding himself increasingly isolated, Argyll looked to alliance with the new king to restore him and his estate. Horror in Scotland at the execution of Charles I and the innate conservatism which prevented the kirk party contemplating a future without a king led to the proclamation of Charles II. But the recovery of the nobility from the shock of the defeat of the Engagement, the great upsurge of royalist sentiment resulting from the execution of Charles I, the growing unpopularity of the kirk party, and the need to resist English invasion, all combined to make it impossible for either the kirk party regime or Argyll to retain control of the king. The kirk party split. The larger part of it gradually recognised the necessity of working in alliance with royalists and Engagers to defeat the English, and the majority of the ministers, the resolutioners, submitted to the desires of the estates in this matter. A minority of the kirk party and ministers refused to surrender the new independence the kirk had won since the fall of Engagers; these remonstrants and protesters virtually disowned the king and the state. This final division among the covenanters hastened the almost inevitable defeat of the movement. Once the royalist nobles had been admitted to a part in the regime they quickly came to dominate it, ousting the disillusioned and demoralised covenanters from power. As Argyll had hoped, restoration of the king had led to restoration of the power of the nobility, but in a way he had never intended. Instead of the covenanting minority of the nobility taking over the regime, the royalist majority had done so. However, the royalist triumph was short lived, for within a few months it was submerged by English conquest. As in 1648, counter-revolution had succeeded in Scotland, only to be destroyed from outside.

By their internal disputes, their failure to find a solution to the problem of what to do with kings who could not be trusted or converted, and by their insistence that Scotland's security demanded that she should be allowed a large part in dictating a settlement in England, the covenanters had destroyed themselves. Yet it is hard to see how else they could have acted if they were determined to preserve what they had achieved up to 1641. Their attempt to 'export' their revolution in the belief that it could not survive 'in one country' proved to be the turning point in their fortunes, but their reasons for making the attempt (though not the tactless way they went about it) were sound. Similarily the Engagers' invasion of England failed, but this does not mean that it was an absurd venture doomed from the start; for a time it was a serious threat to the English parliament. And in 1650–1 Cromwell's victories at Dunbar and Worcester would not have been greeted with such relief and rejoicing by the English commonwealth had it not been feared that it might have been the Scots who would be victorious.[2]

Yet excuses and 'might have beens' cannot alter the fact that the covenanting movement was a failure, and this condemned it in the eyes of most contemporaries as well as in those of posterity. High hopes, raised even further by early success, gave way to disillusionment and despair as triumph gave way to disaster after disaster. The price of the covenanting experiment had been high, both in blood and in material losses; 'No reliable data exist for a calculation of the casualties the Scots suffered in their heroic struggle to enforce the covenants, but if to the known losses in battle are added as many more who died or were disabled by sickness, the total would probably be a staggering percentage of the manhood'.[3] Many of the leading members of all three estates were left virtually bankrupt. Trade had been destroyed. Endless levies, taxes, arbitrary extortions, and plundering and devastation by enemies, had exhausted and demoralised the country. For many the English conquest within the resultant end to fighting and restoration of order must have come almost as a relief. Everything possible had gone wrong, nothing had worked out as intended. In writing that 'all remedies that were applyed did the quite contrary operation' Argyll supplied an epitaph for the covenanting movement as well as for himself.

THE PROBLEM OF UNION

The covenanters sought union with England in order to protect their religious and constitutional revolutions in Scotland by limiting royal power and adding to the union of the crowns ties of union at other levels. It is true that they often used the word 'union' to mean simply an alliance, but it seems clear that usually they meant more than this, using the word in a sense that comes close to the definition of federal union as 'that form of government in which two or more states constitute a political unity while remaining more or less independent with regard to their internal affairs'.[4]

The attempts of the covenanters to add other forms of union to the personal union of the crowns may for convenience be referred to as efforts to bring about closer union, a convenient term justified by phrases used by the covenanters themselves. But it is worth pointing out that in one central respect they sought to weaken the union already existing. The union of the crowns had united executive power in both countries in the hands of a single king. The constitutional reforms and new types of union proposed by the covenanters were specifically designed to limit and check this power, by strengthening internal institutions within each kingdom and creating new links between them. The covenanters thus wanted less union in some respects, more in others.

In 1640–1 the covenanters had failed to achieve closer union. In 1643 circumstances seemed favourable for another attempt; indeed circumstances forced intervention in England on the covenanters in their own interests, thus emphasising the need for permanent links between the two parliaments to curb royal power. Unfortunately the desperate need of the English parliament for their help and their conviction that God would bring them victory as he had done in the past, led the covenanters to expect that they would be able to dictate a peace settlement in England. Naturally such arrogance aroused English resentment, and this helped to make it impossible for the covenanters to achieve even more limited objectives in England to bring their country security. Their enemies, both royalist and parliamentarian, proved skilful in spreading anti-Scots propaganda, exaggerating and distorting the demands made by the Scots and finding a ready audience among those resentful not only of Scots pretensions but of the shameful necessity of having had to beg for Scottish help at all.

The success of anti-Scottish propaganda was most clearly seen in religion; the attitude of the Scots was caricatured (and still is by some modern historians) as a stupid insistence that the kirk in all its aspects, the primitive kirk of a backward country, should be imposed on England without alteration. But the Scots never expected that the reformed church in England would be a carbon copy of the kirk, and were quite prepared to make concessions in matters which were not regarded as essentials. Indeed willingness to compromise led to changes being made in the kirk in Scotland to make it more acceptable to English puritans; the Westminster standards, drafted by an English assembly, were adopted by the kirk for the sake of unity.[5] As Alexander Henderson said 'we are neither so ignorant nor so arrogant, as to ascribe to the Church of Scotland such absolute purity and perfection, as hath not need nor canot admit further Reformation'.[6] Such assurances had little effect, however; the propaganda image of the Scots insisting on a rigid imposition of the kirk on England prevailed. Similarly, the image of presbyterian government as clerical tyranny was widely accepted. The Scots might urge that it provided a middle way between the extremes of episcopal tyranny and sectarian anarchy,[7] but the caricature proved more powerful than reality. It is ironic that in England Scottish style presbyterianism was rejected as leading to clerical tyranny, to theocracy, at the very time that in Scotland it was proving to be a system whereby the laity could successfully infiltrate and control the kirk.[8]

The rigidity of the religious demands of the Scots in England has thus been exaggerated, and the nature of the system they wished to see established has been distorted. Moreover the strength of support for a presbyterian system in England has probably been seriously underestimated in the past.[9] To say that 'Except for a few clergymen, tempted by clerical power, there were no English Presbyterians'[10] is simply not true unless one adopts a remarkably narrow definition of presbyterianism.

All this—the nature of Scots demands in religion and the existence of genuine support for them in England—makes the covenanters' desire for uniformity in religion seem a lot more practical and reasonable than it is often made out to be. It is not 'inconceivable that the Presbyterian system of Scotland would ever have been established in England'.[11] But though not inconceivable it was unlikely, especially since the covenanters, certain of their own righteousness, made no allowance for English reaction against being told how to reform their church by foreigners. Hopes for religious unity, for religion as the basic bond between the two kingdoms, came to nothing. The covenanters had hoped that agreement over religion would provide a firm foundation for closer union in civil matters. Instead failure to achieve religious unity made civil union impossible; 'what a fearfull judgment of God is this upon us, that what we thought should have joyned the nations unseparably, is lyk to be the great separator of them'.[12] As well as the bitterness spilling over from disputes about religion, there inevitably arose differences of attitude and interests between the two kingdoms on civil affairs. But the Scots remained determined that links and guarantees should be established which would prevent developments in England ever again threatening their revolution. To English parliamentarians the Scots seemed to be trying to set up machinery to justify their continued interference in English politics; to the Scots it seemed obvious that they were merely trying to prevent English influence predominating in the union of the crowns. Hatred of the Scots grew in England; 'the whole kingdom in general having a great detestation of the Scots', Cromwell and his supporters (who had done much to stir up this detestation) gained greatly in popularity by excluding the Scots from any say in a settlement in England and persuading them to withdraw their army in 1647.[13]

Despairing of parliament making a satisfactory religious settlement and agreeing to permanent links between the two kingdoms to guarantee Scotland's security, it was hardly surprising that some of the covenanters slowly turned to the king. Betrayed (as they saw it) by the English parliament, they came to believe that the best hope of achieving reformation in England and securing the revolution of 1641 in Scotland perhaps lay after all in alliance with the king. They therefore joined royalists, who now pretended zeal for the covenants, in the Engagement to invade England to restore the king and impose the covenants and closer union. But a strong minority of the covenanters (not surprisingly) could not see the king as a likely instrument of reformation, nor his restoration as likely to secure the revolution in Scotland. On the defeat of the Engagers these extreme covenanters seized power and allied themselves with Cromwell and the Independents as the only alternative to opposing an English invasion on the one hand and the royalists and Engagers on the other. Thus the kirk party regime in Scotland abandoned the mission of imposing covenant and presbyterian church government in England. But this was only intended to be temporary; alliance with the hated

Independents was a matter of expediency and necessity, since the danger from them to the kirk seemed less immediate than the danger from the royalists. The idea of a permanent Independent regime in England was abhorrent to the kirk party and their God, and was thought incompatible with the security of the kirk and state of Scotland.

The kirk party's uneasy alliance with the Independents was brought to an abrupt end by the execution of Charles I. The execution roused universal horror in Scotland, and insult was added to the horror by the argument that since he had been king of both kingdoms the English had had no right to act against him without Scots consent. The abolition of the monarchy in England which followed the execution broke the nominal link of the union of the crowns between the kingdoms. The establishment of the new commonwealth of England had abolished the British state. The covenanters had intervened in the English civil war hoping to strengthen the links between the kingdoms. Instead, the English had now disowned the one certain link. But the covenanters would not recognise England's right to abolish the monarchy; they proclaimed Charles II king of England as well as of Scotland. A variety of motives influenced them in this refusal to consent to England's radical solution of the problem posed by the Gordian knot of the impossibility of making a permanent peace with a deceitful king. Sentiment pointed out that the royal family was Scots in origin and calculation suggested that perhaps the only hope left of imposing a godly reformation in England and destroying the revolutionary regime there which had executed Scotland's king lay in alliance with the new king. Even if Charles II had been proclaimed king of Scotland alone, the country would have inevitably become a centre of royalist intrigue and thus an object of suspicion to the regime in England. In 1643–6 fear for the future and missionary enthusiasm had led the covenanters to intervene in England on behalf of parliament. In 1648 and 1650–1 similar fears and hopes led them to uphold royal claims in England against parliament.

The covenanters' 1650 treaty with Charles II provoked English invasion. Thus the Scots at last got closer union; much closer union than they had ever bargained for, in the form of the Cromwellian union following English conquest. They had forced England to accept their argument that union was vital to the security of both kingdoms by themselves threatening England's security. The wheel had come full circle. The covenanters had revolted against Charles I largely through discontent at unequal union, which was leading to the anglicisation of Scotland. They had tried to add to union of the crowns other forms of union; religious uniformity, military union, and ties between the two parliaments. When this had failed they had turned rather desperately to the king for help in achieving closer union. Failure in this led to complete union based on English conquest. Opposition to anglicisation by the king led eventually to conquest and much more thorough anglicisation by English republicans.

The covenanters had failed to bring about closer union, to redefine the relationship of the two kingdoms, but their attempts to achieve it give an underlying consistency to their four military interventions in England (1640–1, 1644–7, 1648, 1651). This consistency was not evident to the English. The royalist Clarendon believed that from 1640 onwards the Scots acted in opposition to their own interests, culminating in the Engagement which showed 'such a degree of sottishness and a depraved understanding that they can never be looked upon as men who knew what their interest was, or what [was] necessary to advance their own designs'.[14] Clarendon might be right in claiming that the Scots did not understand England, but he clearly had himself little understanding of Scotland; and his charge against the covenanters of stupidity rests on the belief that what they should have done was trust Charles I and fight for him. The covenanters may have been stupid, but they were not quite so stupid as that. To English parliamentarians as well the covenanters seemed bad politicians; they were inconsistent, and indeed treacherous, supporting parliament in 1640–1 and 1644–7, and the king in 1648 and 1650–1. Again this shows a lack of understanding of what the covenanters were trying to do, of their need for security based on a new relationship with England; whether this was achieved in alliance with parliament or with the king was of secondary importance.

What sort of union was it that the covenanters wanted? At times they talked of complete union, of abolishing all distinctions (even of name) between the two countries. Yet in the specific proposals they made at various times they never went so far. They wanted complete free trade, the full rights of natives in one country to be granted to citizens of the other. Constitutionally they wanted to continue the union of the crowns, adding to it close bonds of military cooperation between the parliaments, with meetings between commissioners of the two countries to preserve the peace, regulate armed forces, and discuss other matters of mutual interest. Foreign policy and making war were to be dealt with jointly. When they became disillusioned with the English parliament they tried to ensure that Scotland's interests would be protected by stipulating that Scotsmen should always be about the king to advise him, and that each country should be represented on the privy council of the other. Above all, and most consistently of all, the covenanters demanded unity of religion and uniformity of church government.

But it is of great significance that they never demanded unity of church government; only uniformity. The two countries were to have the same kind of church government, but the two churches were nonetheless to remain separate. Similarly in civil affairs the covenanters never specifically proposed what was later to be called an 'incorporating' union, a union in which the two parliaments would become one. The reason for this is not hard to see. The covenanters were motivated largely by a desire to preserve Scotland's identity, and to prevent arbitrary government by an absentee king. Closer union, they believed, would advance these causes by providing security for the constitutional and religious revolution they had achieved in Scotland. But too close a union would destroy their security for, since the two countries involved were so unequal in size, in population and in wealth, England and her interests would inevitably predominate in an incorporating union. Therefore Scotland had to retain her own parliament and general assembly, however close links were to be with their English counterparts. The union must be a federal one.

Unfortunately, though federal union recommended itself to the Scots, the English parliament showed little interest in it except as a means to gain the help of the covenanters. The trouble was that what seemed equal union to the covenanters seemed most unequal to the English, for it took no account of England's great superiority in size, wealth and population. Would not an equal union be one in which England predominated by right of such superiority? Was not the 'equal union' of the Scots simply justification of Scots interference in England's domestic concerns? This is not to say that the English parliament was against a closer union than that of the crowns, but that, seeing the sort of federal union proposed by the Scots as giving them a disproportionate say in English affairs, they rejected it in favour of full union, an incorporating union with a united parliament whose membership would be largely English. This is what the English parliamentary opposition had done in 1604–7, opposing James' proposed partial union and advocating full union or nothing. This is probably what the English parliamentary commissioners had meant in 1646 when they said that full union was desirable but if it could not be achieved no union was better than partial union.[15]

It has been said that in 1640–8 the English parliament would ideally have liked a full parliamentary union though (as it was a relatively conservative body) it never actually put forward so revolutionary a suggestion.[16] If such an ideal did exist the reason that it was never suggested is more likely to have been that there was no likelihood of agreement being reached on such a union. Nearly all the concessions would have had to have come from Scotland if the union parliament was to be essentially the English parliament with a few Scots members added (and this is what the

English meant by full and equal union). In the 1640s it was the Scots who held (or thought they held) the initiative over union, the Scots whose help the English parliament was forced to beg. The Scots, keen as they were for union, would only contemplate it on their own terms. They wanted a union which would leave the kingdoms separate enough for them to be treated as equals, without account being taken of their inequality in resourses. And the English easily evaded accepting such a union since union did not seem a matter of major importance to them, and they were soon able to dispense with Scots help.

This indeed was Scotland's great difficulty in pressing for union. To her it was frequently a matter of great importance, vital to her future, while to England it was something desirable but not essential, something which could be laid aside if the terms were not right. In 1604–7, in the 1640s, and at the end of the century Scots wishes for partial union met with English demands for all or nothing. Eventually Scotland had to accept that she could not impose her concept of union on her neighbour. The Scots were to get the security and commercial privileges that they sought only once they were ready to accept full parliamentary union and to abandon their plans for religious union. Moreover in order to achieve union the Scots not only had to modify their terms; they had to make England interested enough in union to take action to bring it about, and the only way Scotland could do this was by threatening England's security. Thus full union was only achieved in the 1650s when the threat posed by Scotland provoked English conquest, which the Scots then had no alternative but to accept. Similarly in 1707, though in very different circumstances, full union was achieved only because the weakness of the position of Scotland led her to accept full union, while the threat to England's security which she presented made the English take an interest in union. Throughout the seventeenth century Scotland's position was too weak to impose partial union; only in the 1650s and after 1700 was it so weak that she would accept full union as better than nothing. The 1640s had seen the most sustained attempt of the century by the Scots to bring about an 'equal' federal union. The attempt failed for the very reason that the covenanters felt forced to make it; because England's resources were so much greater than Scotland's.

THE KIRK

Scotland under the covenanters was not a theocracy; far from it being the case that 'as an independent estate the laity simply did not exist' in Scotland,[17] in fact 'the presbyterian system proved admirably adapted to be an instrument of the aristocracy and gentry'.[18] Nobles and lairds dominated the kirk in various roles; as elders, as lay patrons, as payers of stipends, as the richest men in society, as the most powerful men in the covenanting regime. Certainly the church often advised the state, even demanded that certain policies be followed, but such demands were met only if it was expedient. The kirk might be able to persecute more nobles and others of high social status than ever before, but it could do so only because the state permitted it to, as a way of dealing with enemies of the regime. 'What way the Army, and the Sword, and the Countenance of Nobles, and Officers seemed to sway, that way were the [kirk's] Censures carried'.[19]

The great majority of ministers accepted this; to many of them, men of conservative outlook who had accepted episcopacy as passively as they now accepted presbyterianism, such deference to social superiors seemed natural and right. Others perhaps persuaded themselves that since the kirk had freed itself from king and bishops it was now independent; they closed their eyes to its subservience to the state and lay interests. It was at first comparatively easy to do this since state and church had many common interests—in protecting the covenanting reformation and constitutional revolution (if necessary by intervention in England) in suppressing royalists of episcopalian or catholic sympathies. A few ministers were well aware of the extent of lay control of the kirk, and were convinced that it was wrong; lay control had prevented reformation going as far as it should have. But ministers with such radical outlooks were also in touch with the realities of the situation. Powerful lay backing had brought them partial success, and the quickest way to destroy what had been achieved so far would be to alienate the leading lay covenanters. For the time being therefore the radicals contented themselves with minor advances, such as forcing changes in worship on the kirk (and even this was only accepted because such changes were held to be aids to unity with England).[20] Such slow, limited moves towards completing reformation were all that was practicable while the kirk was dominated by laymen and had no chance of freeing itself—unless political circumstances changed dramatically.

The weakness of the kirk was seen after 1645 over the question of what concessions concerning religion might be made to bring about a peace settlement in England favourable to Scotland. Increasing tension between kirk and state culminated in the state making a treaty with the king (the Engagement), ratifying it in parliament, raising a large army, and invading England—and doing all this in the face of bitter opposition from the kirk. It was a defeat for the kirk which astonished those who had believed that the kirk would triumph in any such confrontation.[21] It was by far the greatest setback the ambitions of the radicals to free the kirk and dominate society had experienced since the troubles began. The kirk had defied the state but proved powerless to impose its will.

This defeat was, however, the immediate prelude to their greatest triumph, the establishment of the kirk party regime. This remarkable reversal of fortunes, bringing them victory in their darkest hour, confirmed the conviction of the radicals that God was behind them (even though it was odd that God had used Cromwell's forces, which were also his enemies, to defeat the ungodly Engagers).

The kirk party's seizure of power once the Engagers had conveniently been destroyed in England briefly gave Scotland the experience of something approaching theocracy. But the failure of the kirk party to retain power once it had seized it demonstrated clearly the lack of any social basis for theocracy. The kirk party's determination to exclude malignants of all sorts—including most of the nobility—from power collapsed when it was found how isolated this left the regime. Nobles and many of the greater lairds might be malignant, but the country could not be ruled without them, for there was no adequate alternative base of power in society.

The theocratic experiment failed, but the very fact that it had taken place meant that there could be no return to the pre-1648 situation, with a noble-dominated regime upholding the covenants while the kirk reverted to accepting dependence on the state. The experience of kirk party rule, with its appeal for support to lesser men in society and its radical policies, drove many nobles and lairds back to reliance on the king. Increasingly since 1645 some of them had come to believe that the only hope of a stable peace lay in a settlement based on alliance with the king. Now it seemed that alliance with the king was also necessary to protect the traditional structure of society from the assaults of extremist ministers. The kirk party regime proved more successful than any royalist propaganda in convincing the upper ranks of society that presbyterian church government was inherently dangerous, tending to theocracy.

Changed attitudes among radical ministers who had led the kirk party regime in the kirk also made a return to pre-1648 conditions impossible. Rather than submit, along with the majority of ministers (the resolutioners), to renewed domination by the state, the remonstrant and protester minority defied both kirk and state, claiming that it constituted the true kirk. For the first time the unity of the reformed church in Scotland was broken by a dissident group denying the legitimacy of the established kirk in which its enemies had prevailed. Previously dissidents had always recognised the kirk as a true church of God, in spite of corruptions, which they had worked to reform from within. Now instead the protesters in effect set up a rival structure claiming to be the one true church. The institutional unity of protestantism in Scotland was never to be fully restored.

Why was it that men who had, before the troubles, accepted the need to work within a corrupt kirk now felt it necessary virtually to secede? Perhaps most important was the fact that the radicals had tasted power and success. They had believed themselves to be on the verge of achieving their ambitions, only to have victory snatched from them through the malignancy of the nobility and the timorousness of the majority of ministers. Those who became protesters were those who could not bring themselves to accept defeat and to work within a corrupt kirk—though of course they never admitted that what they were doing amounted to schism, setting up a new sectarian kirk. They believed that they were the true kirk; it was the resolutioners who were guilty of schism.

Moreover even before 1637 the radicals, though working within the corrupt kirk, had taken what might be regarded as a first step towards separation through the holding of prayer meetings or conventicles of the godly separate from the public worship of the kirk. The radicals had indignantly denied that this implied that they had separatist tendencies, but the eventual secession of the protesters suggested that, intentionally or not, they had been moving in this direction. The freeing of the kirk from many of its corruptions in 1638–9 had removed the need for the radicals to continue on potentially separatist paths. The failure in 1649–50 to free it from its remaining corruptions persuaded them to resume their practice of worshipping apart from the ungodly majority, and to go further and claim that they constituted the true kirk.[22]

Unwillingness to accept defeat was one reason for the protesters' refusal to submit; the influence of English puritanism was probably another. The bitterness of the kirk's controversies with English Independents and sectaries over church government has tended to obscure the fact that the two sides to these disputes had much in common where other, more basic, aspects of religion were concerned. As Samuel Rutherford said, errors concerning essentials of theology, such as divine grace, were 'of a far other and higher elevation, then opinions touching Church-Government'.[23] On such essentials the kirk and most English puritans generally agreed. Leading ministers of the kirk found much to say about the godliness and sincerity of the Independents.[24] The effect of years of close contact with English puritanism, diverse and fragmented, on the kirk (and on those who became protesters in particular) has never been investigated, but the willingness of the protesters to secede (in fact if not in theory) from the kirk probably owed a good deal to it.

Other developments since 1637 helped to make secession by a godly minority possible; changes in the concept of the church and of its relation to the nation. The early successes of the covenanting movement led to widespread acceptance of its 'apocalyptic vision', the belief that Scotland was an 'elect nation', specially favoured by God and chosen by him to play a leading part in implementing his plans on earth. The Scots were seen as successors of the Israelites, who would be led from victory to victory; she had the best reformed church in Christendom and was the hope of the world, with the national covenant and the solemn league and covenant forming special bonds between her and God.[25] In the enthusiasm instilled by success the fact that the elect, those chosen by God for salvation, were in orthodox Calvinist theology only a minority of men was temporarily forgotten or ignored. The assumption, though never explicitly stated, was that all, or virtually all, Scots were among the elect,[26] united by the covenants and doing the work of God. The covenants with God could be interpreted almost as a contract, implying that men could help earn their own salvation by keeping their side of the covenant, a serious undermining of predestinarian doctrine[27] which seemed to hold out the hope that all covenanters would be saved. The visible church (all those in the country who acknowledged the kirk and submitted to it, whether predestined for salvation or damnation) could thus be regarded as coterminous with the invisible church, the elect.

Attitudes began to change in the mid 1640s as consistent success gave way to repeated failures. Disillusionment set in; it seemed that the Scots as a people were not so godly after all. The population of Scotland, like that of other countries, now appeared to be a mixture of the elect and the reprobate—with the latter predominating. The more radical ministers reacted by moving towards what might be called exclusive rather than inclusive attitudes. If only a minority was godly, and therefore likely to be among the elect (though there was doubt as to whether or not the elect could be identified on earth), then should not this minority wield power in both church and state? Instead of all joining voluntarily in the work of God it now seemed that most would have to be forced. Such exclusive tendencies (foreshadowed by the conventicles of the godly held before the troubles) were partly justified by developments in covenant theology,[28] and are demonstrated in changing attitudes to admission to the sacrament of the lord's supper. Traditionally the sacrament had been open to all not actually excommunicated or under other kirk censures. Increasingly during the 1640s it appears (though the process has not been traced in detail) that some ministers put more and more emphasis on stringent qualifications necessary for admission. Tests of religious knowledge, repentance for sins and political loyalties were introduced. Thus adherence to the national covenant and the solemn league and covenant became necessary for admission.[29] Instead of a few notorious evil-doers being excluded, the tendency was only to admit the most positively godly. This was seen most clearly among the protesters; 'They will exclude such multitudes for one cause or for another, that the end will be the setting up a new refined congregation of their own adherents' said Robert Baillie.[30] Full church membership was not to be for all the nation but for the godly minority. The tendency for radical ministers thus to separate the godly from the ungodly in their flocks made it easier for them, when the split in the kirk came in 1650, to separate from the ungodly majority of ministers.

This change from an optimistic, inclusive outlook, willing to welcome all ready to offer help without investigating their motives or their morals, to a pessimistic, exclusive outlook, carefully examining men's qualifications (and rejecting those of many) before admitting them as allies, can also be seen in the way the covenants were presented, thus affecting the whole covenanting movement. In 1638 the national covenant was offered to all; it was to be sworn by all subjects[31] 'of what ranke and quality soevir' and refusers were to suffer both ecclesiastical censures and civil penalties.[32] Similarly the solemn league and covenant in 1643 was to be sworn by all; refusers were to be regarded as enemies to religion, peace and the king's honour.[33] Thus at first signature of both covenants was open to all, and was indeed obligatory on all. For it was believed that once all had signed, binding themselves to the cause by solemn oaths, all would be well. If only all could be persuased to swear the covenants, then there would be none to oppose them. This assumption was both naive and optimistic, and did not survive long once things started to go wrong. By the later 1640s it was clear that the covenants, presented in this way, had failed to create, or at least to maintain, a united movement. Some had sworn the covenants hypocritically, to escape persecution, to gain worldly advantage, or so as to be able to work secretly against them. Others might originally have sworn sincerely but had broken their vows later, or proved to have unacceptable ideas about how the covenants should be interpreted. The success of the Engagers in Scotland indicated the dangers of admitting all men willing to sign the covenants to power in church and state. Consequently when, after the Engagers had been defeated, orders were given that the solemn league and covenant should be renewed, the covenant was presented in a new way. Former supporters of the Engagement, far from being forced to swear it, were not to be allowed to do so until they had repented, done penance to the satisfaction of the kirk, and convinced it of their sincerity. Only then were they to be allowed the privilege of taking the covenant.[34] Instead of demonstrating the unity of the elect nation the covenants had become symbols of the division between the sheep and the goats. Men had to prove themselves worthy of taking the covenants, rather than (as had previously been the case) proving themselves worthy by taking the covenants. Only in this way, it was believed, could enemies of the covenants be prevented from creeping, after swearing hypocritically, into office in church and state, thus undermining the covenanting movement from within.

This attempt by the kirk party to substitute a covenanted elite for the covenanted nation failed. Political necessity was soon again forcing the kirk to admit as sincere the obviously false repentances of Engagers and royalists whose help was necessary if English invasion was to be resisted.[35] George Gillespie, the leader of the kirk's resistance to the Engagement, had expressed fears before his death at the end of 1648 that this might happen, seeing it as something which would bring down God's wrath upon them: 'Alas, shall we split twise upon the same Rock?'[36] In accordance with such beliefs the remonstrants and protesters refused to compromise in 1650–1; how could the cause of God be served by handing over power to malignants? As Samuel Rutherford put it 'We are not for an Army of Saints, and free of all Mixture, of ill affected Men: But it seems an high prevarication, for Church Men, to Consel and teach, that the weight and Trust of the Affairs of Christ, and his Kingdom should be laid upon the whole party of such, as have been enemies of our Cause; contrary to the Word of God'.[37] The protesters therefore refused to accept that it was no longer possible to exclude the ungodly from power. This refusal drove them into a sectarian position; they might claim to be the true national church, but in reality they became an exclusive minority sect.[38]

The attempts of the kirk party to impose its will on the country raised doubts in many minds about the value of presbyterian church government. It had been presented to the English as providing a middle way between tyranny and anarchy;[39] strong central control would prevent anarchy, while parity of ministers and election to church courts guarded against tyranny. Yet in its relations with lay society the presbyterian kirk seemed to show symptoms of both extremes. This was true of the internal government of the kirk as well. Presbyterianism had failed to prevent, and indeed had positively contributed to, the first split in the institutional unity of the kirk since the Reformation; it thus seemed that it was no protection against the anarchy of secessions and sectarianism. Moreover it proved tyrannical not only in that it persecuted its enemies, but in that control of the system could be taken over by well organised and determined minority groups—like the radicals (with lay support) after 1637 and the kirk party after 1648. These minorities dominated the general assembly and forced policies upon the more conservative majority of ministers. Increasingly the commission for the public affairs of the kirk emerged as the body through which a minority controlled the kirk. Many ministers came to object to its powers, fearing that it opened 'a door to tyrannie, whilst we think to shut out tyrants out of the Kirk'. Centralisation of power seemed essential if the covenanting kirk was to be successful in its struggle to survive, but it seriously upset the balance of power between central and local courts which was supposed to be the essence of presbyterian government. It is notable, for example, that whereas the presbyteries had power to depose unsatisfactory ministers from office, the majority of ministers purged in 1637–51 were deposed by the general assembly, by the commission of the kirk, or by special commissions appointed by them. Central courts increasingly supplanted local ones, executing policies as well as making them.[40]

The list of charges which can be made against the kirk in 1637–51 is a long one. It seemed consistently to achieve the opposite to what was intended. High ideals of a free kirk contrasted sharply with the reality of lay control; the attempts of the kirk party to evade it proved how inescapable it was. Ideals of a united national kirk led to a kirk more clearly split than ever before. The covenants came to stress the disunity, not the unity, of Scotsmen. Dreams of religious unity with England collapsed, having succeeded only in rousing hatreds that left unity further away than ever. Hopes of avoiding anarchy and tyranny in church government led to a system which gave rise to fears of both. Expectations of moral regeneration came to nothing. The kirk allowed itself to be sidetracked from its spiritual functions into political matters and into repression on behalf of the regime. Endless controversy with Independents and sectarians over church government gave the impression that the kirk thought details of polity more important than other aspects of religion.

The two primary reasons for these failures of the covenanting kirk are closely connected. First, carried away by early successes, the more radical ministers attempted too much; they proved unable to dominate society in Scotland or to export their revolution to England. Secondly, this contributed to the fact that throughout the period the kirk was struggling continually to maintain and secure its position. Emergency followed emergency, and naturally the fight for survival had to take precedence over all else. The kirk was forced to concentrate its attention on some matters and neglect others in ways it did not wish and would not have done in more peaceful conditions. In the course of its struggles, in the ways in which it reacted to emergencies, the kirk developed in ways which could not have been predicted in 1638. As so often happens, the outcome of a revolution was very different from what the revolutionaries had originally hoped and expected—not just in that (in this case) the revolution was ultimately defeated, but in that even before its final failure necessity had forced it in unexpected directions.

THE CONSERVATIVE REVOLUTION

The Scottish revolution was essentially conservative. In the ways in which the covenanters justified resistance to the king and in the policies that they imposed they looked to the past. In both religion and politics they usually claimed to be resisting innovations by the king, not to be innovating themselves. Of course such a conservative looking to the past in theory could be combined with new departures in practice, for years of controversy and conflict produced new circumstances, demanding innovation in practice and extension of old theories to justify it. This does happen in Scotland, but only to a limited extent. There is nothing like the remarkably rich and varied flood of new ideas about church, state and society, about the basis of authority of all sorts, which emerges from the English revolution. Scotland produced in the 1640s no levellers, no republicans, no demands for extension of the franchise, no advocates of religious toleration. Why was this?

First of all, perhaps it is misleading to put the question in this way. The real wonder is not that Scotland produced so few new ideas in this period, but that England produced so many. Thus that Scotland proved less fertile ground for new ideas than England should not lead automatically to the conclusion that this proves that Scotland was suffering from remarkable backwardness that needs to be explained. It is England that shows exceptional features, not Scotland. Moreover, even in England most of those who opposed the king regarded their action as conservative, not innovatory, and in some respects the English revolution was just as backward-looking as the Scottish revolution. Both revolutions, it has been said, were 'two or three generations behind the times', in that on the continent by the 1640s 'political and social revolt lacked the ammunition of religious dissent'. The 'combined political and religious opposition which challenged the government of Charles I therefore looked very much like the belated English version of a kind of movement which was nearly extinct on the continent.'[41]

However, though the aims of resistance to the king in Scotland and in England were both originally conservation and restoration, the problem remains of explaining the very different developments of the revolutions in the two kingdoms. England's revolution may have developed in an unusual way, but if Scotland's had similar origins why did it not show similar originality and diversity? It is true that the difference between developments in the two countries is one of degree rather than of kind; both follow the same basic pattern of limited resistance turning into full scale revolt and revolution, leading in turn to conservative reaction, attempted counter-revolution, a 'move to the left' and displacement of the original revolutionary leadership by more radical elements (though even in England the 'radicalism' of the rump parliament was very limited).[42] Nonetheless, the differences between the two revolutions remain.

One explanation undoubtedly lies in the differences between the societies and economies of the two countries. Economic development had been much slower in Scotland than in England, and had done much less towards undermining the traditional structure of society. The strength of nobles and other landlords in Scotland was much greater than south of the border. In the countryside little basic change had yet to come to the centuries-old organisation and methods of agriculture. Urbanisation in Scotland was much more limited than in England, and Calvinism seemed to have done nothing to inspire capitalism in Scotland (which had tended to lead those seeking to establish a causal connection between the two to ignore Scotland).[43] It was of some significance that Scotland had no great urban centre like London. The importance of this is perhaps most clearly seen in connection with the spread of propaganda and controversial ideas through the printing press. In London, with a large population providing a ready market, printing thrived and proved very hard to control; printers and small presses could easily conceal themselves in the anonymity of a great city. From open and hidden presses poured thousands of pamphlets expressing an astonishing variety of opinions on a great variety of subjects, stirred up by the stimulus of war and revolution. By contrast the few Scottish printers were closely supervised by the covenanting regime. The majority of items printed were official proclamations and declarations of church and state, and uncontroversial religious works. Not only did what works Scottish royalists managed to get published appear from English presses; even the main controversial works of the leading ministers of the kirk were mostly printed in London, for it was there that controversy still raged on matters which had long been settled in Scotland.

This leads to what is perhaps the main reason why the flood of ideas in England had little counterpart in Scotland. When the covenanters rejected episcopacy there was an alternative system of church government available which was generally acceptable because features of it had long existed in the kirk in Scotland—presbyterianism. Moreover there were no separatists in Scotland, no sects outside the established church to confuse the issue by putting forward their own claims once episcopacy was destroyed. In Scotland as soon as bishops were abolished the presbyterian elements already existing in the kirk were extended to provide a presbyterian system. In England by contrast episcopacy was condemned before it was decided what should replace it; years were allowed to pass in controversy, leaving a vacuum in church government. This long delay in agreeing on a settlement encouraged diversity of opinion to blossom, and allowed the sects which already existed to spread. As a result when a presbyterian system was at last imposed, it was impossible to enforce uniformity.[44] As the leaders of the kirk well realised, this period of 'Ecclesiasticall Anarchy'[45] was a fertile breeding ground for Independents and sectaries.

Thus in Scotland the major religious issues were quickly settled. In England such matters were left open for years while a variety of solutions (growing out of existing diversity) were discussed.

To a lesser extent the same is true in constitutional matters. Charles I promptly conceded in 1641 all the constitutional demands made by the Scottish parliament, granting much more than he ever did to the English parliament. He did this because he saw, rightly, that what was really essential to him was power in England, control of the English parliament. In order to help to regain this it was expedient to make all the concessions demanded in a subsidiary kingdom of which he was an absentee monarch. Whatever the motives for Charles' concessions in Scotland, they meant that he had agreed to being reduced to a figurehead of a country ruled by the three estates; and he had agreed to this within little more than a year of detailed demands for constitutional concessions first being made. Undoubtedly problems would occur in implementing the 1641 constitutional settlement in Scotland, in trying to work out in practice what the role of the king in government should be; but the fact that Charles was an absentee ruler and was soon involved in the English civil war deferred controversy over this. Scotland had achieved a constitutional settlement promptly and without a full scale civil war.

In England on the other hand the king's refusal to make such full concessions as he had made in Scotland led to prolonged civil war—over the militia question (control of the armed forces) a matter which had been little debated in Scotland. During the civil war in England there was extended discussion of and controversy over the terms for a constitutional settlement, and over theoretical justification for different types of settlement. But in Scotland in these years there was little such controversy, for the matter was settled already. Large scale civil war did come to Scotland, in 1644–5, but this was (ostensibly at least) on the issue of whether Scotland should help the English parliament against the king. Such intervention in England in 1644 and (so far as many of the Engagers were concerned) in 1648 was concerned not with achieving a constitutional settlement in Scotland, but with securing one already achieved by bringing about a favourable peace in England and thus ensuring that the king respected the 1641 settlement in Scotland. In these circumstances it is hardly surprising that debate over political theory and constitutional settlements thrived in England, but not in Scotland where the terms of a settlement had already been agreed and the problem was enforcing them. Just as most works on religious controversy written by Scots ministers in these years were published in London, so was the most influential Scottish work on political theory, Samuel Rutherford's *Lex Rex*.

It seems reasonable, then, to conclude that the Scots had a less diverse revolution than the English partly because they had a more efficient one, which made controversy unnecessary. The covenanters completed their revolution without losing control of it. Where they then failed was in their unsuccessful intervention in England, which failed to bring them security. Prolonged insecurity led to the royalist revival of the later 1640s, which roused fears that the revolution was being betrayed from within and thus provoked the kirk party's seizure of power. With the kirk party came a realisation that old views on a variety of matters perhaps needed modification in the light of events—a new awareness of social problems and a readiness to contemplate altering the traditional balance of power in society. Even here, however, the covenanters were reactionary in their radicalism, basing it on theocratic ideas.

If the Scottish revolution produced little in the way of entirely novel ideas, old ones were developed in new ways to suit new circumstances. In religion orthodox Calvinism might be reasserted in place of new-fangled Arminianism, but it was a Calvinism altered by a new emphasis on covenant or federal theology.[46] Sectarian ideas did not thrive, but a few sectaries can be identified,[47] and many who were to become sectaries in the 1650s can be seen moving in this direction in the 1640s, driven by circumstances.[48] Schism first comes to Scotland at the end of the 1640s, helped by ideas about church membership new to Scotland. It seems likely, moreover, that further study of the ideas of the leading ministers of the day will prove them to be more original and interesting than is usually assumed. English historians perhaps have tended to approach them with hostility for daring to try to impose ideas stigmatised as alien and backward on England; Scots historians pay lip service to Samuel Rutherford, Alexander Henderson, Robert Baillie and George Gillespie as great men of the kirk, but have produced no systematic and critical studies of their works.

In one field it is obvious that the covenanters were hindered by dogged adherence to old ideas—church-state relations. Ministers clung tenaciously to the Melvillian theory of the two kingdoms in spite of the insuperable problems of demarcation which it raised, insisting that all would be well if only all concerned showed good will; they struggled to get it accepted in England, closing their eyes to the fact that it was only being implemented nominally in Scotland.

In political theory too the covenanters generally held fast to old ideas. In justifying resistance to the king the crude expedient of insisting that they were fighting to free him from his evil advisers proved exceptionally useful (as it did in England). When this wore thin the argument common among Calvinists in the previous century that an ungodly magistrate (one not only personally ungodly, but who also ordered his subjects to do ungodly things) must be resisted, since God's law had precedence over men's, still proved powerful. The difficulty here too was one of definition; who was to judge whether the magistrate was godly or not? What was to be done if the magistrate (like Charles I and Charles II) stubbornly refused to admit either that he was ungodly, or that his ungodliness would justify resistance by subjects to him? The answer lay in limiting royal power to prevent the king abusing it; Scottish tradition justified this, for the belief that the estates of the realm had a right to a share in ruling the country had a long history. John Major and Hector Boece had upheld it in the early sixteenth century, followed by John Knox and George Buchanan after the Reformation. The estates could also be seen as the 'inferior magistrates' whom Calvinist political theory asserted should lead resistance to the ungodly ruler.

Though theories of the powers of the three estates were old, the covenanters were the first to try to put them into practice by converting vague generalisations into detailed constitutional reforms, making parliament the effective ruler of the country and establishing a system of committee government both centrally and locally. So far as they were influenced by any existing political system, the covenanters first looked to the Netherlands.[49] Clement Walker's claim that Argyll 'in conspiracy with certaine his Confederates' intended 'to transforme the Kingdome of Scotland into a Free State like the Estates of Holland'[50] is an exaggeration, but one which probably has a good deal of truth behind it. The Netherlands and Scotland were similar in religion and were strongly linked by trade and culture. The Dutch political system, with a stadholder whose power was limited by the provincial estates, seemed one that might offer solutions to Scotland's problems—especially since the Dutch system was a federal one such as the covenanters hoped to see established to link England and Scotland.[51] The other contemporary political system which was often referred to in relation to Scotland was that of Venice. Charles I complained that 'as long as the Covenant was not passed from, He had no more Power than the Duke of Venice',[52] while Rutherford could 'see small difference between a King, and the Duke of Venice'.[53] In Scotland as elsewhere it seems that the constitution of Venice had (erroneously) become accepted as 'the ideal combination of liberty and order'.[54]

As the Dutch and Venetian examples suggest, what the covenanters sought was mixed monarchy, a government combining the best features of monarchy, aristocracy and democracy. Mixed monarchy was also the generally accepted political theory among parliamentarians in England,[55] where, indeed, one of its best known advocates was Samuel Rutherford.[56] It has been said that this work exhibits 'no originality unless in its phrasing'.[57] This may be true so far as England is concerned, but the work is nonetheless of great interest as the most able and extended Scottish treatment of the theory of mixed monarchy; though published in England it was widely read in Scotland.

Rutherford maintained that no one form of government is inherently superior to another. Monarchy, arsitocracy and democracy are all of divine institution, and in any case the three forms differ only in degree; thus aristocracy is 'diffused and inlarged Monarchy, and Monarchy is nothing by contracted Aristocracy'.[58] A community having 'no Government at all, may ordain a King, or appoint an Aristocracie'.[59] In a monarchy 'The power of creating a man a King, is from the people';[60] they may limit the power they give him and 'they may take again to themselves what they gave out, upon condition, if the condition be violated',[61] for the relation of king and people is a covenant or social contract.[62] A dynasty has a hereditary right to the crown 'only by the suffrages of the people'.[63] So far Rutherford's ideas sound secular and democratic, but this is not the case. Kings hold their crowns from God; God may institute the form of government, not directly but 'mediately by the free will of men'.[64] Similarly God in establishing a king inclines 'the hearts of the States to choose this man, and not this man'.[65] In the same way if a king is deposed 'God doth not take the authority of the King from him *immediately*, but *mediately* by the people their hating and dispising him'.[66] The authority of a king is divine, but in granting or removing it God acts through the people. Thus (in a sermon) Rutherford could sincerely state that 'Princes are Gods Standard-bearers, they beare his Sword by office . . . and they hold Crowne and Scepter of him, as great Landlords of all powers' and that 'In a special manner they are second Gods', God's deputies.[67] James VI had used very similar phrases in justifying absolute monarchy; Rutherford while accepting divine right insisted that it was exercised through the people. But though Rutherford talks frequently of the rights and powers of 'the people' he was not, as has sometimes been claimed, a democrat;[68] for 'he seems never to have meant by the "people" anything but the *pars valentior*',[69] and he uses the term interchangeably with 'the states' or 'estates'. What Rutherford advocated was democratic elements in mixed government, not pure democracy; and by democratic elements he meant no more than a part in government for the three estates, which 'taken collectively doe represent the people'.[70]

Though Rutherford argued that forms of government were a matter of expediency, he had no doubt that the best form was 'A limited and mixed Monarchy, such as is in Scotland and England'. Such a system has glory, order and unity from monarchy; from aristocracy, 'the government of the most and wisest', it has safety in counsel, stability and strength; from the influence of the commons it has 'liberty, priviledges, promptitude of obedience'.[71] Each of the three elements on its own, on the other hand, was liable to abuse; 'absolute Monarchy is Tyranny, unmixed Democracy is confusion, untempered Aristocracy is factious Dominion'.[72] How far the political ideas put forward by Rutherford were shared by the covenanting leaders is hard to say; but probably they do represent the sort of constitutional position which many of them hoped the king's concessions of 1641 would bring about.

Though Rutherford was no democrat, some of what he wrote could be interpreted in democratic ways. His vague talk of 'the people'; his insistence that the right of nobles to sit in parliament was a matter of positive law, which could be changed, not of divine or natural law;[73] and his assertion that resistence to a parliament which abused the power entrusted to it is justified.[74] But though English Levellers on occasion quoted *Lex Rex* with approval[75] there is no evidence that his work was interpreted in a democratic way in Scotland. The radicalism of the kirk party was theocratic, not democratic.

In some ways the covenanters went further in theory than in practice in their political ideas. Rutherford was certainly not alone in believing that a king might be deposed, and a new one created or a non-monarchic form of government established. But when it came to the problems of dealing with Charles I and Charles II this was never openly advocated. It was realised that it might solve some difficulties, but that it would create many more. It would be unacceptable to the great majority of Scots, and thus destroy the covenanting movement, and it would break the link with England which seemed vital to the covenanters. Enemies asserted that the protesters and remonstrants had republican sentiments (like the English enemy they were so reluctant to fight), claiming that they 'will never be satisfied with the proceedings of kirk or state. . . for there is the voice of a king among them',[76] but in fact the protesters went no further than refusing to admit the king to power until he proved himself worthy. This might be illogical, but the failure of the republican experiment in England suggests that the conservatism of the covenanters in refusing to accept the obvious but extreme solution to the problem of the monarchy was justified, and indicated that they were more closely in touch with the sentiments of both the common people and the estates than Cromwell and his supporters were.

REVOLUTION AND RESTORATION

The Scottish revolution failed; and years of confusion and defeat produced a strong reaction in favour of restoration of the monarchy and a return to the pre-1637 situation. But of course when the Restoration came in 1660 complete restoration, as if the unhappy years 1637–60 had never existed, was impossible. The Scottish revolution had failed, but the fact that it had taken place meant that things could never be the same again.[77]

Socially and politically the experience of 1637–51 inclined the upper ranks of society to reactionary conservatism. The nobility in particular concluded that resistance to the king and establishment of presbyterian church government were socially subversive and politically disastrous. Undermining the king undermined the nobility; presbyterianism threatened social hierarchy and deference. The nobility had been offended by the pretensions of the bishops before 1637, but presbyterian ministers had in the end proved even more troublesome. The solution after 1660 was found in moderate episcopacy, strictly controlled by a king who realised the danger of allowing bishops to alienate the nobility. Charles I had broken the alliance of crown and nobility which James VI had used to defeat the presbyterians, and Charles II was well aware of the need to re-establish it, taking advantage of the nobility's disillusionment with presbyterianism. Thus after the Restoration episcopal power was limited and 'office and power lay with nobles'—many of whom had been leading covenanters in the 1640s.[78] Partly no doubt this was simply a reflection of the differences in personality and political wisdom between Charles I and Charles II; but it was also partly a recognition by Charles II and his advisers that the power of the nobility, as it had been demonstrated in 1637–51, could not be ignored (as it had been by Charles I) in the hope that it would go away.

The conservative reaction in favour of the monarchy was shared by the great majority of the lairds, and by most below them in society. But many in the south-west Lowlands refused to submit to episcopacy; they were no longer prepared to follow the lead of the local nobles who had originally helped to stir them up to resist Charles I and who now demanded that they submit to his son. In 1648 many of the men of the south-west had defied the Engagers, and in 1650–1, through the army of the Western Association, they had refused to accept the fall of the kirk party. Now in the Restoration period many of the common people of the west, under the leadership of conventicler ministers and some smaller lairds, were to defy the king in a series of popular rebellions (primarily religious in origin though also owing something to economic and social grievances)[79] of a kind never seen in Scotland before the Scottish revolution. For the first time a Scottish monarch was faced by rebellions not led by nobles or chiefs,[80] and it was the experience of the 1640s that made this possible.

The Scottish revolution confirmed the reputation for religious radicalism which the south-west had held since the Reformation. It also confirmed the reputation of the north-east for religious conservatism, and linked this much more closely than before to support for the Stewarts. In the Highlands the 1640s were decisive in the remarkable change which converted many clans from being a major obstacle of the power of the Stuart monarchy into its staunchest supporters; while the Campbells were transformed from being the dynasty's agents in the Highlands into a serious threat to it. The clans which supported James VII after the 1688–9 revolution were largely the same clans which had fought for Montrose. The conversion of parts of the Highlands into Jacobite strongholds had begun in the 1640s.

The methods by which Scotland was governed were different after 1660 from those of before 1637. Government through the privy council was restored (though with the crown relying in the council more on nobles, less on bishops) but increasingly there emerged a single official responsible to the king for Scottish affairs. The duke of Lauderdale, as secretary of state and king's commissioner in parliament for many years held a position approaching that of viceroy for Scotland. The novelty of this was recognised, and led to his powers as king's commissioner being denounced as unconstitutional.[81] This solving of the problems posed by absentee monarchy by establishing what amounted to a viceregal system (such as had long been employed in Ireland) was carried furthest when after 1679 James, duke of York, the heir to the throne, was given direction of Scottish affairs. James VI had contemplated such a solution to the difficulty of ruling Scotland under the union of the crowns, but had not implemented it. Charles I had been forced into an approximation to it when the troubles began, sending the marquis of Hamilton to Scotland as his commissioner in 1638, the earl of Traquair in 1639. Later Montrose had been given viceregal powers. The speed with which Charles I's regime had collapsed in Scotland when faced with opposition had pointed the need for the concentration of responsibility for Scottish affairs in the hands of one man. Under absentee monarchy such a ministerial system approximated to a viceregal one.

Another lesson Charles II appears to have learnt was that his father's insistence of keeping Scottish and English affairs separate was dangerous.

Charles I had followed anglicising policies in Scotland, but had not given his English advisers any say in, or even information about, Scottish matters. The years of revolution had shown clearly how opposition to the king in one country was likely to spread to the other. It was therefore only prudent that the king's ministers and advisers of both kingdoms should work together.

Legally the Scottish parliament returned after 1661 to its pre-1637 state. The acts of 1640–1 which had reformed its constitution were declared null, even though Charles I had ratified them (whereas in England the early acts of the Long Parliament which Charles had accepted remained in force). Bishops and officers of state were restored to membership. The lords of the articles, through whom the king controlled legislation presented to the full parliament, were revived. The king's right to appoint councillors, judges and officers of state without parliamentary approval was restored. Yet things had changed. Parliament might be firmly under royal control again, but (once the first flush of royalist enthusiasm immediately after the Restoration was over) it was no longer the rubber stamp, with virtually no debate allowed, that it had been in the early seventeenth century. Parliament met more frequently than before (though gaps of several years still occur), and its sessions now often lasted for weeks or months (as in the 1640s), not just for a few days as had happened before 1637. Opposition to official policies appeared and was expressed in prolonged debates in a way not seen before the revolution.[82] Lairds were tacitly allowed to retain the individual votes they had gained in 1640–1; no attempt was made to restrict them again to only one vote per shire. And later, in 1689–90, demands for a revival of the constitution of 1640–1 were made and were partially successful; the lords of the articles were abolished.

Moreover, though all the public legislation of the parliaments of 1640–9[83] was rescinded, many innovations made in these years were soon revived. The main taxes imposed in the Restoration period were excise duties (first imposed by the covenanters in 1644) and the cess based on valued rents, modelled on the monthly maintenance of the later 1640s.[84] The commissioners of supply who raised the taxes in the shires after 1660 were revivals of commissioners appointed by the covenanters in the 1640s.[85] The provisions of the 1646 act for founding schools in every parish were 'substantially embodied' in the 1696 act for settling of schools.[86] A 1645 act was 'the first of a series which established parliamentary protection of industry in Scotland', the other acts being passed after 1660.[87] An act of 1641 in favour of enclosing parks and plantations, the first for this purpose, provided a precedent for acts of 1661 and 1669. The famous commonty act of 1695, providing machinery for the division of common lands, owed several features to a 1647 act for division of commonties in the Lothians, Lanarkshire and Ayrshire.[88]

Finally, the differences in the religious state of Scotland in the 1630s and in the 1660s are very marked. Episcopacy might be restored, but the powers of bishops were limited; in particular, they were little employed in civil affairs. The Five Articles of Perth, the 1636 book of canons and the 1637 prayer book which had sparked off the troubles were quietly abandoned. The court of high commission was not revived.[89] More significant was the fact that it proved impossible to restore the institutional unity of all supporters of reformed religion in Scotland. Whereas before 1637 all protestants, no matter how they hated episcopacy, had accepted the established church as a true (if corrupt) church, now after 1660 a minority of the opponents of episcopacy (like the protesters of the 1650s) refused to work within a corrupt kirk to reform it.[90] The schisms and secessions which were to be such a notable feature of Scottish presbyterianism in the centuries ahead had begun.

Notes

CHAPTER 1: *Civil War in England and Scotland, January 1644–September 1645*

1 C.S. Terry, *The Life and Campaigns of Alexander Leslie, First Earl of Leven* (1899), 181–91.
2 PA.11/2, Register of the Committee of Estates (Army), 1643–4, ff.11–12.
3 Ibid, ff.12v–16v, 18–19v.
4 E.g., PA.11/1, Register of the Committee of Estates, 1643–4, ff.113v–120, 123–4; *APS*, VI.i.78–80.
5 PA.11/2, ff.18–19.
6 *APS*, VI.i.72–3; NLS, MS. Adv. 33.4.8, Transactions of the Scottish Army in Ireland, pp.50–4; J. Turner, *Memoirs of his own Life and Times* (Bannatyne Club 1829), 31–3; PA.11/1, ff.125–126v, 135v–136, 137–8; J.S. Reid, *History of the Presbyterian Church in Ireland* (3 vols., Belfast 1867), i.545–6.
7 Ibid, i.546-50; PA.11/1, ff.139–140v, 148v–149; NLS, MS. Adv. 33.4.8. pp.58–84; Turner, *Memoirs*, 33–4; HMC 29: *Portland*, i.173, 175–6.
8 Terry, *Alexander Leslie*, 190-219; PA.11/2, ff.21–57.
9 C.V. Wedgwood, 'The Covenanters in the First Civil War', *SHR*, xxxix (1960), 9–10.
10 R. Baillie, *Letters and Journals* (3 vols., Bannatyne Club 1841–2), ii.103.
11 L. Kaplan, 'Presbyterians and Independents in 1643', *EHR*, lxxxiv (1969), 249, 251–2.
12 Baillie, *Letters*, ii. 103, 117.
13 *CJ*, iii.264, 279; LJ, vi.288.
14 Baillie, *Letters*, ii.106; *APS*, VI.i.63, 70–1, 72, 83.
15 V. Pearl, 'Oliver St John and the "Middle Group" in the Long Parliament', *EHR*, lxxxi (1966), 494, 498, 508–9, 513, 514; W. Notestein 'The Establishment of the Committee of Both Kingdoms', *American Historical Review*, xvii (1912), 477–95; Baillie, *Letters*, ii.141–2; H.W. Meikle (ed.), *Correspondence of the Scots Commissioners in London* (Roxburghe

Club 1917),2–4.

16 Ibid, 4–31. For the attendances of the Scots on the Committee of Both Kingdoms see L. Mulligan, 'The Scottish Alliance and the Committee of Both Kingdoms', *Historical Studies*, xiv (1970), 174–5.

17 Baillie, *Letters*, ii.156, 166.

18 A.J. and A.M. Macdonald, *The Clan Donald* (3 vols., Inverness 1896–1904) ii.723, 725; T. Carte, *The Life of James Duke of Ormond* (3 vols., 1735–6) iii.214.

19 J. Spalding, *Memorialls of the Trubles* (2 vols., Spalding Club 1850–1) ii.291–2; J. Lowe, 'The Earl of Antrim and Irish Aid to Montrose in 1644, *Irish Sword*, iv (1959–60), 191–4; R. Scrope and T. Monkhouse (eds), *State Papers Collected by Edward Earl of Clarendon* (3 vols., Oxford 1767–86) ii.165–6; G. Hill, *Macdonnells of Antrim* (Belfast 1873), 266–7; Macdonalds, *Clan Donald*, ii.726; HMC 1: *2nd Report*, App, 172.

20 M. Napier, *Memorials of Montrose* (2 vols., Maitland Club 1848–50), ii.119–21; G. Wishart, *Memoirs of Montrose* (1893), 40–2.

21 E.g., W. Fraser, *The Chiefs of Grant* (3 vols., Edinburgh 1883), ii.7–8.

22 E.g., HMC 55: *Various Collections*, v.248.

23 Napier, *Memorials*, ii.128,141.

24 Lowe, 'The Earl of Antrim and Irish Aid to Montrose', *Irish Sword* iv.195–7; C. O'Danachair, 'Montrose's Irish Regiments', *Irish Sword*, iv (1959–60), 61–7.

25 Inveraray Castle, Argyll Transcripts, xii.134; J. Balfour, *Historical Works* (4 vols., Edinburgh 1824–5), iii.198–9.

26 Wishart, *Memoirs*, 36–7; Spalding, *Memorialls*, ii.6, 87, 91–2, 207–8, 290, 301–2, 350–6, 319–20; P. Gordon, *A Short Abridgement of Britane's Distemper* (Spalding Club 1844), 46–7; J. Dennistoun and A. Macdonald (eds.), 'Wigton Papers.' *Maitland Club Miscellany*, 11.ii.439–41.

27 Spalding, *Memorialls*, ii.256, 268, 296, 298, 299, 304–5; *APS*, VI.i.21–2; PA.11/1, ff.59–60, 99; A. Jaffray, *Diary* (Aberdeen 1856), 47–8, 49.

28 *Aber Recs 1643–1747*, 17–18; Gordon, *Britane's Distemper*, 48–9; Spalding, *Memorialls*, ii.324–5; Jaffray, *Diary*, 48; Dennistoun and Macdonald, *Maitland Club Miscellany*, 11.ii.441–2; GD.44/13/5/8, Gordon Castle Muniments.

29 Gordon, *Britane's Distemper*, 48–9; *Aber Recs, 1643–1747*, 19–22; L.B. Taylor (ed.), *Aberdeen Council Letters*, ii (Oxford 1950), 364–5; Spalding, *Memorialls*, ii.329–31, 342, 344–5.

30 PA.11/1. ff.167v–196v *passim*; *APS*, VI.i.84, 86–7.

31 PA.11/2, ff.37v, 38–v; PA.11/1, ff.183v–184; Spalding, *Memorialls*, ii.347, 361–2; H. Guthry, *Memoirs* (Glasgow 1747), 153–4.

32 *APS*, VI.i.89–92, 859; PA.11/1, f.216v; Turner, *Memoirs*, 36–8; Guthry,

Memoirs, 142.

33 Wishart, *Memoirs*, 44–5; Napier, *Memorials*, ii.122, 131, 132; Gordon, *Britane's Distemper*, 49–50; J. Barbour, *The Capture of the Covenanting Town of Dumfries by Montrose* (n.d.), 4–8; PA.11/1, ff.203v, 204, 223v.

34 Ibid, f.234v, PA.11/2, ff. 53v–54v; Wishart, *Memoirs*, 46; J. Somerville, *Memorie of the Somervills* (2 vols., Edinburgh 1815), ii.296–335; Terry, *Alexander Leslie*, 284–6.

35 Spalding, *Memorialls*, ii.334, 336–9, 341, 347–9, 351–77; Gordon, *Britane's Distemper*, 51–3; PA.11/1, ff.231v–232, 236–8.

36 *APS*, VI.i.148–57, 189–92.

37 Baillie, *Letters*, ii.217; *APS*, VI.i.102, 124, 126–30, 158–9.

38 *APS*, VI.i.861; Baillie, *Letters*, ii.214.

39 *APS*, VI.i.98, 100, 103–4, 113, 131, 138, 161–6, 174, 199, 208, 215–20, 245, 247, 278–82, 293. Spalding, *Memorialls*, ii.387–91.

40 *APS*, VI.i.82–3, 192–3, 214–20; *RMS*, *1634–51*, no.1977*.

41 *APS*, VI.i.181–2.

42 *APS*, VI.i.98, 100.

43 PA.11/2, ff.59v–60, 60v; *APS*, VI.i.100–2, 112, 115–16, 133; *LJ*, vi.600–1; *CJ*, iii.539; Turner, *Memoirs*, 38; Terry, *Alexander Leslie*, 287–9.

44 Napier, *Memorials*, ii.145.

45 Terry, *Alexander Leslie*, 228–55, 261–3 266–83, Somerville, *Memorie of the Somervills*. ii.351; R. Douglas, 'Diary', 63–4 in [J. Maidment (ed.)], *Historical Fragments* (Edinburgh 1833); P. Young, *Marston Moor* (Kineton 1970).

46 Baillie, *Letters*, ii.216; PA.11/2, ff.70v–71v, 74; T. Birch (ed.), *A Collection of State Papers of John Thurloe*, i (1742), 43–5.

47 Baillie, *Letters*, ii.201, 203, 204, 208–9, 218; Terry, *Alexander Leslie*, 257–61.

48 D.E. Underdown, *Pride's Purge. Politics in the Puritan Revolution* (Oxford 1971), 65–6.

49 Baillie, *Letters*, ii.195, 211, 234; D. Laing (ed.), *Correspondence of Sir Robert Kerr, first Earl of Ancrum, and his son William, third Earl of Lothian* (2 vols., Edinburgh 1875), i.176.

50 Underdown, *Pride's Purge*, 65, 66–7. See also V. Pearl, 'The "Royal Independents" in the English Civil War', *TRHS*, 5th ser., xviii (1968), 77, 78, and Pearl, 'Oliver St John and the "middle group" in the Long Parliament', *EHR* lxxxi.516 & n.

51 Underdown, *Pride's Purge*, 67–8, 71, 72.

52 J. Bruce and D. Masson (eds.), *The Quarrel of the Earl of Manchester and Oliver Cromwell* (Camden Society 1875), xx–xxiv, xl, lvi–lvii, lx–lxii, lxxviii–lxxx; R. Spalding, *The Improbable Puritan. A Life of Bulstrode*

Whitelocke (1975), 104; W.C. Abbott (ed.), *The Writings and Speeches of Oliver Cromwell* (4 vols., Cambridge, Mass. 1937–47), i.301–14.
53 S.R. Gardiner (ed.), 'A Letter from the Earl of Manchester to the House of Lords', *Camden Society Miscellany*, viii (1883), 2; Meikle, *Correspondence*, 50–1; Baillie, *Letters*, ii.229–30; Terry, *Alexander Leslie*, 344.
54 Meikle, *Correspondence*, 43–4.
55 S.R. Gardiner (ed.) *Constitutional Documents of the Puritan Revolution* (3rd edn., Oxford 1958), 275–86.
56 S.R. Gardiner, *History of the Great Civil War* (4 vols., 1893–4), ii.123.
57 Ibid, ii.121–31; W. Dugdale, *A Short View of the Late Troubles in England* (Oxford 1681), 737–959; Meikle, *Correspondence*, 59–63; L. Mulligan, 'Peace Negotiations, Politics and the Committee of Both Kingdoms', *Historical Journal*, xii (1969), 9–13.
58 Peterkin, *Records*, 418–19, 422; *APS*, VI.i.309, 339; Baillie, *Letters*, ii.242, 485; G.W. Sprott, *The Worship of the Church of Scotland during the Covenanting Period, 1638–51* (Edinburgh 1893), 20–5; D. Stevenson, 'The Radical Party in the Kirk, 1637–45', *Journal of Ecclesiastical History*, xxv (1974), 158–60.
59 Baillie, *Letters*, ii.298.
60 V. Pearl, 'London Puritans and Scotch Fifth Columnists: a Mid-Seventeenth Century Phenomenon', *Studies in London History presented to Philip E. Jones*, ed. A.E.J. Hollaender and W. Kellaway (1969) 317–31; Mulligan, 'Peace Negotiations', *Historical Journal*, xii, 14–18.
61 Baillie, *Letters*, ii.287.
62 *LJ*, vii. 185; Terry, *Alexander Leslie*, 345–8, 350–3, 355–60.
63 Ibid, 362–71, 374–5.
64 Balfour, *Historical Works*, iii.208–9, 215, 217; *APS*, VI.i.159–60, 167, 209–10.
65 Carte, *Ormond*, iii.318–19, 337; O'Danachair, 'Montrose's Irish Regiments', *Irish Sword*, iv.63–5.
66 A. MacBain and J. Kennedy (eds.), *Reliquiae Celticae* (2 vols., Inverness 1894) ii.177–9; Gordon, *Britane's Distemper*, 64–70; Spalding, *Memorialls*, ii.385–6.
67 Wishart, *Memoirs*, 48–56; M. Napier, *Memoirs of Montrose* (2 vols., Edinburgh 1856), ii.412–19; Gordon, *Britane's Distemper*, 70–2.
68 Birch, *State Papers*, i.42–3.
69 Ibid, i.46–7, PA.11/3, Register of the Committee of Estates, 1644–5, ff.9v–10, 24v–25, 32.
70 J.P. Edmond, *The Aberdeen Printers* (Aberdeen 1886), 77; PA.11/3, ff.35v, 36, 38–v, 39v–40.
71 Ibid, f.39.

72 Gordon, *Britane's Distemper*, 73–5; Wishart, *Memoirs*, 57–62; Guthry, *Memoirs*, 163. The best accounts of Montrose's campaigns are in Gardiner, *Civil War*, J. Buchan, *Montrose* (1931) and R. Williams, *Montrose. Cavalier in Mourning* (1975).
73 Napier, *Memorials*, ii.152–3; Gordon, *Britane's Distemper*, 75, 78–81; Guthry, *Memoirs*, 165–6; Wishart, *Memoirs*, 63–5; *A True Relation of the Happy Success of his Majesties Forces in Scotland* ([Oxford] 1644), 9.
74 PA.11/3, ff.40v–41, 44, 46v–47, 81–v, 82, 82v; Terry, *Alexander Leslie*, 301–2.
75 Edmond, *Aberdeen Printers*, 77–8; Gordon, *Britane's Distemper*, 79–80; Spalding, *Memorialls*, ii.399.
76 Taylor, *Aberdeen Council Letters*, ii.383.
77 Spalding, *Memorialls*, ii.406–9; Gordon, *Britane's Distemper*, 80–4; *Aber Recs, 1643–1747*, 28–9.
78 Spalding, *Memorialls*, ii.410–12.
79 Ibid, ii.416.
80 Wishart, *Memoirs*, 70–2; Gordon, *Britane's Distemper*, 85–6.
81 MacBain and Kennedy, *Reliquiae Celticae*, ii.179–81; Laing, *Correspondence*, ii.172–5, 177–8; Wishart, *Memoirs*, 72–80; Gordon, *Britane's Distemper*, 89–94; Spalding, *Memorialls*, ii.414–34; T. Carte (ed.), *A Collection of Original Letters and Papers, Concerning the Affairs of England* (2 vols., 1739), i.74.
82 See map in Gardiner, *Civil War*, ii.158.
83 PA.11/3, ff.48v–49, 126–v, 127v, 129v–131; Baillie, *Letters*, ii.234, 262, 417; Birch, *State Papers*, i.49–50.
84 Baillie, *Letters*, ii.234.
85 Terry, *Alexander Leslie*, 322–35; Turner, *Memoirs*, 39.
86 MacBain and Kennedy, *Reliquiae Celticae*, ii.181; Gordon, *Britane's Distemper*, 94-6; Birch, *State Papers*, i.53–4, 56, 61.
87 Carte, *Original Letters*, i.75, MacBain and Kennedy, *Reliquiae Celticae*, ii.182–3; Wishart, *Memoirs*, 80–2; Gordon, *Britane's Distemper*, 96–8
88 PA. 11/3, ff.148v, 158v; Baillie, *Letter*, ii.417.
89 Napier, *Memorials*, ii.172–4, 176.
90 Ibid, ii.175–9; Balfour, *Historical Works*, iii.256; Birch, *State Papers*, i.60–1; Wishart, *Memoirs*, 82–5; Carte, *Original Letters*, i.75–6; Gordon, *Britane's Distemper*, 99–102; Spalding, *Memorialls*, ii.443–5; MacBain and Kennedy, *Reliquiae Celticae*, ii.183–5.
91 GD.248/46, Seafield Muniments, bundle 4, two letters of 7 March 1645, Huntly to Lewis Gordon; Spalding, *Memorialls*, ii.446–8; Wishart, *Memoirs*, 87–8; Gordon, *Britane's Distemper*, 105, 109–10.
92 *APS*, VI.i.287, 297, 356–7, 363–4, 371–2.
93 *APS*, VI.i.290–1, 313–23, 334, 345–50, 302–8; Balfour, *Historical Works*,

iii.250–1, 271, 272, 282.
94 *APS*, VI.i.351–4. See D. Stevenson, 'The Financing of the Cause of the Covenants, 1638–51', *SHR*, ii (1972), 106–23.
95 Baillie, *Letters*, ii.263, 417–18; *APS*, VI.i.356, 363–4.
96 *APS*, VI.i.380–3.
97 R. Steele (ed.), *Tudor and Stuart Proclamations* (Oxford 1910), ii.236; PA.11/3, ff.85v–86, 91v–92, 142, 142v, 150–v; *APS*, VI.i.291, 303; C. Creighton, *A History of Epidemics in Britain* (Cambridge 1891), i.562–4; J.F.D. Shrewsbury, *A History of Bubonic Plague in the British Isles* (Cambridge 1970), 426–32; PA.11/4, Register of the Committee of Estates, 1645–6, ff.54v–55.
98 PA.11/4, ff.29–30v.
99 PA 11/4, f.8v; Spalding, *Memorialls*, ii.447, 449–50; Fraser, *Chiefs of Grant*, ii.16.
100 Ibid, ii.15–17; Gordon, *Britane's Distemper*, 110–17; Spalding, *Memorialls*, ii.450–63; PA.11/4, ff.35–v; Wishart, *Memoirs*, 88–95.
101 C. McNeill, *Tanner Letters* (Dublin 1943), 185–7.
102 Gordon, *Britane's Distemper*, 117–20; Wishart, *Memoirs*, 96–7; Spalding *Memorialls*, ii.462, 463, 465–8.
103 Baillie, *Letters*, ii.418
104 Spalding, *Memorialls*, ii.468–74; Gordon, *Britane's Distemper*, 120–7; MacBain and Kennedy, *Reliquiae Celticae*, ii.185–93; Wishart, *Memoirs*, 97–103, 502–3.
105 Ibid, 104–6; Gordon, *Britane's Distemper*, 127–8; Baillie, *Letters*, ii.418, *The Copie of a Letter showing the True Relation of the Late and Happie Victorie . . . at . . . Alfoord* ([Oxford 1645]), 3–4; Spalding, *Memorialls*, i.474–9.
106 Ibid, ii.478; Reid, *History of the Presbyterian Church in Ireland*, ii.555–9.
107 Napier, *Memorials*, ii.178–9.
108 McNeill, *Tanner Letters*, 177–8; Scrope and Monkhouse, *Clarendon State Papers*, ii.186; Carte, *Ormond*, iii.380–1, 384.
109 *The Lord George Digby's Cabinet* (1646), 11, 40, 41–2, 57–9; *The King's Cabinet Opened* (1645), 10; Gardiner, *Civil War*, ii.221, 203–4, 290–1; Wishart, *Memoirs*, 501–2; HMC 1: *2nd Report*, App.172; E. Hyde, earl of Clarendon, *History of the Rebellion* (6 vols., Oxford 1888), iv.77.
110 PA.11/4, ff.65, 68v–69, 90v, 94v, 97v, 105v–109; Baillie, *Letters*, ii.417–18; Guthry, *Memoirs*, 185–6; Wishart, *Memoirs* 106–7.
111 Ibid, 107–12; Gordon, *Britane's Distemper*, 128–35; MacBain and Kennedy, *Reliquiae Celticae*, ii.193–5; W.D. Simpson, 'The Topographical Problem of the Battle of Alford', *Aberdeen University Review*, vi (1918–19), 248–54; *The Copie of a Letter showing the True Relation of the Late and

Happie Victorie. . . . at. . . . Alfoord, 4–8; Baillie, *Letters*, ii.419.
112 Ibid, ii.304–5; Meikle, *Correspondence*, 97.
113 PA.11/4, ff.114v–115, 121v; *APS*, VI.i.431–2, 439; Baillie, *Letters*, ii.419; Guthry, *Memoirs*, 189–90.
114 Wishart, *Memoirs*, 113–18; Gordon, *Britane's Distemper*, 135–7; *The True Relation of the Late and Happie Victorie . . . at Kilsyth* (1645), 3–5; Balfour, *Historical Works*, iii.298–9, 301; *APS*, VI.i.446, 447, 449, 451.
115 *APS*, VI.i.448, 460; Baillie, *Letters*, ii.419.
116 Gordon, *Britane's Distemper*, 137–9; Wishart, *Memoirs*, 119–22; *The True Relation of. . . . Kilsyth*, 5–6.
117 Baillie, *Letters*, ii.420, 423–4.
118 Ibid, ii.420–4; Wishart, *Memoirs*, 122–5; Gordon, *Britane's Distemper*, 139–45; MacBain and Kennedy, *Reliquiae Celticae*, ii.199–201; *The True Relation of. . . . Kilsyth*, 6–8.
119 Meikle, *Correspondence*, 107.
120 Napier, *Memorials*, ii.222 PA.7/23/2/42, Supplementary Parliamentary Papers; Guthry, *Memoirs*, 191; Birch, *State Papers*, i.70–1; HMC 1: *2nd Report*, App.172.
121 Guthry, *Memoirs*, 195; Gordon, *Britane's Distemper*, 146; Wishart, *Memoirs*, 134.
122 T. McCrie (ed.), *The Life of Mr Robert Blair* (Wodrow Society 1848), 175–6.
123 Guthry, *Memoirs*, 195; Meikle, *Correspondence*, 108; Napier, *Memorials*, ii.325–32; Gordon, *Britane's Distemper*, 145–6.
124 Ibid, 145; Guthry, *Memoirs*, 196.
125 PA.7/23/2/38, 39.
126 J. Fraser, *Chronicles of the Frasers* (SHS 1905), 301–2; Gordon, *Britane's Distemper*, 153–4; Wishart, *Memoirs*, 137–8; MacBain and Kennedy, *Reliquiae Celticae*, ii.203; J. Burns, 'Memoirs,' 14, in [Maidment], *Historical Fragments.*
127 Wishart, *Memoirs*, 140; Gordon, *Britane's Distemper*, 154–5; Napier, *Memorials*, ii.233.
128 Gardiner, *Civil War*, ii.349; HMC 29: *Portland*, i.245–6.
129 Napier, *Memorials*, ii.229, 231; PA.7/23/2/38, 39; Wishart, *Memoirs*, 136–7.
130 Ibid, 140–1; *LJ* vii.581; *APS*, VI.i.592–3; HMC 29: *Portland*, i.267–8; Gordon, *Britane's Distemper*, 156–7.
131 Ibid, 146; Napier *Memorials*, ii.231–2, 234; Wishart, *Memoirs*, 139.
132 Ibid, 142–4; Gordon, *Britane's Distemper*, 157–8.
133 HMC 10: *10th Report*, App, i.55; HMC 29: *Portland*, i.259–60; Meikle, *Correspondence*, 110.
134 Bodleian Library, Oxford, Carte MSS, vol.80, Wharton Correspondence

and Papers, ff.247, 248; *CSPD, 1645–7*, 107.
135 J. Rushworth (ed.), *Historical Collections.* (8 vols., 1659–1701), IV.ii.125–6; HMC 29: *Portland*, i.259; Meikle, *Correspondence*, 107, 108, 110.
137 Ibid, 109; *CSPD, 1645–7*, 94.
138 HMC 29; *Portland*, i.271–3; Gardiner, *Civil War*, ii.309–10.
139 Meikle, *Correspondence*, 108, 109, 111, 113, 118–19; HMC 15: *10th Report*, App, vi. 159–63.
139 *LJ*, vii.581; HMC 29: *Portland*, i.267–8; Wishart, *Memoirs*, 143.
140 *Three Great Victories* (1645).
141 W. Thomson, *Montrose Totally Routed at Tividale in Scotland* (1645), 5; Wishart, *Memoirs*, 143–7; Gordon, *Britane's Distemper*, 158–63; Guthry, *Memoirs*, 201–4.
142 D. Robertson (ed.), *South Leith Records* (Edinburgh 1911), 54–69; H.P. Tait, 'Two Notable Epidemics in Edinburgh and Leith', *Book of the Old Edinburgh Club*, xxxii (1966), 8–21.
143 Spalding, *Memorialls*, ii.403–75 passim Taylor, *Aberdeen Council Letters* iii.44–7, 50.

CHAPTER 2: *The End of the Civil War in England, September 1645–January 1647*

1 Guthry, *Memoirs*, 207; McCrie, *Life of Blair*, 178; *CSPD, 1645–7*, 149; PA.12/1, Warrants of the Committee of Estates, 1640–6, minutes for 16–18 October 1645; PA.11/4, ff. 131–176v; Bodleian Library, Carte MSS vol. 80, Wharton Correspondence and Papers, ff.244, 253v.
2 Meikle, *Correspondence*, 119–20, 121–3; *Glasgow Recs, 1630–62*, 79, 80–1, 82–3; Burns, 'Memoirs', 13–14 and J. Spreul, 'Some Remarkable Passages', 7–8, both in [Maidment], *Historical Fragments.*
3 PA.12/1, minutes for 16 October 1645; PA.11/4, ff.131, 144v–145, 145v; Burns, 'Memoirs', 11–12, in [Maidment], *Historical Fragments*; Wishart, *Memoirs*, 157–9.
4 PA.11/4, ff.142v–143, 144–v; Meikle, *Correspondence*, 133.
5 Rushworth, *Historical Collections*, IV.i.128–9, 133–4; McNeill, *Tanner Letters*, 196–7; Scrope and Monkhouse, *Clarendon State Papers*, ii.199–200; *A True Relation of the totall Routing of the Lord George Digby . . .* (1645).
6 PA.11/4, ff.144–v, 150v; Meikle, *Correspondence*, 128–9, 136; Terry, *Alexander Leslie*, 379, 382–90.
7 NLS, MS Adv.33.4.8, pp.95–8; PA.11/4, ff.162v–163, 164–v.
8 MacBain and Kennedy, *Reliquiae Celticae*, ii.203; GD.112/40/2,

Breadalbane Muniments, 6 October 1645, Sir Robert Campbell to John Campbell.
9 Gordon, *Britane's Distemper*, 89, 164–8; Napier, *Memorials*, ii.237–8; *Aber Recs, 1643–1747*, 58; Taylor, *Aberdeen Council Letters*, iii.46; Wishart, *Memoirs*, 150–7, 160.
10 Sir R. Gordon, *A Genealogical History of the Earldom of Sutherland* (Edinburgh 1813), 530–1; Wishart, *Memoirs*, 160–4, 175; Gordon, *Britane's Distemper*, 168–74; Napier, *Memorials*, ii.260–70; GD.84/2/202, Reay Muniments.
11 Baillie, *Letters*, ii.345; McCrie, *Life of Blair*, 178–9.
12 APS, VI.i.474–5, 476, 478, 496, 863–4; Balfour, *Historical Works*, iii.307–12, 314, 316.
13 Ibid, iii.325; *APS*, VI.i.502; Napier, *Memorials*, ii.245–51.
14 *APS*, VI.i.492–3; Balfour, *Historical Works*, iii.341.
15 Ibid, iii.346, 352–3; *APS*, VI.i.503–5.
16 *APS*, VI.i.505–16, 521–33. Lord Ogilvie would probably have been executed but escaped from St Andrews Castle, *APS*, VI.i.503; Balfour, *Historical Works*, iii.358–64.
17 *APS*, VI.i.532, GD.6/1107, Beil Muniments; *Treason and Rebellion Against their Country justly rewarded upon severall Traitors and Rebels lately executed in Scotland* . . . (1646); McCrie, *Life of Blair*, 179–80.
18 *APS*, VI.i.477–8, 486–7, 489, 490, 496–7, 546, 550, 559–63, 581–3, 596; Balfour, *Historical Works*, iii.336, 367, 370–1, 372; PA.11/4, ff.196v–199.
19 *APS*, VI.i.567–72, 611–12, PA.11/4, ff.181–190v, 193; PA.14/3, Register of the Committee for Moneys (South); PA.14/4, Register of the Committee for Moneys (North).
20 Taylor, *Aberdeen Council Letters*, iii.36–7, 46; *Aber Recs, 1643–1747*, 60–1; Guthry, *Memoirs*, 213–15; Wishart, *Memoirs*, 165–6; PA.11/4, ff.199–v; Baillie, *Letters*, ii.513.
21 PA.12/1, papers dated 5, 11, 14, 15, 18 and 20 April 1646; Gordon, *Britane's Distemper*, 176–7; Gordon, *History of Sutherland*, 531–2; Taylor, *Aberdeen Council Letters*, iii.48, 50–1.
22 Gordon, *Britane's Distemper*, 173–4, 175, 177–84; Wishart, *Memoirs*, 176–8; Napier, *Memorials*, ii.270–4; Gordon, *History of Sutherland*, 531–2; Fraser, *Chronicles of the Frasers*, 313–14.
23 PA.12/1, papers dated 11 and 18 April 1646; Gordon, *Britane's Distemper*, 174.
24 PA.11/4, ff.202, 208v–209, 213v–214, 214v; Meikle, *Correspondence*, 170–1; PA.7/24, Parliamentary and State Papers, f.227v.
25 *A Declaration Against a Late Dangerous and Seditious Band under the Name of a Humble Remonstrance*. . . (Edinburgh 1646), 3–10, 16–17; Baillie,

Letters, ii.513.
26 PA.7/23/2/44, 45, Additional Parliamentary Papers.
27 Middleton dated letters from Tolquhon on 6 and 8 May, Taylor, *Aberdeen Council Letters*, iii.48, 51.
28 Wishart, *Memoirs* 178–9; Gordon, *Britane's Distemper*, 184–7; Fraser, *Chronicles of the Frasers*, 315–17; Gordon, *History of Sutherland*, 532.
29 Ibid, 533–4; Gordon, *Britane's Distemper*, 188–9; Wishart, *Memoirs*, 180–1; *Aber Recs, 1643–1747*, 68.
30 In a commission to his son Lord Reay gives himself the title of lieutenant governor of the northern shires of Scotland; it is not clear when he acquired it, GD.84/2/203, Reay Muniments; I. Grimble, *Chief of Mackay* (1965), 146–7; Wishart, *Memoirs*, 179.
31 Napier, *Memorials*, ii.277; Wishart, *Memoirs*, 179, 182–3, Gordon, *Britane's Distemper*, 194–5; GD.44/13/4/15, Gordon Castle Muniments.
32 G. Mackay (ed.), 'Two Unpublished Letters from . . . Montrose', *Juridical Review*, liii (1941), 310–11; Napier, *Memorials*, ii.278; HMC 21: *Hamilton*, i.110–11.
33 Napier, *Memorials*, ii.279–80.
34 PA. 11/4, ff. 196–v; Baillie, *Letters*, ii.512–13; PA. 12/ 1, 17 June 1646.
35 PA.7/24, ff.269–72.
36 PA. 12/1, 9 July 1646; Wishart, *Memoirs*, 183.
37 Ibid, 184–5; Napier, *Memorials*, ii.282; Guthry, *Memoirs*, 223.
38 McCrie, *Life of Blair*, 187; *RCGA*, i.14–19, 21, 30, 31–3, 41–2, 44–5; Burnet, *Hamilton*, 280–1; PA.7/23/2/46; Wishart, *Memoirs*, 185–8.
39 Gordon, *Britane's Distemper*, 196–9; Gordon, *History of Sutherland*, 535–6.
40 Hill, *Macdonnells of Antrim*, 446–8.
41 NLS, MS Adv.33.4.8, pp.101–8.
42 Rushworth, *Historical Collections*, IV.ii.399–401.
43 *APS*, vii.248–50; H. McKechnie, *The Lamont Clan* (Edinburgh 1938), 168–93; W. Cobbett (ed.), *Complete Collection of State Trials*, v (1809), 1379–87.
44 D.C. Mactavish (ed.), *Minutes of the Synod of Argyll* (2 vols., SHS 1943–4), i.99.
45 HMC 21: *Hamilton*, i. 111–13; Scrope and Monkhouse, *Clarendon State Papers*, ii.237–8; Inveraray Castle, Argyll Transcripts, xii. 149; Hill, *Macdonnells of Antrim*, 273; MacBain and Kennedy, *Reliquiae Celticae*, ii.203.
46 *LJ*, vii.442–3, 620–2, viii. 9.
47 [D. Buchanan], *Truth its Manifest: or a short and true relation of divers main passages . . .* (1645), 110–11.

48 *CSPD, 1645–7*, xviii, 130.
49 *A Speech of the Right Honourable The Earle of Louden . . . upon the 12 of September 1645* (1645); Gardiner, *Civil War*, ii.339–40; *CJ*, iv.273; Meikle, *Correspondence*, 118–19.
50 Baillie, *Letters*, ii.301; *LJ*, vii. 514–15, 581, 593; *APS*, VI.i.457; Bodleian Library, Carte MSS, vol.80, Wharton Correspondence and Papers, ff.244, 245v–249v, 251–254v; *CSPD, 1645–7*, 107–8, 113–16, 149, 174–5, 177–8, 182, 193–5, 197–8, 199; PA.11/4, ff;131v–138v, 143–4.
51 *CSPD, 1645–7*, 226–7; *LJ*, vii.689–95, 703.
52 D. Holles, 'Memoirs', in F. Maseres (ed.), *Select Tracts relating to the Civil Wars* (2 vols., 1815), i.217.
53 Meikle, *Correspondence*, 82–3.
54 Gardiner, *Civil War*, ii.285–6; *LJ*, vii.514; J. Webb, *Memorials of the Civil War as it effected Herefordshire* (2 vols., 1879), ii.379–82; HMC 29: *Portland*, i.362–3. HMC 7: *8th Report*, App. i.212.
55 Scrope and Monkhouse, *Clarendon State Papers*, ii.189–92.
56 *LJ*, vii.638.
57 *LJ*, vii.639.
58 D.A. Bigby, 'An Unknown Treaty between England and France, 1644', *EHR*, xxviii (1913), 337–41; L. Ranke, *History of England* (6 vols., Oxford 1875), ii.455–8, v.472–9.
59 J.G. Fotheringham (ed.), *The Diplomatic Correspondence of Jean de Montereul and the Brothers de Bellièvre* (2 vols., SHS 1898–9), i.3n. ii.564–5; Gardiner, *Civil War*, ii.338–9.
60 Fotheringham, *Montereul Correspondence*, i.3–4, 6–7.
61 Ibid, i.7, 16, 23.
62 Ibid, i.14– 17, 21–2.
63 Ibid, i.35–6, ii.569–72.
64 Ibid, i.68–9, 78, 83–4, ii.575–9.
65 J. Bruce (ed.), *Charles I in 1646. Letters of King Charles the First to Queen Henrietta Maria* (Camden Society 1856), 2, 5, 11; Scrope and Monkhouse, *Clarendon State Papers*, ii.196–7, 209–10; Fotheringham, *Montereul Correspondence*, i.103–6.
66 Gardiner, *Civil War*, iii.12, 15–16, 17, 20–2, 24–5.
67 Fotheringham, *Montereul Correspondence*, i.126, 143, 152.
68 Bruce, *Charles I*, 15, 17, 19, 22–5, 27.
69 Scrope and Monkhouse, *Clarendon State Papers*, ii.226–7.
70 *APS*, VI.i.575–9.
71 Meikle, *Correspondence*, 160; PA.13/4, Register of Instructions to the Scots Commissioners in London, f.42v.
72 Fotheringham, *Montereul Correspondence*, i.163–4, 173, 176; Gardiner,

Civil War, iii.73–6.

73 *LJ*, viii. 163, 164, 186, *APS*, VI.i.578, PA. 13/4, f.35v; Terry, *Alexander Leslie*, 389–90; Baillie, *Letters*, ii.347. The original muster rolls are at PRO, SP.41/2.

74 *APS*, VI.i.578; McNeill, *Tanner Letters*, 206.

75 *LJ*, viii. 123–5, 152, 1934; HMC 10: *10th Report*, App i.37.

76 V. Pearl, 'London's Counter-Revolution', in G.E. Aylmer (ed.), *The Interregnum: The Quest for a Settlement, 1646–1660* (1972), 33–6.

77 J.N. Figgis, 'Erastus and Erastianism', *Journal of Theological Studies*, ii (1900), 66, 78–81, 83; W.M. Lamont, *Marginal Prynne* (1963), 155–6, 173.

78 C.H. Firth and R.S. Rait (eds.), *Acts and Ordinances of the Interregnum* (3 vols., 1911), i.749–54, 789–97; Gardiner, *Civil War*, iii.6–8.

79 Ibid, iii. 10–11, 76–7; Firth and Rait, *Acts and Ordinances*, i.833–8.

80 Baillie, *Letters*, ii.360–1.

81 *LJ*, viii.217–20, 258, 265; Meikle, *Correspondence*, 169–70, 171–2, 173; C.L. Hamilton, 'Anglo-Scottish Militia Negotiations', *SHR*, xlii (1963), 87–8.

82 *Some Papers of the Commissioners of Scotland, given in lately to the Houses of Parliament concerning the Propositions of Peace* (1646), 1–4.

83 Meikle, *Correspondence*, 173–4, 176; *LJ*, viii.272, 274, 276, 277, 281; Baillie, *Letters*, ii.348, 361, 366–7.

84 *CJ*, iv.513– 15.

85 Meikle, *Correspondence*, 175, 176–7; PA. 13/4, f.44.

86 Gardiner, *Civil War*, iii.83–4, 86; Scrope and Monkhouse, *Clarendon State Papers*, ii.218–20.

87 Bruce, *Charles I*, 31–3.

88 Fotheringham, *Montereul Correspondence*, i.180, 185; Bruce, *Charles I*, 33, 35; Scrope and Monkhouse, *Clarendon State Papers*, ii.221.

89 Ibid, ii.22 1–4; Fotheringham, *Montereul Correspondence*, i.180–1; Gardiner, *Civil War*, iii.89, 89n.

90 Ibid, iii.95, 102; Bruce, *Charles I*, 36–8, Fotheringham, *Montereul Correspondence*, i.192–3. F. Peck (ed.), *Desiderata Curiosa* (2 vols., 1779), ii.359–66; HMC 29: *Portland*, i.368–84.

91 Turner, *Memoirs*, 41; J. Ashburnham, *A Narrative. . . of his Attendance on King Charles* (2 vols., 1830), ii.75–7; Fotheringham, *Montereul Correspondence*, i.193–4.

92 *CSPD*, 1645–7, lxv; *LJ*, viii, 305, 306.

93 Rushworth, *Historical Collections*, IV.i.268–9.

94 Baillie, *Letters*, ii.514; Meikle, *Correspondence*, 180.

95 Ibid, 181–2, 183; Baillie, *Letters*, ii.514, *CJ*, iv.537–8, 541, 547–8, 550–1; *LJ*, viii.308, 309.

96 GD. 18/3 1 10, Clerk of Penicuik Muniments.
97 Meikle, *Correspondence*, 180–1, 185.
98 Gardiner, *Civil War*, iii. 103–4; Terry, *Alexander Leslie*, 404–11; Burnet, *Hamilton*, 274–5; *LJ*, viii.329; HMC 29: *Portland*, i.361–2; Steele, *Tudor and Stuart Proclamations*, ii.331.
99 Bruce, *Charles I*, 40, 41–3.
100 Burnet, *Hamilton*, 272; HMC 21: *Hamilton*, ii.70; Fotheringham, *Montereul Correspondence*, i.202–3.
101 Ibid, i.196, ii.583–7.
102 Ibid, i.212–13, ii.582; Guthry, *Memoirs*, 217–18, 220; Burnet, *Hamilton*, 286–8.
103 Meikle, *Correspondence*, 183–4, 185–6; *CJ*, iv.551; *LJ*, viii.319.
104 Carte, *Ormond*, iii.455; *LJ*, viii.364–5; *CJ*, iv.567; Baillie, *Letters*, ii.374–5.
105 *LJ*, iv.356–8.
106 Meikle, *Correspondence*, 191, 193–4.
107 PA.13/4, f.44v; *RCGA*, i.57–8.
108 Meikle, *Correspondence*, 194–6; Baillie, *Letters*, ii.376; Guthry, *Memoirs*, 220.
109 Meikle, *Correspondence*, 196.
110 Rushworth, *Historical Collections*, IV.i.298–301; *LJ*, vii.392–4; For further evidence of Argyll's enthusiasm for union see Fotheringham, *Montereul Correspondence*, ii.95.
111 Gardiner, *Constitutional Documents*, 297–306.
112 J. Aiton, *The Life and Times of Alexander Henderson* (Edinburgh 1836), 633–60.
113 Peterkin, *Records*, 450; McCrie, *Life of Blair*, 186, 187; Terry, *Alexander Leslie*, 4 16– 17.
114 Bruce, *Charles I*, 48–9.
115 Guthry, *Memoirs*, 220.
116 Terry, *Alexander Leslie*, 417.
117 Bruce, *Charles I*, 50, 53, 79; Gardiner, *Civil War*, iii.117–18; Scrope and Monkhouse, *Clarendon State Papers*, ii.243, 247.
118 Rushworth, *Historical Collections*, IV.i.319–20.
119 Fotheringham, *Montereul Correspondence*, i.244, McCrie, *Life of Blair* 187–8; Terry, *Alexander Leslie*, 419–20; Gardiner, *Constitutional Documents*, 306–8.
120 Baillie, *Letters*, ii.386; PA. 13/4, f.49; Burnet, *Hamilton*, 283–4.
121 Meikle, *Correspondence*, 203–4, *LJ*, viii.461–2, Baillie, *Letters*, ii.390–1; Gardiner, *Civil War*, iii.137.
122 *CJ*, iv.659, 660; *LJ*, viii.487–8.
123 Burnet, *Hamilton*, 284; Guthry, *Memoirs*, 228.

124 Meike, *Correspondence*, 207n.
125 McCrie, *Life of Blair*, 188; Guthry, *Memoirs*, 229–30.
126 Burnet, *Hamilton*, 285–6; S.R. Gardiner, (ed.), *Hamilton Papers* (Camden Society 1880), 112; Terry, *Alexander Leslie*, 423–4; GD.248/556, Seafield Muniments, bundle 1, 9 September 1646, committee of estates to Findlater.
127 Fotheringham, *Montereul Correspondence*, i.269–70.
128 Scrope and Monkhouse, *Clarendon State Papers*, ii.249; Bruce, *Charles I*, 64.
129 Meikle, *Correspondence*, 208.
130 *Papers from the Scots Quarters, Containing the substance of Two Votes by the Estates* (1646), 1–2; *RCGA*, i.75.
131 Meikle, *Correspondence*, 216–18, 220–2; *CJ*, iv.672; *LJ*, viii.498, 499; Burnet, *Hamilton*, 29–34.
132 Rushworth, *Historical Collections*, IV.i.329–72.
133 Bruce, *Charles I*, 72, 73; Gardiner, *Hamilton Papers*, 119.
134 Baillie, *Letters*, ii.390; *APS*, VI.i.614–15, 656–7, 673; Napier, *Memorials* ii.288–90, GD.45/i/69, Dalhousie Muniments.
135 *APS*, VI.i.6 16.
136 *RCGA*, i.116–22, 130–3, 168–7 1; *APS*, VI.i.623–4, 669–71; Burnet, *Hamilton*, 294–5.
137 McCrie, *Life of Blair*, 192.
138 Lanark speaks of 'the grand Committee (the whole Parliament being present)', Burnet, *Hamilton*, 306, and I take this to refer to the committee of burdens. All members of parliament had the right to be present at committee meetings, *APS*, VI.i.6 16.
139 *RCGA*, i.147–54; *APS*, VI.i.634; Baillie, *Letters*, iii.4–5.
140 *APS*, VI.i.636–7, 638, 641–2, 645–6.
141 *CJ*, v. 12–14; Gardiner, *Civil War*, iii.184–5.
142 Gardiner, *Hamilton Papers*, 121–2; Gardiner, *Constitutional Documents*, 308–9.
143 Fotheringham, *Montereul Correspondence*, i.364.
144 C.S. Terry, 'The Visits of Charles I to Newcastle', *Archaeologia Aeliana*, 2nd ser. xxi (1899), 136–9; Burnet, *Hamilton*, 307.
145 Fotheringham, *Montereul Correspondence*, i.374–5, 393; Gordon, *History of Sutherland*, 536; Gardiner, *Civil War*, iii.187–8; Baillie, *Letters*, ii.511; D. Dalrymple (ed.), *Memorials of . . Charles the First* (Glasgow 1766), 186, 188–9.
146 Burnet, *Hamilton*, 310– 12; *APS*, vii.33, app.14.
147 *APS*, VI.i.659–60; *LJ*, viii.699–700.
148 *APS*, VI.i.660, 864.

149 *APS*, VI.i.669.
150 Terry, *Alexander Leslie* 436; Fotheringham, *Montereul Correspondence*, i.440; Gardiner, *Civil War*, iii.188; *LJ*, viii.686, 691–2; *CJ*, v.36, 65.
151 Terry, *Alexander Leslie*, 434–43; Gardiner, *Civil War*, iii.188; Fotheringham, *Montereul Correspondence*, i.444.
152 Dalrymple, *Memorials*, 190–1.
153 J. Kirkton, *The Secret and True History of the Church of Scotland* (Edinburgh 1817), 40n.

CHAPTER 3: *The Engagement, January 1647–September 1648*

1 Guthry, *Memoirs*, 240; Baillie, *Letters*, ii.511; *APS*, VI.i.672–6, 681–91, 708–11.
2 Reid, *History of the Presbyterian Church in Ireland*, ii.539–43; NLS, Adv. MS.33.4.8, pp.127–8, 146, 148–9, 151–3; *CJ*, v.113– 14, 172, 292, 296–7; *LJ*, ix.401, 404–5, 425, 428, 474–5.
3 *APS*, VI.i.653, 654, 680–3, 691–3, 717, 753–4, 765–6, 768–9, 780; *RCGA*, i.206; I. Grimble, *Chief of Mackay* (1965), 123–4, 150.
4 *APS*, VI.i.697–8, 722–3, 725; Birch, *State Papers of John Thurloe*, i.89–90; PA. 11/5, Register of the Committee of Estates, 1647–8, ff.6v–7, 16, 17v–18; PA. 12/2, 16 and 20 April 1647, Leslie to committee of estates; Gordon, *Britane's Distemper*, 199–200; Gordon, *History of Sutherland*, 537; Guthry, *Memoirs*, 422.
5 PA. 12/2, 16 April 1647, Leslie to committee of estates; *RCGA*, i.227; PA.7/23/2/5 1; PA. 11/5, ff. 18v– 19v; Guthry, *Memoirs*, 243.
6 *Glasgow Recs, 1630–66*, 101, 113, 119–20, 123, 146; Baillie, *Letters*, iii.5, 6, 18; W. Kennedy, *Annals of Aberdeen* (1818), i.270–1; *Aber Recs, 1643–1747*, 81–5; D.B. Thoms, *The Kirk of Brechin in the Seventeenth Century* (Brechin 1972), 86–9; PA. 11/5, ff.42v–43, 44v–45, 49v, 121v–122v; *RCGA*, i.286; J.H. Pagan, *Annals of Ayr in Olden Times* (Ayr 1897), 72–4.
7 PA. 11/5, ff. 17v–18v; Fotheringham, *Montereul Correspondence*, ii.140.
8 Reports in English pamphlets in February 1647 that Macdonald had marched within thirty miles of Edinburgh were false, *A Declaration of the Proceedings of the New Moddl'd Army in the Kingdome of Scotland* (1646/7); *Papers Concerning the Debates of the Parliament of Scotland* (1646/7).
9 A. McKerral, *Kintyre in the Seventeenth Century* (Edinburgh 1948), 53–6; D. Stevenson, 'The Massacre at Dunaverty, 1647', *Scottish Studies*, xix (1975), 27–37.
10 PA. 11/5, ff. 14, 25v–26, 28–v; Birch, *State Papers of John Thurloe*, i.91–2; PA. 12/2, 23 June 1647, Leslie to committee of estates; Rushworth,

Historical Collections, IV.i.561–2; PA.7/23/2/49.
11 PA.7/23/2/54; Turner, *Memoirs*, 47–8; McKerral, *Kintyre*, 69–72.
12 Guthry, *Memoirs* 246; Fotheringham, *Montereul Correspondence*, ii.261; Cobbett, State Trials, v.1391–2, 1396, 1411, 1462; McNeill, *Tanner Letters*, 275–6.
13 PA.7/23/2/54; Turner, *Memoirs*, 49; Hill, *Macdonnells of Antrim*, 111–13; Gordon, *Britane's Distemper*, 204–5; Guthry, *Memoirs*, 251–3; PA. 11/5, ff. 128v 130v, 137v, 161–v, 174v, 180; Fotheringham, *Montereul Correspondence*, ii.288, 289, 295, 299–300, 313, 323, 331, 339.
14 Grimble, *Chiefs of Mackay*, 150–5.
15 McKerral, *Kintyre*, 74–9; PA. 11/5, ff. 183v.
16 *APS*, VI.i.731, 764–5.
17 Fotheringham, *Montereul Correspondence*,.ii.51, 71, 83, 93, 175.
18 Laing, *Ancrum and Lothian Correspondence*, i.212–13.
19 Fotheringham, *Montereul Correspondence*, ii.70–1, 83; *APS*, VI.i.766–8, 856.
20 Baillie, *Letters*, iii.16.
21 Gardiner, *Civil War*, iii.213–14, 216, Pearl; 'London's Counter-Revolution' in Aylmer, *The Interregnum*, 434.
22 Gardiner, *Civil War*, iii.217–37.
23 Gardiner, *Constitutional Documents*, 311–16; Gardiner, *Civil War*, iii.252–4.
24 Ibid, iii.252 alleges that Lauderdale had secret instructions (from whom?) to be content if the king agreed (as he now did) to presbyterian government for three years and to give up the militia for ten. But Gardiner cites no authority for this and there appears to be no evidence to support it.
25 Ibid, iii.259–60.
26 Ibid, iii.237, 254, 260–73, 277; *LJ*, ix.244, 245–6.
27 Gardiner, *Civil War*, iii.278; Fotheringham, *Montereul Correspondence*, ii.163.
28 PA. 11/5, ff.31, 34, 36, 38v, 40; *LJ*, ix.302–3, 305, 319, Fotheringham; *Montereul Correspondence*, ii.182.
29 Ibid, ii.182–3.
30 Ibid, ii.188.
31 Gardiner, *Civil War*, iii.286–9, 301, 304, 307, 336–9; Underdown, *Pride's Purge*, 76–83; Pearl, 'London's Counter-Revolution' in Aylmer, *The Interregnum*, 46–56; Baillie, *Letters*, iii.17.
32 Fotheringham, *Montereul Correspondence*, ii.210–11; Gardiner, *Civil War*, iii.323–5, 329–34, 342; *LJ*, ix.367–8, 387, 416; PA. 11/5, ff.76–v, 60–v; Rushworth, *Historical Collections*, IV.ii.796–7.
33 PA.11/5, ff.47v–48, 55v–60v Fotheringham, *Montereul Correspondence*,

ii.175, 189, 193, *RCGA*, i.289–94, 297–8; Burnet, *Hamilton*, 319; Peterkin, Records 472–4, 476; Baillie, *Letters*, iii.15.
34 PA.11/5 ff.61, 71–72v, 74v–75; Fotheringham, *Montereal Correspondence*, ii.240; Baillie, *Letters*, iii.17.
35 PA.11/5, ff.77–78, 89–90v, 92v, 93v–95v; Fotheringham, *Montereul Correspondence*, ii.207–8, 233, 260, 264–5; Guthry, *Memoirs*, 246–7.
36 Burnet, *Hamilton*, 320– 1, 322.
37 Ibid, 321.
38 Gardiner, *Civil War*, iii.354–5, 357; *LJ*, ix.420, 422, 424–5; PA.11/5, ff.88v–89; Burnet, *Hamilton*, 322.
39 Gardiner, *Constitutional Documents*, 326–7; *Calendar of Clarendon State Papers*, i.388; Gardiner, *Civil War*, iii.361, 366–7.
40 PA.11/5, ff.102–v, 106v–110, 112; *Calendar of Clarendon State Papers*, i.391; Fotheringham, *Montereul Correspondence*, ii.275.
41 PA.11/5, ff.107, 113.
42 NLS, Wodrow MS, Folio LXVII, f.122.
43 PA. 11/5, ff.116v, 117, 118–119v, 132–134v; Fotheringham, *Montereul Correspondence*, ii.287–8, 294; Baillie, *Letters*, iii.23; Guthry, *Memoirs*, 248; *RCGA*, i.3 14–18.
44 NLS, Wodrow MS, Folio LXVII, f.118.
45 Scrope and Monkhouse, *Clarendon State Papers*, ii.380–1; Burnet, *Hamilton*, 323–4.
46 HMC 36: *Ormonde*, N.S. ii.353–5.
47 Burnet, *Hamilton*, 324; Gardiner, *Civil War*, iv.1–2, 9–10, 13–15, 17–19.
48 Ibid, iv.24–5; Gardiner, *Constitutional Documents*, 328–32.
49 Burnet, *Hamilton*, 326–7; *LJ*, ix.532, 542.
50 *LJ*, ix.532; Burnet, *Hamilton*, 328; Gardiner, *Civil War*, iv.31–4.
51 *LJ*, ix.582–4, 591–601, 605.
52 H. Marten *The Independency of England Endeavored to be Maintained . . . Against the Claim of the Scottish Commissioners. . .* (1648), 4, 5, 10–11, 24–5.
53 This name had sometimes been used by James V when travelling incognito, and had survived as an indirect way of referring to the king of Scotland.
54 NLS, Wodrow MS, Folio LXVII, f.128.
55 Burnet, *Hamilton*, 328–32; Gardiner, *Civil War*, iv.37.
56 Burnet, *Hamilton*, 333, 334.
57 Gardiner, *Civil War*, iv.38.
58 Gardiner, *Constitutional Documents*, 347–53. Hyde, *History of the Rebellion*, iv.294, stated that the king also agreed to give the Scots Berwick and Carlisle and made 'some other concessions which trenched. . . upon

the honour and interests of the English'. G. Burnet, *History of My Own Times*, ed. O. Airy (2 vols., Oxford 1897– 1900), i.59, 72, claimed that Lauderdale had toed him that the king promised to unite Northumberland, Cumberland and Westmorland to Scotland, and that he had first offered this to the Scots when seeking their help in 1643. There had been similar rumours that the king in 1641 and the English parliament in 1643 had offered to cede the northern counties to Scotland (ibid, i.59n.). It seems wildly improbable that such offers were made; they would be bound to be universally unpopular in England. But it is possible that Charles made limited concessions in December 1647 relating to Berwick and Carlisle (it had been agreed in 1641 that neither country should place garrisons in them), or that Hamilton's army which was to invade England would he allowed to remain in occupation of the northern counties until peace was settled (as the Scots had done in 1641, and had tried to do in 1646–7).

59 Gardiner, *Civil War*, iv.41, 50–3.

60 PA.11/5, f.188. The previous master of requests, Sir James Galloway, seems to have resigned on being created Lord Dunkeld in 1645, Guthry, *Memoirs*, 255.

61 PA.11/5, ff.199v, 205v; Baillie, *Letters*, iii.32–3; Guthry, *Memoirs*, 256.

62 Gardiner, *Civil War*, iv.56, 86–7; C.H. Firth (ed.), 'Narratives Illustrating the Duke of Hamilton's Expedition into England in 1648', *Miscellany*, ii (SHS 1904), 302; Gardiner, 'Hamilton Papers, Addenda', *Miscellany*, ix (Camden Society 1895), 1–2.

63 PA. 11/5, ff.210, 211–v; Fotheringham, *Montereul Correspondence*, ii.392, 399, 407.

64 Ibid, ii.407–8; PA.11/5, ff.210v–211, 212, 212v, 216; *RCGA*, i.352–3, 355–6, 357, 360, 364, 367–8, 370–2; Burnet, *Hamilton*, 337, 340.

65 Ibid, 319; Fotheringham, *Montereul Correspondence*, iii.386, 402, G. Gillespie, *An Useful Case of Conscience Discussed* (Edinburgh 1649), 1; W. Rosse, *A Message from the Estates of Scotland* (1648), 3.

66 Ibid. 2, W. Rosse, *The Lord Loudouns Speech to the English Commissioners at Edinburgh* (1648), 3.

67 Fotheringham, *Montereul Correspondence*, ii.388.

68 Gardiner, *Hamilton Papers*, 158; Guthry, *Memoirs*, 257–8, 260; *LJ*, x.7–8, 11; *Copies of all the Letters, Papers, and other Transactions* (1648), 5–14; Fotheringham, *Montereul Correspondence*, iii.399–400.

69 Ibid, ii.288, 419–20, 426; Baillie, *Letters*, iii.35; *APS*, VI.ii.5–9, 13–14, 19; *CSPD*, 1648–9, 26; Guthry, *Memoirs*, 259–60.

70 *RMS, 1634–51*, no.1863; H. Campbell (ed.), *Abstracts of the General Register of Sasines for Argyll* (Edinburgh 1934), 251.

71 *APS*, VI.ii.5; W. Rosse, *A Declaration of the Kirk of Scotland presented to the Parliament of that Kingdom* (1648), 2.
72 *APS*, VI.ii.9.
73 *RCGA*, i.373–82, 384, 385; *APS*, VI.ii.9–10, 11–12.
74 Fotheringham, *Montereul Correspondence*, ii.426, 428; *APS*, VI.ii.10.
75 PA.11/5, ff.156, 159, 181v, 218; *APS*, VI.ii.5; Fotheringham, *Montereul Correspondence*, ii.331, 359, 370, 374, 427–8; Baillie, *Letters*, iii.35–6; Guthry, *Memoirs*, 261; Balfour, *Historical Works*. iii.396
76 Baillie, *Letters*, iii.35, 36; *RCGA*, i.390, 392–3, 394–5, 400, 405–6, 408–9, 411–12.
77 Baillie, *Letters*, iii.36; Fotheringham, *Montereul Correspondence*, ii.425–6, 433.
78 *APS*, VI.ii. 13; Rushworth, *Historical Collections*, IV.ii.1049.
79 Fotheringham, *Montereul Correspondence*, ii.414, 434–5; Guthry, *Memoirs*, 262–4; Baillie, *Letters*, iii.37–8; Bodleian Library, MS Clarendon 2742; RH.2/8/15, Minutes of Parliament, 11 March–8 April 1648, pp.8–10 (transcript from Hamilton MSS; informal notes by a member of parliament rather than formal minutes).
80 *RCGA*, i.399, 404–5, 420–3; Baillie, *Letters*, iii.36–7, 38; *APS*, VI.ii. 14–15, 16–18, 19–21.
81 Fotheringham, *Montereul Correspondence*, ii.439, 455–6; HMC 72: *Laing*, i.224; Baillie, *Letters*, iii.45; Turner, *Memoirs* 52–3; [J. Dennistoun and A. Macdonald (eds.)], 'Royal Letters and Instructions . . . from the Archives of the Earl of Wigton', *Maitland Miscellany*, II.ii (1840), 647.
82 Fotheringham, *Montereul Correspondence*, ii.408–9, 458, 465, 466, 477; HMC 21: *Hamilton*, i.120, ii.70; Gardiner, 'Hamilton Papers, Addenda', *Camden Miscellany*, ix.26; *Maitland Miscellany*, II.ii.457–9; Burnet, *Hamilton*, 346, 347.
83 Baillie, *Letters*, iii.40; *Maitland Miscellany*, II.ii.464–7.
84 Burnet, *Hamilton*, 336.
85 *APS*. VI.ii.23–5; Fotheringham, *Montereul Correspondence*, ii.451.
86 Gardiner, 'Hamilton Papers, Addenda', *Camden Miscellany*, ix.29–30; Bodlian Library, MS Clarendon 2758.
87 *RCGA*, i.442–4, 446–7, 452–5; *APS*, VI.ii.28–9, 434.
88 *APS*, VI.ii.30–9, 40–3, 45, 47, 48; Fotheringham, *Montereul Correspondence*, ii.459.
89 *RCGA*, i.485–512.
90 *APS*, VI.ii. 10, 12, 20, 22, 25–6, 52; *Copies of all the Letters, Papers, and Transactions*, 16–29; Fotheringham, *Montereul Correspondence*, ii.409, 421.
91 Gardiner, *Civil War*, iv.122–3; Firth, 'Narratives', *SHS Miscellany*, ii.302–5; *APS* VI.ii.67, *Copies of all the Letters, Papers, and Transactions*,

29–30, 34–8, 39–43, 59–60; *LJ*, x.394, 396.
92 *APS*, VI.ii.53–6, 67–8; NLS, MS Adv.33.4.8, pp.154–6, 159–61; Fotheringham, *Montereul Correspondence*, ii.483.
93 *APS*, VI.ii.68, 724, 85–6, 88, 120– 1; Baillie, *Letters*, iii.40, 44–5.
94 *RCGA*, i.528–31.
95 *APS*, VI.ii.86–7; *RCGA*, i.547–56.
96 A. Henderson, *A Sermon preached before the Right Honourable House of Lords . . . the 28 May 1645* (1645), 12–13, 18–19.
97 G. Gillespie, *Works*, ed. W.M. Hetherington (2 vols., Edinburgh 1846), i.12–19; G. Donaldson, *Scotland: James V to James VII* (Edinburgh and London 1965), 197.
98 *APS*, VI.ii.69–71, 87; PA.11/6, Register of the Committee of Estates, 1648, ff.1–v.
99 HMC 72: *Laing* i.225–36; *Edin Recs, 1642–55*, 403–4, Mactavish, *Minutes of the Synod of Argyll*, i.107–12; *APS*, VI.ii.90–1.
100 PA.11/6, ff.5v, 7v, 8, 8v, 13v, 14; Gardiner, *Hamilton Papers*, 202–3, 205; Guthry, *Memoirs*, 270–1.
101 Bodleian Library, MS Tanner LVII.i, f.80.
102 Fotheringham, *Montereul Correspondence*, ii.492, 494 497, 503; HMC 21: *Hamilton*, ii.74–5; Baillie, *Letters*, iii.48; Guthry, *Memoirs*, 271–2, 273, 275; Turner, *Memoirs*, 53.
103 Ibid, 52–5; PA.11/6, ff.9v–10, 15–v; Baillie, *Letters*, iii.47–8; *APS*, VI.ii.90, 92, 93, 105–6; *Glasgow Recs, 1630–62*, 137–41.
104 NLS, MS Adv.33.4.8, pp.156–9, 164; PA.11/6, ff.12v–13; PA.12/2, 10 June 1648, Lord Cochrane etc. to Committee of Estates.
105 *APS*, VI.ii.98–9, 106–9.
106 *LJ*, x.247; Gardiner, *Civil War*, iv. 124.
107 *APS*, VI.ii.94. Gardiner, *Civil War*, iv.95n, took Loudoun to refer to the rejection by the Engagers of some secret approach by the Independents for a peace treaty as his reason for abandoning the Engagement, but it seems clear that he meant the refusal to negotiate with the English commissioners in Edinburgh on the English parliament's vote of 6 May.
108 *APS*, VI.iii. 102–5; PA. 11/6, f.27v; PA.12/2, 21 June 1648, letters of Argyll, Loudoun and Wariston to the committee of estates; Guthry, *Memoirs*, 276–7.
109 Turner, *Memoirs*, 55–7, 242; *Information of the Public Proceedings of Scotland* [Edinburgh 1648], 2–4. For two previously unpuhlished accounts of the 'battle' see D. Stevenson, 'The Battle of Mauchline Moor, 1648', *Ayrshire Collections*, XI.i. (1973), 1–24. PA.11/6, ff.23v, 41, 43v, 99.
110 Turner, *Memoirs*, 57; Baillie, *Letters*, iii.49; PA.11/6, ff.29–v, 30v, 32v; [J. Robertson (ed.)], *Selections from the Registers of the Presbytery of Lanark*

(Abbotsford Club 1839), 60.
111 PA.11/6, ff.32, 118v; Guthry, *Memoirs*, 275–6; HMC 21: *Hamilton*, i.125–6.
112 PA.12/2, papers of 16, 29 June 1648, Lord Cochrane etc. to committee of estates; PA. 11/6, ff.28, 34–v, 73–v, 92–v, 126– 7; NLS, MS Adv.33.4.8, pp. 165–6.
113 Gardiner, *Civil War*, iv. 118, 126, 133–4, 137–42, 146, 147–54; Burnet, *Hamilton*, 351–3.
114 PA.11/6, ff.46v–48, 70v, 72v, 75v; *The Designs and Correspondencies of the Present Committee of Estates* (1648), 7–11; *CJ*, v.640, 643, 664; *LJ*, x.421, 423, 437, 440.
115 PA.11/6, f.64.
116 Burnet, *Hamilton*, 355–6; Turner, *Memoirs*, 59; Gardiner, *Civil War*, iv.165–6.
117 *Maitland Miscellany*, II.ii.459–63; Burnet, *Hamilton*, 351–2; Fotheringham, *Montereul Correspondence*, ii.529; PA.11/6, ff.79, 98v; *The Designs and Correspondencies*, 12– 13.
118 Ibid, 15– 17; PA.11/6, ff.92v, 156–61; Gardiner, *Hamilton Papers*, 232–3.
119 Ibid, 237–53; Gardiner, *Civil War*, iv.135; *Calendar of Clarendon State Papers*, i.412– 15, 433–5.
120 PA.11/6, ff.81–2, 83v–84v, 87v, 88, 89v, 90–1; HMC 72: *Laing*, i.237; Peterkin, *Records*, 496–506, 509, 517; Baillie, *Letters*, iii.57.
121 PA.11/6, f.93v.
122 Baillie, *Letters*, iii.51.
123 PA.11/6, ff.93, 94–v, 96–8, 100v; Fotheringham, *Montereul Correspondence*, ii.530.
124 Burnet, *Hamilton*, 357–8; Turner, *Memoirs*, 242–3.
125 Ibid, 62–3; Burnet, *Hamilton*, 357; Gardiner, *Civil War*, iv. 180, 182.
126 Ibid, iv. 183–93; Turner, *Memoirs*, 63–76, 243–5; Baillie, *Letters*, iii.455–7; W.C. Abbott (ed.), *The Writings and Speeches of Oliver Cromwell* (4 vols, Harvard 1937–47), i.630–46.
127 Guthry, *Memoirs*, 286; Burnet, *Hamilton*, 376; *RCGA*, ii.90. The term 'Whiggamore Raid', or rather originally 'road' or 'inroad', was in use by the end of 1648. It was apparently derived from the habit of men from the western Lowlands of spurring on their horses with shouts of 'whiggam', *Scottish National Dictionary* under 'whig,' 'whiggam,' and 'whiggamore'; Balfour, *Historical Works* iii.388, 420; Burnet, *History of My Own Times*, i.72–3.
128 PA.11/6, ff.133v–136, 192v, 193v; *RCCA*, ii.34.
129 PA.11/6, ff.136v–137; Burnet, *Hamilton*, 368.
130 PA.12/2, papers of 2, 3 and 4 September 1648.

131 *RCGA*, ii. 36–43.
132 Ibid, ii.47–51, 53–5; G. Gillespie, *An Usefull Case of Conscience Discussed* 29–30, 33–4.
133 PA.12/2, papers of 9 and 10 September 1648; Guthry, *Memoirs*, 289; Burnet, *Hamilton*, 370.
134 *LJ*, x.519; Guthry, *Memoirs*, 290–1; Burnet, *Hamilton*, 370–1; Gordon *Britane's Distemper*, 211.
135 Birch, *State Papers of John Thurloe*, i.99–100; PA.12/2, papers of 13 and 14 September 1648; Guthry, *Memoirs*, 294.
136 *LJ*, x.518; Abbott, *Cromwell*, i.653–4, 656–8.
137 *RCGA*, ii.61, 63–4; Birch, *State Papers of John Thurloe*, i.102; PA.12/2, papers of 20 and 21 September 1648.
138 Abbott, *Cromwell*, i.659–61; HMC 15: *10th Report*, App vi.169–70.
139 PA.11/7, Register of the Committee of Estates, 1648–9, ff.1–v.
140 PA.12/2, paper of 25 September 1648.
141 Eg, Gardiner, *Civil War*, iv.230; Burnet, *Hamilton*, 372; Cobbett, *State Trials*, v. 1375, 1402, 1418, 1426.
142 Wishart, *Memoirs*, 215–16; PA.11/7,ff.1v–2.
143 PA.12/2, papers of 14–25 September 1648; *LJ*, x.518: Burnet, *Hamilton*, 371–5; *The Last Declaration of the Committee of Estates* (1648), 15–19.
144 Ibid, 22–4; Birch, *State Papers of John Thurloe*, i.104.
145 Aylmer, *The Interregnum*, 5.
146 Donaldson, *Scotland: James V to James VII*, 337.

CHAPTER 4: *The Rule of the Kirk Party, September 1648–September 1650*

1 Guthry, *Memoirs*, 296; Birch, *State Papers of John Thurloe*, i.105; Abbott, *Cromwell*, i.661.
2 PA.11/7, f.7.
3 McCrie, *Life of Blair*, 209–10; *A True Account of the great Expressions of Love from . . . the Kingdom of Scotland unto Lieutenant General Cromwel* (1648), 3–6.
4 Abbott, *Cromwell*, i.661, 662, 663–4, 668, 669; PA.11/7, ff.8v–10; C.H. Firth (ed.), *The Clarke Papers* (4 vols., Camden Society 1891–1901), ii. pp.xxiv–xxv; HMC 15: *10th Report*, App vi. 172.
5 Ibid, vi.172, 173; Abbott, *Cromwell*, i.669; PA.11/7. ff.11–v, 15v, 17–v, 42v, 75, 76v–77; Rushworth, *Historical Collections*, IV.ii.1305, 1313–14, 1329.
6 E.g., Guthry, *Memoirs*, 298.
7 PA.11/7, ff.11–v, 20v–27v, 28v–34; *RCGA*, ii.77–96, 106–7.
8 G.D.112/39/880, Breadalbane Muniments. See also *Glasgow Recs*,

1630–62, 153, 155, 157; PA.11/7, ff.111–v; D. Stevenson, 'The Western Association', *Ayrshire Collections*, XIII, iv (1982).
9 PA.11/7, ff.53v–55, 64v–65.
10 PA.11/7, ff.2v–3, 20v, 55v–57, 58v–59, 149–50; *Glasgow Recs, 1630–62*, 149–50.
11 *RCGA*, ii.98–105, 109–11.
12 Burnet, *Hamilton*, 375–7; PA.11/7, ff.35–39v, 146–v; *LJ*, x.564–5, HMC 72: *Laing*, i.237–8, Scrope and Monkhouse, *Clarendon State Papers*, ii.422–3.
13 Underdown, *Pride's Purge*, 95–105.
14 Ibid, 142–72.
15 Abbott, *Cromwell*, i.677–8.
16 *RCGA*, iii.112–13.
17 PA.11/7, ff.96v–98.
18 *APS*, VI.ii.692–3.
19 *APS*, VI.ii.129–30, 140–1, 143, 694–5; Gardiner, *Civil War*, iv.288–92.
20 Laing, *Ancrum and Lothian Correspondence*, i.236–8; *APS*, VI.ii.697–8; F.P.G. Guizot, *History of the English Revolution* (2 vols., Oxford 1838), ii.396–7, 404.
21 *APS*, VI.ii.3–4, 124–6; Balfour, *Historical Works*, iii.374, 377; Gillespie, *An Usefull Case of Conscience Discussed*, 31–2.
22 *APS*, VI.ii. 143–8.
23 W.L. Mathieson, *Politics and Religion* (2 vols., Glasgow 1902), ii.107n.
24 *APS*, VI.ii.153–4.
25 PA.11/7, ff.112v–113v, 116, 131, 151; PA.11/8, *Register of the Committee of Estates*, 1649 f.2; *APS*, VI.ii.150–1; Scrope and Monkhouse, *Clarendon State Papers*, i.460, 162–4; Guthry, *Memoirs*, 298.
26 Scrope and Monkhouse, *Clarendon State Papers*, ii.460–1; HMC 51: *Leyborne-Popham*, 9–11; Carte, *Original Letters*, i.238.
27 *Calendar of Clarendon State Papers*, i.460, 462–4; *RGCA*, ii.125–32.
28 Balfour, *Historical Works*, iii.386–7; Burnet, *Hamilton*, 377–8; Sir Walter Scott (ed.), *Somers Tracts* (13 vols., 1809–15), viii.508–10.
29 *APS*, VI.ii.156, 157; Baillie, *Letters*, iii.114.
30 *RCGA*, ii.196–8.
31 *APS*, VI.ii.211–12.
32 *APS*, VI.ii.159–60, 706–8; McCrie, *Life of Blair*, 216–17. The commissioners are often said to have intended to sail to Holland (ibid, 217–18; S.R. Gardiner, *History of the Commonwealth and Protectorate* (4 vols., 1903), i.21), but as the Scots parliament had only passed the instructions for them to go to Holland the day before (23 February) they presumably intended to return to Scotland.

33 *CJ*, vi. 151, 152; *APS*, VI.ii.276–7, 706; Laing, *Ancrum and Lothian Correspondence*, i.245–6; HMC 29: *Portland*, i.511–12; PA.11/8, ff.16v–17, 21.
34 *APS*, VI.ii.232, 300, 317; J. Lamont, *Diary* (Maitland Club 1830), 1; Balfour, *Historical Works*, iii.388; *RCGA*, ii.212–15, 236.
35 It had at first been intended that Cassillis should be joint secretary with Lothian but he refused to accept that office. Cesnok refused the office of justice clerk and was replaced by Sir Robert Moray in March 1651. *APS*, VI.ii.174–8, 179–83, 195–200, 270–5, 277, 283, 316, 317, 321, 458, 495–6, 547–9, 551–2, 648, 653, 656; Balfour, *Historical Works*, iii.389–90, NLS, Gordon-Cumming of Altyre Correspondence, no.661; PA.11/8, ff.17v–18.
36 D.E. Underdown, 'The Independents Reconsidered', *Journal of British Studies*, iii. (1963–4), 81; Underdown, *Pride's Purge*, 243, 354.
37 *RCGA*, ii.184–5, 205–11; Baillie, *Letters*, i.240–1, ii.450–60; A. Henderson, *Government and Order of the Church of Scotland* (1641), 11.
38 Peterkin, *Records*, 37, 321–3, 353; Baillie, *Letters*, i.240–1, ii.47–8, 94, 476; *APS*, v.262–3, 348, VI.i.66, 195–6, 554.
39 *RCGA*, ii.184–5, 205–11; Balfour, *Historical Works*, iii.391; *APS*, VI.ii.261–2. According to R. Wodrow, *Analecta* (4 vols., Maitland Club, 1842–3), ii.160 Argyll had argued before the vote against the abolition of patronage.
40 *APS*, v.480, 566, VI.i.774–6; Laing, *Ancrum and Lothian Correspondence*, i.212–13; Fotheringham, *Montereul Correspondence*, ii.80–1.
41 PA.11/5, ff.202v–203v; J. Scot, 'Trew Relation', *SHR*, xi (1913–14), 79–80; *APS*, VI.ii.15–16, 20; RH.2/8/15, Minutes of Parliament, pp.10–11, 12, 27–8, 32–3.
42 Scot, 'Trew Relation', *SHR*, xii (1914–15), 76–83, 174–83, 408–12; *APS*, VI.ii.244–6, 708–9, 717–18.
43 *APS*, VI.ii.287.
44 Eg, *RCGA*, ii.107, 205, 291–5.
45 Lamont, *Diary*, 6; R. Mitchison, 'The Movement of Scottish Corn Prices in the 17th and 18th Centuries', *Economic History Review*, 2nd ser. xviii (1965), 283; Balfour, *Historical Works*, iii.409; *Fife Fiars, from 1619 to 1845* (Cupar 1846), 5–9; H. Arnot, *History of Edinburgh* (Edinburgh 1816), 481; 'Fiars Prices, East Lothian', *Archaeologia Scotica*, i (1792), 91–5.
46 *APS*, VI.ii.220–1.
47 *APS* VI.i.812, VI.ii.268, 388, 449, 464–7, 502; *RCGA*, ii.290–5; PRO, SP.46/129, State Papers, Domestic, Supplementary, Documents relating to Scotland, 29 June 1649.
48 *APS*, v.611.
49 *APS*, VI.ii.299–300. S. Rutherford, *Lex Rex* (1644), 223–4, D. Stevenson, 'The Covenanters and the Court of Session', *Juridical Review*

(1972), 243–4, 245.
50 *RCGA*, ii.240–1; *APS*, VI.ii.152–3, 173–4, 184, 185.
51 J. Nicoll, *Diary* (Bannatyne Club 1836), 3–4, 5–6.
52 K. Thomas, *Religion and the Decline of Magic* (Harmondsworth 1973); A. Macfarlane, *Witchcraft in Tudor and Stuart England* (1970). My comment on th dearth of witchcraft studies in Scotland of courses relates to the position in the 1970s. Since then, much has been published on the subject.
53 Thomas, *Religion and the Decline of Magic*, 521–34, 537, 542–3, 546–8, 595–7, 697.
54 G.F. Black, *A Calendar of Witchcraft Cases in Scotland* (New York 1938) states that 'The three great periods of witchcraft persecutions in Scotland were 1590–1597, 1640–1644, and 1660–1663', but the numbers of cases he records for each year show no rise in the 1640s until 1644, and the numbers recorded for 1649–50 greatly exceed those for 1643–4, even though Black did not use the registers of the committee of estates, one of the main sources for the 1649–50 craze.
55 See C. Larner, 'James VI and I and Witchcraft', in A.G.R. Smith (ed.), *The Reign of James VI and I* (1973), 74–90; T.C. Smout, *History of the Scottish People* (1969), 198–207.
56 Eg, Peterkin, *Records*, 279, 354, 407, 432, 553; *RCGA*, i.123, ii.307, 329, 337, 393, 414, 417.
57 Thomas, *Religion and the Decline of Magic*, 597–8.
58 Ibid, 667–8.
59 Black, *Calendar*, 14.
60 W. Ross, *Aberdour and Inchcolme* (Edinburgh 1885), 337, 343; W. Stephen, *History of Inverkeithing and Rossyth* (Aberdeen 1921), 440–3.
61 E.g., PA.11/8, ff.49, 62v-63, 72, 90, 90v; *APS*, VI.ii.453, 463, 479, 484, 490, 497, 498, 506, 516, 518, 538; *RPCS*, *1544–1660*, 198–205.
62 *APS*, VI.ii.490, 538; Black, *Calendar*, 56.
63 PA.11/8, ff.101–96 *passim*; PA.11/9, Register of the Committee of Estates, 1649–50, ff.2v–7v; PA.12/5, Warrants of the committee of estates, 1650, minutes of 1 March and 2 April 1650; *APS*, VI.ii.565; Balfour, *Historical Works*, iv.22; A. Johnston of Wariston, *Diary*, 1650–4 (SHS 1919), 14.
64 *APS*, VI.ii.490, 510, PA.11/8, ff.134v–135, 157–v; Ross, *Aberdour and Inchcolme*, 342–3; Stephen, *Inverkeithing and Rossyth*, 442–4; Lamont, *Diary*, 12; *RCGA*, ii.348–9, 356.
65 J. Kirkton, *The Secret and True History of the Church of Scotland* (Edinburgh 1817), 49–50.
66 *APS*, VI.ii.141, 155; Gordon, *History of Sutherland*, 546; Grimble, *Chief*

of Mackay, 156–7, 186–95; D. Warrand (ed.), *More Colloden Papers* (Inverness 1923), i.90–1.
67 PA.11/8, f.3.
68 PA.11/8, ff.3v, 4.
69 Fraser, *Chronicles of the Frasers*, 336–8; Gordon, *History of Sutherland*, 547; *APS*, VI.ii.216–19; PA.11/8, ff.4v-5; *RCGA*, ii.249–51.
70 C.F. Mackintosh (ed.), *Antiouarian Notes* (Stirling 1913), 167–8; Gordon, *History of Sutherland*, 547; *APS*, VI.ii.705; PA.7/24, f.248; PA.11/8, ff.6v–7, 20, 206–v.
71 NLS, MS Wodrow, Folio LXVII, ff.151–2; Fraser, *Chiefs of Grant*, ii.18–19; Gordon, *History of Sutherland*, 547–8; PA.11/8; ff.18v–20, 46–v.
72 *RCGA*, ii.225; *APS*, VI.ii.327; PA.11/8, ff.15v–16; Gordon, *Britane's Distemper*, 223–6.
73 PA.11/8, ff.15v, 26.
74 PA.11/8, ff.50, 64–65v; Balfour, *Historical Works*, iii.401–5.
75 *RCGA*, ii.263, Gordon, *History of Sutherland*, 548–9, Fraser, *Chronicles of the Frasers*, 338–41; PA.11/8, ff.73v, 74, 76–v, 207–v; *APS*, VI.ii.380, 394–5.
76 PA.11/8, ff.12v, 13, 14–v, 20, 22v–23, 27, 75v.
77 Burnet, *Hamilton*, 384–405; Cobbett, *State Trials*, iv.1155–94; Carte, *Original Letters*, i.232, 238.
78 Ibid, i.232, 238, 243, 244; Baillie, *Letters*, iii.79, 81; HMC 51: *Leyborne Popham*, 9–11; HMC 1: *2nd Report*, App, p.173.
79 Carte, *Original Letters*, i.263–4; Baillie, *Letters*, iii.84–5.
80 *APS*, VI.ii.728–9; Baillie, *Letters*, iii.87, 88, 512–14; Carte, *Original Letters*, i.271.
81 *APS*, VI.ii.729–30; Baillie, *Letters*, iii.515–16.
82 HMC 1: *2nd Report*, App, p.173.
83 *Calendar of Clarendon State Papers*, ii.12.
84 Napier, *Memorials of Montrose*, ii.376–82.
85 Ibid, ii.383; *APS*, VI.ii.731–2; Baillie, *Letters*, iii.87, 88, 516–20; Carte, *Original Letters*, i.300.
86 *APS*, VI.ii.435–6.
87 *RCGA*, ii.290–4; Wishart, *Memoirs*, 302–3; for the date of Strachan's letter see Gardiner, *Commonwealth and Protectorate*, i.213n.
88 *APS*, VI.ii.446–7, 527–8.
89 Peterkin, *Records*, 556–8; Baillie, *Letters*, iii.91, 97; Lamont, *Diary*, 10; Balfour, *Historical Works*, iii.430; D. Stevenson, 'Deposition of Ministers in the Church of Scotland Under the Covenanters, 1638–51', *Church History*, xliv, (1975), 329–32.
90 Baillie, *Letters*, iii.94–5; Peterkin, *Records*, 550–1.

91 Balfour, *Historical Works*, iii.417–18.
92 Peterkin, *Records*, 544–9; *APS*, VI.ii.514.
93 Baillie, *Letters*, iii.99–100; *APS*, VI.ii.538; Scrope and Monkhouse, *Clarendon State Papers*, iii, app, lxxxix–xc; Balfour, *Historical Works*, iii.417.
94 Baillie, *Letters*, iii.98–9; Stevenson, 'The Financing of the Cause of the Covenants', *SHR*, li.116–18.
95 E.g., PA.11/8, ff.123–v; PA.11/9, f.17.
96 E.g., PA.11/8, ff.100–171v *passim.*
97 *APS*, VI.iii.486; Balfour, *Historical Works*, iii.424–5; PA.11/8, ff.100, 127v–142v *passim* 154–v.
98 PA.11/8, f.169v, PA.11/9 f.26, *RCGA*, ii.353, 360, 364–5, 411–12; F.B. Bickley (ed.), 'Letters Relating to Scotland, January 1650', EHR, xi (1896), 113–15.
99 *APS*, VI.ii.739–40; PA.11/8, ff.118v, 142v, 146–148v, 169; Balfour, *Historical Works*, iii.432; Bickley, 'Letters Relating to Scotland', *EHR*, xi.114.
100 Baillie, *Letters*, iii.522; Gardiner, *Commonwealth and Protectorate*, i.184.
101 Ibid, i.12–13, 105–44.
102 G.F. Warner (ed.), *Nicholas Papers*, i (Camden Society 1886), 160–1.
103 Carte *Original Letters*, i.338–9, 355–6, 357–8; HMC 5: *6th Report*, App, 612; *RCGA*, ii.354–5.
104 Balfour, *Historical Works*, iv.2; PA.11/8, ff.50v–51.
105 Kirkton, *History of the Church of Scotland*, 50.
106 Bickley 'Letters Relating to Scotland', *EHR*, xi.115–17; Balfour, *Historical Works*, iii.437–9; *RCGA*, ii.355; PA.11/9, f.54.
107 Gardiner, *Commonwealth and Protectorate*, i.191–2; PA.11/9, f.65v; J. Nickolls (ed.), *Original Letters and Papers of State addressed to Oliver Cromwell* (1743), 3–4; E. Walker, *Historical Discourses* (1705), 157.
108 *RCGA*, ii.367–73; PA.11/9, f.66v; J. Livingstone, *A Brief Historical Relation* (Edinburgh 1848), 115–16.
109 *APS*, VI.ii.557–61.
110 Gardiner, *Commonwealth and Protectorate*, i.189–91; J.N.M. Maclean, 'Montrose's Preparations for the Invasion of Scotland and Royalist Missions to Sweden, 1649–51' in R. Hatton and S. Anderson (eds.), *Studies in Diplomatic History in Memory of D.B. Horn* (1970), 7–31.
111 J. Mooney (ed.), *Charters and Other Records of the City and Royal Burgh of Kirkwall* (Kirkwall [1948]), 88–9; Balfour, *Historical Works*, iii.431, 433–4; J. Gwynne, *Military Memoirs of the Great Civil War* (Edinburgh 1822), 88; Gordon, *History of Sutherland*, 550; S.R. Gardiner (ed.), *Charles the Second and Scotland in 1650* (SHS 1894), 38–9, 49; Napier, *Memorials of Montrose*,

ii.394–6,413–15.
112 Ibid, ii.410–12.
113 PA.11/8, ff.164v–165, 172v–173.
114 PA.11/8, ff.101–99 *passim.*
115 PA.11/8, ff.180–v, 183–v; PA.11/9, ff.15v–16.
116 Steele, *Tudor and Stuart Proclamations,* ii.342; Gwynne, *Military Memoirs,* 86–7; Balfour, *Historical Works,* iii.432; PA.11/8, ff.180–v, 191v–192, 197; Gordon, *History of Sutherland,* 550–1.
117 Gardiner, *Charles II and Scotland,* 41; Scrope and Monkhouse, *Clarendon State Papers,* ii, app, li–liv; Livingstone, *Brief Relation,* 117–19, 123–4; *RCGA,* ii.381–5.
118 Scrope and Monkhouse, *Clarendon State Papers,* ii. app, liv–lv; RCGA, ii.38 1–2; Gardiner, *Charles II and Scotland,* 74–5.
119 Ibid, 141; Scrope and Monkhouse, *Clarendon State Papers,* ii. app, lv–lix; *RCGA,* ii.389–92; Livingstone, *Brief Relation,* 123–4.
120 *RCGA,* ii.392–3; Kirkton, *History of the Church of Scotland,* 51; Livingstone, *Brief Relation,* 124–5.
121 Napier, *Memorials of Montrose,* ii.400–1, 405–6, 413–15, 478; Gardiner, *Charles II and Scotland,* 49–50, 68.
122 Ibid, 49; Gwynne, *Military Memoirs,* 89–91; Gordon, *History of Sutherland,* 551–3; HMC 1: *2nd Report,* App, pp. 176–7; Wishart, *Memoirs,* 294–9.
123 PA.12/5, minutes for 16 and 18 April 1650.
124 Gordon, *History of Sutherland,* 553; Balfour, *Historical Works,* iv.9–10; Fraser, *Chronicles of the Frasers,* 351–2.
125 Ibid, 352; Balfour, *Historical Works,* iv.9–12; Wishart, *Memoirs,* 305–9, 493–501; Gordon, *History of Sutherland,* 554–7; Gwynne, *Military Memoirs,* 91–3.
126 Fraser, *Chronicles of the Frasers,* 352–6; Wishart, *Memoirs,* 522–33; Gordon, *History of Sutherland,* 555, 557.
127 Laing, *Ancrum and Lothian Correspondence,* ii.262.
128 *APS,* VI.ii.563 564, 565; *Maitland Miscellany,* II.ii.481–7; Balfour, *Historical Works,* iv.12–13, 15–16.
129 J. Willcock, *The Great Marquess* (Edinburgh 1903), 233; Cobbett, *State Trials,* v.1427; Burnet, *History of My Own Times,* i.225.
130 Gardiner, *Charles II and Scotland,* 114; Livingstone, *Brief Relation,* 115; HMC 5: *6th Report,* App. pp.112–13; Kirkton, *History of the Church of Scotland,* 50.
131 *Maitland Miscellany,* II.ii.489–90; Balfour, *Historical Works,* iv.19–22; Fraser, *Chronicles of the Frasers,* 357–62.
132 Laing, *Ancrum and Lothian Correspondence,* ii.262; G. Mackenzie,

Memoirs of the Affairs of Scotland (Edinburgh 1821), 47; Wodrow, *Analecta*, ii.139.
133 *APS*, VI.ii.562, 564, 565, 566, 568, 569, 575, 577, 579, 582; Balfour, *Historical Works*, iv.18–19, 23, 27, 28–31, 32, 34–7, 50, 56; Lamont, *Diary*, 18, 19; Nicoll, *Diary*, 15, 16.
134 Gardiner, *Commonwealth and Protectorate*, i.201, 206; A. Lang, *A History of Scotland*, (Edinburgh 1907), iii.221–4.
135 *Maitland Miscellany*, II.ii.472–81.
136 A.G. Reid (ed.), 'Notice of an Original Letter of Instructions for Sir William Fleming', *Proceedings of the Society of Antiquaries of Scotland*, xxxiv (1899–1900), 201.
137 E.g., Lang, *History of Scotland*, iii.224, Buchan, *Montrose*, 362–3 and Williams, *Montrose*, 347–8. Williams argues that the king wrote no letter to parliament on 12 May, the letter presented in his name probably being a forgery by Argyll or William Murray.
138 There is no reliable direct evidence as to the date Fleming arrived. English reports give dates ranging from 8 to 18 May (Napier, *Memorials of Montrose*, ii.762n.; Gardiner, *Commonwealth and Protectorate*, i.230 and n.). The first date is obviously wrong—Fleming was still in Breda on 8 May—but that he arrived before Montrose's death has generally been accepted. Gardiner believed that he arrived on 15 May, not knowing that he had been in Breda as late as 12 May when he received new instructions from the king. Gardiner did know of the 12 May letter from the king to the Scottish parliament which Fleming was to deliver, but he assumed that this letter was sent after Fleming in the hands of William Murray. But the instructions of 12 May were clearly not sent after Fleming, to be delivered to him in Scotland, for they tell him what to do immediately on arriving there. Moreover the instructions of 5 and 9 May order Fleming to consult Murray, whom they imply would reach Scotland before him (*Maitland Miscellany*, II.ii.477, 480). Gardiner's belief that Murray carried the letter of 12 May led him to confuse matters further by identifying a summary of an undated earlier letter from the king to parliament which was carried by Murray as being a summary of the letter of 12 May—though as the summary was inconsistent with other reports of the contents of the 12 May letter he had to claim that it was an inaccurate summary! (*Charles II and Scotland*, 103; *Commonwealth and Protectorate*, i.233). Unfortunately Gardiner failed to make it clear that the summary was undated, the date being added by him, thus leading later writers to accept the date of 12 May as certain (Lang, *History of Scotland*, iii.225; Buchan, *Montrose*, 363n.).

So Murray evidently set out for Scotland before Fleming; and did not arrive until 24 May. It is possible that Fleming had somehow overtaken him and had already arrived, but it is much more likely that Fleming arrived after Murray, on 25 May, the day he presented the king's letter of 12 May to parliament. Assuming he had left Breda on 12 May this would mean the journey had taken him thirteen days; this seems a long time, but it is notable that a letter from the Scottish commissioners in Breda to parliament dated 11 May was not read in parliament until 25 May (*Charles II and Scotland*, 101–2; Balfour, *Historical Works*, iv.25). Whatever reasons might be invented for Fleming failing to deliver the king's letter immediately on his arrival, there is no reason why delivery of the commissioners' letter should have been similarly delayed. The least tortuous interpretation of the evidence is surely that Fleming was delayed by unfavourable winds, and found that Montrose was already dead when he landed. The story that he cynically stood by without intervening while Montrose was executed has grown up from no better evidence than rumours in London about when Fleming had landed.

139 *APS*, VI.ii.568; Balfour, *Historical Works*, iv.24–5.

140 *APS*, VI.ii.562, 563, 564; PA.7/7/10; Balfour, *Historical Works*, iv.12.

141 Ibid, iv.14, 41–4; Scrope and Monkhouse, *Clarendon State Papers*, ii. app, lix–lxi.

142 *RCGA*, ii.399–404; *APS*, VI.ii.565, 566; Balfour, *Historical Works*, iv.18.

143 Cuningham, *Journal*, 231–3; Livingstone, *Brief Relation*, 125–8.

144 Gardiner, *Charles II and Scotland*, 141–2; Carte, *Original Letters*, i.396.

145 Livingstone, *Brief Relation*, 128–30; Scrope and Monkhouse, *Clarendon State Papers*, ii. app, lxiii–lxv; Walker, *Historical Discourses*, 158.

146 *RCGA*, ii.436–8; Balfour, *Historical Works*, iv.61–2.

147 A Jaffray, *Diary*, (Aberdeen 1856), 32–3; Livingstone, *Brief Relation*, 130–1.

148 Gardiner, *Commonwealth and Protectorate*, i.231; *APS*, VI.ii.568; Balfour, *Historical Works*, iv.25.

149 *APS*, VI.ii.577, 586–7, 594.

150 Abbott, *Cromwell*, ii.263, 265, 267–72.

151 *APS*, VI.ii.584–5.

152 *Edin Recs, 1642–55*, 238–9, 240, 241, 244.

153 *APS*, VI.ii.579, 582–3, 586, 587, 588–90, 597–600; Balfour, *Historical Works*, iv.58, 70, 79–80; *RCGA*, ii.418, 419, 425.

154 Nicoll, *Diary*, 16–17.

155 HMC 5: *6th Report*, App. 613; Laing, *Ancrum and Lothian Correspondence*, ii.269–71; *RCGA*, ii.439–40; *APS*, VI.ii.594, 602, 603–4; Walker, *Historical Discourses*, 160–2; Balfour, *Historical Works*, iv.64–6; PA.12/5, 3 July 1650, Lauderdale to Loudoun; GD.25/9/30, *Ailsa Muniments*, 2 July 1650, Hamilton to Cassillis.

156 *APS*, VI.ii.601–2, 607; Balfour, *Historical Works*, iv.73, 78; *RCGA*, ii.440.
157 *Calendar of Clarendon State Papers*, ii.69, 70; Gardiner, *Charles II and Scotland*, 130; PA.12/5, minutes of 17 July 1650.
158 Lamont, *Diary*, 21–2; Peterkin, *Records*, 591; Scrope and Monkhouse, *Clarendon State Papers*, ii. App. lxiii; Livingstone, *Brief Relation*, 124–5, 131–2.
159 *APS*, VI.ii.587, 808; Balfour, *Historical Works*, iv.58–9; PA.7/24, f.5; Johnston, *Diary, 1650–4*, 4; Warner, *Nicholas Papers*, i.189.
160 Gardiner, *Commonwealth and Protectorate*, i.271–2; Abbott, *Cromwell*, ii. 294–301.
161 Ibid, ii.302–5.
162 Johnston, *Diary, 1650–4*, 5; PA.7/24, f.7.
163 Scrope and Monkhouse, *Clarendon State Papers*, ii.74; Walker, *Historical Discourses*, 163–4.
164 Johnston, *Diary, 1650–4*, 5.
165 E.31/19, Minute Book of the Board of the Green Cloth, 1650–1, f.10v; Johnston, *Diary, 1650–4*, 5,6; Balfour, *Historical Works*, iv.86; Warner, *Nicholas Papers*, i.188, 193–4; PA.7/24, f.7v.
166 Balfour, *Historical Works*, iv.89; Johnston, *Diary, 1650–4*, 6.
167 Ibid, 7–9, 11, 19–20; Burns, 'Memoirs', 15–16, in [Maidment], *Historical Fragments*; Walker, *Historical Discourses*, 165; Warner, *Nicholas Papers*, i.193–4; *CSPD, 1650*, 309.
168 Johnston, *Diary, 1650–4*, 8, 10, 11–12, 15.
169 *Glasgow Recs, 1630–62*, 192.
170 W.S. Douglas, *Cromwell's Scotch Campaigns, 1650–1* (1898), 58; Abbott, *Cromwell*, ii.307–8 and n., 309n.
171 *RCGA*, iii.26, 33–40; Johnston, *Diary 1650–4*, 11–12, 13–14, 15, 17; PA.12/5, minutes of 8, 10 and 13 August 1650; Balfour, *Historical Works*, iv.95–6; R. Wodrow, *History of the Sufferings of the Church of Scotland* (4 vols., Glasgow 1828–30), i.47–8; Baillie, *Letters*. iii.114.
172 Balfour, *Historical Works*, iv.90–1.
173 *Calendar of Clarendon State Papers*, ii.74; PA.12/5, minutes of 15 August 1650, *CSPD, 1650*, 310; Gardiner, *Charles II and Scotland*, 131–2, 133–4; Laing, *Ancrum and Lothian Correspondence*, ii.280–6.
174 Ibid, ii.289–90; PA.12/5, minutes of 16 August 1650.
175 *RCGA*, iii.33–40, 42–3; E.31/19, f.15.
176 PA.12/5, minutes of 14 August 1650; Balfour, *Historical Works*, iv.96–7.
177 Gardiner, *Hamilton Papers*, 255; Gardiner, *Charles II and Scotland*, 143–4.
178 Gardiner, *Commonwealth and Protectorate*, i.275–6, 279–82; Abbott,

Cromwell, ii.305–14.
179 Ibid, ii.314.
180 Gardiner, *Commonwealth and Protectorate*, i.284–8; Baillie, *Letters*, iii.111.
181 Birch, *State Papers of John Thurloe*, i.167–8.
182 Abbott, *Cromwell*, ii.326, Laing, *Ancrum and Lothian Correspondence*, ii.297–8.
183 C.H. Firth, 'The Battle of Dunbar', *Transactions of the Royal Historical Society*, n.s. xiv (1900), 19–52; Abbott, *Cromwell*, ii.315–25; Gardiner, *Commonwealth and Protectorate*, i.290–5. Firth and Gardiner, arguing from a nearly contemporary print of the battle, suggest that the Scots were not drawn up along the Brox Burn when Cromwell attacked but parallel to the coast. But the order to Leslie to storm Broxmouth House (though this was not done) and skirmishing along the burn on 2 September show that at least some of Leslie's forces were ranged along the burn. The print therefore probably shows the Scots position once Cromwell had driven their right wing back from the burn.
184 HMC 51: *Leyborne-Popham*, 75. Many of the colours are illustrated in British Library, MS Harleian 1460, A Perfect Registry of all the Colours taken from the Scotts at Preston and Dunbar.
185 Abbott, *Cromwell*, ii.327. See also *Mercurius Politicus*, no. 15, 12–19 September 1650, 230, 'now the Kirk–party are down, the Scotch Cavaliers will begin to shew their Teeth againe, and then what will become of the Covenant'.

CHAPTER 5: *The Cromwellian Conquest, September 1650–December 1651*

1 D. Robertson (ed.), *South Leith Records* (Edinburgh 1911), 92; H. Paton (ed.), *The Register of Marriages in the Parish of Edinburgh, 1595–1700* (Scottish Record Society 1905), iii–iv; PA.7/24, Parliamentary and State Papers, f.142; McCrie, *Life of Blair*, 238; Walker, *Historical Discourses*, 183, 186.
2 Ibid, 183, 187, 189; PA.7/24, f.142; McCrie, *Life of Blair*, 241; Baillie, *Letters*, iii.111–14; *Glasgow Recs, 1630–62*, 192. For this whole section see D. Stevenson 'The Western Association', *Ayrshire Collections*, XIII. iv(1982).
3 Walker, *Historical Discourses*, 183; Birch, *State Papers of John Thurloe*, i.163–4; Laing, *Ancrum and Lothian Correspondence*, ii.298–9.
4 *RCGA*, iii.48–58, 63–5.
5 Ibid, iii.61–2; Walker, *Historical Discourses*, 189.
6 Balfour, *Historical Works*, iv.107–8; McCrie, *Life of Blair*, 239–40.
7 Hyde, *History of the Rebellion*, v.149; D.E. Underdown, *Royalist*

Conspiracy in England, 1649–1650 (New Haven 1960), 12, 18, 42.
8 J. Evelyn, *Diary and Correspondence* (4 vols., 1852), iv. 195–6.
9 GD.112/39/882–5, Breadalbane Muniments; Walker, *Historical Discourses* 188; HMC 5: *6th Report*, App, 606–7.
10 Balfour, *Historical Works*, iv.109–12.
11 Walker, *Historical Discourses*, 196–7; J. Murray, Duke of Atholl, *Chronicles of the Atholl and Tullibardine Families* (Edinburgh 1908), i.140.
12 Ibid, i.140; Walker, *Historical Discourses*, 197–9; Evelyn, *Diary and Correspondence*, iv.197; Balfour, *Historical Works*, iv.112–13.
13 HMC 72: *Laing*, i.250–1.
14 Laing, *Ancrum and Lothian Correspondence*, i.306–7; PA.7/24, f.30; Balfour, *Historical Works*, iv. 115–16.
15 Ibid, iv.112–15; Walker, *Historical Discourses*, 199.
16 Ibid, 200–1; Murray, *Chronicles*, i.140.
17 PA.7/24, ff.30v–31, 32; Hyde, *History of the Rebellion*, v.171; Balfour *Historical Works*, iv.117–19.
18 Ibid, iv.123, 125–8; PA.7/24, ff.39–v; Walker, *Historical Discourses*, 203; Laing, *Ancrum and Lothian Correspondence*, ii.317–18.
19 Ibid, ii.501*–502*; Balfour, *Historical Works*, iv.129–32.
20 Ibid, iv.132–5, 160; HMC 5: *6th Report*, App, 613.
21 Abbott, *Cromwell*, ii.335–6, 340, 342–3, 345, 348; Laing, *Ancrum and Lothian Correspondence*, ii.301–2, 305–6; Nicoll, *Diary*, 30–1, 33–4; Walker, *Historical Discourses*, 201; Baillie, *Letters*, iii.118–20.
22 HMC 72: *Laing*, i.251–2.
23 Abbott, *Cromwell*, ii.352, 354, 355–7; Walker, *Historical Discourses*, 189; Balfour, *Historical Works*, iv.122, 125.
24 *RCGA*, iii.557–62; Baillie, *Letters*, iii.115–16.
25 *RCGA*, iii.95–107; Balfour, *Historical Works*, iv.141–60.
26 Baillie, *Letters*, iii.112–14, 118, 120.
27 Balfour, *Historical Works*, iv.309–10; PA.11/11, Register of the Committee of Estates, 1651, ff.64v–65v, 68v–69, 70v–71v, 76v.
28 PA.7/24, ff.42, 42v, 45; *RCGA*, iii.94–5, 106–8.
29 Balfour, *Historical Works*, iv.136–7; Baillie, *Letters*, iii.122–3.
30 Ibid, iii.120–2; PA.7/24, ff.57–60; *RCGA*, iii.108–9, 111–15; Balfour, *Historical Works*, iv.166–8; W. Stephen (ed.), *Register of Consultations of the Ministers of Edinburgh* (2 vols., SHS 1921–30), i.298–9.
31 PA.7/24, f.57; *RCGA*, iii.113–14; Balfour, *Historical Works*, iv.98, 109, 127, 129, 166.
32 Ibid, iv.170, 172–4; Johnston, *Diary, 1650–4*, 28, 29, 30; Baillie, *Letters*, iii.123.
33 *RCGA*, iii.123–5; Balfour, *Historical Works*, iv.176–8.

34 *RCGA*, iii.126–33; Balfour, *Historical Works*, iv.160–1; Stephen, *Register of Consultations*, i.299–301.
35 *RCGA*, iii.137–41.
36 Laing, *Ancrum and Lothian Correspondence*, ii.319–20.
37 *APS*, VI.ii.609, 613; Somerville, Lord J., *Memorie of the Somervills* (2 vols., Edinburgh 1815), ii.437.
38 Abbott, *Cromwell*, ii.359–63; Balfour, *Historical Works*, iv.165–6, 209–10.
39 Abbott, *Cromwell*, ii.363, 364, 366; Somerville, *Memorie of the Somervills* ii.442–50; Nicoll, *Diary*, 36–7; Baillie, *Letters*, iii.125.
40 *APS*, VI.ii.621, 630.
41 *RCGA*, iii.157–60; Baillie, *Letters*, iii.125–6.
42 *APS*, VI.ii.620, 623, 624–6; *RCGA*, iii.267–71; Balfour, *Historical Works*, iv.212.
43 *RCGA*, iii.85–474 *passim*; Turner, *Memoirs*, 94.
44 *RCGA*, iii.216–29.
45 Ibid, iii.173–431 *passim*; McCrie, *Life of Blair*, 264–6.
46 *RCGA*, iii.232–4, 252, 260, 295, 328–35; McCrie, *Life of Blair*, 257–8; PA.11/10, Register of the Committee of Estates, 1651, ff.70v–71, 79, 86v, 95–v, 100; *APS*, VI.ii.641–2, 647; Balfour, *Historical Works*, iv.248.
47 Abbott, *Cromwell*, ii.366–7, 370, 372; *RCGA*, iii.160–70; Fraser, *Chronicles of the Frasers*, 372.
48 PA.11/10, f.47; [Maidment], 'Collections by a Private Hand at Edinburgh', 30–1, in *Historical Fragments.* (Edinburgh 1833); Jaffray, *Diary*, 38–41; W.I. Hoy, 'The Entry of Sects into Scotland', in D. Shaw (ed), *Reformation and Revolution* (Edinburgh 1967), 178–211; G.D. Henderson, 'Some Early Scottish Independents', in *Religious Life in Seventeenth Century Scotland* (Cambridge 1937) 100–17; M.V. Hay, *The Blairs Papers* (1929), 187–8.
49 Balfour, *Historical Works*, iv.222, 250; Burns, 'Memoirs', 17–18 in [Maidment], *Historical Fragments.*
50 PA.11/10, ff.23v, 24v; Balfour, *Historical Works*, iv.238–40, 246; Carte, *Original Letters*, i.410–11, 469–70; Laing, *Ancrum and Lothian Correspondence*, ii.325–6.
51 See D. Stevenson, 'The English and the Public Records of Scotland, 1650–1660', *Miscellany One* (Stair Society 1971), 156–70.
52 *RCGA*, iii.142–54.
53 G. Hillier, *A Narrative of the Attempted Escapes of Charles the First* (1852), 327–34; Warner, *Nicholas Papers*, i.221–2, 238; Johnston, *Diary, 1650–4*, 97–8, 218.
54 *Coronation of Charles the Second, King of Scotland, England, France and Ireland, as it was acted and done at Scone* (Aberdeen 1651); P.C. Stuart, Marquis of Bute, *Scottish Coronations* (Paisley 1912), 141–217.

55 *APS*, VI.ii.631–3; Baillie, *Letters*, iii.129.
56 *APS*, VI.ii.640; PA.11/10, ff.52v–53, 82v; Balfour, *Historical Works*, iv.253–4; Nicoll, *Diary*, 50.
57 PA.11/10, ff.54v–55v; Burns, 'Memoirs', 19 in [Maidment], *Historical Fragments*; Balfour, *Historical Works*, iv.297.
58 Abbott, *Cromwell*, ii.393; [Maidment], 'Collections by a Private Hand', 33; in *Historical Fragments*.
59 Abbott, *Cromwell*, ii.393–6, 408, 410, 411–12, 415, 419, 420; *Ancrum and Lothian Correspondence*, ii.339, 344–5.
60 Abbott, *Cromwell*, ii.393–6, 408, 410, 411–12 415, 419, 420; Baillie, *Letters*, iii.165–6; Nicoll, *Diary*, 51, 52, Fraser, *Chronicles of the Frasers*, 381; Burns 'Memoirs', 18, 19 in [Maidment], *Historical Fragments*.
61 HMC 72: *Laing*, i.257; *APS*, VI.ii.647; McCrie, *Life of Blair*, 269.
62 HMC 72: *Laing*, i.258–9. See also *Mercurius Politicus*, no.38, 20–27 February 1651, 621, 622.
63 *RCGA*, iii.356–8; *APS*, VI.ii.652, 654–5; Balfour, *Historical Works*, iv.275, 277
64 *APS*, VI.ii.655–6, 662–3, 666; *RCGA*, iii.361.
65 *RCGA*, iii.367–70.
66 PA.11/11, ff. 1–45v.
67 PA.11/11, ff.3v, 19–20, 25v, 29v–31v, 40.
68 *APS*, VI.ii.651, 663; PA.11/11, f.109v; British Library, Egerton Charter 422, Commission to the duke of Buckingham; Balfour, *Historical Works*, iv.297, 299–301.
69 Nicoll, *Diary*, 51; PA.7/8/9; Baillie, *Letters*, iii.160; *RCGA*, iii.388.
70 *RCGA*, iii.404, 432, 439–46.
71 *APS*, VI.ii.672–3, 676–7.
72 *APS*, VI.ii.648, 652, 677, 679–81.
73 *RCGA*, iii.450–9, 476–9; PA.11/11, ff.86v–87.
74 *APS*, VI.ii.683–4; PA.11/11, ff.64v–65v, 68v–69, 69v, 70v–71v, 76v; Balfour, *Historical Works*, iv.309, 310; Burns, 'Memoirs', 20 in [Maidment], *Historical Fragments*.
75 Peterkin, *Records*, 626–7, 632–4; McCrie, *Life of Blair*, 273n., 274–5.
76 Ibid, 277; Peterkin, *Records*, 628, 631–2; Lamont, *Diary*, 33.
77 Ibid, 40; Peterkin, *Records*, 628–9; McCrie, *Life of Blair*, 239, 278; Stevenson, 'Deposition of Ministers in the Church of Scotland under the Covenanters', *Church History*, xliv (1975), 332.
78 Peterkin, *Records*, 630–1, 635–6; *RCGA*, iii.495–6.
79 Stevenson, 'The Radical Party in the Kirk', *Journal of Ecclesiastical History*, xxv. 162–3.
80 Laing, *Ancrum and Lothian Correspondence*, ii.360.

81 Nicoll, *Diary*, 53; PA. 1 1/1 1, ff.97v, 100v, 101v; Abbott, *Cromwell*, ii.427–9.
82 Balfour, *Historical Works*, iv.308.
83 Abbott, Cromwell, ii.430–1; Gardiner, *Commonwealth and Protectorate* ii.26–8, Nicoll, *Diary*, 53–4; Fraser, *Chronicles of the Frasers*, 383–4; Balfour, *Historical Works*, iv. 313.
84 Ibid, iv. 313–14; Abbott, *Cromwell*, ii.434–5, 439–42; Nicoll, *Diary*, 54–5.
85 Ibid, 55; PA. 11/11, ff.88–v; HMC 29: *Portland*, i.610–11.
86 Burnet, *Hamilton*, 426; HMC 21: *Hamilton*, ii.77–8.
87 Turner, *Memoirs*, 94; H. Cary (ed.), *Memorials of the Great Civil War* (2 vols., 1842), ii.305, 308, 309.
88 Underdown, *Royalist Conspiracy in England*, 49–52; Turner, *Memoirs*, 95; Abbott, *Cromwell*, ii.456, 458–65; Gardiner, *Commonwealth and Protectorate*, ii.35, 36–9, 41–6.
89 Ibid, ii.57.
90 Abbott, *Cromwell*, ii.422–3; C.H. Firth (ed.), *Scotland and the Commonwealth* (SHS 1895), 1–6, 316–17; Cary, *Memorials of the Great Civil War*, ii.330–1.
91 Firth, *Scotland and the Commonwealth*, 21–3; D.G. Barron (ed.), *In Defence of the Regalia, 1651–2* (1910), 94; A. Maxwell, *The History of Old Dundee* (Edinburgh 1884), 545; PA.7/24, ff.136–v.
92 HMC 29: *Portland*, i.615.
93 Barron, *In Defence of the Regalia*, 5, 91–2, 164.
94 Cary, *Memorials of the Great Civil War*, ii.345–6; Balfour, *Historical Works*, iv.314–15; Firth, *Scotland and the Commonwealth*, 8–9, 320; Nicoll, *Diary*, 56–7.
95 Ibid, 57–8; Cary, *Memorials of the Great Civil War*, ii.351–2, 366; Gardiner, *Commonwealth and Protectorate*, ii.66–8.
96 *RCGA*, iii.513; Barron, *In Defence of the Regalia*, 93–4; *Aber Recs, 1643–1747*, 122, 123; Taylor, *Aberdeen Council Letters*, iii.169–70; Firth, *Scotland and the Commonwealth*, 325–6.
97 Ibid, 23–4; Murray, *Chronicles*, i.142; Barron, *In Defence of the Regalia*, 98; NLS, MS Adv.29.2.9, Balcarres Papers, ff.213, 215, 216.
98 *Stirling Recs, 1519–1666*, 199; HMC 4: *5th Report*, App, 645; NLS, MS 5155, Erskine Papers, f.130; Firth, *Scotland and the Commonwealth*, 24–6, 26n.
99 Ibid, xxi, xxii, 19–21, 26–7, 333, 335, 338–9.
100 Ibid, 337–8, 340–1; Balfour, *Historical Works*, iv.345–6; Gordon, *History of Sutherland*, 561–2.
101 Ibid, 562.

CHAPTER 6: *The Scottish Revolution*

1 A. Campbell, Marquis of Argyll, *Instructions to a Son* (1661), 4–5, 6.
2 See B. Worden, *The Rump Parliament* (1974), 226, 251, 262.
3 G. Davies, *The Restoration of Charles II, 1658–1660* (1969), 219.
4 *Oxford English Dictionary, s.v.* 'Union'.
5 D. Stevenson, 'The Radical Party in the Kirk, 1637–45', *Journal of Ecclesiastical History*, xxvi (1974), 158–60.
6 [A. Henderson], *Reformation of Church Government in Scotland cleared from some Mistakes. . .* (1644), 15.
7 Ibid, 14, 17; A. Henderson, *A Sermon Preached Before the Right Honourable the House of Lords, 28th of May 1645. . .* (1645), preface 'To the Christian Reader'; [A. Henderson], *The Government and Order of the Church of Scotland* (Edinburgh 1641), 64.
8 D. Stevenson, 'Church and Society under the Covenanters', *Scotia: American–Canadian Journal of Scottish Studies*, I.i (1977), 24–41.
9 See V. Pearl, 'London's Counter-Revolution' in *The Interregnum*, ed. G.E. Aylmer (1972), 29–56.
10 H.R Trevor-Roper 'Scotland and the Puritan Revolution', in *Religion, the Reformation and Social Change* (1967), 407.
11 H.R. Trevor-Roper, 'The Union of Britain in the Seventeenth Century', ibid, 460.
12 Baillie, *Letters*, iii.82.
13 Hyde, *History of the Rebellion*, iv.307.
14 Ibid, iv. 302–4, 308–10.
15 D.H. Willson, 'King James and Anglo-Scottish Unity' in *Conflict in Stuart England*, ed. W.A. Aiken and D.B. Henning (1960), 52; Trevor-Roper, 'The Union of Britain', 451n.
16 Ibid, 459.
17 Trevor–Roper, 'Scotland and the Puritan Revolution', 440.
18 Donaldson, *Scotland: James V to James VII*, 321.
19 S. Rutherford, *A Testimony. . . to the Work of Reformation in Britain and Ireland* (Glasgow 1719), 6. See D. Stevenson, 'Church and Society under the Covenanters, 1638–51', 24–41.
20 Stevenson, 'The Radical Party in the Kirk', 159–60.
21 Baillie, *Letters*, iii.51.
22 Stevenson, 'The Radical Party in the Kirk', 135–65; and Stevenson, 'Conventicles in the Kirk, 1619–37. The Emergence of a Radical Party', *Records of the Scottish Church History Society*, xviii (1972–4), 99–114.
23 S. Rutherford, *The Tryal and Triumph of Faith. . .* (1652, first published 1645), 'The Epistle Dedicatory'.

24 See Stevenson, 'The Radical Party in the Kirk', 158–9.
25 S.A. Burrell, 'The Covenant Idea as a Revolutionary Symbol: Scotland 1596–1637', *Church History*, xvii (1958), 342–4, 348. For similar ideas in England see e.g. B.S. Capp, *The Fifth Monarchy Men. A Study in Seventeenth Century Millenarianism* (1972), 33–4.
26 Burrell, 'The Covenant Idea', 348.
27 Ibid, 342; J.B. Torrance, 'Covenant or Contract? A Study of the Theological Background of Worship in Seventeenth Century Scotland', *Journal of Scottish Theology*, xxiii (1970), 51–76.
28 Ibid, 70.
29 G. B. Burnet, *The Holy Communion in the Reformed Church of Scotland, 1560–1960* (Edinburgh and London 1960), 103–4.
30 Quoted in ibid, 129: See Torrance, 'Covenant or Contract?', 68–9.
31 Except that at first it was not thought expedient to press the covenant on officers of state, lords of session, privy councillors and some advocates, Baillie, *Letters*, i.109.
32 *APS*, v.270–7.
33 *APS*, VI.i.148–55.
34 *RCGA*, ii.78–80, 136–9, 181–2.
35 See Turner, *Memoirs*, 94.
36 *RCGA*, ii.53–5.
37 Rutherford, *Testimony*, 7–8.
38 Stevenson, 'The Radical Party in the Kirk', 164.
39 See above, n.7
40 Baillie, *Letters*, iii.81–2. See Stevenson, 'The General Assembly and the Commission of the Kirk', *Records of the Scottish Church History Society*, xix.59–79 and Stevenson, 'Deposition of Ministers. . . 1638–1651', *Church History*, xliv (1975), 321–35.
41 J.H Elliott 'England and Europe: A Common Malady?' in C. Russell (ed.), *The Origins of the English Civil War* (1973), 247–8.
42 See Worden, *The Rump Parliament.*
43 S.A. Burrell, 'Calvinism, Capitalism and the Middle Classes: Some after-thoughts on an old problem', *Journal of Modern History*, xxxii (1960), 134–7.
44 See C. Cross, 'The Church in England, 1646–1660' in G.E. Aylmer (ed.), *The Interregnum*, 99–120.
45 R. Baillie, *Errours and Indurations, are the Great Sins and the Great Judgements of the Time. Presented in a Sermon Before the Right Honourable House of Peers . . . July 30 1645* (1645), 21.
46 See Torrance, 'Covenant or Contract?', 51–76.
47 See Stevenson, 'The Radical Party in the Kirk', 154–5.

48 Ibid, 162–3.
49 S. Rutherford, *Lex Rex* (1644), 211–12.
50 C. Walker, *Relations and Observations, Historicall and Politick, upon the Parliament. . . together with An Appendix, touching the Proceedings of the Independent faction in Scotland* (1648), 8.
51 See D.H. Pennington, *Seventeenth Century Europe* (1972), 45–6, 212.
52 Burnet, *Hamilton*, 46.
53 Rutherford, *Lex Rex*, 387; G.D. Henderson, *Religious Life in Seventeenth Century Scotland* (Cambridge, 1937), 62.
54 Pennington, *Seventeenth Century Europe*, 47.
55 C.C. Weston, 'The Theory of Mixed Monarchy Under Charles I and After', *EHR*, lxxv (1960), 426–43.
56 Weston makes no mention of Rutherford, presumably because he was a Scot.
57 J.W. Allen, *English Political Thought, 1603–44* (1938), 285, 424.
58 Rutherford, *Lex Rex*, 7.
59 Ibid, 9.
60 Ibid, 10–11.
61 Ibid, 10.
62 Ibid, 96–105.
63 Ibid, 14.
64 Ibid, 53.
65 Ibid, 16.
66 Ibid, 45.
67 S. Rutherford, *A Sermon preached to the Honorable House of Commons. . . Wedenesday Janu. 31 1643* (1643/4), 3, 4.
68 W.M. Campbell, 'Lex Rex and its Author', *Records of the Scottish Church History Society*, vii (1941), 204, 212, 224.
69 P. Zagorin, *A History of Political Thought in the English Revolution* (1954), 6.
70 Rutherford, *Lex Rex*, 178.
71 Ibid, 387.
72 Ibid, 212.
73 Ibid, 170.
74 Ibid, 152; Zagorin, *History of Political Thought*, 6; Allen, *English Polltical Thought*, 464; G.P. Gooch, *English Democratic Ideas in the Seventeenth Century* (New York, 1959), 98–9.
75 Zagorin, *History of Political Thought*, 6.
76 J. Burns, 'Memoirs. . . 1644–1661', 19–20; in [J. Maidment (ed.)], *Historical Fragments relative to Scottish Affairs* (Edinburgh 1833).
77 T.K. Rabb, *The Struggle for Stability in Early Modern Europe* (New York 1975), 147–51 has urged the need in assessing the significance of the mid-

seventeenth century 'crisis' for paying much more attention than has been done in the past to the aftermaths of revolution, instead of concentrating on their causes.

78 Donaldson, *Scotland: James V to James VII*, 358–9.

79 See I. B. Cowan, 'The Covenanters: A Revision Article', *SHR*, xlvii (1968), 46–52.

80 R. Mitchison, 'Restoration and Revolution', in G. Menzies (ed.), *The Scottish Nation* (1972), 135.

81 Donaldson, *Scotland: James V to James VII*, 375–6.

82 Ibid, 359–60; W.C. Dickinson and G. Donaldson (eds.), *A Source Book of Scottish History*, iii (1961), 252–4, 501.

83 The 1661 act recissory is usually stated to have annulled all public legislation in 1640–51 (e.g. ibid, iii.153). In fact it only annulled acts of parliament of 1640–8 (*APS*, vii.86–7). A separate act annulled legislation passed in 1649–50 (*APS*, vii.30–2) but there was no general annulment of acts passed in 1650–1 when Charles II had been present in parliament.

84 D. Stevenson, 'The Financing of the Cause of the Covenants, 1638–51', *SHR*, li (1972), 122; Dickinson and Donaldson, *Source Book*, iii.297–302; Donaldson, *Scotland: James V to James VII*, 360.

85 Ibid, 399.

86 S.H. Turner, *The History of Local Taxation in Scotland* (Edinburgh and London, 1908), 66–7.

87 T. Keith, *Commercial Relations of England and Scotland, 1603–1707* (Cambridge, 1910), 32; *APS*, VI.i.367.

88 I.H. Adams, 'Division of the Commonty of Hassendean, 1761–1763', *Miscellany One* (Stair Society, 1971), 172.

89 Donaldson, *Scotland: James V to James VII*, 362–3.

90 Ibid. 365–6.

Bibliography

I Sources
  (i) Manuscripts
  (ii) General Printed Works

II Secondary Material
  (i) Bibliographies and Catalogues
  (ii) General Works

All printed works are published in London unless otherwise stated.

I SOURCES: (i) MANUSCRIPTS

National Archives of Scotland (formerly the Scottish Record Office)

E. EXCHEQUER RECORDS

E.31/19, Minute Book of the Board of the Green Cloth of Scotland, 1650–1.

PA. RECORDS OF PARLIAMENT

PA.7/3–8, Supplementary Parliamentary Papers, 1643–60.
PA.7/23/1–2, Additional Parliamentary Papers.
PA.7/24, Parliamentary and State Papers, 1581–1651.
PA. 11/1–11, Registers of the Committees of Estates, 1643–51.
PA.12/1–7, Warrants of the Committee of Estates, 1641–51.
PA.13/1, Papers relating to negotiations with the King and the English Parliament, 1641–6.
PA.13/3, Register of Letters to and from the Scots Commissioners in London, 1642, 1644–5.
PA.13/4, Register of Instructions to the Scots Commissioners in London, 1644–6.
PA.13/5, Register of Negotiations, 1643–7.

National Library of Scotland

ADV. ADVOCATES MANUSCRLPTS
Adv. 33.4.8, Transactions of the Scots Army in Ireland, 1643–8.

WODROW MANUSCRIPTS
Folio, xxxi, Church and State Papers, 1618–85.
Folio, lxv, Church and State Papers, 1639–50.
Folio, lxvii, Letters, 1641–53.
Quarto, lxxvii, Church and State Papers, 1584–1648.

Argyll Manuscripts, Inveraray Castle

Argyll Transcripts, vol. xii.

Public Record Office

SP.41/2, State Papers, Domestic, Military: Muster Rolls of the Scottish Army in England, 1646.
SP.46/129, State Papers, Domestic, Supplementary; Documents relating to Scotland, 1546–1653.

Bodleian Library, Oxford

MS. Carte 80, Wharton Correspondence.
MSS. Tanner, liv–lxvii, Letters and Papers, 1638–51.

(ii) GENERAL PRINTED WORKS

Abbott, W.C. (ed), *The Writings and Speeches of Oliver Cromwell* (4 vols., Harvard 1937–47).
The Acts of Parliament of Scotland, ed. T. Thomson and C. Innes (12 vols., Edinburgh 1814–75).
Baillie, R., *The Letters and Journals*, ed. D. Laing (3 vols., Bannatyne Club 1841–2).
Balfour, Sir J., *Historical Works* (4 vols., Edinburgh 1824–5).
Barron, D.G. (ed.), *In Defence of the Regalia*, 1651–2; *Being Selections from the Family Papers of the Ogilvies of Barras* (1910).
Bickley, F.B. (ed.), 'Letters relating to Scotland, January 1650', *EHR*, xi (1896), 112–17.

Birch, T. (ed.), *A Collection of State Papers of John Thurloe*, vol.i (1742).
Bruce, J. (ed.), *Charles I in 1646. Letters of King Charles the First to Queen Henrietta Maria* (Camden Society 1856).
Burnet, G., *History of My Own Times*, ed. O. Airy (2 vols., Oxford 1897–1900)
Burns, J., 'Memoirs by James Burns, Bailie of the City of Glasgow, 1644–1661' in [J. Maidment (ed.)] *Historical Fragments* (Edinburgh 1833).
Calendar of Clarendon State Papers in the Bodleian Library (4 vols., Oxford 1872–1932).
Calendar of State Papers, Domestic, Charles I, vols. xix–xxiii (1888–97) and *Commonwealth*, vols. i–iv (1875–8).
Carte, T. (ed.), *A Collection of Original Letters and Papers, Concerning the Affairs of England* (2 vols., 1739).
Clarendon, Earl of, *see* Hyde, E.
Dalrymple, D., Lord Hailes (ed.), *Memorials and Letters relating to the History of Britain in the Reign of Charles the First* (Glasgow 1766).
[Dennistoun, J., and Macdonald, A. (eds.)] 'Royal Letters and Instructions and other Documents from the Archives of the Earl of Wigton', *Maitland Club Miscellany*, II.ii (1840), 361–490.
Dickinson, W.C., and Donaldson, G. (eds.), *A Source Book of Scottish History*, vol.iii (1961).
Douglas, R., 'The Diary of Mr Robert Douglas when with the Scottish Army in England' in [J. Maidment (ed.)] *Historical Fragments* (Edinburgh 1833).
Firth, C.H. (ed.), 'Narratives Illustrating the Duke of Hamilton's Expedition to England in 1648', *SHS Miscellany*, ii (1904), 291–311.
Firth, C.H. (ed.), *Scotland and the Commonwealth*, 1651–3 (SHS 1895).
Firth, C.H. and Rait, R.S. (eds.), *Acts and Ordinances of the Interregnum*, 1642–1660 (3 vols. 1911).
Fotheringham, J.G. (ed.), *The Diplomatic Correspondence of Jean de Montereul and the Brothers de Belliévre* (2 vols., SHS 1898–9).
Fraser, J., *Chronicles of the Frasers. The Wardlaw Manuscript*, ed. W. Mackay (SHS 1905).
Gardiner, S.R. (ed.), *Constitutional Documents of the Puritan Revolution* (Oxford 1958).
The Hamilton Papers (Camden Society 1880).
'Hamilton Papers. Addenda', *Camden Miscellany*, ix (1895).
Letters and Papers Illustrating the Relations between Charles the Second and Scotland in 1650 (SHS 1894).
Gordon, P., of Ruthven, *A Short Abridgement of Britane's Distemper*, ed. J. Dunn (Spalding Club 1844).

Gordon, Sir R., of Gordonstoun, and Gordon, G., of Sallagh, *A Genealogical History of the Earldom of Sutherland* (Edinburgh 1813).
Guthry, H., *Memoirs* (2nd ed., Glasgow 1747).
Hailes, Lord, see Dalrymple, D.
Hyde, E., Earl of Clarendon *The History of the Rebellion and Civil Wars in England Begun in the Year 1641*, ed. W.D. Macray (6 vols., Oxford 1888).
Jaffray, A., *Diary*, ed. J. Barclay (Aberdeen 1856).
Johnston, A., of Wariston, *Diary. . . 1650–4*, ed. D.H. Fleming (SHS 1919).
Journals of the House of Commons, vols. iii–vi.
Journals of the House of Lords, vols. vi–x.
Laing, D. (ed.), *Correspondence of Sir Robert Kerr, first Earl of Ancrum, and his son William, third Earl of Lothian* (2 vols., Edinburgh 1875).
Lamont, J., *The Diary of Mr John Lamont of Newton, 1649–71*, ed. G.R. Kinloch (Maitland Club 1830).
Livingstone, J., *A Brief Historical Relation. . .*, ed. T. Houston (Edinburgh 1848).
Macbain, A., and Kennedy, J. (eds.), *Reliquiae Celticae. Texts, Papers and Studies in Gaelic Literature and Philology left by the late Rev. Alexander Cameron* (3 vols., Inverness 1894).
McCrie, T. (ed.), *The Life of Mr Robert Blair, Minister of St Andrews, Containing his Autobiography* (Wodrow Society 1848).
Mackay, G. (ed.), 'Two Unpublished Letters from James, 5th Earl, (later) 1st Marquis of Montrose', *Juridical Review*, liii (1941), 298–317.
[Maidment, J. (ed.)] 'Collections by a Private Hand at Edinburgh', in *Historical Fragments* (Edinburgh 1833).
Marwick, J.D. (ed.), *Extracts from the Records of the Burgh of Glasgow*, vols. i–ii (SBRS 1876–81).
Meikle, H.W. (ed.), *Correspondence of the Scots Commissioners in London, 1644–1646* (Roxburghe Club 1917).
Mitchell, A.E., and Christie, J. (eds.), *The Records of the Commissioners of the General Assemblies of the Church of Scotland, 1646–52* (3 vols., SHS 1892–1909).
Napier, M. (ed.), *Memorials of Montrose and his Times* (2 vols., Maitland Club 1848–50).
Nickolls, J. (ed.), *Original Letters and Papers of State, addressed to Oliver Cromwell . . . found among the Political Collection of Mr John Milton* (1743).
Nicoll, J., *A Diary of Public Transactions and other Occurences, chiefly in Scotland*, ed. D. Laing (Bannatyne Club 1836).
Peck, F. (ed.), *Desiderata Curiosa or a Collection of divers scarce and Curious Pieces* (2 vols., 17325).

Peterkin, A. (ed.), *Records of the Kirk of Scotland, Containing the Acts and Proceedings of the General Assemblies* (Edinburgh 1838).

Registrum Magni Sigilli Regum Scotorum: The Register of the Great Seal of Scotland, 1634–1651, ed. J.M. Thomson (Edinburgh 1897).

The Register of the Privy Council of Scotland, 2nd series, viii, 1544–1660 (Edinburgh 1908).

Reid, A.G. (ed.), 'Notice of an Original Letter of Instructions for Sir William Fleming by King Charles II, dated at Breda, 22nd May 1650', *Proceedings of the Society of Antiquaries of Scotland*, xxxiv (1899–1900), 199–202.

Renwick, R. (ed.), *Extracts from the Records of the Royal Burgh of Stirling* (SBRS 1887).

Rushworth, J. (ed.), Historical Collections (8 vols., 1659–1701).

Rutherford, S., *Lex Rex: The Law and the Prince* (1644).

Scot, Sir J., of Scotstarvet, *The Staggering State of Scottish Statesmen from 1550 to 1650*, ed. C. Rogers (Edinburgh 1872).

'Trew Relation of the Principall Affaires concerning the State', ed. G. Neilson, *SHR* xi 164–91, 284–96, 395–403, xii 76–83, 174–83, 408–12, xiii 380–92, xiv 60–8.

Scrope, R., and Monkhouse, T. (eds.), *State Papers Collected by Edward, Earl of Clarendon* (3 vols., Oxford 1767–86).

Simpson, H.F.M. (ed.), 'Civil War Papers, 1643–1650', *SHS Miscellany*, i (1893), 143–225.

Somerville, Lord J., *Memorie of the Somervills; being a History of the Baronial House of Somerville*, ed. Sir W. Scott (2 vols., Edinburgh 1815).

Spalding, J., *Memorialls of the Trubles in Scotland and in England, a.d. 1624–A.D. 1645*, ed. J. Stuart (2 vols., Spalding Club 1850–1).

Spreul, J., 'Some Remarkable Passages of the Lord's Providence towards Mr John Spreul, Town Clerk of Glasgow, 1635–1644', in [J. Maidment(ed.)] *Historical Fragments* (Edinburgh 1833).

Stephen, W. (ed.), *Register of Consultations of the Ministers of Edinburgh and some other Brethren of the Ministry, 1652–60* (2 vols., SHS 1921–30).

Stuart, J. (ed.), *Extracts from the Council Register of the Burgh of Aberdeen, 1625–1747* (2 vols., SBRS 1871–2).

Taylor, L.B. (ed.), *Aberdeen Council Letters*, vols. ii–iii (Oxford 1950–2).

Terry, C.S. (ed.), *Papers Relating to the Army of the Solemn League and Covenant, 1643–1647* (2 vols., SHS 1917).

Turner, J., *Memoirs of his own Life and Times*, ed. T. Thomson (Bannatyne Club 1829).

Tweedie, W.K. (ed.), *Select Biographies* (2 vols., Wodrow Society 1845).

Walker, Sir E., *Historical Discourses upon Several Occasions* (1705).

Warner, G.F. (ed.), *The Nicholas Papers. Correspondence of Sir Edward Nicholas*, vol.i (Camden Society 1886).
Wishart, G., *The Memoirs of James Marquis of Montrose, 1639–1650*, ed. A.D. Murdoch and H.F.M. Simpson (1893).
Wood, M. (ed.), *Extracts from the Records of Edinburgh, 1626–55* (2 vols., Edinburgh 1936–8).

II SECONDARY: (i) BIBLIOGRAPHIES AND CATALOGUES

Aldis, H.G., *A List of Books Printed in Scotland before 1700* (revised ed. Edinburgh 1970).
Davies, G., and Keeler, M.F., *Bibliography of British History, Stuart Period* (2nd ed., Oxford 1970).
Gouldesbrough, P., Kup, A.P., and Lewis, I., *Handlist of Scottish and Welsh Record Publications* (British Records Association 1954).
Hancock, P.D., *A Bibliography of Works relating to Scotland, 1916–1950* (2 vols., Edinburgh 1959–60).
Livingstone, M., *Guide to the Public Records of Scotland* (Edinburgh 1905).
Matheson, C., *A Catalogue of the Publications of Scottish Historical and Kindred Clubs and Societies. . . 1908–27* (Aberdeen 1928).
Mitchell, A., and Cash, C.G., *A Contribution to the Bibliography of Scottish Topography* (2 vols., SHS 1917).
Steele, R., *A Bibliography of Royal Proclamations of the Tudor and Stuart Sovereigns* (2 vols., Oxford 1910).
Stuart, M., *Scottish Family History* (Edinburgh 1930).
Terry, C.S., *A Catalogue of the Publications of Scottish Historical and Kindred Clubs and Societies, 1780–1908* (Glasgow 1909).
Thomason, G., *Catalogue of the Pamphlets. . . collected by George Thomason, 1641–1661*, ed. G.K. Fortescue (2 vols., 1908).

(ii) GENERAL

Aylmer, G.E. (ed.), *The Interregnum: The Quest for Settlement, 1646–1660* (1972).
Buchan, J., *Montrose* (1931).
Burnet, G., *The Memoires of the Lives and Actions of James and William Dukes of Hamilton* (1677).
Burrell, S.A., 'Calvinism, Capitalism, and the Middle Classes: Some

Afterthoughts on an Old Problem', *Journal of Modern History*, xxxii (1960), 129–41.
Campbell, W.M., *The Triumph of Presbyterianism* (St Andrews 1958).
Cowan, E.J., 'Montrose and Argyll', in *The Scottish Nation*, ed. G. Menzies (1970).
Cowan, I.B., 'The Covenanters: A Revision Article', *SHR*, xlvii (1968), 35–52.
Donaldson, G., 'The Emergence of Schism in Seventeenth Century Scotland', in *Schism, Heresy and Religious Protest*, ed. D. Baker (Cambridge 1972), 277–94.
Scotland: James V to James VII (Edinburgh and London 1965).
'Scotland's Conservative North in the Sixteenth and Seventeenth Centuries', *TRHS*, 5th series, xvi (1966), 65–79.
The Scottish Reformation (Cambridge 1960).
Douglas, W.S, *Cromwell's Scotch Campaigns, 1650–1* (1898).
Firth, C.H., 'The Battle of Dunbar', *TRHS*, new series xiv (1900), 19–52.
Cromwell's Army (1962).
'Marston Moor', *TRHS*, new series xii (1898), 17–79.
Forster, R., and Greene, J.P. (eds.), *Preconditions of Revolution in Early Modern Europe* (Baltimore and London 1971).
Gardiner, S.R., *History of the Great Civil War* (4 vols. 1893–4).
History of the Commonwealth and Protectorate (4 vols. 1903).
Hamilton, C.L., 'Anglo-Scottish Militia Negotiations, March–April 1646', *SHR*, xlii (1963), 86–8.
Henderson, G.D., *The Burning Bush: Studies in Scottish Church History* (Edinburgh 1957).
Religious Life in Seventeenth Century Scotland (Cambridge 1937).
Hewison, J.K., *The Covenanters* (2 vols., Glasgow 1913).
Hill, G., *An Historical Account of the Macdonnells of Antrim* (Belfast 1873).
Kirkton, J., *The Secret and True History of the Church of Scotland* (Edinburgh 1817).
Lamont, W.M., *Godly Rule. Politics and Religion*, 1603–60 (1969).
MacCormack, J.R., *Revolutionary Politics in the Long Parliament* (Cambridge Mass. 1972).
McCoy, F.N., *Robert Baillie and the Second Scots Reformation* (Berkeley, Los Angeles and London 1974).
McKenzie, W.C., *The Life and Times of John Maitland, Duke of Lauderdale, 1616–1682* (1923).
McKerral, A., *Kintyre in the Seventeenth Century* (Edinburgh 1948).
Mathieson, W.L., *Politics and Religion, A Study in Scottish History from the Reformation to the Revolution* (2 vols., Glasgow 1902).

Napier, M., *Memoirs of the Marquis of Montrose* (2 vols., Edinburgh 1856).
Ogilvie, J.D., 'A Bibliography of the Resolutioner – Protester Controversy, 1650–1659', *Proceedings of the Edinburgh Bibliographical Society*, xiv (1926–30), 57–86.
Rait, R.S., *The Parliaments of Scotland* (Glasgow 1924).
Rubinstein, H.L., *Captain Luckless. James, First Duke of Hamilton, 1606–1649* (Edinburgh and London 1975).
Scott, H., *Fasti Ecclesiae Scoticanae* (9 vols, Edinburgh 1915–50).
Shaw, D., (ed.), *Reformation and Revolution. Essays presented to the Very Reverend Principal Emeritus Hugh Watt* (Edinburgh 1967).
Smout, T.C., *A History of the Scotish People, 1560–1830* (1969).
Sprott, G.W., *The Worship of the Church of Scotland during the Covenanting Period, 1638–61* (Edinburgh 1893).
Stevenson, A., *History of the Church and State of Scotland* (Edinburgh 1840).
Stevenson, D., 'The Battle of Mauchline Moor, 1647', *Ayrshire Collections* XI.i (1973), 3–24.
'Church and Society under the Covenanters, 1638–51', *Scotia: American-Canadian Journal of Scottish Studies*, I. i(1977), 24–41.
'Conventicles in the Kirk, 1619–37. The Emergence of a Radical Party', *Records of the Scottish Church History Society*, xviii (1972–4), 99–114.
'The Covenanters and the Court of Session, 1637–51', *Juridical Review* (1972), 227–47.
'Deposition of Ministers in the Church of Scotland under the Covenanters, 1638–1651', *Church History*, xliv (1975), 321–35.
'The English and the Public Records of Scotland, 1650–1660', *Miscellany One* (Stair Society 1971), 156–70.
'The Financing of the Cause of the Covenants, 1638–51', *SHR*, li (1972), 89–123.
'The General Assembly and the Commission of the Kirk, 1638–51', *Records of the Scottish Church History Society*, xix (1975) 59–79.
'The King's Scottish Revenues and the Covenanters, 1625–51', *Historical Journal*, xvii (1974), 17–41.
'The Massacre of Dunaverty, 1647', *Scottish Studies*, xix (1975), 27–37.
'The Radical Party in the Kirk, 1637–45', *Journal of Ecclesiastical History*, xxvi, (1974), 135–65.
The Scottish Revolution, 1637–44. The Triumph of the Covenanters (Newton Abbot 1973). [RRPTD. 2003]
'The Western Association, 1648–50', *Ayrshire Collections*, XIII. iv(1982).
Terry, C.S., *The Life and Campaigns of Alexander Leslie, First Earl of Leven* (1899).

'The Scottish Campaigns in Northumberland and Durham between January and June 1644', *Archaeologia Aeliana*, 2nd series, xxi (1899), 146–79.

The Scottish Parliament, its Constitution and Procedure, 1603–1707 (Glasgow 1905).

'The Siege of Newcastle-upon-Tyne by the Scots in 1644', *Archaeologia Aeliana*, 2nd series, xxi (1899), 180–258.

'The Visits of Charles I to Newcastle in 1633, 1639, 1641 and 1646–7', *Archaeologia Aeliana*, 2nd series, xxi (1899),83–145.

Trevor-Roper, H.R., 'Scotland and the Puritan Revolution', in *Religionm the Reformation and Social Change* (1967), 392–444.

Underdown, D.E., *Pride's Purge. Politics in the Puritan Revolution* (Oxford 1971).

Wedgwood, C.V., 'The Covenanters in the First Civil War', *SHR*, xxxix (1960), 1–15.

The King's Peace (1955).

The King's War (1958).

Willcock, J., *The Great Marquess. Life and Times of Archibald . . . Marquess of Argyll* (Edinburgh and London 1903).

Williams, R., *Montrose. Cavalier in Mourning* (1975).

Wodrow, R., *Analecta, or Materials for a History of Remarkable Providences*, ed. M. Leishman (4 vols., Maitland Club 1842–3).

The History of the Sufferings of the Church of Scotland, ed. R. Burns (4 vols., Glasgow 1828–30).

Worden, B., *The Rump Parliament*, 1648–53 (1974).

Maps

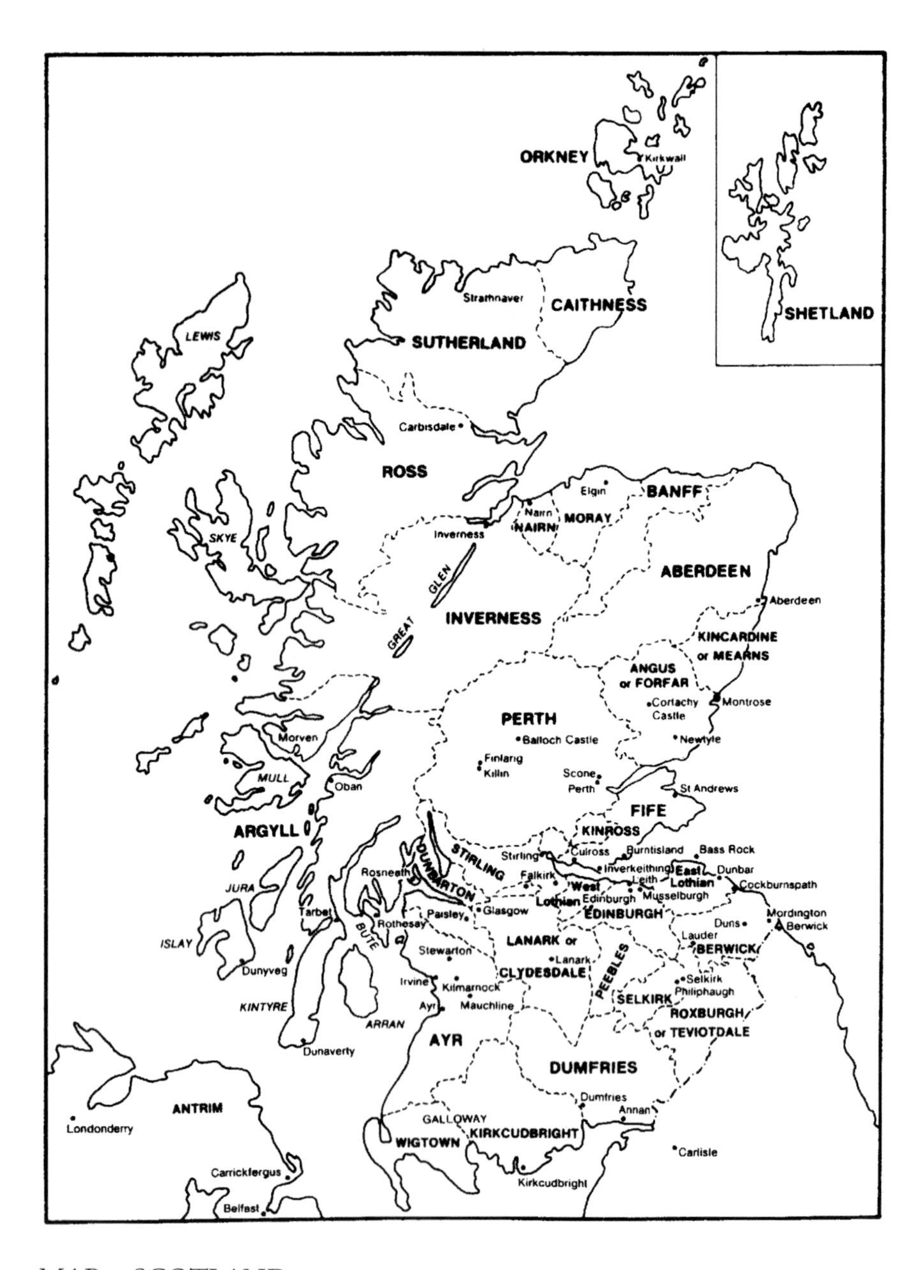

MAP 1: SCOTLAND

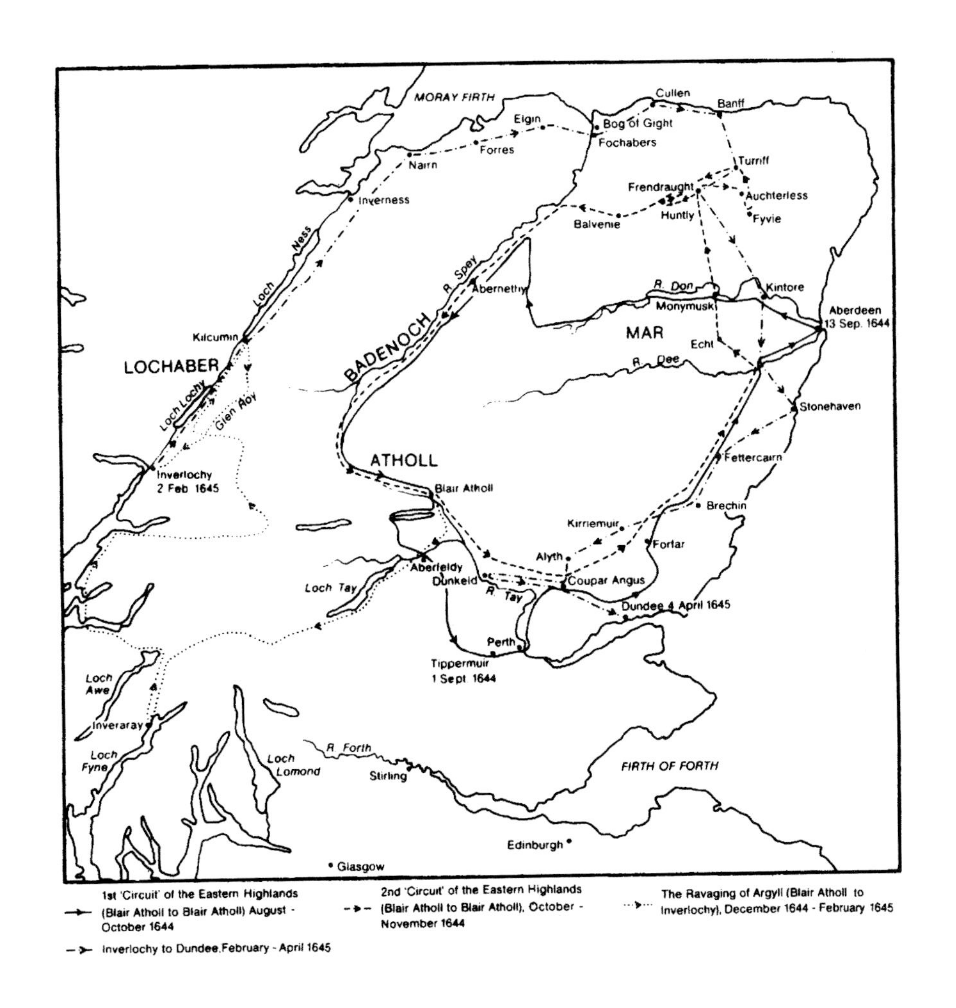

MAP 2: MONTROSE'S CAMPAIGNS AUGUST 1644–APRIL 1645

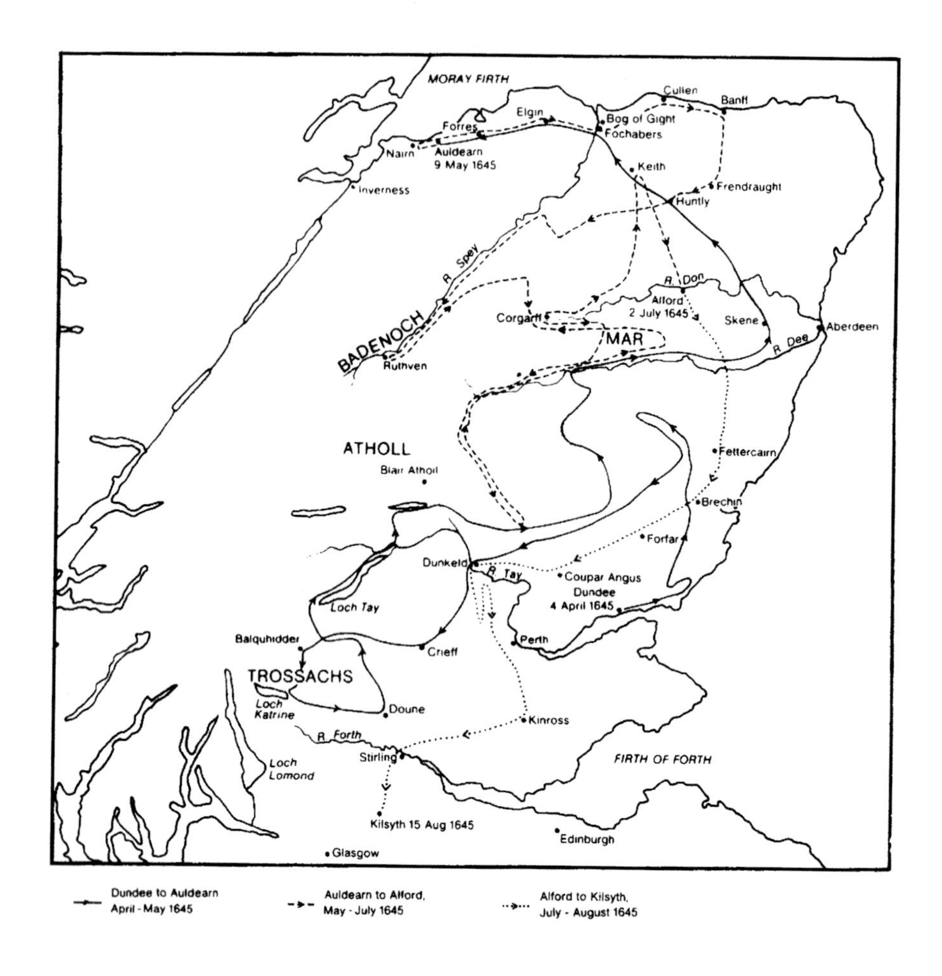

MAP 3: MONTROSE'S CAMPAIGNS APRIL–AUGUST 1645

1640: Second Bishops' War The advance to Newcastle

1644-5: The Scottish Army in England. Marston Moor, the capture of York and Newcastle,and the advance to Hereford (the Scottish army withdrew from Hereford to Yorkshire in September 1645.From November 1645 to May 1646 it laid siege to Newark).

1648: The Preston Campaign

1651: The Worcester Campaign

MAP 4: SCOTTISH CAMPAIGNS IN ENGLAND 1640–51

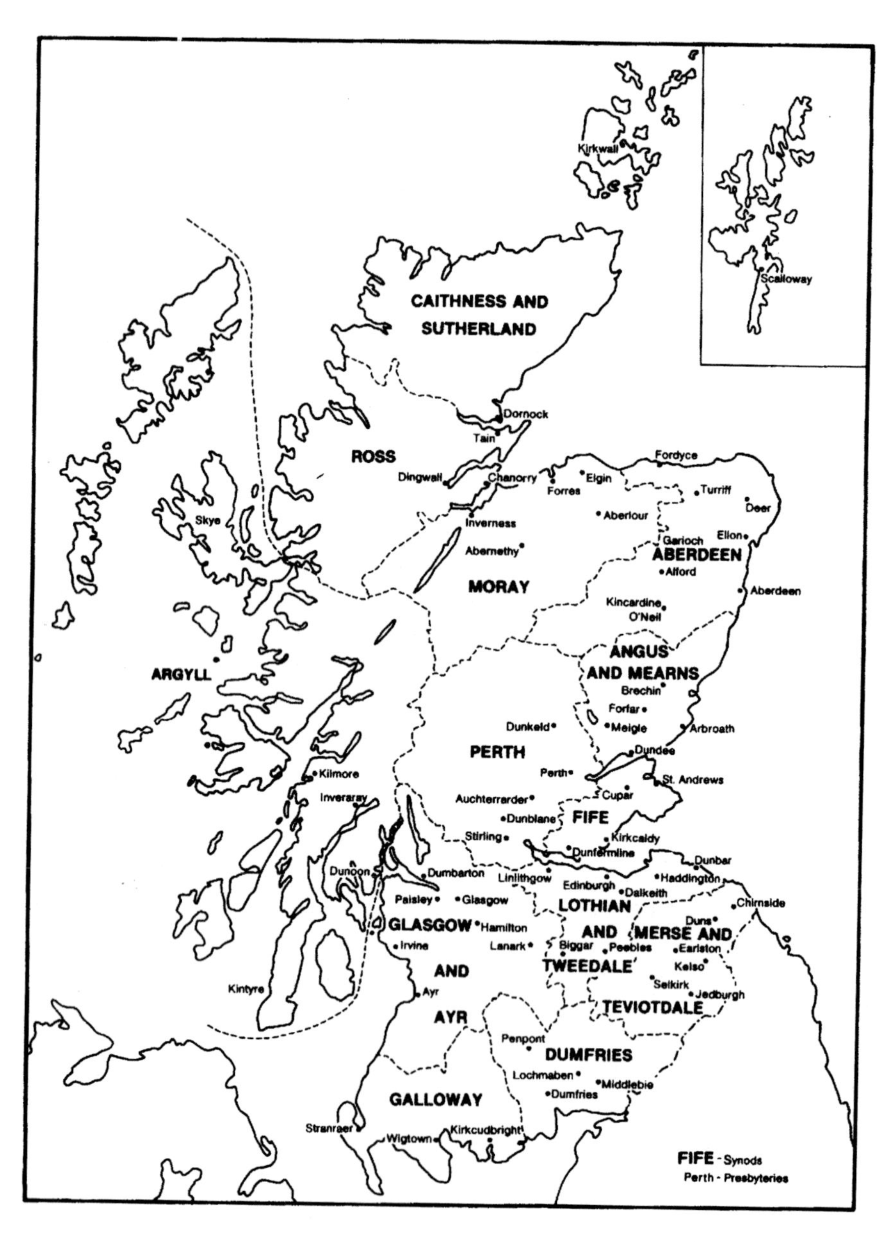

MAP 5: SCOTLAND—SYNODS AND PRESBYTERIES IN THE 1640s

NOTES ON THE MAPS

MAPS 2 and 3 have been compiled mainly from the accounts of Montrose's movements given in Wishart, *Memoirs*, Gordon, *Britane's Distemper* and Spalding, *Memorialls*. Where the sources fail, Montrose's exact route must remain conjectural; this applies especially to some of his marches through the mountains. The maps in Buchan, *Montrose*, 190, 218, 238, 252, 262 are useful (and are an improvement on those in Gardiner, *Civil War*, ii.141, 151, 217, 278, 293), but at many points indicate different routes from the present maps (and, indeed, in some instances Buchan's maps show routes which are not the same as those he describes in the text of his book). Where Montrose's route between two places is unknown it has been assumed that he would take the easiest and most direct route that military considerations left open to him; previous maps seem, at some points, to be based on the assumption that from time to time Montrose gave way to a taste for dramatic mountaineering exploits with his army for which there was no practical necessity.

MAP 4: Terry, *Alexander Leslie* describes the routes taken by the Scottish armies in 1640 and 1644–6, and has a map of the 1640 and part of the 1644–5 campaigns. There are maps of the 1648 and 1651 campaigns in Gardiner, *Civil War*, iv.177 and Gardiner, *Commonwealth and Protectorate*, ii.33 respectively.

MAP 5 is based on the list of synods and presbyteries approved by the general assembly in 1638 (Peterkin, *Records*, 37–8), with the following alterations in conformity with later acts:—

In 1640 the presbytery of Melrose was transferred to Selkirk (H. Scott, *Fasti Ecclesiae Scoticanae* (Edinburgh, 1915–50), ii.168).

In 1644 a new presbytery was created at Biggar out of parts of the presbyteries of Peebles and Lanark. It was assigned to the synod of Lothian and Tweeddale (Peterkin, *Records*, 297, 333, 361, 397–8).

In 1645 the presbyteries of Aberlour and Abernethy were conjoined, though they still sometimes met separately (Scott, *Fasti*, vi.334, 351).

In 1646 Kirkwall and Scalloway presbyteries, formerly forming the synod of Orkney and Shetland, were joined to the synod of Caithness and Sutherland (Peterkin, *Records*, 447).

In 1648 the presbytery of Scalloway or Shetland was disjoined from the synod of Caithness and Sutherland and declared to be immediately subordinate to the general assembly (Peterkin, *Records*, 511).

Glasgow and Ayr were listed in 1638 as separate synods which were to meet together *pro hac vice*, but they always met together in this period. Several of the more remote presbyteries are sometimes referred to under different names to those given on the map. Dornoch was also known as Sutherland; Caithness as Wick or Thurso; Kilmore as Lorne; Dunoon as Cowal; and Kintyre as Kinloch or Saddell.

Index